MOREAU DE ST. MÉRY'S
AMERICAN JOURNEY
1793–1798

Moreau de St. Méry's American Journey

[1793–1798]

Moreau de Saint-Méry

TRANSLATED AND EDITED BY

Kenneth Roberts
Anna M. Roberts

PREFACE BY KENNETH ROBERTS
INTRODUCTION BY STEWART L. MIMS

Frontispiece painting by James Bingham

DOUBLEDAY & COMPANY, INC.

Garden City, New York

1947

PREFACE

by Kenneth Roberts

ONE of the most troubled periods of my life was that during which I was writing *Lydia Bailey;* for in it I was confronted with problems that at the time seemed insuperable. One of these was Moreau de St. Méry.

Lydia taught French in her father's Philadelphia school in 1796. When her father died, her uncle got her a position as private tutor in the home of a wealthy planter in San Domingo—now known as Haiti. As I struggled with Lydia's vicissitudes in San Domingo, I became increasingly conscious of Moreau de St. Méry. Moreau de St. Méry had said thus and so about life in San Domingo. Moreau de St. Méry had said this and that about the creoles, the colonials and the Negroes of San Domingo; about its Free Men of Color; about mulattoes, griffes, sacatras and other light-skinned Negroes; about the Little Whites and the Big Whites of San Domingo; about serpent worship, zombis, voodoo rites, yellow fever, coffee plantations and various other things. Almost everyone who had written about San Domingo had quoted extensively from Moreau de St. Méry. Apparently his book was as important as it was powerful, so I took steps to add Moreau's *Description topographique, physique, civile, politique et historique de la partie française de l'isle Saint-Domingue* to my library.

I advertised extensively for it in the *Publishers' Weekly,* and wrote pleading letters to innumerable bookdealers, but never a copy was offered. I then discovered that there were

v

only a few copies in existence, all in the rare-book departments of large libraries. Milton Lord, director of the Boston
Public Library, produced a copy for me. The *Description
topographique,* and so on, *of the French Part of San Domingo* was an enormous two-volume tome of 1500 pages,
and not only had it never been translated into English, but
it had been published, as well as written, by Moreau de St.
Méry in Philadelphia in 1796.

I was indignant that such an important book had never
been translated; but its weight and size were so staggering
that I was able to control my indignation.

I had to know more about Moreau de St. Méry, however—
how, for example, he had got to America and to Philadelphia; how he had happened to enter the publishing business;
how long he lived in Philadelphia; with whom he consorted.
That was how I first came across Moreau de St. Méry's
Voyage aux Etats-Unis de l'Amérique, 1793–1798.

But when I got my hands on that book in turn, I found
that it too was in French and untranslated. Yet this book
was short—a mere 403 pages—and was widely acclaimed
by French students as containing information of tremendous value about New York, Philadelphia and the habits
and customs of Americans. My indignation at this unhappy
state of affairs knew, as the saying goes, no bounds. I complained to Mrs. Roberts about it. Why, I asked her, shouldn't
she take up a part of the white man's burden by translating
this powerful and penetrating account of early America?
The task would be absorbing and amusing—she could make
a strictly literal translation without bothering to polish it;
and each night I'd be glad to look over what she'd done during the day and touch it up here and there if touching should
be necessary. Here, I told her, was an opportunity to be of
genuine service to literature! What are we waiting for?
Allons! Let's go!

To make a long story short, she agreed to do it; so I asked

the Yale University Press, which had published the French version, what I should do in order to get translation rights. The Yale University Press conferred with Mr. Stewart Mims, who had discovered Moreau de St. Méry's manuscript while assistant professor of history at Yale in 1913, and had edited and annotated it. Both the Yale University Press and Mr. Mims promptly and graciously replied that they were happy to relinquish to me all rights in Moreau de St. Méry's book, and that Mrs. Roberts and I could proceed with the translation whenever we wished.

A week later Mrs. Roberts placed upon my desk the first five typed pages of her literal translation of Moreau de St. Méry's *American Journey;* and with that there began, for me, a trying period that was rewarded by the uncovering of unexpected information about early America.

So far as I am aware, no American or foreign author has ever written with such startling frankness about the habits, manners and garb of American women during the last decade of the eighteenth century; and Moreau's statements about prostitution, houses of assignation, streetwalking, contraceptives, frigidity and allied subjects came as a complete surprise to everyone who had a hand in the translation.

But there were times, after racking my brains for endless hours, trying to make Mrs. Roberts' literal rendering of Moreau into readable English, when I feared I would become a gibbering idiot if I persisted in my original intention of seeing the book completely translated.

Mrs. Roberts' sister Katharine, head of French House at Smith College, had the kindly idea of lightening Mrs. Roberts' labors by presenting her with a literal translation of Moreau's description of Philadelphia. She started blithely enough; but she confessed to me that after she had done twenty pages, she had a feeling that attendants from a madhouse might call for her at any moment and roll her in a wet sheet.

I was frequently and generously helped, in my attempts to overcome Moreau's complexities, by Major A. Hamilton Gibbs, whose school days had been spent in Moreau's adopted town of St. Malo. For hours I read Moreau in translation to him and Mrs. Gibbs, while the major followed in the French version. At frequent intervals we called Moreau some pretty hard names, and prayed to be given understanding; and there were times when, like women in labor, we wondered whether it was worth the struggle.

When we'd done as well by Moreau as we could, Peter Grant, translator of *War Diary* by Jean Malaquais, kindly consented to check our own version against the original. It was then apparent that Moreau had given us a glimpse of an America that we couldn't possibly have got from anyone else, and that he emphatically had been worth the time and the trouble we'd devoted to him. We hope that others will find Moreau equally enlightening.

INTRODUCTION

by Stewart L. Mims

MÉDÉRIC-LOUIS-ELIE MOREAU de SAINT-MÉRY was born at Fort Royal, Martinique,*[1] on January 13, 1750. His ancestors had emigrated from Poitou, in the seventeenth century, to settle in the island and had come to occupy a place of prominence by furnishing in succeeding generations judges to the superior courts. His father died before the young Moreau had reached the age of three, which prevented him from being sent, according to custom, to France for his early education. For this early training he was indebted to his mother, who seems to have succeeded well in laying a solid foundation for the future development of her son. His grandfather, a *sénéchal* of Martinique, also took a deep interest in the boy's development and at his death left a legacy of 66,000 francs which he had carefully laid aside to enable his grandson to seek legal training in Paris and thus to equip himself to follow in the footsteps of his fathers. It was not until three years after his grandfather's death, how-

*Thus Moreau, having been born in the French West Indies of white parents, was a creole. His ancestors, having come there from France, were colonials. Colonials weren't creoles: creoles weren't colonials. This distinction should be kept in mind when reading Moreau.—K. R.

[1]The above sketch has been based upon the following material: Silvestre, *Notice Biographique sur Moreau de Saint-Méry*, Paris, 1819; Fournier-Pescay, *Discours prononcé aux obsèques de Moreau de Saint-Méry, le 30 janv. 1819*, Paris, 1819; *Idem*, article on Moreau in *Biographie Universelle*; L. Chassin, *Les Elections et les Cahiers de Paris en 1789*; S. Lacroix, *Actes de la Commune de Paris pendant la Révolution*; P. Robiquet, *Le Personnel Municipal de Paris pendant la Révolution*, pp. 114–117 and Index.

ever, at the age of nineteen, that Moreau sailed for France on this mission.

At Paris he found a cordial reception at the hands of rich relatives, who opened the doors of society in the capital to him. Tall, of goodly proportions, of pleasing presence and of ready wit, he seems to have created an excellent impression wherever he went. He did not permit himself, however, to be led astray by the attractions of a brilliant society, but began at once to follow courses in mathematics and law. Finding himself deficient in Latin, he began alone the study of that language, reading the classic authors with such zest that he learned to quote freely from them, and so familiarizing himself with Roman law that he could cite it with precision. The success of his study is shown by the remarkable fact that at the end of fourteen months he wrote and sustained, in Latin, a thesis for the bachelor's degree in law. At the end of three years he won the coveted honour, for which he had come to France, of attaining the rank of *avocat au parlement.*

With the creditable record of these three years behind him, he returned to his native isle, equipped to follow his chosen profession. During his absence his mother had died and the remnant of the family fortune had been dissipated. The outlook apparently discouraged him, for he decided to remove to Cap François,[2] a thriving port of French St. Domingo, the richest and most prosperous of all the West Indies. There he began the practice of law and met with such success that at the end of eight years he was made a member of the *conseil supérieur* of the colony.

It was during this experience as lawyer and judge that Moreau began to make the great collection of laws whose publication a few years later made his name immortal to all students of West India history. He himself has left us a record of his own embarrassments in trying to determine

[2]Now Cape Haitien, Haiti.

points of law, which led him to undertake the task. But the work of collecting data for his own personal use opened a field of wonderful possibilities for public service, and he continued his work with the view of rendering such a service. Investigation showed that the *conseil supérieur* itself had made attempts in 1716, 1738 and 1757 to codify its laws, and that, more recently, royal orders had been issued in 1762 and again in 1771 for the work to be done. In obedience to these orders, de la Rivière had for some time been engaged in the work, but had found it slow and discouraging. Hearing of Moreau's undertaking, he gracefully gave way to the younger and more competent man. On his recommendation, the royal government gave its sanction and support to Moreau and enabled him to pursue his work. He visited all parts of St. Domingo, Martinique, Guadeloupe and St. Lucia to rescue from a devastating climate and hungry insects the records of the past. "*Quelles fatigues, quelles dépenses dans les voyages qu'il faut entreprendre pour découvrir ceux qu'on désire. Quelles recherches et quel temps pour les trouver dans les Dépôts publics où ils sont mal en ordre. Que de dégouts à essuyer, que d'obstacles à surmonter!*" The zeal of a historian in search of the truth inspired him and set his mind upon the evolution of that larger plan of work which later gave us his printed works upon St. Domingo and the many manuscripts of unpublished works upon the French West Indies, which go to make up the monumental *Collection Moreau de Saint-Méry* in the *Archives Coloniales* at Paris today. Called to Paris to aid in the administration of the colonies and to complete and publish the results of his work, he was able to give to the world from 1784 to 1790 the six volumes of his famous collection of laws, entitled, *Loix et Constitutions des Colonies françaises de l'Amérique sous le Vent.*

At his return to Paris, Moreau became an active member of the *Musée de Paris*, being chosen its secretary in 1784 and then president in 1787. He found delight in the company of its members. He read before them selected chapters from his *Description de la partie espagnole de St. Domingue*, the writing of which was absorbing much of his attention at the time.

At the outbreak of the Revolution, Moreau became one of its ardent champions and defenders. Among the four hundred and seven *électeurs* of Paris who assembled on April 23, 1789, Moreau was one of the representatives sent from the district of St. Eustache. From the first he became one of the leading spirits and exerted a decisive influence on the course of events. By July 1 he had defined his leadership to such an extent that he was easily elected president of the body. The *électeurs*, from the force of circumstances, had by then become a provisional governing body for the city. As the Parisian populace grew restless, Moreau sent out the clarion call for union and order, urging all to keep inviolate the character and self-respect of the nation. When the storm broke on the 13th and 14th, he remained constantly at the Hôtel de Ville, on the one hand watching jealously over the interests of the city and taking measures to protect it from royal troops, and, on the other, trying to stay the ravages of lawlessness and devastation. In the organization of the Parisian militia of 48,000 men, voted on the 13th, he played a prominent part and was in charge of the distribution of arms and ammunition on the eventful 14th. When the Bastille had fallen, he received at the Hôtel de Ville the keys of the fortress from the hands of its conquerors. In the night session of the *électeurs*, he sent a message of triumph to the National Assembly of Versailles beseeching it to beg His Majesty *"de faire vivre son autorité en n'employant d'autre arme que l'amour de ses peuples: cette arme suffit et toutes les autres seraient inutiles."* Dusaulx, one of his colleagues in these trying times, has left, in his *L'Oeuvre de Sept Jours*, a vivid description of Moreau on duty at the Hôtel de Ville on the night of the 14th:

"As to M. Moreau de Saint-Méry, whose prudence and *sang-froid* grew stronger in the midst of excitement and who was in a certain sense the arbiter of our destiny, immovable as a rock beaten upon by a storm, he remained at his post while everyone else deserted. This American-born Frenchman, a stranger in a way to France and grown famous within a short lapse of time, declared afterwards . . . that he had given three thousand orders without leaving his chair."

On the 15th, in the discussions concerning the choice of an efficient commander for the guard of Paris, Moreau seized upon the psychological moment by pointing to the bust of Lafayette in the hall and thus effecting a most enthusiastic election of that patriot. In the choice of Bailly as mayor, he exerted the same decisive influence—a fact cordially referred to by Bailly in a letter addressed to Moreau on July 16.

It was undoubtedly to the unique position of authority which he occupied during these eventful days of July 13–15 that he referred, when he playfully remarked afterwards, during his exile, that he had been "King of Paris during three days."

As the provisional government gave way to the permanent government of the Commune, the *électeurs,* in their final session of July 30, put on record their appreciation of Moreau's services by ordering a gold medal to be struck in honor of their president "who from the first outbreak of the Revolution had not ceased to show the coolest courage, the most courageous foresight and the most unvarying devotion to the cause."

From this provisional government, Moreau passed into the permanent governing body of the Commune and was elected first secretary and then vice-president on July 27. After resigning, on August 10, he was re-elected vice-president on September 26. This election to the vice-presidency was equivalent to an election to the presidency, as Bailly, being, *ex officio,* titular president, seems not to have performed the function. A study of the records printed by Lacroix (*Actes de la Commune de Paris pendant la Révolution*) will reveal Moreau's constant activity and important influence as presiding officer. At the reception of Necker at the Hôtel de Ville on July 30, he presented the *cocarde* to Necker by saying, "These colours are dear to us, they are the colours of liberty." In the eventful days of October, during which the populace of Paris brought the king and the National Assembly to Paris and made them captive, the Commune became almost supreme. Moreau as its head occupied a place of great prominence. He was one of the committee of twenty which escorted Louis XVI to the Hôtel de Ville and addressed the king in a most graceful speech at the reception there accorded him.

Moreau seems, however, to have been disturbed by the course of events, or, for some reason, to have debated at this time a departure from Paris; for, after refusing an election as chief of the Parisian police on October 4, he resigned from the Commune on October 10, on the grounds that "pressing reasons made his return to America imperative." At his resignation the Commune passed a resolution of regret at the loss of a member "who from the beginning had never failed to give the capital and the nation proofs of a most enlightened, most courageous and most indefatigable patriotism."

Moreau decided, nevertheless, to remain at Paris, and became a member of the *Constituante* as deputy from Martinique. Although he was not destined to play a capital rôle in this body, he proved a leader and constructive statesman in all discussions relating to the colonies, for there he spoke with an authority and conviction that few possessed. His ability and training as a lawyer and judge were recognized

by his selection as a member of the *comité judiciaire* to aid
the Minister of Justice. Ardent champion of reform as he
was, however, he was no less an ardent opponent to lawlessness, and in fact so incurred the hostility of the radical elements that he was savagely attacked on July 30, 1792 (see
p. 123, below), and left for dead in a café where he had
taken refuge.

With the close of the *Constituante*, Moreau's work in the
Revolution came to an end. At the accession to power of
Robespierre, whose hostility Moreau had incurred in the
Constituante, he fled from Paris to hide in Normandy. On
being discovered, he fled to Le Havre where he was fortunate
enough to board a vessel bound for New York and to clear
the port on November 9, 1793, just before the order for his
arrest and deportation to Paris arrived. Had he not escaped,
he would have been counted among the victims of the
guillotine.

With him sailed his wife and two children to bear him
company and consolation during his exile. . . .

Moreau had planned to return to St. Domingo, but the
hosts of refugees which he found at Norfolk and the news
which they gave him of the condition of affairs in the colony
convinced him that it would be unwise to do so. He decided, accordingly, to remain for the present in the United
States. Through the kindness of a fellow-passenger, Goynard, of St. Malo, he obtained a position at Norfolk as
shipping agent for the firm of Daniel Merian & Co., which
was engaged in the surreptitious shipment of provisions to
the French government. He remained at Norfolk until
May 15, when he went by way of Baltimore, Newcastle,
Wilmington and Philadelphia to New York, where he arrived on the 25th. He resided at New York until August
21, being forced to earn his living as shipping clerk at
hard work which weighed heavily both upon his pride and
upon his strength. During his residence in New York he

made the acquaintance of de la Roche, a German nobleman, with whom he formed a partnership for the establishment of a bookstore and printing press at Philadelphia.

He accordingly removed to Philadelphia, where he remained from October 14, 1794, to August 23, 1798, when he set sail for France. Of the many interesting facts connected with Moreau's sojourn in this city and in the United States, the reader is referred to the pages herewith published.

These four years of his life mark an epoch in his career as an author. He published from his own press two of his most important works. *Description topographique et politique de la partie espagnole de l'isle Saint-Domingue*, 2 vols., appeared, in French and in English translation (by William Cobbett), at the beginning of 1796. This was followed in 1797 by the publication of his best-known work, under the title of *Description topographique, physique, civile, politique et historique de la partie française de l'isle Saint-Domingue*, 2 vols. In these two works he made his most important and permanent contributions to historical work. Into both of them are crowded the results of many years of indefatigable research and of observation which make them invaluable to all students of West India history. These were accompanied by the publication, also in 1797, of two smaller works, *De la danse* and *Idée générale ou abrégé des Sciences et des Arts*, published in French and in English; the former a study of dances among the slaves of the West Indies, which drew forth enthusiastic praise from no less a personage than Talleyrand, and the latter, an abstract of the arts and the sciences, which became more or less popular as a text-book for schools. During his residence at Philadelphia thus appeared nearly all of his most important published works. These years of exile were the harvest season for his work as an author.

Moreau became associated with some of the most learned men in Philadelphia in the American Philosophical Society.

Elected to non-resident membership on January 16, 1789, before he left France, he became, on arrival, resident member of the society and attended its meetings regularly throughout his sojourn in the city. He spent many delightful evenings in its halls, had a high respect for its work, and was proud enough of his membership in it to subscribe himself on the title pages of his works as one of its members.

It will become apparent to the readers of the diary that Moreau became the person around whom some of the most distinguished French *émigrés* were grouped. His bookstore and printing press, located at the corner of Front and Walnut streets, became the rendezvous for many of them. Talleyrand, de Noailles, Talon, de Beaumetz, Démeunier, La Colombe, La Rochefoucauld Liancourt and the duc d'Orléans (the future Louis Philippe) all frequented his shop and sought Moreau's company. Some of them frequently remained for supper and like boys scuffled and played pranks upon one another about the store.

In regard to Talleyrand, the most notable of the many *émigrés* who found a temporary refuge in "the ark of Noah," as Philadelphia was happily called by one of them, the diary contains some important data. Moreau's first meeting with Talleyrand in America is recorded under the date of May 22, 1794. . . .

At his departure for Europe on June 11, 1796, Talleyrand took with him some two hundred copies of Moreau's *La description de la partie espagnole de St. Domingue* to find sale for them at Hamburg and in France. He offered to take Moreau's son with him back to Paris and to provide for his education. After his return to Europe Talleyrand did not forget the friend of his days of exile, for the diary contains letters written in affectionate terms from Hamburg and Paris.

It is pleasant to dwell upon these pages of the diary, because they throw a pleasing light upon Talleyrand's character. He is generally thought of as the prince of diplomats, employing human speech to conceal his own thoughts, but here we have him unveiling his very soul to a kind and sympathetic friend.

The diary shows, however, that Moreau de Saint-Méry's shop became something more than the rendezvous for such notable *émigrés*. From his printing press went forth many notable works published in French, such as Liancourt's study on the prisons of Philadelphia, and many of his own notable works, as has been shown above. At his press also was published from October 15, 1795, to March 14, 1796, a daily newspaper in French entitled *Courrier de la France et des Colonies,* edited by Gatereau, an *émigré* from St. Domingo. In its pages were printed the latest news of the great revolution in France and of the most recent developments in the French West Indies. How eagerly the numerous *émigrés* then at Philadelphia and in other cities must have read it! It must have come as a messenger to them in their exile. It served also as a social organ for them, for it contained notices of balls and concerts and meetings of French societies. Moreau's press, therefore, in publishing such a paper must have occupied an important place in the lives of the wider circle of French exiles in Philadelphia.

Moreau's experience as a bookseller and printer must have proved interesting to him. In the catalogue which he published at the opening of his shop, the following announcement was made:

Moreau de Saint-Méry & Co. take the opportunity of their Catalogue to repeat that they are established in the general business of Stationers, Booksellers and Dealers in most fashionable and choice Engraving. They will also have connected therewith a Printing Office and Book-bindery, adding thereto a select collection of Music.

They purchase French Books, and deal in every kind of business on commission.

They will also continue to fulfill orders for Books (or other things) from several parts of Europe, on the most reasonable terms.

In short, they will not spare any Care to accomplish their enterprize intended to propagate and diffuse knowledge.

The catalogue advertised for sale many books published in English, Dutch, Italian, Spanish and French, a fact which must have attracted many cultured Philadelphians to his store. But his business did not prosper and he was forced to move into more humble quarters at the corner of Front and Callowhill streets. This lack of prosperity was due partly to the quarrels which he had with his partner, de la Roche, partly, perhaps, to poor management, and partly to the ravages of yellow fever which drove hosts of Philadelphians from the city. In Bache's *General Advertiser* of July 2 and days following appeared the advertisement of the sale of his stock and fixtures together "with several works of his own library and some of his maps," indicating that he had not been doing a very profitable trade.

The picture which the comte de Moré (*Mémoires du comte de Moré*, pp. 148–149) has drawn for us of Moreau in his shop, though somewhat unsympathetic and sarcastic, is inimitable.

I went into a shop one day to buy some paper and pens and there found Moreau de Saint-Méry, one of the famous electors of Paris. After I had made my purchases he addressed me: "You do not suspect," he said with emphasis, "who I am and what I was in days gone by?" "Why, no," I replied. "I, who speak to you now, such as I am, was once king of Paris for three days and today I am forced to earn my bread by selling ink and pens and paper at Philadelphia." I was not so much surprised at this striking illustration of the freaks of fortune, as I was to see this little *bourgeois* suppose that he would startle posterity. I was not even more surprised to learn a few months later that he failed in business. The most remarkable thing was that it was for 25,000 francs and I would not have given 3,000 francs for the shop of M. Moreau de Saint-Méry.

The diary does not bear out the count's statement that Moreau failed, but it does indicate that he was hard pressed for money on sailing for France.

The last days of Moreau's sojourn at Philadelphia were embittered by the hostility which was shown toward Frenchmen. President John Adams, though friendly in earlier days, grew hostile and put Moreau's name upon the list of undesirable foreigners against whom the Alien Bill might be enforced.

Sailing from Newcastle on August 23, 1798, Moreau arrived at Bordeaux on September 28 and at Paris on October 14. His exile was at an end, and he was ready to enter upon a brief, but rather notable career.

After overcoming, through the aid of Talleyrand, the opposition of the director, Merlin de Douai, who insisted on considering him as an *émigré*, without rights of residence in France, he obtained the position of historiographer at the Ministry of the Marine. At the establishment of the consulate, he was made a *conseiller d'état* and a commander in the Legion of Honour. He seems to have been received immediately with open arms by the learned in Paris. Thus, on November 24, he was elected member of the *Société libre des sciences, des lettres et des arts;* on December 6 he addressed the Institute on the subject of yellow fever and was later elected member of the *Société libre d'agriculture* and of the *Lycée des Arts et des Sciences.*

In 1801 Moreau was entrusted with the protection of the interests of France in Northern Italy as guaranteed by the Treaty of Lunéville. He went to Parma as ambassador at the court of Duke Ferdinand, and at the death of the duke in 1802, he became the administrator of the states of Parma, Piacenza and Guastalla. In this capacity he exercised almost kingly powers, and, according to Fournier-Pescay, acquitted himself with credit. Hidden away somewhere in the Archives of the Foreign Office at Paris, or in the papers of Moreau which have not yet come to light, must be the records of his official life in Parma, which contain an interesting story. We only know that he incurred, by his leniency, the disapproval of Napoleon and was recalled in 1806. Napoleon refused to continue his pension as *conseiller d'état* and even refused to reimburse him for the 40,000 francs due him.

Moreau was thus reduced to selling many personal belongings in order to meet expenses, and did not receive relief until he was granted a small pension in 1812 through the influence of Josephine, to whom he was related. In 1817 Louis XVIII showed his generosity by relieving his poverty by a gift of 15,000 francs, which enabled him to live, for the remaining two years of his life, in more comfort.

During these last thirteen years of his life (1806–1819), Moreau worked indefatigably upon various studies in French colonial history, the manuscripts of which have remained in part in the great *Collection Moreau de Saint-Méry*. He died on January 28, 1819, at the age of sixty-nine.

Such in brief was the career of the author of the diary which is here offered for perusal and study. The variety of his experiences, the scope of his work and the charm of his personality all make him a worthy subject of a complete biography. Enough has been said, it is hoped, to make it possible for the reader to appreciate more deeply the personality reflected in the succeeding pages.

MOREAU DE ST. MÉRY'S
AMERICAN JOURNEY
1793–1798

MOREAU DE ST. MÉRY'S
AMERICAN JOURNEY
1793–1798

EARLY on the morning of November 9, 1793, I went on board the brig *Sophie* of Portland, which lay in the harbor of Le Havre, to see Captain Lowther about sailing for America. Captain Lowther claimed that two circumstances were unfavorable: not only was the wind adverse, but it was Saturday, a day on which Americans did not like to start a voyage; and so he sent me away until the following Monday.

I returned to the house extremely annoyed by this new delay; but while we were dining the captain sent word at 2 P.M. that he had decided to sail after all, and that the brig had already been warped outside the basin.

We hastily collected the few personal belongings remaining to us; and our good friends escorted us to the vessel, carrying the remainder of our interrupted dinner. Foremost among these good people was the mother of a numerous family named La Dentu. They saw us on board, and showered us with blessings as they left.

But not even then had we escaped France and her dangers; for a small boat, carrying several town officials, rowed out to us; and the officials, after ransacking the vessel, seized my nephew Dupuy, who had no reason for hiding and was making no effort to do so. The officials, insisting that Dupuy was of military age, since he wouldn't be twenty years old for another ten days, refused to let him sail. Even when shown his passport and the sailing permit issued by the

Convention,[1] they still insisted that he must appear in person before the town authorities; and, disregarding my own and my sister's distress, they took him away.

The *Sophie* stood off and on outside the jetties, waiting for further word from Dupuy. When the little boat finally brought him back to us, we were as happy as though our own child, hopelessly lost, had unexpectedly been rescued and restored.

Nearby lay the American vessel *Sussex*, bound for Philadelphia, aboard which was Baron de Cambefort, ex-colonel of the Regiment of the Cape [Cap François].

Finally we were ready to set off, in spite of the unfavorable wind from the southeast, the unlucky day of the week, and being in the Channel in the month of November, most dangerous of months at sea, as the records of all insurance companies testify. But how much more terrifying a season for all the world had been the months during which the Convention had ruled France.

Beginning that evening, everybody began paying his greater or lesser stomachic debt to seasickness.

November 10, 1793. I shall many times interrupt the recital of our voyage to tell things which we learned only after our arrival in the United States of America, for these things are better when chronologically arranged.

On Sunday morning policemen arrived (at Le Havre) from Paris with an order to arrest me and mine and to take us back to the capital, where we would promptly have been

[1]In September, 1792, the monarchy was abolished in France and all government passed into the hands of a National Convention composed entirely of republicans (749 members), but divided into two parties, the Gironde (right) and The Mountain (left). September 22 was the first day of the year 1 of the French Republic. Emigrants, by decree, were perpetually banished—a fact that got Moreau de St. Méry into grave difficulties when he returned from America to France in 1798. In the following months, Louis XVI was executed on January 21; the Girondists fought The Mountain; the Committee of Public Safety and its nine dictators took charge of France; Robespierre became head of the state; commissaries of the Committee were guilty of unheard-of atrocities

counted among the number of the victims of the guillotine. But the distance covered during the last eighteen hours, slowly though we had sailed, was enough to have saved me from my executioners.

Such was the disappointment of the police at their failure to capture me that they softened the sting of their disappointment by seizing one of my neighbors in Le Havre, Brother Bonnechose, one of the King's pages. He was beheaded in Paris.

Learning these details later, when we were safe, we trembled at the risks to which one more day of delay would have exposed us.

November 15. We were in the Channel from November 11–15. On the eleventh Bailly, first Mayor of Paris, suffered ignominious death, but with a courage worthy of a hero. On that day the wind became so adverse that Captain Lowther decided to put in at St. Aubin in England. As I was the only passenger who understood English, he gave me this news.

We laid our course accordingly, and were well in the harbor, with ships behind us, when the wind changed suddenly, and we had to return to the Channel, which we left the next day.

November 17. We received a polite visit from a frigate of Admiral Howe's fleet, composed of thirty sail, including three ships of the line.

November 18. A heartfelt *te deum* expressed not only

---

in Bordeaux, Nantes, Arras, Lyons; in August a levy was made on the whole male population capable of bearing arms; in September a law was passed authorizing the imprisonment of all persons suspected of being unfriendly to the Republic; fifteen thousand persons were put to death at Nantes; on October 16 Marie Antoinette was guillotined; in the same month the heads of the Girondists, defeated by the leftists, rolled in the dirt of the Place de la Concorde; the Cult of Reason came into being; the worship of God was abolished; the royal sepulchre at St. Denis was profaned; Mme. Roland, Bailly, thousands of others were executed; the inhabitants of Lyons were massacred; priests were ordered transported, every tenth day was a holiday. . . . Terror reigned. . . .

our gratitude for the blessings vouchsafed to us by the Almighty, but our prayers for the unhappy people of France where, at this very moment, all churches and places of worship were being closed by governmental decree.

As the weather was calm up to the end of November and the voyage uneventful, I shall fill in the time with a discussion of our sea life and the things that went to make it up.

November 19–30. Judging from the lack of foresight which seems to be the outstanding characteristic of American sailors, they rely on luck more than on anything else in making a voyage. They fear neither fatigue nor danger; but the care necessary to prevent accidents, especially desirable in a calling where everything is hazardous, is practically unknown to them.

In general, North American ships are strongly built, and the practice of keeping the upper works low adds greatly to their strength. However, the wood used in their construction is far inferior to that used in Europe, which lasts twice as long.

American ships are good sailers, but badly fitted out, and the owners have the insane idea that they can effect a saving by refusing to equip their vessels with many useful and some necessary things.

The French are always terrified at the carelessness with which fires are lighted on American ships. No precautions are taken, either with fires or lights. As soon as darkness falls a lamp is lit in the crews' sleeping quarters, and there it burns all night.

American vessels are equipped with Great Cabins that are strikingly clean and well furnished. Among their decorations are mirrors, pictures, curtains, mahogany furniture, excellent copper stoves, and even rugs; but such things are largely for show when in port, and they frequently disappear into storage when the vessel puts to sea. In such a well-appointed cabin, it is something of a shock to find that needs which might offend the nostrils must be satisfied through a hole in the floor, near the starboard windows. Cleanliness condemns this practice, and its practicability is so doubtful as to make one prefer a bottle.

In the matter of navigation the Americans are equally careless. The log-line is seldom run out; a helmsman often reckons his course by the manner in which the wind strikes his sails rather than by the compass; often the binnacle is left unlighted. Since he thus guesses at his course, without the help of hourglass or chronometer, considerable errors in longitude often can, and must, result from such negligence.

Americans returning to their fatherland from any country abroad pretend to have an infallible check on their longitude by means of the Gulf Stream, as they call it.

The Gulf Stream, to hear them tell it, is a current which starts in the Gulf of Florida.

Its effects, according to the celebrated Franklin and these returning Americans, are extremely noticeable. They are felt soon after a vessel gets out of soundings, and its flow is into the northeast from the southwest; but I can assure you that nothing is less accurate than this information. I have heard Americans say that we were in the Gulf Stream at entirely different times, and they are forever contradicting each other, even whalers having the same absurd notions as the others.

A more certain sign of the Gulf Stream is an alteration in the color of the water. At certain spots, one hundred and twenty miles out in deep water, it changes successively from a deep blue shade to the most tender light green. The indications are strengthened by the appearance of many birds not seen up to now, among which one sees a bird very much larger than the sea mew, its body all white, the ends of its wings black and its beak yellowish. The Americans call it a gannet.

Then there are burgomasters and mangs.[2] All these birds rarely go beyond soundings.

Other indications that accompany the change in color, etc., are clumps of floating weed, driftwood and trash.

The ordinary food of the American sailor is salt beef and biscuit, both of excellent quality. The beef is firm and red; and Americans, like the English, eat more of it than of bread. This simple fare is common to both officers and crew, and it is a rare occurrence on board an American vessel to have fresh food. They eat four meals. The first is breakfast, about seven or eight in the morning; dinner is between noon and two o'clock; the third is a snack at six o'clock; supper is around eight.

Tea is always served at the first meal; and it is this leaf, passionately loved by the Americans, which constitutes the entire third meal. Salt beef, butter, onions, cheese and potatoes make up the rest of the menu, and it is quite common for the officers, in their moments of leisure and even at night, to devour even more of these simple dishes.

The usual drink is water, which salt beef makes highly essential. When they have rum, they put it in their tea. They use it also to liven up the water a little. The crew drinks a great deal of tea, in which sugar is never spared.

A painful form of American shortsightedness is shown by the wretched clothing worn by the sailors. When ashore, not being under surveillance in this matter, they squander all their pay without a thought of the bad weather that will later make them regret bitterly, but too late, their failure to purchase extra garments to protect them from the cold as well as from the penetrating damp that tortures those forced to sleep in wet garments.

There is no form of religious service on board American ships. Nevertheless one can tell when it is Sunday, because when the weather is fine they pay a little more attention to

[2]The Manx shearwater, now extinct.

their appearance, and refrain from tasks not absolutely necessary. The most devout read some chapters from the Bible.

I shall repeat often that lack of foresight is the most conspicuous trait in the American character. Instead of foreseeing a thousand little annoyances caused by lack of care aboard ship, whether it be the breaking of dishes by the rolling, or the loss of provisions, or a thousand other incidents of this nature, they wait for the accident to occur; then hunt, sometimes in vain, for a way to remedy it. The lesson of today is lost for tomorrow, as was yesterday's for today.

The trip from France to North America is almost always long and painful because the prevailing south and west winds grow stronger as one nears the coast of the continent from which they blow. Thus American sailors speak fearfully of the waters near the Bermudas, and still more of those off Cape Hatteras, at 35 degrees.

It would be a good thing if they were equally apprehensive of sailing to the north of the Azores, as they frequently do when returning from Europe, and would learn that the storms to be found there are just as destructive as the rocks of the Bermudas and the shoals of Cape Hatteras.

American seamen have a mania for considering themselves more skillful than French sailors. They regard the careful precautions of the latter as a form of timidity, and when they learn that a trip will be longer than they anticipated, they are not at all distressed at the prospect of running out of food in mid-ocean. It is especially on coasting vessels that this American genius for shortsightedness reaches astonishing heights; and it is not unusual for such vessels, traveling without compasses, to find themselves blown out to sea by a gale and forced to speak another vessel in order to find out the longitude and latitude to which they have been driven.

The captain maintains strict discipline over the crew. The sailors are under a firm hand and their misdemeanors are sometimes severely punished. This discipline, very noticeable and unusual in a free people, does not prevent the captain from toiling with the others, including the first and second mates. My voyage from Le Havre to North America enabled me to verify these things I have just described, and which are confirmed by other reports and my own observation.

As I have said, I embarked on November 9, 1793, on the brig *Sophie* of Portland, one hundred and eighty tons, built two years previous and now returning from its second voyage to France. Her captain was M. George Lowther, and others of her crew were Reuben Howland, the first mate; Franklin, the second mate; a boatswain; Mathew, whom we nicknamed Cadet Roussel; Tom, the carpenter; Grim (a seaman) ; Dutchman (a seaman) ; Ned (Edouard), the cook; David, the cabin boy—ten men in all.

The passengers were myself, my wife and my two children; my sister Mme. Dupuy with her three children; Riene, their servant; M. Baudry Deslozières, my brother-in-law, his wife, sister of my wife; their young daughter Eléanore; Adelaïde, their servant; Mlle. de Marle, their friend; M. Goynard, former sea captain of St. Malo; and M. Brière, a youthful resident of Martinique, son of one of my friends.

Thus there were sixteen passengers and ten in the crew, making twenty-six persons on board. The cost of the passage was fifteen pounds sterling apiece or three hundred and seventy-five francs, without wine. The servants paid two thirds as much, or two hundred and fifty francs apiece.

December 2, 1793. From the Channel up to a point west of the Azores (where we arrived on December 2, the twenty-third day of our trip), we had weather as good as could be expected at that season; but our captain unfortunately had the opinion that he could make better time between France and America by going north of the Azores.

December 3. From December 3 onward we met winds violent beyond the imagination of any of the passengers except M. Goynard. They came just when we thought we had found our sea legs, and gave us a painful lesson in the undreamed-of hardships which the sea can inflict.

We contrived to be lively; my eleven-year-old son sometimes dispelled our ennui by playing upon his violin; and hopes of a short crossing helped us endure the numerous discomforts of a sea voyage. In our ignorance we thought our journey would last no more than fifty days; and we thought nothing of it when M. Goynard constantly spoke of a trip of ninety-six days which he had made in October, 1792, when in command of a packet boat plying between l'Orient and New York.

December 5. We spoke the ship *Jewel*, coming from Faro, Portugal, to Baltimore.

December 8. Our discomforts grew as the weather worsened. The sea came into my berth through the companionway hood. Our chickens suffered: they had been put aboard at Le Havre eight days before our departure; but since Americans are unaccustomed to taking such luxuries on their voyages, the fowl were unintelligently and carelessly crated. They were housed in unprotected cages and placed where rain could flood them. Even before our departure we had lost more than eighty birds, about a third of our total stock; with bad weather this trouble increased, and on December 13, our thirty-fifth day at sea, we killed our last chicken.

The turkeys lasted the longest, but their scrawniness was proof of how much they had suffered.

We had been in the habit of eating three chickens a day, either boiled or stewed. The stew was prepared in the stove of the cookhouse, in a square pan made of tin; and in the making of this dish the cook employed all his skill. He was also an American, engaged before the vessel left Charlestown, as caulker or cook at the captain's choice. I do not know what fitting test the captain gave him before deciding to make him cook; but in Le Havre the captain had boasted to me about his cooking ability. I am inclined to believe that an American captain's knowledge of culinary proficiency isn't overly profound, otherwise one would have had to conclude that Ned's talents were erratic; for as his masterpiece he offered us a dish that would have wrecked the reputation of even the lowest of restaurants. He was signally slovenly in appearance; and a malignant ulcer on one of his legs made walking difficult, so that his movements when tending the fire in the galley were so blundering as to give us cause for alarm.

We had some beetroots, which we always found pleasing and nourishing, but these vanished almost as soon as the poultry. Then onions took first place in our cuisine.

M. Goynard, who as a French sailor had made frequent fishing trips to Newfoundland and developed a well-trained palate, was even more filled with horror at our way of life than were the rest of us, so he took it upon himself to make our onion soup. This was rapturously received by nearly everybody, and benefited the health of many of us, myself included. For five weeks I had been able to take only a little nourishment, and from now on the foulness of the weather made it impossible for me to have recourse to the fresh air which I had been breathing each day on deck.

December 15. The stove in the cabin, only lighted hitherto on the first night after our departure, became our kitchen; for the heavy seas and the exhausting rolling of the *Sophie* made it impossible to venture on deck to reach the galley. Waves frequently broke over the deckhouse: on the eighth they flooded my berth; on the fifteenth they carried away the after gangways.

On less stormy days we went again to the galley to boil rice, or to prepare onion soup or *turlutine*,[3] a kind of stew made by Newfoundland fishermen from biscuit cooked with fat from salt beef; but these rare attempts were hindered by the

[3]Lobscouse to an American sailor.

jealous interference of the cook, who objected to sharing his galley, even though boiled salt beef had become the only dish to which this celebrated chef could aspire. He was forced, nonetheless, to endure the presence of the captain when the latter prepared puddings, or ricepounds. This delicacy was made with eggs, according to the supply on hand, flour or rice, and raisins. Some orange-flower water, that had been brought on board as a remedy for upset nerves, and a small jar of allspice belonging to the farseeing M. Goynard, added greatly to this dish; but eventually we saw all these good things vanish one by one, and for a long time before we reached America, our only remaining ingredient for pudding was wheat flour.

Each day the strengthening and restorative onion soup lost a little of its merit, since we were obliged to make this useful vegetable last as long as possible. Specimens which would have been rejected in times of prosperity were now regarded as not too rotten: for a long time we were able to use the young shoots of those too soft to eat; but eventually this resource vanished, too.

M. Goynard, whose ingenuity was always sharpened by hunger, recalled the pancakes of Brittany, and thanks to a little frying pan I had been inspired to bring, we saw the birth of this epicurean dish—and in our state of dire want it was truly that. With the addition of brandy, a little allspice, eggs, and an abundant supply of sugar from our private stock, it was ambrosia to our creole palates. But the eggs went first, then the brandy, then the allspice, and finally the oil, which we had replaced for some time with butter from which we had removed the salt.

The sugar was a consolation to almost everyone. "Almost everyone" is not a rash statement, for M. Goynard—assisted after a while by my nephew Dupuy, whom he had instructed in the happy (though difficult on shipboard) art of flipping over a pancake in the pan, and still later by the captain—

made enough pancakes so that every passenger could have several. He even sent some to the crew, or at least to the helmsman, and to the cook, whose willingness to supply a bit of wood was thus repaid. The sugar, I repeat, was used prodigally, as though it were inexhaustible; and successive evenings of four, five and even six dozen pancakes used up, in turn, this agreeable provision, the lack of which was perhaps our most grievous cross.

December 16–31. Fish, desirable even on the fastest of crossings, now became, as anyone can imagine, the object of our yearnings. M. Goynard, in the belief that American laziness could be overcome by the bait of a reward, offered the crew one dollar for each fish caught which was two feet long, and double for one of three feet. The captain posted a proclamation to that effect at the foot of the mainmast, but the offer of a reward was scorned. M. Goynard wished to drop a line, but he had no hook, there were not enough tallow candles to sacrifice for this worthy project, and besides, the weather was so bad it would hardly have been possible to catch fish, though we saw several porpoises, some dolphins, one day a turtle, and on other days many whales.

January 1, 1794. We spoke the brig the *Lively,* which had been out fifty-eight days, we having been out fifty-four.

Man is happily denied the baleful knowledge of the future, so on the seventy-third day after our departure, January 21, we thought we must be nearing the end of our troubles and so persuaded the captain to take soundings. Alas for all the stories of the Gulf Stream! There had been a genuine alteration in the color of the water, which excited our impatience; but the sounding lead disappointed us.

On the twenty-second the non-believers of the preceding day were forced to another period of waiting, but this only increased the number of the discontented.

On the twenty-third, when an observation was taken at noon, we found ourselves a little to the north of the latitude of Sandy Hook, so soundings were taken again. So firmly did we believe that bottom would be touched that the heaver of the lead imagined he actually felt it; and this news swept through the vessel like an electric shock. But when the lead was drawn up, it brought us nothing but alarm and despondency. The disappointed passengers cursed the Gulf Stream, the green water, the shearwaters we had seen the previous day, and most of all the wind, which now turned and forced us to head south.

January 24–31. For ten days, counting from that moment, we were the playthings of a tempest. During the month of January we saw the deadlights of the main cabin put up eighteen times. In other words, the cramped space in which we lived became a somber prison. The candles were used up, barring the few we must have against the time when we would land, so that the only gleam to cheer our nights and our deadlighted days came from the uneven and vacillating flame of a goblet-shaped oil lamp; and even that was sometimes extinguished by our terrific rolling.

The foul air of our little retreat was further enriched by the smoke from the stove, which had no outlet when the deadlights were on, and when the wind, which came from the hatch, prevented it from escaping. The evil increased until it became almost unbearable when the hatch was closed— which seldom happened until an inrushing wave reminded us only too well that someone had forgotten to shut it.

Seldom would one experience two sensations as dolorous and as contradictory as those we now endured. Hunger told us that we must eat, in spite of the smoke; and we wept scalding tears while we prepared something to deceive our hunger, which there was no way of satisfying, and at the same time the smoke suffocated us in our berths or put us out of them, when the rolling and the darkness would have made it less painful to be there than elsewhere.

It was during those ten days of misery that we found our-

selves deprived of all spirituous liquor. We discovered that
the captain's brandy supply had leaked away, since our departure from the Azores, because of carelessness in protecting the big bottles from rolling in their cases. All outside
the cases had been consumed. My sister and M. Goynard,
being unable to get along without wine, had brought some
bottles aboard, as had the captain. He, however, tossing it
off with gusto with the ship's company, seemed to forget
that he was obligated to supply M. Brière with wine during
the entire crossing. M. Goynard's supply might have com-
forted—even if it hadn't satisfied—a Breton, if, on top of
miscalculating the length of our voyage, he hadn't been over-
generous. And now all of us wanted a restorative, not only
those who had been forced by lack of funds to believe that
water was sufficient for a crossing, but even I who never
drank anything but water, and so had thought it would
suffice as on land. But it wouldn't, for our stomachs were dis-
ordered, the water had a slight odor and very often a disagreeable taste.

We spoke with chagrin of our meeting with the New-
buryport brig the *Lively* out of Lisbon, already fifty-eight
days at sea when we came up with her on the first of January. We recalled also the ship *Jewel* from Faro in Portugal
to Baltimore, which we had met on December 5; but regrets
were a waste of time and the wine of Portugal was far away.
I knew that M. Longuemare de la Salle, a merchant of Le
Havre, passenger on the *Sussex,* had put aboard the *Sophie*
about one thousand bottles of good wine; and having confirmed it by examining the bill of lading, we formed a plan
to procure a case.

The plan was feasible, considering our situation, the personal knowledge that I had of the extremely obliging character of M. Longuemare, and our determination to pay for
the wine in any case; but when I proposed it to the captain,
he refused on the grounds that he would be held responsible.

It was necessary to play the role of lawyer with him, and to dispel his fears by pointing out to him in a book of congressional maritime laws that a cargo could be drawn on in case of distress—and our distress was evident.

But when a propitious moment arrived and we opened the hold, it was impossible to find a single one of the forty cases of wine belonging to M. Longuemare. No news ever brought greater unhappiness. A second search was contemplated, but the futility of the first was discouraging and the captain apparently had no intention of giving the matter another thought.

February 1–3, 1794. The wind rose the next day and increased until we were again forced to put the deadlights on the Great Cabin.

The third of February was noteworthy. A little after sunrise a tremendous sea came out of the southwest, though the wind did not blow at all from that direction, and continued for more than an hour, bringing with it myriads of all sorts of fish, some of them six feet long. They seemed distressed and almost carried away by the sea, which was, so to speak, alive with them and at the same time solidified by them. When the ship plunged between two waves, the fish on each side threatened to overwhelm us; and when a wave subsided, the fish, over an area of many yards, were left without water and slid noisily over one another. What a prodigious spectacle! Never will it be erased from my memory!

I do not know what connection this occurrence could have had with the weather of the following evening, but never was there a more dreadful storm. The wind blew from the southwest with incredible violence; and for eight hours the vessel suffered such torture from keel to masthead that the sound alone was enough to shake the most courageous soul. We were afraid to see fish, because everyone feared a new omen.

I was on deck the morning of February 3, looking at those innumerable fish, when M. Goynard came and begged me—since I spoke English and enjoyed the captain's confidence—to prevail upon the captain to make a second search for the wine. Never was a service of the highest importance solicited in a more persuasive or pressing manner. M. Goynard had lost his flourishing embonpoint, he had courageously struggled against hunger, but the horrible necessity of drinking nothing but water had shattered his spirit and already changed his features.

Warmed by his prayers, I spoke to the captain about it, and once again a search was made for the wine; but again without success. Yet heaven, not wishing to abandon us to despair, let us discover some hampers of liquor belonging to M. de la Motte, a merchant in Le Havre and the American Consul. The captain agreed to take one. It was opened and the forty-four bottles were divided between him and the passengers.

What a spice is need! Never was nectar more delicious than this drink, which was nothing but ordinary *eau de vie* embellished with the smallest quantity of the brandy named on the label. One drank it from necessity, but I almost said with delight. A few applications to the bottle, and hope seemed reborn with strength. It took the place of sugar in our tea, also in our pancakes. It gave us, too, the courage to endure a new misfortune—that of being reduced, on the same day, to one bottle of water per person every twenty-four hours.

I wasn't a stranger to liquor, and if I had been fond of it I could have borne the distress of finding a chest filled with my literary works (which had arrived on board too late to be put in the hold and so had been put between decks) exposed and soaked to the point of damaging all my papers, engravings and drawings. One must have the soul of an author to understand the agonizing despair that comes with such a discovery; if ever I'd had any fear that one's sensibilities would be damaged by a long and fatiguing voyage, this experience would have proved that they can withstand the severest tests. I salvaged my materials as well as I could; but some of them will forever bear witness to how greatly they suffered.

February 4. In the evening we suffered a violent tempest; our deadlights were on; the captain was ill. In the midst of these horrors a terrific sea struck us on the larboard quarter. We thought we were sinking; the sea yowled, as it were, and the crashing of the waves echoed like the ringing of great bells in every ear.

At that moment, in my berth, I felt a long, heavy body thrown in from the left—the body of a living, breathing human being.

"Who is it?" I cried.

A voice replied, "It's I, Papa!"

It was my daughter!

On each side of the ship were two tiers of bed-places, one above the other and separated by an alleyway or passage. On the inner wall of our compartment, therefore, there were two bed-places, one above and one below for my wife and myself. But instead of this arrangement we preferred to use only half of our side as a bed-place, and devote the remainder to our belongings.

But on the outer side, toward the sea, two bed-places remained. My son occupied the lower and my daughter the one above, higher than ours. It was from there that this blow from the sea threw her on me, but so neatly that neither she nor I was in any way hurt, whereas she might have been killed, and I killed as well. Our dear Amenaïde spent the rest of the night, as well as part of the fifth, with us in our bed-place.

Among the frightful tempests at this period, one must include the decree of the Convention, by which slavery was suddenly abolished in the colonies.

February 6–12. From the sixth to the tenth, we had, with brief intervals, almost the same conditions as during the last of January; then the weather became easier, and on the eleventh we had a copious rain and the water was carefully saved. Although it was highly charged with electricity, and although its laxative quality was no benefit to our already bad health, and although it caused the greatest discomfort to those who drank it raw, we found it, and rightly so, much superior in taste to that of our water ration. Some of those who drank it vomited, some had colic, others were hopelessly incapacitated.

From the twelfth I was among those last. After the sharp pains of constipation, which almost universally afflicts those who travel by sea, and from which I suffer at all times, it was distressing to experience continued straining and evacuations that exhausted one's strength. And to what diet can one turn for relief when one is reduced to water, biscuit and salt beef?

Fortunately I had a stomach powder especially prescribed for loose bowels (such as that caused by laxative water like that of the Seine) and for weak stomachs. Someone had elegantly named it Powder of St. Germain, after a man whose singularity was well known, and who enlivened a jovial life with recitals of adventures in various centuries, even pretending, like Pythagoras, to have taken part in the siege of Troy. An American or an Englishman, because of childish prejudice, would die rather than use this remedy; and even the instrument for applying an infusion made from the powder, if seen by them, would cause a great scandal. However, it eased my colic and sometimes kept it from recurring, and I have no doubt that it saved my life; for this latest incident afflicted me more distressingly than any that had gone before, and prostrated me for more than fifteen days.

On February 14 we had been at sea ninety-seven days and

had never found ourselves so far south, our latitude now being 34 degrees. Since the twenty-first of January we had never stopped losing longitude, for whenever we tried to bear north, a squall soon took us in the opposite direction. Five or six times at least we had been in the latitude of Cape Hatteras, which, as I have said, fills Americans with an even greater fearfulness than that of the Bermudas. We didn't know whether we were threatened by this latter danger, and all was discouragement and uneasiness.

There was talk on the same day of the necessity of putting in at Charleston. Some of the passengers didn't like the idea at all. The wicked weather, however, which had blown us from north to south made it impossible to say whether we'd ever get to Charleston or not. It was hard for us to reckon our position because we had been continually blown off our course by the violent winds. At times we had been under full sail; at other times under bare poles. And to cap the climax our American sailors were always arguing about their tiresome Gulf Stream.

The weather had been good enough, all day, to allow us to spend the afternoon on deck enjoying the sight of many porpoises. And when the moon rose that night, we saw that it was in eclipse. We consulted the almanac, which announced a total eclipse for Paris; but because of the difference in latitude, the eclipse for us was only partial. With the help of the figures for Paris, our own midday observations and my excellent spyglass, I was able to make some calculations, from which I deduced that our longitude at noon had been 70 degrees, 0′ 8″ 45″′ from the meridian of Paris. After all our sufferings it was a disappointingly distant position, but at least it placed us to the west of the Bermudas, which was more than we had dared hope. I re-set my excellent timepiece to correspond with the hour of my observation, and I will anticipate a little here to say that when we sighted

land, this showed that my calculation had been only twelve
and a half leagues[4] out of the way.

February 15–19. Almost everyone had acclaimed me as a
good astronomer, since I was raising their hopes of an early
arrival, and the next two days, February 15–16, confirmed
this hope. But bad weather returned on the night of the
sixteenth; the sea was extremely rough and we became the
prey of new anxieties.

The gusts of wind from the Azores had broken the dolphin striker, supporter of all the masts, since it braces the
bowsprit, which is itself the key of the support. By one of
those happy strokes of fortune which we had often encountered, we had a good day in which to repair this loss.
In our brig the dolphin striker was fastened to the cutwater,
and since the piece had been carried away by the sea, there
was nothing to do but make another. A hole had to be made
for the new dolphin striker, and tools invented for the work.

The first mate, a twenty-two-year-old American, strong
and zealous, made the necessary contrivances, and bored
this hole in spite of having to do so with his body partly sub-
merged by every pitch and roll of the ship.

Toward three o'clock in the morning on that same night
the tiller of the rudder gave way. The wedges which should
have held the rudder steady, after this break, had previously
been displaced and worn out, but nobody had taken the
trouble to replace them; consequently the helmsman of the
vessel was shaken horribly. Helpless before the battering of
frightful seas, she shipped waves on both sides. One terrifying roll threatened to wrench out her masts, and never were
fears for them better founded. Our rigging, already old before our departure, had been repeatedly damaged, and even
one who had no knowledge of seamanship could see that its
alarming condition was a constant threat to our masts. We
were forced to remain several hours in this distressing situa-

[4] A French league is three miles.

tion, so that the steering gear could be repaired; and then it was done badly, so that it broke again the next day. Fortunately the second break occurred during the daytime, and new wedges had been made: thus the repairs were more quickly effected, were much stronger than before, and we were spared our former terrors.

February 22. Stormy weather struck us afresh. Our courage ebbed again: our health was worse than ever; and Mlle. de Marle, one of the passengers, who had been ill even before we left Le Havre, and had never ceased vomiting, became extremely feeble.

Deprived of any real nourishment, because some bouillon tablets, brought on board by the farsighted M. Goynard and finally cut into eight pieces, were exhausted, her end seemed near at hand—and a prolongation of our stay aboard threatened more than one among us with the same fate.

We were worn out with listening to endless arguments as to whether we should put in at New York or at Charleston, and all this uncertainty was terrifying. We felt it was indispensable to give the captain a clear picture of our voyage, and cap it with an urgent prayer to make the first land to which the wind would carry us. Since this had to be put into English for the captain, I was chosen to draw it up and translate it.

I painted a picture of all we had suffered, the inclemency of the season, the perverse obstinacy of contrary winds, the continual fatigues that had exhausted our own health as well as that of the officers and crew. I explained the sad state to which we had been reduced by lack of food and of sleep, perhaps the first of all foods, by the lack of air in our cabins and the water that poured in upon us daily during bad weather to add dampness to our other misfortunes. And then, as a final crown to our misery, which would have been sufficiently overwhelming without it, I told him that for several days we had been attacked by bedbugs, those hideous insects which excel all others in disgustingness and filth.

The captain was moved by this picture, even though it was no news to him. But he told us that the wind held out no hope for early improvement: he spoke a great deal about his shipowner's interests; also of the risks that an interrupted trip might cause to his own fortunes in a country where, according to him, the owners of vessels believe that non-success is a proof of incapacity (which they condemn) or of bad luck (which they avoid). He impressed upon me how important it was that any request to break the trip should come from the crew, since in that case their wages would not be paid during the stop, whereas the contrary would result if he stopped of his own accord.

I vainly observed that the shipowner, resting tranquilly in Portland, should be concerned only with the preservation of our existence; that nothing was less likely to add to a captain's reputation for wisdom and success than being dismasted and thus being forced to stop in the colonies; that lastly his crew must know that the passengers wished to reach the continent, no matter where, and were urging the captain to do so, and consequently wouldn't be crazy enough to take a step which would cost them wages.

I wasn't able to persuade him. The captain, who otherwise deserved the greatest praise for his equanimity, his amiability, his kindness, and the courage he showed in the face of danger, persisted in saying he would remain at sea as long as there were provisions aboard. He ignored the fact that our so-called provisions, which may have been passable fare for an American sailor, were hastening our end. Our only good fortune, that day, was getting a second hamper of M. de la Motte's liquor. It was, however, worse than the first, and the labels did not fool us in this respect.

February 26. We had some small consolation in temporary breaks in the bad weather. Most notable of these, a calm on February 26 following three days of raging seas, permitted work to be done on the replacement of tattered portions of our sails with other strips. The sails had been in bad condition when we left France, and the poor quality of the only spares we possessed—one mainsail and one foresail—had reduced us to a most terrifying state. Our two topsails were in such miserable condition that they tore to shreds if an effort was made to do better than three knots an hour, even when the wind was favorable.

To add to this improvidence, not a single ell of canvas was aboard for repairs, nor an inch of sail twine for the same purpose. My son was forced to sacrifice a ball of string that he had brought with him for his own amusement, and the passengers hunted everywhere for scraps with which papers and packages had been tied, and even unraveled the cover of the logbook to provide thread for sail-patching in an attempt to make serviceable that which actually was only lint. Nothing could have been more appalling than the appearance of the ship from a point where the eye everywhere encountered rotten and broken rigging, and holes in every sail. Ah, that anyone should so carelessly pretend to subdue a fierce element and aspire to a place among commercial people!

In the midst of all these perils and uncertainties we had preserved a sort of confidence, due to the sturdiness of the vessel's hull and the strength of her masts. Even in the moments of our greatest crises, one heard singing, or the strains of my son's violin, or a conversation usually accompanied by merriment. Indeed, one would truly be able to say that the character attributed to the French had never been more evident than with us. Our troubles usually ended happily, and never did one of us lose courage. The captain, whose disposition to have faith in his destiny was strikingly similar to our own, often expressed admiration for our cheerful endurance, and liked to repeat that English and American passengers would not have been capable of a similar strength of mind.

Beginning with the middle of December I conceived the idea of relieving our boredom by once again giving lessons in English. While on shore I had given them to my nephew and my son, never dreaming at that time that events would soon make the study of English imperative for them.

M. Goynard wished to join in the lessons, since English would be useful to him; and my brother-in-law and M. Brière made for me a full school. The resulting benefits— my own among them, since one cannot teach without learning something himself—grew by emulation. The school was increased by my two nieces, who were taught by my son. This pursuit, which occupied many hours, was a lifesaver for all, and without it I surely would have died of tedium.

Over and above all that, my gaiety did more than my courage or my strength of character, and we regretted the days when heavy rolling or deadlights in the cabin made our English lesson impossible. It was a singular spectacle: a Frenchman teaching students of widely differing ages a language which I wouldn't have dared to teach before those whose language it was, except that the teaching required knowledge with which American sailors are even less equipped than others.

My daughter occupied herself in sketching, and while I don't wish to be guilty of overenthusiastic praise of her mastery of this delightful talent, I'm free to say that we could hardly believe—even though we saw her doing it—that she could be so successful in making a crayon drawing of Juno. This she did for Captain Lowther, and the framed sketch was hung in the cabin of the *Sophie,* where she had done it.

Music, too, was a constant enjoyment to us. My daughter was unaffected by tempests that silenced the guitar of M. Goynard, expert as he was at predicting bad weather and foreseeing its effects—which in a way confirmed the views of those who considered ignorance one of the ingredients of happiness. One must add that youth, with its ever-evident bent for pleasure, either refuses to torture itself with a thousand imaginary annoyances, or resists those annoyances with an imagination undimmed by experience and anxieties.

How often did we envy the lot of the young and only cabin boy aboard the *Sophie*. He was barely fourteen; life for him was play; each day he learned French words by the hundred and laughed at everything. Charmed by the loose, easy manner in which the French passengers relieved themselves, with boyish eagerness he turned it to his own profit. This quadrupled his labors, but new objects and customs had become so many amusements to him. He even was enchanted with the repulsive duty of cleaning the chamberpots—which creole cleanliness makes awkwardly numerous. We sometimes wished—for even we were occasionally unjust—that he would be more zealous in his disgusting duties; but a moment's reflection, his smiling face and the knowledge that he was the captain's cousin combined to overcome our moments of temper, and there was no one who refused a just tribute of praise to this child who not only understood French as well as he did his own language, but already spoke it with astounding fluency.

The twenty-sixth of February, which I have already mentioned as so favorable for our much-needed repairs, brought us, however, a new sorrow, for on that day we were reduced to two biscuits a day per person. This was a blow that forced us to summon all our courage; but that courage was strengthened the next day, when we spoke the schooner *Amelia* of and for Boston. She had left Madeira only forty-five days before and was already short of water, so that we felt ourselves fortunate by comparison. To our regret we were unable to help the improvident Americans, even though they offered in exchange a little Madeira wine which we would have mightily enjoyed.

Two days later, the twenty-eighth, there was a violent storm, and lightning-torn clouds drenched us with water which we collected with the idea of boiling it before drinking. Doubtless the *Amelia* also received the same help, which she needed even more than we.

March 1, 1794. For the fourth time since our departure we counted the last day of a month. Every moment was long, yet the days flew by with a rapidity which we couldn't help regretting.

Then came March, the month so feared by sailors because of its equinoctial convulsions. Our hopes had been dashed so often that we had expected this new epoch to bring fresh furies upon us; but the day was beautiful, and only our craving for good news kept us from being affected by a truly heartbreaking scene: the public distribution, made March 1 to every individual on board, without distinction, of the remaining biscuits. To each one was allotted twenty-seven and three-quarters, and it took a trained philosopher to figure how many days he could make his portion last, even by exercising a starvation economy. One hid away his portion like a treasure, then one was gay and sang as usual. A few days later the interesting first mate Howland, the same who had repaired the dolphin striker, made it possible for us to economize on our biscuit ration by cooking pieces of wheat flour dough over the coals. We called the result "cakes"; but their appearance and flavor was such that only our hunger prevented them from being repulsive to our sight, our sense of smell and our palates.

On March 2, encouraged by the changing color of the water, we sounded, but without results. We thought of trying again on the following day, but a Norfolk brig, seventeen days out of St. Bartholomew, told us that she had not been any more fortunate in the morning than we had been the day before, so we decided to wait for the next day.

When that fortunate moment arrived, five o'clock in the afternoon, our sounding lead touched bottom; and at sunset the outlook at the masthead sighted land, the American land, the promised land! If we could have done so, we would have convinced ourselves with our own eyes of its existence, which we had begun to doubt; but darkness fell and left us at least the certainty that the sounding had been successful. The wind was favorable and we went to our berths with hearts filled with hope.

March 5. Daybreak showed us land close at hand; but its very nearness was a handicap, not only because the wind had turned to the east, but because with our insecure rigging and our tattered sails we might not be able to bear off from the coast. This thought also occurred to M. Goynard, who was on deck at an early hour; so—exercising the initiative which he had more than once employed during the voyage, both in preventing and repairing accidents—he urged me to persuade the captain to put in at Norfolk, in order to escape further trouble from the bad weather that threatened. The captain agreed with him, but suggested waiting an hour and a half in the hope that the wind would change. At half past seven in the morning it was decided to put into Norfolk. This decision, which meant that we would probably land that day, delighted all of us and filled our breasts with gratitude to God for His mercies.

After having obtained the captain's permission, as we had done when we left the Channel on November 17, we united in singing a *te deum* with a fervor understandable only to those who have endured such a voyage as ours and find themselves at the end of their tribulations.

It was not long before we made out Schmidt's Island close at hand. We hunted eagerly but vainly for a pilot boat, which we needed urgently, since nobody aboard was familiar with the Chesapeake, barring M. Franklin, our second mate, and one of the crew named Grim. We had no confidence in M. Franklin, who was a relative of Benjamin Franklin but failed to resemble him in any way; and from a sharp rebuke that the captain had given Grim on February 17, we knew beyond question that Grim couldn't be relied on for anything of the least importance.

It was necessary to tack into the river: fog and a rising wind made it impossible to double either Cape Charles or Cape Henry.

Under the guidance of M. Franklin we raised Cape Charles before noon. By following the course of nearby ships and tacking when they did, we presently made out Cape Henry, low and wooded like Cape Charles, then the high, square Cape Henry lighthouse, whose lime-whitened bricks stand out against the slightly reddish sand of the beach from which it rises.

Although pilotless, we entered the river a little after midday, having Cape Charles on the right, Cape Henry closer on our left. The thickening fog increased our need for a pilot, but the two or three pilot boats we saw were bound for Baltimore and moved away from us as soon as they heard us mention Norfolk. The captain was extremely uneasy, and we also regretted that we weren't able to see more of the land, which we hadn't seen for one hundred and fifteen days. At times it even disappeared entirely, at which our alarm increased.

But guided by a French map which the captain mistrusted because he was unable to understand its legends and warnings, and with the aid of constant soundings and of M. Franklin, we reached Point Comfort about three miles offshore and there were spoken by a pilot boat. Everything led us to think that it would pilot us: from its position, above the Baltimore turnoff, it had to be a Norfolk boat; and more than that, we saw the word "Norfolk" written on its stern; but when it learned who we were it headed upriver without a word of explanation and put into Point Comfort where several small vessels at anchor made a pleasing prospect.

We were therefore obliged to proceed as before by our own light, which the absence of the light of the heavens

made very uncertain. Because of this uncertainty and because this latter part of the journey required even more
specialized knowledge than the first part, we lost so much
time that we were unable to reach Norfolk by day. We then
decided to spend the night at anchor in Hampton Roads.
After we had passed Point Comfort we discovered some warships—two ships-of-the-line and five frigates—in Hampton
Roads, and felt sure that they must be the two French ships-
of-the-line and the frigates which had convoyed the unfortunate refugees from Cap François into the Chesapeake, so
we steered toward their anchorage.

As we passed one of the frigates, we were hailed in English. M. Goynard, to whom the captain had given the speaking trumpet with the thought that we would have to talk to
Frenchmen, told them to speak to us in French. They replied in bad English, telling us to go to hell and that they
couldn't understand us. A few moments later we were astern
of one of the two ships-of-the-line, from which we were
hailed in excellent English.

We thought we understood them to tell us to drop anchor. Since we had planned to anchor, we weren't annoyed
by the suggestion; but the imperative tone of the order
struck us as despotic, and captain and passengers alike
feared that we were anchoring in the midst of an English
squadron. Somebody thought he had heard, from the ship,
the shout of "You are with the French!" We were disturbed
by doubts, feared each moment to be visited by a longboat,
and had no way of knowing the nationality of the vessels.

March 5. It was windy and rainy during the night, but the
anchorage is such that there was no need to fear the weather,
which only becomes violent and a trial during the winter.
Hampton Roads is on the south bank of the James River,
about twenty-four miles from Cape Henry. Warships of
every sort can anchor there and even proceed upriver as far
as Mulberry Island. The James River at this point is under

two and a half miles wide, so that both banks are in sight, though there is nothing to see except pines and occasional stretches of felled trees. Hampton is the name of the small settlement at the end of the roadstead.

March 6. At seven the next morning a boat from one of the ships-of-the-line, flying the French tricolor and manned by sailors in French uniform, came alongside. From it we learned that the fleet had been sent in search of the convoy from San Domingo. It was made up of the 80-gun *Tiger,* Captain L'Hermitte; the 74-gun *Jean-Bart,* Captain Pillet; and 40-gun frigates *Concorde* and *Sémillante;* the frigate *Embuscade;* the frigate *Charente,* Captain La Brière; the frigate *Normande,* and the gun-brig *Papillon.* The fleet, under orders from Admiral Vaustable, had left Brest December 26 and reached Hampton February 10. The *Charente* had left Rochefort later and reached Hampton on the eighth.

They questioned us about the surrender of Toulon,[5] which it was impossible for us to know about, since we had left Le Havre November 9. They had thought we had mentioned this the night before, when we hailed the *Jean-Bart,* because the Englishman who replied to us had asked us about Toulon. We thought he was telling us to anchor, and had said "Yes" to him; and he thought we were saying "Yes, Toulon has surrendered." It was not without reason that I had suspected our questioner of the night before of being extremely British, for he was an English officer captured on the ship

[5]In 1792 after great and sanguinary disorder, the royalists of Toulon sought the support of the English and Spanish fleets cruising in the neighborhood. The Convention having replied by putting the town "outside the law," the inhabitants opened their harbor to the English. The army of the Republic now laid siege to the town late in 1793, and on this occasion Napoleon Bonaparte first made his name as a soldier. In December the forts commanding the town having been taken, the English ships retired after setting fire to the arsenal. The conflagration was extinguished by the prisoners, but not before thirty-eight out of a total of fifty-six vessels had been destroyed. Under the Directory Toulon became the most important French military fort on the Mediterranean; and it was here that Napoleon organized his Egyptian campaign.

Scorpion, which was returning to England with news of the capture of Pondichéry, the flags from there, and a sum of money.

We could tell them nothing except about our endless misfortunes, and they only needed to look at our vessel and us to know that we were telling the truth. The boat's officer, who was a Swiss volunteer from the *Jean-Bart's* marines, and the boat's crew were so struck by our thinness and our pitiable condition that they returned at once to the *Jean-Bart* to get food for us. Captain Lowther went with them, hoping to arrange for a fleet pilot to take us into Norfolk.

They were gone an hour and a half, during which we were spoken by a pilot boat with nine pilots on board, but it was too busy to bother with us, and left us for the *Jean-Bart.*

When the *Jean-Bart's* boat came back, it brought twenty pounds of fresh beef, a demijohn of good Bordeaux wine, several pounds of fine sugar, thirty pounds of bread and half a pound of chocolate.

I won't try to express the joy this help gave us. Everyone fell upon it voraciously, and while M. Goynard put on the proper clothes for frying things on the stove, we wolfed down the bread and sugar. We shared our gifts with the crew, and they gave in return the pleasure they manifested. The bits of broiled meat were gobbled as soon as cooked, and the French who had so generously brought us such wealth were delighted by our satisfaction. All would have been perfect if Mlle. de Marle had not been in a state of real danger, a state which had grown steadily worse on our approach to land.

The boat had also brought us a pilot from one of the frigates. Our natural desire to take advantage of this, since the shifting sands in the channel of the James require skilled knowledge and constant sounding, made us refuse a kind invitation for all of us to spend the day aboard the *Jean-Bart.* We expressed our regrets and gratitude in a note addressed to the *Jean-Bart's* commandant and signed by all the passengers.

At eleven in the morning we raised anchor, and since it is only fourteen miles from Hampton Roads to Norfolk, we expected to arrive there shortly.

But the weather, which had been clear since daybreak, became so foggy that we instantly lost sight of the fleet. Our pilot was therefore forced to sound constantly, as we had done the night before. The lead was cast by a sailor standing on the gangway outside the bulwarks, and announcing the depths in a singsong voice. The pilot questioned a passing schooner as to the location of the channel; she was astern, so that the pilot may have heard incorrectly, or the schooner in a spirit of roguish play may have misdirected us: at all events we ran aground a few minutes later, near the mouth of the Elizabeth River, no more than about seven miles from Norfolk.

Our depression at this mishap was slightly alleviated when the pilot assured us that we would soon be afloat and would reach Norfolk that same night. The captain and M. Brière had gone ahead in the *Jean-Bart's* boat: all the rest of us made preparations for disembarking.

The slow movements and drawling speech of our pilot made us doubt his ability, and with reason, for we remained aground until eight o'clock the next day.

Even then, we weren't long afloat. We knew from the song of the lead heaver that we were still in shoal water, and we soon ran aground for the second time, almost in the same place. The crew made every effort to get clear, but in vain. Sailors and officers alike cursed the pilot, but nothing disturbed his phlegmatic nature.

March 7. The need of waiting for the next flood tide made no appeal to M. Goynard, any more than it did to me or my son, because we were determined to go ashore. This we couldn't do because there was no way of getting action from any of the five sailors aboard the *Sophie*. We tried to hail boats from the fleet but without success, since the wind prevented them from hearing our cries. Not until noon did a boat come alongside—a boat from the *Jean-Bart*, sent from Norfolk by its commander with the thought that we might find it useful!

Not all of us could board it, for Mlle. de Marle's condition made it impossible for her to make such a trip or to be left alone aboard the *Sophie*; but M. Goynard, myself, my son and my two nephews Dupuy set off in it. We were determined that the captain should return to the ship with provisions, for it was hard indeed that those on board should have to exist on salt beef, water and biscuit and go without candles, when they were only nine miles from Norfolk.

As we left the *Sophie* I could scarcely believe the prospect before us. To have escaped all the perils of our dreadful crossing, to find myself approaching an enormous continent concerning which I knew nothing, to arrive on the heels of occurrences that must inevitably influence my entire life—these things joined to fill my mind with profound gratitude to the Being who holds the universe in the palm of His hand and hearkens to the prayers of those who have faith in His majesty.

Somewhat recovered from this first troublous thinking, which also had its joyous aspects, I studied the nearby shores of the Elizabeth River. With their inlets, in which I could see limekilns, cabins and fishermen's houses set down along the monotonous and uncultivated banks, they rather recalled certain shore lines in the Windward Islands. All along the river were pines whose permanent green was soothing to eyes that had so long looked upon nothing but water, which is so wearying to the imagination. Eventually we saw the houses of Portsmouth; then those of Norfolk. These two settlements face each other, the latter on the northern shore of the Elizabeth River; the other on the southern, at a point where the river, which flows from east to west, turns toward the west, making an elbow. We passed to windward of the English frigate *Daedalus*, almost close enough to touch her. She was commanded by M. Knowles, son of the Knowles who captured the fort of St. Louis in San Domingo in 1748. How stupid it is that enemies who become neighbors in a neutral port should go out to fight each other again.

At last I am on this hospitable soil, on this land of freedom, this land which, if the inhabitants are wise, should one day astound the rest of the universe by its power and perhaps impose upon the universe the law of being happy like itself.

My foot trembles in touching it, my head swims, my heart beats faster, the purest joy penetrates it; but at the same time, alas, I was confronted by the unfortunate San Domingo colonists, those charming people who were perhaps too proud of their wealth, but are now the very picture of misery. Dear God! Their pitiable condition, so much more distressing than my own, showed me that I had small cause for complaint!

Business matters took us to the home of M. Myer, a Norfolk merchant, whose praises had been sung to us even before we disembarked. Everyone had spoken of his kindness to the French and his espousal of their cause, and even before we met him we felt that we knew him and had many things in common. It was nearly half after one when we came ashore, and we were wondering where we should dine, when M. Myer's kind invitation solved the problem for all of us—even for M. Brière, who had joined us.

For us, whose stomachs had been wrecked by the *Sophie's* miserable fare, that meal was like a wedding feast. The excellent food, the simple and flattering welcome, the sight of a fond mother who even suckled a lusty infant during the meal, M. Myer's four pretty children—everything charmed us. I couldn't forget, however, that those we had left aboard the *Sophie* were in need; and M. Goynard, too, made every effort to find lodgings that would accommodate all the passengers under one roof.

The only house he could find—because of the influx of colonists from San Domingo and of persons from the fleet— was in Portsmouth. He engaged it, but we couldn't take possession until the tenth.

A happy circumstance had brought to Norfolk, the night before, M. Longuemare de la Salle, a passenger on the *Sussex,* which had left Le Havre the same day as we, but had fortunately failed to follow our example. Sailing to the south, she had arrived in Philadelphia after seventy-eight days.

M. Longuemare and his companion M. Marcel, another San Domingan, had lodgings, and when they found we could find no lodgings in Norfolk, they kindly deprived several sailors of their beds so that the six of us who had come ashore from the *Sophie* might have a place to sleep. Even then we had to sleep two in a bed.

March 8. Early the next day we went to the river to see whether the *Sophie* had arrived, and found her at anchor. A ship's boat loaned to M. Longuemare by a French merchant vessel took me and my son on board, where we learned that the *Sophie* had reached Norfolk around midnight, and that Mlle. de Marle had been so near death that an English doctor had been called to attend her.

It had been decided that everyone, even the invalid, must land; and thanks to the kindness of the sailors from this same French vessel, the landing was effected. The unhappy invalid received almost no harm from being taken ashore.

We took the entire group to the pension where we had slept, thinking it would be easier and more agreeable if we stayed together until the Portsmouth house could receive us. Already the night before I had arranged with our host,

M. Farrhit, an English citizen, for the reception of additional guests. But when he saw Mlle. de Marle carried in on a stretcher by four sailors, he flew into a rage, and absolutely refused to take her in.

Shocked and angry at his behavior, which I couldn't possibly understand in view of his gentle and kindly reception of us on the preceding night, I told him what I thought of it.

Philadelphia had suffered grievously from an epidemic, so I assured him that Mlle. de Marle's illness was not contagious, and that her condition was due solely to the hardships of our voyage. Even when I showed him the ravaged features of this dying person, he was more terrified than ever and declared again that he would never consent to take her in.

I heaped reproaches upon him, I even insulted him, accusing him of inhumanity; but he said my abuse made no difference to him: Mlle. de Marle must leave the house.

I asked for a day, at least, in which to find lodgings. He refused me even an hour. Furious at his hardheartedness, I had the invalid brought into the parlor on the stretcher, and immediately went in search of a place for her.

I saw M. Myer, who was touched by our predicament and made arrangements with Mlle. Eléanore Bynn, who had another boardinghouse, and she agreed to take Mlle. de Marle if we paid in advance. Much as every refugee from San Domingo needed money, my brother-in-law made this sacrifice for Mlle. de Marle, since she had accompanied his family ever since they had fled from Léogane. Happy would he have been if he had been able to save the life of this unhappy woman, but she died on the seventh day after she landed.

Thus our passage on the *Sophie* ended on the one hundred and nineteenth day, for the last passengers didn't go ashore until the morning of March 8. The great lessons to be drawn from our voyage were not lost upon us, and I note a few of them here in the hope that others, too, may learn something from them.

It seems to me that any Frenchman who plans to come to North America in an American vessel should make sure that the vessel is not old and also that her rigging and sails can withstand the perils of the crossing—which is not easy at any time of year.

In addition to this primary precaution, it is essential to learn from the ship's captain the amount of provisions carried, and the captain's statements should be verified.

I should add here that we have nothing but praise for Captain Lowther, for he not only made every effort to see that we had ample provisions, but even begged us to add to his list whatever we desired. It is true that supplies were unfortunately difficult to find when we left Le Havre, but what hurt us most was the lack of care in the handling of our stores. The Americans are not familiar with the disposition and care of such supplies, and so stow them without thought, give no attention to perishable goods, and leave them unprotected from dampness, from rats, from ruinous spoilage or from gluttony, which spares nothing. Care must therefore be taken to prevent such neglect.

Aboard the *Sophie* we experienced the results of the lack of this systematic economy, which, when it is present, seems to multiply the resources and consequently the enjoyment of them. Although we had enough water and biscuit to satisfy everyone's needs for five months, we consumed seven eighths of the supply in eighty-five days. Even when we then rationed those two articles, we had almost enough, from February 3 on, to let each one have a large pint bottle a day.

In truth, as all the passengers, as it were, were one big family, the economies of some of them supplied the needs of the others.

I have said enough about the waste of our fresh provisions. A captain must carefully calculate how much butter, oil, salt, candles, pepper, vinegar and eggs can be consumed by each person, and he must make sure that each person stays within his allowance—especially as regards sugar, which the French, particularly creoles, cannot do without. This is also true of Americans, who use great quantities in their tea. Officers and passengers alike will use fifteen pounds per person.

A traveler, too, must make certain that spare canvas is aboard for sail repair, and must remember that sail thread is necessary for this work; he must remember, too, that fish can't be caught without lines and hooks. He must make sure there are utensils with which to prepare food as well as on which to eat it. The saucepans in which we cooked our own meals were enough to make anyone shudder. They were copper and looked as if they had been made in a region that knew nothing whatever of the tinsmith's art. One of the three most dangerous stewpans had been brought on board by me, and in first-class condition. I had brought a good stock of plates and other things with me, as had M. Goynard; but even so we hadn't nearly enough to take care of our needs. I will say, too, that without my frying pan we would have almost died from hunger—though the ship's personnel would have got along all right.

Finally, after the traveler has taken every measure both to assure his own comfort during the voyage and to spare himself numerous privations, by carrying a private stock of provisions, of which he himself will be caretaker and steward, he must still not lose sight of the fact that any livestock put on board will be badly housed and fed if proper precautions are not taken. He must remember that meals will never be ready at the proper hour unless he insists upon it, and that if he fails to oversee the activities of those whose duty it is to place the food on the table, and make them exercise the greatest care, the rolling of the ship will destroy the food for which everybody is waiting. To complete the list of obligations on which one's life depends, a passenger must even be perpetually alert to the seamanship of the ship's personnel: must insist that the binnacle be lighted, that sextant and compass be picked up and boxed when not in use; that there be spare marine compasses aboard. He must ask frequently for the longitude and latitude, so that days won't pass without a reckoning being taken; must see with his own eyes that there are proper maps and charts of the ship's course and destination; must remind them to put out the log; must make them care for the tools which he will have seen to it that they put aboard for the carpenter, the caulker, the cook, for sweeping, scraping, et cetera; must forever urge upon them the necessity of promptly repairing anything that is damaged or spoiled, of putting on deadlights in a storm, before the sea has a chance to come in. In a word, a passenger must carry upon his own shoulders all the anxieties of a voyage, and at the same time never lack in gaiety, courage, patience and above all a constant resolve to get along harmoniously with everyone on shipboard. Without these last provisions, of which we never ran short, we'd have been done for.

After having brought up all these details, which may seem unimportant to most of my readers, I wish to express one great truth and one great hope. The truth is that my pen has not been guided by any wish to depreciate the great people who have given to the world the magnificent spectacle of men who successfully fought for liberty: the hope is that everyone will believe that anything I write about North America will be truthful—for I dare to say that all my writings are fundamentally truthful. For a Frenchman who lived in Paris during a period when that city astounded all nations by its love for science and the arts and by the urbanity of its inhabitants—who has seen, even though he has not enjoyed, the innumerable opportunities and pleasures which this capital offered—who has had occasion to admire what France offered within its interesting and enchanting confines—for such a Frenchman it may be difficult not to draw invidious comparisons between such a unique state and one that is just, so to speak, in process of being born. But such comparisons are not, and never will be, made with any intention of humiliating Americans. States rich in luxury have their disadvantages, and great vices can exist alongside great virtues and the most sublime knowledge.

March 9. We are writing to M. Gauvain, whom we understand to be in Baltimore, and to M. Clarkson of New York, to whom we had consigned our belongings.

The raw foods we had eaten, above all the milk, completely wrecked my stomach, already greatly upset for a matter of fifteen days, to such a degree that when I weighed myself at M. Myer's house, on scales on which provisions for the French fleet were being weighed, I found that I only weighed one hundred and thirty-four pounds instead of one hundred and eighty-six, which had been my weight in Harfleur. In a crossing of one hundred and twenty days I had lost fifty-two pounds, a loss evidenced by my thinness, the hollowness of my stomach which had replaced its usual rotundity, and a swelling of the legs that accompanied my wasting away.

March 11. We went to live in Portsmouth in the house M. Goynard had rented. It was a huge house, and if it had been completed in the same manner in which it had been begun, it would have been one of the pleasantest in town. It was a frame house, on the bank of the Elizabeth River on the outskirts of Portsmouth, near Gosport.

This is a good time to speak in detail about M. Goynard.

He came from St. Malo, where his parents, wife and children still lived. He was a ship captain by profession, and had made many trips to New York as master of a French packet. On this journey he was the confidential agent of M. Daniel Merian.

Goynard was a small man, fat and jovial, with all the vivacity and amiability of a Breton. He had a good voice and, as I have said, played agreeably on the guitar. He had a quick wit, a frank nature, manners somewhat brusque for a man about town, but very gentle for a sailor. Obliging and sensible, he detested ceremony and made himself fast friends easily.

From the moment of our meeting aboard the *Sophie* in the harbor of Le Havre, he inspired me with a confidence that was confirmed by my wife, my children and by our misfortunes. The fact that I had been made an honorary citizen of St. Malo, and that M. de Varenne of that town was my friend, established a sort of bond between us.

He asked me what I intended to do in the United States. When I said I had no plans, he promised to help me in every possible way. His kindly disposition toward me grew with the crossing. We were congenial. He told me that the *Sophie's* cargo ostensibly belonged to Daniel Merian, a Swiss, but in reality to the French Republic; that as Merian's representative he would do a business of several millions in New York; and if agreeable to me, he could offer me a position with Merian's firm and pay me at the rate of two hundred and forty piastre-gourdes or dollars a year. This, at the rate of five francs ten centimes per piastre-gourde, meant one thousand two hundred and sixty francs. What unexpected good luck! What happy fortune! In Goynard I saw a man of parts, a true friend, an angel sent from heaven to shower me with kindness.

In proof of my gratitude I presented him with my gold repeater watch, an extremely beautiful one whose accuracy had been demonstrated during our voyage; and on its cover I had engraved this thought, which seemed to me appropriate: "It is always the hour for a good deed." M. Goynard was delighted with the gift.

From the ships of the French fleet we had learned that they had brought another representative of Daniel Merian, M. Guerlain of Le Havre, but Goynard assured me he could make Merian fulfill all promises made to me. Behold me, therefore, changed into a clerk in a commercial house.

The same day, going in search of our most useful belongings, which had been left on the *Sophie,* I met several colonists whom I had known in Cap François. None of them seemed to me to be enduring our common ruin with as much courage as I, and I couldn't help smiling scornfully when I heard one of them bewailing the fate that had reduced him to only two Negro servants. His father, I knew, had had no servants, either white or black, whereas I had seventeen when I left Cap François, and now had none at all.

March 13. I called upon the Vice-Consul of the French Republic, at the home of Citizen Oster in Norfolk, to announce my arrival with my family and our intention to return to San Domingo if a favorable opportunity presented. Then I took up the task of rescuing M. Guerlain's belongings, which had been left in Norfolk and had been greatly damaged. On our return to Norfolk we witnessed the death of our poor friend Mlle. de Marle.

The Baudry family as well as my sister's joined us in the Portsmouth house.

March 16. Each day I go to Norfolk on business matters connected with my clerkship; and bring back to Portsmouth different effects to make up for the losses suffered on the voyage.

Every day we meet many colonists whose pitiful condition makes our hearts bleed.

March 19. The English seize Guadeloupe.

March 20. The English seize Martinique.

March 26. I gave my daughter her first English lesson and received a letter from my friend Berlin from Baltimore.

I received one from Gauvain.

April 2, 1794. We were greatly chagrined to discover that a young American girl fifteen or sixteen years old, who had been befriended by my niece Uranie, had repaid the kindness by stealing several small articles from the house.

April 3. We met Denard from Cap François. He dined with us the following day.

April 4. My mother-in-law reached Baltimore from Charleston.

April 5. Boussenat died as a result of persecutions by Jacobins aboard the French fleet in the Chesapeake, which was in sympathy with the American Jacobins. He had been forced to hide in the woods and swamps.

Denard left for Edenton, capital of North Carolina.

April 7–10. It was cold.

High winds made it dangerous to cross the river.

April 14. Guadeloupe captured (see March 19 for the same event).

Gauvain wrote us that my mother-in-law had arrived at Baltimore.

The ashes of J. J. Rousseau were placed in the Panthéon.

We gave a dinner for Captain Lowther and the owner of the *Sophie*.

May I be permitted to cite that on the same day the Lycée of Paris, to which I belong, performed a most courageous act by visiting the prison of the Conciergerie and placing a crown upon the head of Lavoisier, who was awaiting the death to which the most atrocious ignorance had condemned him.

The French fleet in the Chesapeake left Hampton Roads on the fifteenth, and Cape Henry the seventeenth at two in the afternoon.

My friend Claudot was guillotined.

I escorted Mme. Boussenat to the Vice-Consul in Norfolk on the occasion of her husband's death.

April 20. My mother-in-law and Gauvain arrived from Baltimore after a three-day voyage. With my mother-in-law was her little Héloïse, born at Cap François May 22, 1785, and her griffon Sylvie. What joy her arrival gave us! How many things they had to tell us and to hear! All this took some time.

On the same day the English, aided by a group of renegade Frenchmen, seized Martinique (see March 20 for the same event).

I saw an American tarred and feathered in punishment for causing the death of M. Guspin, killed by the discharge of a cannon that was saluting the frigate *Commerce.* The American seemed not to care that he had killed a man.

So many were congregated in our house that we were obliged to employ a cook—a young Negress named Louise belonging to M. Crousielles, a refugee from San Domingo, living in Portsmouth.

April 26. Gauvain went alone to Baltimore. By the same packet which had brought Gauvain, Howland, the young mate of the *Sophie,* wrote my daughter, offering her his hand and his heart.

April 27. The arming of the Revolutionary army.

May 1, 1794. We saw a review of the militia at Norfolk. Each infantryman wore a sprig of laurel or pine in memory of this day, which is celebrated in America just as it is in France.

At the table my brother-in-law Baudry had a slight difference of opinion with my niece Uranie. Her brother took offense, and showed it. My brother-in-law wished to show a sort of superiority over him because of his age; but my nephew immediately offered him the chance to prove whether he was also superior with the pistol.

Fortunately the plan was discovered and Goynard, at my request, put an end to this folly.

May 4. Easter was extremely hot. We went to Norfolk to

celebrate the solemn event and sing O *Filii* in the Roman Catholic church, which really was a barn. But of course the majesty of the Creator dwelt therein.

May 7. I rented lodgings near Norfolk for my sister.

May 9. We paid all the bills for our respective expenses and packed our baggage. Goynard, my family and I were leaving for New York; my sister, the Baudry family, and also my mother-in-law, were remaining in Norfolk.

A letter from M. Guerlain, written April 29, told me that the *Sophie* had reached New York, and assured me that he would carry out Goynard's wishes concerning me. The schooner *L'Espérance*, of New York, sailed from Portsmouth with our belongings.

May 12. In the evening we took a walk in the woods, and M. Goynard was startled for a moment at the sight of flickering fireflies, which were new to him.

We bought some pineapples.

May 14. Mme. Bayard, born Mlle. Fage, died. She was the wife of the former assessor-counselor to the Council of Cap François.

My mother-in-law, M. Baudry, my wife, my sister, her second son and I dined at M. Myer's.

May 15. We paid several goodbye calls, including one to Colonel Wilson at Gosport. It was a sorrowful time. At ten in the morning we took leave of our own people who remained in Norfolk, knowing that we were perhaps leaving them forever; and my wife, my children, Goynard, Brière and I embarked for Baltimore on the schooner *President*.

NORFOLK

MAY, *1794*. Norfolk is situated in the county of the same name, and on the right bank of the Elizabeth River, just below the mouth of its eastern branch, four miles above the mouth of the western branch and nine miles from its juncture with the James. The Elizabeth River has an east, west and a south branch, the last being its principal artery. Ships can go up it for almost four miles, provided they are familiar with the channel.

Norfolk, which is 36 degrees 35 minutes latitude north and 1 degree 10 minutes longitude west of the meridian of Philadelphia, provides anchorage for three hundred vessels. The roadstead is from two to three hundred yards wide, and the average rise of the tide at Norfolk is about eighteen feet.

The principal landing place is on docks which border an indentation at the foot of an open square. The docks, which are extremely narrow, are reached by ladders or ramps made of thick planks to which crossbars are nailed for footholds.

The open square is a long one, quite deep, with shops and taverns along both sides. All the way across the upper end of the square is the market, which is open every day except Sunday, when it closes at nine in the morning. Through a gap in the market one sees an imposing brick house that looks like a public building, especially since the word "Southport" is lettered over its main entrance. "Southport," however, is only the name of the merchant whose shop is housed in it. Its steeple is topped by a weather vane whose direction irons bear the initials, brilliantly gilded, of the four cardinal points of the compass.

The street on which this beautiful house stands is the widest and longest in Norfolk, with the exception of one other at right angles to it that leads straight out into the country. The other streets are laid out helter-skelter, though the sides of each street, generally speaking, are parallel. None of the streets are paved, which makes them unpleasantly dusty or muddy, according to whether it is dry or rainy. The sewage ditches are open, and one crosses them on little narrow bridges made of short lengths of plank nailed on crosspieces.

Most of the houses in Norfolk are made of wood and are mostly one story high, though some have two or three stories, big barns and even lightning rods. We saw one whose top had been made into a terrace. Every day new houses spring up in the direction of the Elizabeth River. New wharves completely fill the river front. These wharves, like all the others in America, are put up solely for the convenience of the owner, are built without any general plan, and inconsiderately shut off the view of the river without a thought for the future needs of the town. On the wharves are warehouses built on piles or on squared timbers set on planking or on brick piers. Some of the warehouses are three stories high. It is commonly thought in Norfolk that pine buildings seldom last more than ten years, and for this reason they are never repaired.

Norfolk contains about five hundred houses, set close together except near the upper part of the town. Formerly there were fewer, and most of them were brick. But on January 1, 1776, during the War of Independence, Lord Dunmore, Royal Governor of Virginia, ordered the British ship *Liverpool* to set them afire. The many charred ruins that still remain are a forceful reminder of Norfolk's destruction, and must long make it rankle in the minds of Americans.

Norfolk has three churches, Anglican-Episcopal, Presbyterian and Methodist. The last-named has the largest congregation. The Methodists, for the most part, are Negroes whose Sunday grimaces, sobs and inarticulate cries attract the curious[1] when the minister, wearing everyday clothes and with transfigured features, addresses them upon the sufferings they must expect in the Life to Come. Sometimes his voice is gentle: more often his thunderous warnings fill the Negroes' superstitious souls with terror.

Although the minister teaches that all must suffer alike in the hereafter, everything in this church harps upon class distinction. The women sit on the right, the men on the left; there are separate sections for free colored men and for slaves, and these are again divided according to their sex. The church is built of wood.

I cannot keep from comparing the religion of the Methodist slaves in the United States with that of slaves in French colonies. Among the latter the religious ceremonies are conducted by missionaries drawn from various denominations, even from the Capuchins.

The monks are usually stricter and less worldly in appearance than the secular priests, and their simplicity is better adapted to the manners and thoughts of Negroes. The Capuchins, in particular, when the slaves complain of their unhappy state, tell them: "You think you are downtrodden because you are black; but we who are white like your masters are equally abject in your masters' eyes. But if you have been good, there will be no difference in the Life to Come between you and your masters: with them you will share eternal bliss; when you enter the Lord's House, you will enjoy the presence of God in exactly the same way as your masters. If you are sufficiently pure to approach the sacred table, you use the same table as those who are white; and

---

[1]"La troisième est une église de méthodistes, où comme dans toutes celles de la même espèce, on fait beaucoup de grimaces, de hurlemens et de contorsions." La Rochefoucauld Liancourt, IV, 277. One of several cases where La Rochefoucauld "borrowed" from Moreau without giving credit.

on your deathbed you receive, like them, the sacred viaticum. Console yourselves, then, for the ills you suffer: because of them you will merit heaven."

Such words are at least consoling. But the Methodist priest says to the Negro slaves, "Unhappy creatures, you are condemned to suffering in this world and to eternal torment in the next!" How can such a doctrine, which gives birth only to despair, attract even an unfortunate slave!

There is a bishop of the Protestant Episcopal Church for the state of Virginia (M. James Madison)[2] who exercises authority over Episcopal ministers. When he thinks fit to dismiss one, he sends his mandate to the mayor of the town, who reads the order in the Episcopal church.

There is also, as I have said before, a place consecrated to the practice of the Roman Catholic religion. A room in extreme disorder has been used for this purpose ever since a zealous, red-faced Hibernian came among the unhappy French San Domingan refugees to preach humility and submission to the will of God and the necessity of accepting gladly a miserable lot with which the Church and the priest are in harmony. This priest was appointed by M. Carroll, a Maryland creole. M. Carroll was consecrated a Roman bishop in London, named Vicar General of the Holy See, and held his See in Baltimore for one year, during which time the Irish priest was in Norfolk. He lives on charity, and every Sunday money is collected for him during Mass by the San Domingan colonists who attend his church. What a miserable fate!

These unhappy colonists, ruined by the disasters in their island, which not long since was known everywhere as being the richest in America, are proportionately more numerous in Norfolk than in any other part of the continent, and for various reasons.

[2]James Madison (1749–1812), a second cousin to the President, elected president of William and Mary College in 1777 and first bishop of the Protestant Episcopal Church of Virginia in 1790.

The first is that the convoy which left Cap François when the town was in flames came to anchor in Hampton Roads, so that Norfolk was the first asylum for these unfortunates. The second is that most of them lacked the means to proceed elsewhere. The third is that many who had brought Negro servants with them remained because the laws of Virginia permit slavery. Fourthly, the winter season, distressing to people from a warm climate, is less severe in Norfolk than in most places. And lastly the inhabitants of this place evinced a warm sympathy for the French.

The Norfolk newspaper, on July 10, 1793, announced the arrival from Cap François of a convoy of one hundred and thirteen sail, including two ships-of-the-line and six frigates or small gunboats, and told of the tragic situation of those who had been snatched from death.

Subscriptions were immediately started. Richmond, Petersburg, York, Hampton, Portsmouth and Williamsburg competed with each other in expressing their generous compassion, the three last places alone subscribing one thousand and seventy-five dollars, or about six thousand francs.

In the newspaper of the seventeenth, Rear Admiral Combis expressed his gratitude to the magistrates and to the citizens of Norfolk; and on the thirty-first M. Cassan, deputy of the French Minister to the United States, added his thanks, not failing to say how deeply touched Admiral Combis had been by the affectionate reply made by the mayor on the twenty-seventh.

I wish to mention here a remarkable fact: the influence that political writings may have on any occurrence whatever.

A deputation from Williamsburg arrived in Norfolk by water to bring aid to the French colonists of San Domingo, and came aboard the ship-of-the-line *Jupiter* to pay their respects to her commander, M. de Jerçay.

Protruding from the pocket of one of the deputies was

a packet bearing a Jamaica address. This caused shouts of
"Treason!" and the suggestion that the deputies be hanged.
They were only saved because they agreed to the opening
of the packet, which contained nothing but business letters
from merchants.

What a horrible example of suspicious minds, which can
see treason even in kindliness!

Norfolk, which is Virginia's foremost commercial port,
does a considerable business with the Antilles, sending them
lumber, barrel staves, shingles, flour, cattle, Indian corn, potatoes, etc. At the moment eighty deep-water vessels and
ten coasters operate out of Norfolk, and one hundred more
ply in the rivers and in the Chesapeake. Norfolk-built vessels are highly esteemed for their speed, especially the brigs
and the schooners.

Unfortunately a dangerous worm attacks ships' bottoms
in these waters from June until September.

In Norfolk, as elsewhere in America, everything is sold in
the same store, and the townspeople gladly follow this custom because farmers who bring their products to Norfolk
generally sell them to merchants at whose stores they can
find everything they need.

Norfolk has little direct commerce with England (to
which it sends, however, tobacco for which the freight
charge is five dollars a hogshead), and the merchants of this
section get their drygoods from Baltimore, Philadelphia and
even from New York. It is the usual custom for such Norfolk merchants as have no correspondents to fill their order
to go at least once and sometimes twice a year to one of those
three cities to purchase a stock of goods.

Norfolk also has a Court House, in which County Court
meets on the third Monday of each month, a prison, a theater
built of brick, and an academy. The town is incorporated,
and is managed by a mayor and several aldermen.

There are reckoned to be three thousand inhabitants.

Norfolk has two printing houses and two newspapers. The printing houses are used almost entirely for the printing of broadsides advertising Negroes for sale, to let or to farm out, Negro fugitives, notices of the departure of persons who plan to leave town. Norfolk also has a bookdealer who makes quite an advantageous affair out of the rental of books. This bookseller is M. Hunter who, coming from England to Jamaica, left that island twice by the doctors' orders to try to recover his health, first in India and then in Africa, and it is probable that Virginia will complete its ruin, even though the doctors advised this as a third resort. M. Hunter is affable and well educated.

The Norfolk women are pretty. Their eyes are expressive but their complexion is dull, bad teeth disfigure their mouths and the length of their feet is also unpleasing. In general they are tall and graceful, and among their charms one should not overlook their pretty bosoms.

The men are large and well built.

The love of luxury is universal in this locality, as is the case in all places where people own slaves. One sees unemployment even among the population of three thousand— a considerable number for the size of the place:—since ten or twelve people are often seen chatting idly at certain street corners.

The house furnishings are simple; the houses are without plate glass or carpets. Tables, sideboards, mahogany bureaus and chairs are always in the English taste, and floors are always carefully washed.

Because of the warm climate the houses are built with a sort of corridor called a hall. In this the residents live when the cold season is over, because the doors at the two ends admit a flow of air which helps one to breathe during the sometimes suffocating heat, especially on a day when the atmosphere is filled with lightning, and claps of thunder succeed one another with dreadful reverberations.

These hot spells make the climate of Norfolk quite deadly. Bilious fevers, ague and putrid bilious fevers are common. There are also slow fevers which persist for many years. Stoppage, swelling of the legs, and illnesses resulting from lack of exercise (such as those called bellyache in the Antilles) are common. This may be due to the excessive use of quinine, which is taken recklessly and often without following any directions. Verminous diseases are frequent. The residents fear their climate to such an extent that those who have the means take a trip, and even go out to sea, during the hot season. It is true that the surrounding country is swampy and even more unhealthy than Norfolk itself, and everywhere are pools of stagnant water from which rise emanations which impregnate the air and in which swarms of mosquitoes breed to such an extent that during the summer, even in daylight hours, they are a veritable torture.

The fear of yellow fever, fairly general in America, was so widespread and firmly fixed in Norfolk in 1794, on account of a violent epidemic of it in Philadelphia, that in one instance a boardinghouse refused to admit a young San Domingan woman who was brought ashore from Le Havre in a dying condition as a result of the sufferings endured on a crossing of one hundred and nineteen days. Only after great difficulty were her friends able to find a lodging for her—a lodging where she died eight days later.

The farmers who have lived a long time in Virginia are always careful to purge themselves in the month of August.

Summer causes the death of a large number of people in Norfolk, and funerals there are far more sumptuous than elsewhere on the continent. The dead are shaved and dressed, and vanity demands that they be provided with beautiful coffins. The minister comes to the house of the deceased and delivers a discourse, after which everyone goes to the cemetery. A singular peculiarity of Norfolk funerals is the manner in which the physician always attends, giving his arm to the minister. If the deceased is sufficiently important, his body is taken to the church before interment. The graves are marked by upright stones engraved with the names of the person beneath, and above some of them brick walls support large marble slabs on which are written eulogies that nobody bothers to read.

Second marriages are frequent in Norfolk, and since the climate is harder on men than on women, it is not unusual to find one woman with children of various last names. It is thought here, however, that nowhere is so much tenderness shown toward children as in Virginia; all their whims are indulged, especially those of going barefoot a great part of the time, and beating slaves with rawhide whips.

Norfolk weddings are extremely gay. A dear female friend of the bride prepares pastries of all kinds for the occasion, and does the honors at the fête which follows the consecration of the marriage which the minister celebrates in the house. At this repast, as at all others, the women seat themselves first, but always leave the table the moment the men announce they prefer Bacchus to Venus.

In the summer Norfolk has theatrical performances given by comedians who play in Richmond during the winter. The theater is built of brick. In the spring of 1794, Ricketts and MacDonald visited Norfolk and gave an exhibition of horsemanship which drew a large crowd who, according to the location of their seats, paid a dollar or three quarters of a dollar. There was a separate place for people of color.

In other respects life in Norfolk is monotonous, and the throng of young girls who came to hear my niece, a young French creole from Paris, play the harp was definite proof that this instrument was absolutely new to them. The men are greatly attached to Freemasonry—or at least the many lodges known to be in Norfolk would indicate that this is the case.

In spite of the great number of French in Norfolk, the prices are not high. The cost of living at a good boardinghouse is 4½ dollars a week (about 1 louis), but one who remains more than three days must pay the full amount.

The charge for one day is a dollar, and dinner alone costs ½ a dollar.

Choice beef costs ⅛ of a dollar a pound, less than 14 sous; a quarter of mutton 3 to 5 francs, a pound of pork 15 sous; a pair of young fowl from 50 sous to 3 francs; a duck 15 sous; a hen turkey 5 francs; a dozen eggs 9 French sous; a pint of milk 1/16 of a dollar, or 6 sous.

The ordinary drink of Norfolk is cider, which comes from New England and is improved by the voyage. Sometimes one pays only a louis (4½ dollars) for a barrel which holds 120 French jugfuls (about 30 gallons).

But what sells for an absurdly low price in Norfolk is fish. A weakfish weighing more than 20 pounds costs only 4 or 5 francs, and sometimes one that weighs three times as much may be purchased for 1 dollar, or 5 francs 10 sous. Drumfish are also cheap. Sturgeon, which here weigh up to 60 pounds, cost 6 French sous a pound, and one pays no more for little cod, which are sold alive and are delicious eating. Shad are innumerable. There are also perch, sea hog, herring, sole, plaice, flounder, mullet, trout, blackfish, eels, the cofferfish, the garfish, etc., etc. In a word, fish are so abundant that the police are frequently obliged to order unsold fish to be thrown into the sea.

At any moment one may see fish jumping in the Elizabeth River off Norfolk, and various sorts of birds choose this place to do their fishing. The crows show a delicacy not usually associated with them by preferring live fish, and refusing to touch the dead ones that float on the surface. Many boats engage in oyster fishing, using an iron scissors-shaped instrument ending in two rakes to scrape the oysters from the bottom of the river. The oysters are large but have little taste because the water is not sufficiently salty.

I have eaten asparagus in Norfolk on March 24. By April

10 young peas and beans are in blossom. Around April 3 the maple-sugar tree shows its blossoms, as does the hawthorn. By the twenty-third red roses are displaying all their spring beauty, and so is the honeysuckle.

I have eaten strawberries on May 15; and by the twenty-ninth wild white- and red-heart cherries are found in the woods and are sold at 24 French sous a pint.

An hour after noon on April 2 there was a fall of yellow dust like sulphur, pollen from the stamens of the pines. This lasted several minutes, and was so heavy that it covered the streets. This same phenomenon had been observed twenty years before.

Sweet potatoes in Norfolk are delicious and extremely cheap. They are smaller than those of the Antilles, but they are more sugary, more mealy and less soggy.

The geese grow to an astonishing size. I measured one of their eggs: it was four inches long, seven inches in circumference and weighed more than seven ounces.

A little upriver from Norfolk are several municipal buildings. One is the Court House, which is also used as a town hall during elections. It is built of brick, as is the prison which stands between it and the building of which I am about to speak.

The latter is the hospital which was started about twenty years ago by withholding nine French sous a month from the pay of sailors whose ships were anchored in Norfolk. It faces northwest. It was completed in 1793, and now takes care of eight hundred patients, due to French needs since the arrival of the convoy from Cap François. It was then managed by M. Lynham, a merchant of Norfolk, who, during the first month of operation, spent fourteen thousand dollars (seventy-one thousand francs). There have been only thirty-nine deaths, even though the convoy had many wounded.

The fleet, which had been sent by Vaustable to pick up

the convoy in the Chesapeake and guide it to France, was not so fortunate. The two ships-of-the-line, the *Tiger* and the *Jean-Bart*, particularly the former, lost many of their crews. They may have hesitated to send their men to the hospital because of the inconvenience of getting them from Hampton Roads to Norfolk, the hardship of such a trip, and the wish to keep the crews as large as possible. At all events, they lost a great many. The illness, which quickly gave signs of gangrene, was thought to be due to the wood used in the construction of the vessels.

Many of the Negroes employed in the hospital to care for the sick were also victims of this disease, which proved that the malady was not yellow fever, to which Negroes are not subject.

Near the hospital is a boozing ken or bottle-tipping place which attracts the poorer elements in the hot weather.

The temperature of Norfolk is extremely uneven. From one day to another, and even in the interval of a few hours, one experiences, so to speak, a change of season.

When the wind is between east and northeast, there is a feeling of considerable coldness, whereas winds from other directions seem almost scorching. One would think that in a place as hot as this, where there is, as it were, no dividing line between winter and summer, the first day of May, which announces the approach of hot weather, would be no occasion for rejoicing. On this day, so delicious in France, however, all the Norfolkians put a tuft of deer's tail in their hats, and all their faces express joy. The ships also show that they share in the general festivity by fastening green branches to the ends of their yards.

It is on this same day, the first of May, that the annual grand review of the Norfolk Militia takes place.

Most of the companies are ununiformed, poorly armed and untrained; some wear uniforms which are blue with red collar and trimmings. The general uniform is green, white buttons, infantryman's cap adorned with plumes and ribbons of cerulean blue which makes them look like toy soldiers.

The gunners wear blue coats with scarlet collars, revers and facings, yellow pipings, a turned-up hat and a flame-colored cockade. The general officers wear a blue coat with gold epaulettes and yellow weskits, breeches, collars, facings and linings.

After the review everyone repairs to the common behind the town, where there is a barbecue—animals roasted whole on crisscrossed pieces of wood over a great fire, in the open air.

The combination of May 1 with the reunion of brothers-in-arms results in boisterous joy, with the usual finish: not every citizen-soldier is able to conquer the charms of the bottle.

Colonel Matthew commands the militia of Norfolk and the counties.

The seizure of American vessels going to and leaving French ports has caused Congress to take defensive measures of its own. As a result, in May, 1794, fortifications were started at Norfolk, chief among them a fort with earth ramparts on the left bank of the Elizabeth River, about a mile below Plymouth. In it the militia maintains a twenty-four-hour guard made up of fourteen men. The fortifications were built under the direction of M. de Rivard, an Italian engineer.

It was from this fort that on the night of May 8 or 9, 1794, three shots were fired at the anchored English frigate *Daedalus* at such close range that one of the shots was found embedded in a plank at the frigate's waterline.

This unfortunate incident proves what I have already reported about the liking of the inhabitants of Norfolk for the French. It is apparent in their speech, in the affectation which leads large numbers to wear the tricolored cockade, and in the eagerness they showed on April 22 to tar and feather an American who had spoken disrespectfully of the French and make him ride an entire day through the streets in a cart. Although M. Robert Taylor, their mayor, publicly begged them to cease this popular punishment, they persisted in their resolution.

I can cite a similar act. When the French convoy was leaving Hampton Roads and setting sail for Europe, it was secretly noised about that pilot boats were being dispatched with the news to Halifax. That very evening, every pilot boat in Norfolk had its rigging destroyed.

This sort of enthusiasm is not universal. At many market stalls the French are overcharged, and more than one heart obviously loves money more than it does the French.

In spite of all this I repeat that nowhere on the continent do the French receive so many signs of affection as in Norfolk, nor such a cordial reception. The state of Virginia voted the colonists of San Domingo twenty-six hundred gourdes or fifteen thousand francs, and Congress voted them another fifteen hundred gourdes or eight thousand francs.

I wish now to speak of the slaves who are found in great numbers in this section. They are held in a state of debasement which astounds even the inhabitants of the colonies. They are beaten for the slightest faults with whips made of rawhide and cord, and a slave-owner can always find constables willing to execute his desires in this respect.

In Norfolk the Negroes are ugly and dirty, whereas the mulattoes (who are also numerous) are comely, as are those that are the fruit of the mixture of Negroes and mulattoes.

It is claimed that these slaves, as well as those of all Virginia, are more intelligent than those of more southern states, and they are said to be greatly attached to their families and their masters.

Ignorance and its unhappy results prevail among the Negroes of Norfolk and all other sections: they are quick to believe in sorcerers, and their superstitious weakness of mind makes them a ready prey to the Methodists, who are the greatest converters here below. Thus the unfortunate Negro, already convinced that his lot in this life can never be good, is even taught to believe that only in hell can he ever be on equal terms with his master. Alas that human reasoning can fall so low!

Free Men of Color are no better treated than the slaves, except for the fact that no one is allowed to beat them. They too are in an abject condition, and there is no intercourse between them and the whites—barring the favors extended to white men by colored women. On December 10, 1793, the Virginia legislature passed a law requiring every such person to carry a certificate from the Governor, certifying to his liberty. This has to be renewed every three years under penalty of imprisonment. There is a fine of five dollars for employing as a free man any colored person who cannot produce such a certificate.

Although they are never allowed to forget their dependent state, the free people of color and the slaves are not strangers to the pleasures of life, the dance and finery.

It is chiefly on Sunday that they take advantage of the last. On that day they don their finest clothes, including boots and knickerbockers, and the women put on their brightest dresses and their prettiest shoes. They repair, particularly the Methodists, to church where their voices blend with those of the whites; the evening is spent in dancing, for which the Negroes have a mania.

At Christmas and Easter, when slaves are given three days vacation, they vie with each other in every form of indulgence—including, unfortunately, drunkenness.

The Negroes do all the manual labor, and fill all the domestic positions. They can be rented by the day for thirty-three French sous apiece, food included. Negresses can be had for a third less.

Among the Negroes one finds chimney sweeps of an odd type, the only ones employed in Norfolk. To the end of a cord they tie a bundle of brushwood the size of the chimney flue; then pull it up and down inside the chimney and scrape off the soot.

Even this precaution does not prevent houses from occasionally taking fire. When this occurs, people quickly mount to the roofs on ladders, which almost always stand ready on every house, and from there try to put out the fire with pumps which are never sufficiently numerous to cope with a large fire, or with one that is driven by a strong wind.

Although Virginia is noted for its fine horses, one seldom sees anything but wretched animals in Norfolk, nor are the carriages particularly elegant.

In Norfolk there are great numbers of African ducks,[3] notable for their great size, the red and fleshy excrescences which cover their heads, and their strong odor of musk.

The country around Norfolk is not interesting. The slaughterhouses are on the outskirts of the town. The beeves are killed with a sledge hammer, their throats cut with a knife, and almost before they have stopped breathing they are skinned. In ordinary times one beef sufficed for the town's daily needs. After the arrival of the convoy from Cap François, two or three had to be killed daily; but when the French fleet anchored in the Chesapeake, from eight to twelve had to be slaughtered each day. Other foods were needed in similarly increased proportions.

I repeat that the land around Norfolk is swampy, and almost entirely covered with brushwood and pines. Nowhere is there the slightest elevation; nowhere does one see a single pebble. The soil is everywhere sandy, occasionally mixed with pulverized fragments of quartz. Occasional plantations of Indian corn break the monotony, but not noticeably; and the frequency with which one encounters swamps

[3]Muscovies.

and stagnant water in the space of a few miles shows clearly why Norfolk, like all places that are both hot and damp, is unhealthy.

Everything in Norfolk conforms to English measurements and small purchases are weighed on scales that aren't models of accuracy. This stupid custom, combined with the difficulty of computing in currencies whose values in relation to the dollar are not definite, leads to frequent disputes between shopkeepers and customers. The dollar is worth 6 shillings, which makes the pound worth 3⅓ dollars, or 17 francs 13 sous, and the shilling 17⅓ sous.

The few other details of interest concerning Norfolk will be found under my remarks about Portsmouth, which has many things in common with Norfolk, in addition to the spectacle of the animated marine activities of the river that separates the two towns. If I wished to be captious, I could complain of the handling of letters by the postal service which, at this time, was subject to the whims of a clerk who willingly delivered letters to anyone who would pay for them, without taking the trouble to find out whether or not they belonged to him.

The future growth of Norfolk as a commercial center depends upon the depth of the Elizabeth River. If, as some think, it is constantly growing shallower, Norfolk's future would be a sad one; for a time would inevitably come when deep-water vessels could no longer be brought up to the town.

M. Plum, in 1788, built a rope factory in the upper part of Norfolk, and in it made a cable for the French ship-of-the-line *Jupiter,* 74 guns. The business was so profitable that M. Plum built a charming house, costing about thirty thousand francs. The walls are plastered, and it is tastefully furnished.

It would, of course, be too presumptuous to conclude that Norfolk alone is responsible for the character of Virginians, which is not highly esteemed outside the province. In general they have the reputation of being vain and insolent. It is said that these traits are most noticeable in public houses, which are worse in the slave states, because the slave-owners are as I have described them. Lower-class Virginians cultivate extremely long fingernails, with which to scratch out the eyes of those with whom they fight, the fighting being done with bare fists. Gentlemen fight with the pistol, and I know of one case where both of the participants in such a duel were killed.

These peculiarities have given rise to the saying that Virginians are to the rest of the United States what Spaniards are to the rest of Europe. It is generally acknowledged that they love display, and that the pleasure of paying their debts is not the one they seek most eagerly.

All this is natural to men who are surrounded by slaves and consequently develop exaggerated opinions of themselves, as men must when all their wishes are law. One citizen of Norfolk claims to be a descendant of William the Conqueror.

The price for a passage by water for one person from Norfolk to Richmond, Virginia, is two dollars, and one feeds himself.

Passage from Norfolk to New York costs eight dollars without food, and twelve if the captain supplies it.

Norfolk is one hundred and forty-four miles south of Richmond and four hundred and ninety-five miles southwest of Philadelphia.

I will conclude my remarks on Norfolk by saying that nowhere does the English language have such sweetness and charm as on the lips of a pretty Virginian. Happy is he who can bring her to use it in the expression of those sentiments which make for the happiness of man!

Since details concerning Portsmouth and Gosport are, in a way, a complement to those concerning Norfolk, it is natural and logical for me to give them immediately.

PORTSMOUTH AND GOSPORT

PORTSMOUTH is directly across from Norfolk, on the left bank of the Elizabeth River. Its three hundred houses do not border the streets. They are so spaced that the impression is of wide and beautiful avenues. These are all grass-covered, and the houses are built of wood for the most part, though a few extremely pretty ones are brick.

The Portsmouth market, also built of brick, fronts on the river. Although small, it is large enough for the town's needs. This market is on an open square or very wide street which runs to the outskirts of the town. On the left side of this street, going up, is the brick Anglican church, neat and well kept up. It has a rood loft, and benches throughout its entire length. Next to the door, on both sides, are two benches painted black. These are for blacks, who are not allowed to mix with the whites.

Prior to American independence, the minister of this church had a fixed salary of one thousand five hundred dollars (nearly eight thousand francs). Now he has only his perquisites and attractive lodgings.

There are both Methodists and Anabaptists in Portsmouth. This place is down-at-heels because it has no commerce of its own. Vessels can come to Portsmouth as readily as to Norfolk, since the port is formed by the two banks of the Elizabeth River; but the greater age of Norfolk and the very nature of the establishments already founded there, which must necessarily determine the character of those yet to be formed, prevent Portsmouth from being a rival. There was a time when such a thing might have been possible, but Portsmouth didn't know enough to take advantage of the opportunity. It was at the beginning of the quarrels in America, when fire drove the population of Norfolk over to Portsmouth. The residents of Portsmouth were so stupid as to express displeasure at the influx, and even to talk of burning the houses where the strangers had sought refuge if they did not get out within eight days. They immediately abandoned Portsmouth.

However, its location has some genuine advantages over that of Norfolk. The water is deeper at the wharves, and its drinking water is better than Norfolk's. It is better arranged, less hot and swampy, and therefore healthier. Because of this a hospital for convalescent French was set up there while Vaustable's fleet was at Hampton Roads.

House rents are much less in Portsmouth than in Norfolk, proving the inferiority of Portsmouth, which must import everything from Norfolk. The need of crossing the Elizabeth River when coming to Norfolk from the upper part of Virginia or the states situated to the east or west, because the stages and even the mail-coach end their routes at Portsmouth, brought about a special means of communication between Norfolk and Portsmouth.

This consists of six ferry-boats, two of them large ones. Each boat is propelled by two men, who steer the boat by their manner of rowing. Six people travel comfortably in the small boats, eight in the others. This number is almost always exceeded, one reason being because people don't want to wait for the next boat, and another that the Negro rowers, by taking aboard as many as fifteen, hope to get a longer wait on the other shore.

The rule is that a boat must leave after even one passenger has waited for five minutes; but the boatmen, wishing to make less frequent crossings, often leave their boats on the beach and hide.

There must always be boats on the two shores; for that reason, when a third boat comes in the one which is there the longest is supposed to go to the other side, even if empty. But the carrying out of these rules is not rigorously enforced. Each boat leaves exactly in its turn, in the order in which it arrived at the wharf.

When the water is calm and the tide high, it takes eight minutes to go from Portsmouth to Norfolk, and vice versa; seven minutes from Norfolk to the hospital; another seven from the hospital to Portsmouth. The crossings take twice as long when wind or tide, or both, are contrary.

The fare is five and a half French sous a person. A yearly ticket costs six dollars.

On one of these boats I met a Negro called Sem, a slave of Colonel Wilson's, one of the lessors of the ferries. He had learned to read and write all by himself. He was about thirty years old. His conversation showed clear thinking and an ardent desire for education.

In addition to the six passenger ferries there are two large oar-propelled horse boats which carry wagons, animals and heavy articles. The fare is half a dollar for an invalid's chair, eleven French sous for a horse, and half that for a man. As for baggage, one generally makes a price.

It is difficult to get the chairs and horses on the ferry-boat. They are pushed on, after the side of the ferry-boat is against the wharf.

The ferry privilege is leased to two people for ten years, at the rate of three hundred and sixteen and two thirds dollars a year, about two thousand francs, with the stipulation that town officials and those having to do with sessions at the Norfolk court shall ride free.

In addition to these boats, the town of Portsmouth maintains one of its own for those who live above the hospital on the Norfolk side and wish to bring goods, provisions or anything else to the Portsmouth market. It also carries anyone else who wishes to make the trip.

One may also hire scows for transporting goods between

Norfolk and Portsmouth. These scows, carrying from fifteen to twenty tons, cost a dollar a day, exclusive of the Negroes employed by the day to run them.

In Norfolk and Portsmouth baggage is carried in carts at a cost of eleven French sous a trip. There are twelve in Norfolk, and only two in Portsmouth. They are always driven by Negroes.

In view of the poverty of Portsmouth and its inhabitants, it is surprising to find that it supports one of those places where one sex prostitutes itself to the bestial desires of the other. The convoy increased the number of those loathsome creatures who, in drunkenness, lose all sense of modesty and shame.

Portsmouth has seventeen hundred inhabitants, six hundred of whom are slaves.

GOSPORT

GOSPORT, half a mile from Portsmouth, depends entirely on Portsmouth for its livelihood.

It is reached by a levee built across a marsh flooded at high tide.

Gosport is made up of several houses placed helter-skelter, among them an old distillery rented by refugees from San Domingo.

Colonel Wilson lives in Gosport. He is the commandant of the place, a wealthy man, a great friend of the French, and one of the two lessors of the ferry-boats between Portsmouth and Norfolk. Though his house is built of wood, it is attractive, and all the rooms have a cheerful view of the river, to which his land extends.

On September 6 Colonel Wilson's wife lost a daughter by a former marriage, Miss Janet Craig. She lies in the garden, where a tablet gives the details of her life and death. This only daughter, stricken in the prime of life, was mourned by all who knew her, and eight months later her mother is still inconsolable, while Colonel Wilson himself still wears mourning for his stepdaughter.

The custom of indicating outwardly one's grief at the cruel loss of those to whom one has given life seems to me natural and praiseworthy, and I greatly regret that France has never adopted a similar custom.

Eels are caught from the wharf at Gosport and Portsmouth. You can get more than a dozen for half a dollar, but this price is paid only by the French to French fishermen, for Americans are not interested either in catching or eating them.

The surroundings of Portsmouth and Gosport are no different from those of Norfolk—flooded, sandy, barren. Many of the houses are wretched, and frequently an extensive piece of fenced ground will have nothing on it but a miserable dwelling made of logs or planks. The fire-blackened stumps of trees which have been left in the fields do not noticeably improve the picture.

The fences add to the depressing outlook. They are always made of rails split triangularly, four or five inches thick and about eight feet long. Generally the rails are placed in a zigzag manner, so that the fence is a series of projecting and inverted angles. The rails are placed on top of each other, sticking out a little where they cross in order to strengthen the point of support. Sometimes uprights are used to hold the crosspieces, in which case the fence is straight.

The roads leading to Portsmouth are mere tracks large enough for wagons, occasionally bridged, across ditches, streams or mudholes, by small tree trunks placed close together.

One meets coaches, wagons and carts on these roads, the carts sometimes drawn by yoked oxen; and occasionally one passes a horse with a husband in the saddle and his wife riding behind, which indicates that the horses are stronger than they seem.

Deer are found twenty miles from Portsmouth. Fawns are brought in and sold for two dollars apiece, and some people amuse themselves by raising them. The ships sell skins of rabbit and hare, which are also found in the surrounding country.

I will close my account of Norfolk, Portsmouth and Gosport by remarking that the women in these places, as elsewhere in Virginia, have the sweetest of voices; and this charm, perhaps one of the greatest the fair sex can possess, is so pronounced that the English language, ordinarily far

from sweet, becomes something quite different on their se-
ductive lips.

Since we left Norfolk, Portsmouth and Gosport to go to
Baltimore, I will now speak about this journey.

TRIP FROM NORFOLK TO BALTIMORE BY WATER

MAY 15, 1794. Two packets or passenger boats ply from Norfolk to Baltimore, and two from Baltimore to Norfolk.

These boats are schooners, excellent sailers, well built and with pretty cabins. The trip costs eight dollars and a half (forty-eight francs). When the voyage is short, passengers eat well, since fresh provisions are always stocked with a quick trip in mind. As I have said, we left Norfolk May 15, 1794, at ten in the morning, on the schooner *President*, belonging to M. Moses Myer, a Norfolk merchant, and commanded by Captain Gold.

When we reached the fort we spoke a ship hailing from Jérémie, quarantined because of having smallpox aboard. Regardless of this circumstance, our captain took several passengers from her onto his own boat for Baltimore. Among this number was M. le Sassier, the son of the counselor of Louisiana and hence a compatriot of my wife, and M. Sompérat of Jérémie.

A little beyond the fort, on the right bank, is a large distillery which has been allowed to go to ruin.

Craney Island, which always seems to be midway of the route coming from Norfolk, made a beautiful screen for us for a long time because of a calm which struck us almost as soon as we had left the wharf. We were not able to double this island until a quarter past twelve.

At a quarter before two we were at Sowels Point; at quarter past two we were abreast of the French frigate *La Concorde* at anchor in Hampton Roads. It then took us fifteen minutes to round Point Comfort.

At three o'clock the lighthouse of Cape Henry was far off on our right. The view from this point is beautiful, as the eye sees the James River on one side, and on the other the true entrance to Chesapeake Bay.

We chose this hour to dine. We numbered thirty-nine passengers, of all ages, sexes and even colors. Many of them, who hadn't paid to eat at the captain's table, had already eaten all over the boat. Many of the passengers, whose appetite might have been stimulated by a gentle movement of the schooner, found themselves unable to eat on account of seasickness.

So slow was our progress that we were only off Back River Point at four o'clock.

The heat of the sun, the slatting of the schooner's boom in the calm, the cooler night air, the boredom brought about by our slow progress, everything made us decide to look for a place to sleep, although not until we had taken tea, following the custom of taking this rather than an American supper.

The schooner had only ten berths, into which those who were married or had small children—fifteen in all—were crowded. The rest stretched out on the floor, on the deck or on hatches.

May 16. At five o'clock on the morning of the sixteenth we were off the mouth of the Potomac in Chesapeake Bay, the Potomac here being seven or eight miles wide. We could see the right bank. The Potomac is the boundary between Virginia and Maryland. During this entire day we were becalmed and drifted with the tide, so that the captain decided to anchor at seven o'clock.

A favorable wind sprang up at seven o'clock at night. We got under sail, and when we went back to our berths we flattered ourselves that we would regain all the distance we had lost in the past thirty hours; but at eleven o'clock the wind turned into the north and became very fresh. It constantly increased, and at two in the morning we were extremely distressed by the heavy seas. The schooner, being loaded beyond measure, wholly belied its reputation as a good sailer.

The waves came over the bow and wet all those who had the deck only as a shelter. One by one they came to the cabin, looking for a better one. The Negresses with their children were the last who dared to beg for refuge, but were finally forced to it. A colonist, his heart wrung by their plight, pleaded for them, and particularly for a little child. His tenderness toward this child and the color of its skin indicated that the child's mother had favored this particular colonist to the detriment of her marriage vows.

The state of these unfortunate people was too painful not to receive them, even though it was apparent that all of them, including the suspected father, were covered with a beautiful itch. Finally the storm made us come about and, after losing fourteen miles, seek shelter in a little bay at the mouth of the Patuxent River, which enters the Chesapeake eighteen miles north of the point where the Potomac comes in, and on the same side. Nine sloops, boats and schooners had preceded us to this haven, where we dropped anchor early in the morning.

May 17. Several passengers, including my son and I, went ashore. We found it to be a wretched place, and we had gone scarcely half a mile before one of us killed a snake two and a half feet long. It was black, of the dangerous sort that the country people call a moccasin. As each one vied with the other in hitting it with a stick we saw about twenty eggs of varying sizes come out of its stomach.

Several points of the shore of the bay which opened to the east and west had slight elevations, particularly to the north where they reached the height of forty feet. The shore is sandy and bordered with pines. Here we saw and inspected several miserable buildings. The passengers who had brought guns killed some little birds, which paid with their lives for the adverse winds we had experienced. We were kindly offered some excellent milk by a farmer's wife, who did not wish to take any money from us.

The lands in the vicinity of the Patuxent are used to raise rye, oats and tobacco. At present they are trying to raise the cotton plant.

May 18. Since the weather seemed propitious, we left at eight o'clock at night, and in the morning arrived at the wharf in Baltimore. We much enjoyed the approach to this city, whose appearance, as it revealed itself little by little, agreeably fed our curiosity.

We were particularly struck by the contrast between the two sides of the river. The right side, called the Point, very prettily built up; the buildings are new, and their numbers are constantly increasing. The opposite side has a precipitous bank, rising to a height of fifty feet. The port was well equipped; vessels, decked with flags because the day was Sunday, were preparing to get under way; all was gaiety and enjoyment, all was interesting, in spite of the rude distraction caused by the captain, who waited until we had almost arrived to demand of each his passage money.

Negroes, eagerly awaiting the small remuneration which the passengers' belongings would bring, took our baggage. Everyone said goodbye to the others as though they had been acquainted for a long time; and we repaired to the Indian Queen Inn which had been pointed out to us as the one we would find most suitable.

It had taken us ninety-two hours to cover the one hundred and ninety miles between Norfolk and Baltimore by Chesapeake Bay, which has all the characteristics and even all the dangers of an arm of the sea.

May 19. In the evening we walked to the Point to see the colonists from Cap François and some friends. Others came to visit us.

The next day we dined with Gauvain at Mlle. Ridgley's pension.

We went in our turn to see more colonists: Séguin, Cambefort; Geanty, my friend and former colleague, counselor at Cap François; Paradé, Commissioner of Marine.

I was disappointed to learn that my dear friend Berlin had gone down the Chesapeake, returning to San Domingo, while we were traveling from Norfolk to Baltimore.

In the afternoon we went walking in Howard's Park.

May 22. We left Baltimore in the morning to go to Philadelphia.

Let us then speak here of Baltimore.

BALTIMORE

THIS rather large city, situated on an arm of the Patapsco River, is the county seat and the most extensive and flourishing commercial center in Maryland. It extends from Harris Creek in the south to the great branch of the Patapsco, and increases each day amazingly.

It is divided into two parts by Jones Falls and the northwest branch, over which there are three wooden bridges.

In 1787 there were two thousand houses. The number had increased to three thousand in 1795, the greater part brick and elegantly built; and there were more than fifteen thousand inhabitants, ten per cent of them slaves.

In general the houses have two stories. They are of brick with fine sidewalks in front of them, but the entrances to the cellars, which are used as stores and kitchens, are halfway across the width of the sidewalks. The sidewalk of the main street is ten feet wide.

The streets are spacious, paved, and arranged in a straight line. They run from east to west the entire length of the north side of the basin, and are cut by others at right angles, except for some that run every which-way. It is the same at the point which is called Fells Point. The principal street running east and west is about eighty feet wide and is called Baltimore Street. The others vary from thirty feet to eighty feet. Holyday Street, where the new theater is, is nearer one hundred. Some of the streets bear names which seem to be monuments of gratitude. Lafayette Street is a good example of this.

Carts collect the litter in the streets.

From Baltimore Street one sees to the north the Court

House, under which there is an archway and a passage through which even vehicles can pass. This building is two stories high with a wooden balcony. Its pediment fronts on and forms the end of Calvert Street. The prison is west of the Court House. There are gardens in the outskirts of the city, which are not yet built up. It is divided into one hundred and thirty streets, alleyways and paths, although future streets have already been staked out and even named, so that eventually the number of buildings may be tripled. The easterly part is the most built up, from Howard Street to Jones Falls.

There are many dove-cotes in Baltimore, as well as little houses made to shelter swallows, due to the belief that their attachment for a house will bring prosperity to those who live there. There is also an idea that hospitality to timid creatures is somehow connected with and will be rewarded by long life. One would gladly forgive superstition if it never gave rise to worse errors.

Public buildings in Baltimore, in addition to the Court House and the prison, are three markets, one Poor House, two banks (one of Maryland and the other of the United States), a stock exchange and a theater. The Court House is built of brick.

The larger streets of Baltimore are lighted by lanterns of an English type, similar to those found in other American cities.

In Baltimore one sees fairly good driving-horses, but the draught horses are more remarkable. They are hitched two, four, five and even six to a wagon or cart by means of iron chains, and every detail of the harnesses and carriages evidences care and neatness.

There are stallions in Maryland whose pedigrees are elaborately advertised. Stud fees are twenty-four francs for the covering of the mare, and thirty or forty sous to the stableman. Food for a horse costs three francs a week.

Baltimore is built on two slopes, one from west to east, the other from north to south. The first has a forty-foot elevation, the second is also considerable.

The port is at the southern end of this latter slope. Due to the configuration of the terrain it is a sort of basin which consists of three successive indentations formed by points of land which face each other: it extends from the city to the place where, in relation to the city itself, Chesapeake Bay really ends. This basin is about three miles long and runs more or less northwest and southeast.

If the plans for this basin are entirely carried out, it will have houses on three sides, and the outermost section, called the Point, will have houses on a major part of the fourth. Already wharves or quays have been built on portions of all four sides.

The port is from six to seven feet deep. Ships of five hundred tons can anchor at the Point.

The wharves (for there are no quays in Baltimore) are always made for the convenience of their owners, who always build them out into the harbor. Hence in the direction of the town there are spaces where the water still fills large indentations, while the nearby wharves stick out like jetties. This gives an air of disorder to a place to which a rigorous alignment would bring added charm.

There are three markets in Baltimore, the principal one being at the eastern end of the great street, going toward the Chesapeake. Wednesday and Saturday are market days. On other days one finds only scrap meat and vegetables.

There are eleven churches or houses of worship in Baltimore itself and one in the sort of small elbow of land formed by Fells Point, or simply the Point. These include one German Reformed, two German Lutheran, one German Calvinist, one Anglican, one Presbyterian, one Mennonite, one Roman Catholic, two Methodist, one Anabaptist, and one Nicolite or new Quaker.

How admirable is this liberty of religion, this respect for conscience! And if the Creator, in the wonders which excite our continual admiration, speaks in a thousand ways to the heart of man, why should we not find a thousand ways to sing His praises and express our most profound gratitude?

Baltimore also has a theater situated, as I have said, on a street one hundred feet wide.

At the Point the buildings are much more modern than those in Baltimore, and are increasing prodigiously. The reason for this is due to its situation, which is purely commercial. As the Point expands, the closer to it are the houses of Baltimore, and it won't be long before they meet. The space that separates them, like that which corresponds to it on the other shore of the basin, is still marshy, but constant work lessens this inconvenience—at least on the side of the Point.

The outskirts of the city to east and west are no different from those to be seen elsewhere in the United States of America.

The increase in population due to the influx of colonists from San Domingo (who, let me say in passing, have received marked evidence of kindness from the inhabitants of this city), has also benefited nearby farmers; and many gardens have sprung up in these outskirts to beautify them. Many of the gardens are cultivated by the French themselves.

But what gives Baltimore a pleasant air, peculiar to itself, is the hill which dominates it on the north. This belongs to Colonel Howard, whose residence and out-buildings are situated on the front portion. The rear portion is beautified by a park. Its elevated situation; its groves of trees; the view from it, which brings back memories of European scenes: all these things together fill every true Frenchman with both pleasure and regret; his mind and heart alike rejoice in the vistas and the sensations they inspire.

On the eastern slope of this height is a rivulet called Jones

Falls, the sound of which is as charming as its appearance. Its rocky bed, the windmill which it turns, the combination of rustic simplicity with the nearby commerce and marine activity of the city, constantly fascinate one who follows its course back to the city. It flows into the basin east of the great market.

Baltimore has two banks, one named after the province, of which this place is the capital. It was established in 1701, with resources of three hundred thousand dollars (one million six hundred and fifty thousand francs). The other is a branch of the Bank of the United States, properly so called.

Baltimore-owned vessels, which in 1790 were only one hundred and two, comprising 13,564 tons, have more than doubled in 1794, when exports were valued at five million three hundred thousand dollars, equal to more than twenty-nine millions of our francs.

But Baltimore is subject to the scourge of yellow fever, which has inflicted frightful ravages almost every year since 1793, particularly in the vicinity of the Point, which is nearest to the sea and the lowest part of the town.

An interest stronger than love of life, however, holds those there who place the doubtful rewards of fortune above the danger of certain death. If this terrible disease does not cease to harvest by the thousands the inhabitants of these wretched regions, they will eventually arm themselves against it with the sole expedient of predestination, and will fall back upon it as do the Turks when confronted by the pest.

There are large hotels in Baltimore where one eats well, either at the ordinary or at private tables.

In them one finds an enormous collection of large slippers, to which one helps himself on going to bed, so that he may find, on waking the next day, his cleaned shoes or boots outside his door.

It is difficult to obtain water in the rooms. Ice is kept in order to cool it in summer.

The newspapers offer rewards of from thirty to three hundred francs for the capture of fugitive slaves.

The inhabitants have a rather strong liking for the French.

[The river at Baltimore (the Patapsco) was frozen from the beginning of January through February 11, 1809.

[A journalist of this place, having offended Americans on the occasion of their declaration of war against England in 1812, had his house pulled down, though he had the good fortune to escape. Other outrages were committed.]

In Baltimore there are refineries, distilleries, tobacco factories, rope works, paper mills, cotton mills, nail, shoe and boot factories, lumber yards, tanneries, etc., etc.

Baltimore is governed by commissioners and overseers.

This city is thirty-six miles northwest of Annapolis, two hundred and twenty-five miles north-northeast of Richmond, and one hundred and twenty-nine miles west-south-west of Philadelphia.

Its latitude is 29 degrees 18 seconds north, and its longitude 1 degree 35 minutes west of Philadelphia.

I ate green peas at Baltimore the eighteenth of May, 1794.

VOYAGE FROM BALTIMORE TO PHILADELPHIA

By the Chesapeake, Frenchtown, Newcastle
and the Delaware

MAY 20, 1794. The commerce which requires trans-portation between Baltimore and Philadelphia would be too costly if carried by land; whereas if carried by way of the Chesapeake, it would be too long, too uncertain, and sometimes, during the winter, even perilous. A middle course, therefore, has been adopted.

Goods are loaded on cargo boats bound for Frenchtown. From Frenchtown wagons and carts carry them to New-castle. At that place other packets pick them up and take them to Philadelphia. It is by the same means, but employed in the contrary direction, that this latter city forwards goods to Baltimore.

However, they are usually in a state of inactivity from Christmas to March 15 because the Chesapeake is ice-bound.

Having left Baltimore on May 20, 1794, at half past eight in the morning with a wind from the east, on the schooner *Peggy* of Frenchtown, thirty-five tons, we stopped at the Point, where passengers are always taken on. We finally left this place after having lost considerable time, and we had trouble getting out of the basin at Baltimore and reaching the Chesapeake because the wind would allow us to proceed only by tacking.

On leaving Virginia for Baltimore we had been warned that we would have to take the precaution to reserve berths on board the packets, and even to mark our names on them with chalk, because custom gave a sort of sacred right of

possession to those who had first engaged the places. We had
found this custom well respected in the voyage from Norfolk to Baltimore; and in engaging our places in the latter
place for Frenchtown, the captain himself gave me the chalk
with which to mark the six berths I had reserved.

When we arrived on board we found that the marks on
two of them had been rubbed out, and when we wished to
take possession of our quarters, some were occupied. Our
complaints stirred up a lively quarrel and we only got the
the best of it by showing a grim determination not to let
ourselves be robbed. The captain himself sided against us,
which increased our irritation, because we were so indignant
at his duplicity in favoring his compatriots above ourselves.

The price for the passage for one person when the captain
supplies the food is a dollar and a quarter, about seven French
francs. A Negro pays only three fourths of a dollar (four
francs). You pay extra for drink, giving one eighth of a
dollar, sixteen sous, for a glass of brandy; five sixteenths,
about forty-five sous, for a bottle of porter or heavy English beer, and a dollar (five francs ten sous) for a bottle of
Madeira wine.

On the boat, as elsewhere, drink is a dominating idea. We
wouldn't have known that any regulations of any sort existed
aboard if we hadn't seen a little fly-bill which said that whoever gets into his berth with shoes or boots on must pay a
fine of a bottle of porter.

Fortunately the prohibition did not speak of dirty feet,
else the berths would have been almost entirely unoccupied,
or would have been a rich source of fines.

At half past one the captain's table was served. A dish of
beef, one of potatoes, one of cabbage and one of ham made
up the dinner—which may have been designed to encourage
drinking.

At half past three we were still only twelve miles from the

city of Baltimore; at half past five we were only off Fall Island.

But the varied scenery of the Chesapeake, the ever-changing plantations of wheat, maize, tobacco and potatoes, consoled us for this slowness.

Everything, too, aboard the boat—the twenty-five passengers traveling for different reasons, for the most part strangers to one another, perhaps meeting only this once in their entire life; the diversified talk; the slumberers, the snorers, the tobacco chewers, the tipplers who packed this floating smoking-den—made time pass rapidly for one who knew how to contemplate it with profit.

The boat touched bottom two or three times, but without being held there.

At nightfall we retired in the hope of being in Frenchtown in a few hours.

May 21. In fact, we reached this place at 1 A.M., May 21. We remained on board until a quarter to five, when a sort of ferry-boat or scow came to take the passengers and their luggage to land.

Frenchtown, or La Ville Française, consists of a large dwelling house, its kitchen and out-buildings and a warehouse. It is on the left bank of the pretty Elk River, which enters the Chesapeake several miles farther down. It is said that the name, Ville Française, was given to this place because it was the site of a settlement of Acadians who had been exiled by the English, founded in 1715.

(It was burned by the English in 1813.)

There are two stages at Frenchtown, one with twelve places, drawn by four horses, the other with nine places drawn by two horses. There is also a wagon to carry travelers' luggage that cannot be put in trunks of the stage or behind the carriages.

A seat from Frenchtown to Newcastle costs three quarters of a dollar (four francs).

At half past five the driver cracked his whip, the signal for departure.

Fifteen minutes later we saw on our left a steeple and about thirty brick houses—Elkton or Head of Elk; and at half past six we reached Glascow. From Frenchtown, whose location is pleasant and whose surroundings are neat, up to Glascow both sides of the road as far as the eye can see are thickly planted with flax, wheat and corn. The trees are oaks and walnuts. Birds looking like large blackbirds, and turtle-doves brighten the scene. The soil is heavy, and a bit clayey. This section is said to be somewhat subject to destructive droughts.

Glascow, where the stage stops for a scant fifteen minutes to water the horses, is made up of several houses. It is eight miles from Frenchtown.

Beyond Glascow the road is as pleasing as before. One catches frequent glimpses of horses, cows, sheep, pigs, geese, fowl of all kinds. Two-horse plows turn up the fields; and young girls hoe them.

Three miles outside Glascow one reaches the boundary between Maryland and Delaware.

After another ten miles we arrived at a house where, according to the American custom, there was a fresh stop of a half quarter-hour to regale the stage horses with a huge bucket of cold water, after their bridles had been taken off. At this point, which is six miles from Newcastle, milestones begin to tell the distances from Newcastle and from Philadelphia.

But what gives the eye the greatest pleasure in the eight or nine miles before reaching Newcastle are the living hedges peculiar to this section.

They are formed of white thorn, whose flower is beautified at this moment by the charms which the month of May seems to give to all nature.

In order to judge the keen pleasure caused by these hedges,

one must be acquainted with the United States and their fences or dry hedges, of which one never ceases to have a boring view.

We reached Newcastle at half past nine. The Court of Justice was assembled here. We had the curiosity to go and see the tribunal in session. One would not know how to express in words the majesty of the place, but looking at the jurors one cannot help admiring an order of things which entrusts the judgment of lawsuits to men who are in a position to know how they were caused, and in whom the study of law does not replace the study of the human heart. And moreover whatever might be the simplicity of the temple consecrated to justice, it wakens always in the man who loves it ideas of respect.

Newcastle, one of the oldest cities of the state of Delaware, of which it has also been the capital, is built on the right bank of the river of the same name. It is thirty miles from Philadelphia by land, and forty by water. The houses are brick, and about eighty in number, but not adjoining.

This place has a Court House and prison, a Supreme Court of Justice, an English Episcopal and a Presbyterian church.

It was first settled around 1627 by Swedes, who named it Stockholm.[1] Falling later into the hands of the Dutch, it received from them the name of New Amsterdam. Finally the English gave it the name which it has today. Newcastle had declined, but it has bloomed again, and when its breakwater (for whose construction a toll has been levied) is completed, vessels can lie there safely in the winter.

Newcastle is a stop for all deep-water ships sailing from Philadelphia, in order to take aboard their poultry and other fresh provisions. If the weather seems unfavorable to let them get well beyond the Delaware Capes, they can stay

[1]Moreau was apparently misinformed in regard to the early history of Newcastle. Amandus Johnson, in his recent study, *The Swedish Settlements on the Delaware, 1638–1664,* gives no account of any Swedish settlement named Stockholm or New Stockholm.

there safely awaiting a propitious moment, and can replace the provisions consumed during the wait.

The halt at Newcastle is so much a custom that a vessel is not considered ready to leave until it has come down to Newcastle with a pilot. It is at this anchorage that a captain joins his ship when he has completed in Philadelphia all necessary details.

After having lunched at a hotel where the session of the court had brought many people together, we went to the wharf or quay to board the passenger boat for Philadelphia. Four of these passenger boats are constantly engaged in this navigation. The one that awaited us was the *Morning Star*, Captain Thomas Moore.

Here we found three or four passengers who had been our companions on the trip from Baltimore, among them M. A. Murray, a merchant of Philadelphia, whose kindnesses we would not be able to praise too highly. The others were complete strangers to us, up to that moment.

The Newcastle packets are very fine, and far more pleasingly arranged than those from Norfolk to Frenchtown.

The price of a passage for one person is three fourths of a dollar (four francs). One pays separately for food and drink. The slaves pay only half a dollar (fifty-five sous). Two of the four passenger boats, which differ in no way from each other except in their names, the *Morning Star* and the *Rising Sun,* are considered the fastest sailers of the whole Delaware River. They have been known to make the forty-mile trip in less than three hours when wind and tide are favorable.

We left Newcastle at eleven in the morning to go up the Delaware, which at this point is far from having the same width as the Chesapeake, for it is scarcely two miles wide.

At noon we were abreast of Wilmington, having made about six miles from Newcastle.

Wilmington is situated seventeen hundred toises up the Delaware between Christiania Creek and Brandywine Creek, the first of which accommodates boats drawing eight feet of water. The two join about nine hundred toises below the city and their mouth in the Delaware is one hundred toises wide.

Wilmington presents an interesting aspect with its six or seven hundred houses, brick for the most part, its public buildings and the Work House which has been built here, and whose extent and steeple draw attention to it. The elevated situation of Wilmington makes it even more pleasing, seen from the river. The creek which flows in here is navigable by boats of light draught.

Wilmington has six places of worship, two for Presbyterians, one for Swedish Episcopalians, one for Quakers, one for Anabaptists and one for Methodists. There are also two markets, a Poor House and the Work House. It had an academy, destroyed during the War of Independence.

Wilmington is the most important city in Delaware. The mills are magnificent and their manner of loading and unloading grain is most ingenious.

Its founding does not go back further than 1735. This city also has passenger boats, which are the means of regular commerce between it and Philadelphia.

From Newcastle to Wilmington and above, the Delaware shore is charming and varied, the eye always finds something of interest, while the opposite shore, which is New Jersey, is sad in contrast with the other.

Toward noon we were at Marens Hook, the name of a rich inhabitant which was given to his wharf. There the land is less cultivated, but there are green fields here and there, some of them thinly wooded.

Five miles farther along is Chester, a small market town of about six hundred houses. We reached there at two o'clock.

At three o'clock Fort Mifflin, mounting ten cannons, showed itself, and at half past three we had sighted the city of Philadelphia.

At this distance it offers a very interesting prospect and the fort seems to indicate that it is important. As one proceeds, one sees more and more of the southern part of the town and when finally you get a view of the whole town, the steeple of the Anglican Christ Church gives this town indeed the appearance of a city. North Second Street runs through the center of the town.

At four o'clock we came abreast of the landing place, but the wharves happened to be so encumbered that we were over an hour getting in to them. Our packet had taken only five hours to make the trip from Newcastle to Philadelphia, even though we had left with the tide against us.

One feels real sadness when docking at Philadelphia, of which one had received such a favorable impression from the river. The entire view is blocked by the construction of the wharves, which clearly show that their builders, moved solely by their own greed, had no consideration whatever for good taste, the appearance or well-being of the city, or anything else of that nature. All that Philadelphia has of beauty in its magnificent design preceded the influence of mercantile and narrow-minded speculations, which can never give birth to anything either beautiful or great.

One must praise the great speed of the Newcastle packets, but like everything planned in America for public use they have a defect. It has been overlooked that those who are continually bringing merchandise consigned to Philadelphia ought to have a central depot on the docks. As it is, the boat is supposed to wait for the consignee to come and get his goods. But, when he comes, either the boat has gone, or the captain is not on board. It is impossible for him to know when to come back again because the boat's sailing depends each time on the tide, and its docking on weather conditions. If a passenger should happen on a favorable moment and find the packet at its wharf, rain will be falling and no carriage will be available to transport his belongings. Thus the opportunity is again lost. Never anywhere in the world is the public shown less consideration; yet it is claimed that the packets exist only for the public's convenience. One cannot mourn the absence of police supervision over all individual movements on the pretext of safety; but a country that has no police at all is ridiculous, and indeed uncivilized, because in a thousand instances nobody bothers to look out for anything and neglect becomes an ideal.

When we finally landed at Philadelphia, Goynard and I took great pains to find lodgings, aided in the effort by Messrs. Longuemare and Marcel, our Norfolk traveling companions. After many wasted steps, and innumerable refusals, we were directed to a miserable haven in North Second Street, near the Anglican church. We received here L'Ami and Milhet from Cap François; then went to Sureau's house where we saw Prior Mad Seur, Aubert and his family, and a crowd of our unfortunate colonist friends.

May 22. Goynard, my son and I visited the Congress, which was in session. I had a letter of recommendation from Colonel Wilson for Colonel Parker, representative from Virginia in this chamber; and when Colonel Parker left his bench and went to refresh himself at a table where there were earthen pots and bottles of molasses liquor for the members, I gave him my letter. On reading it, he received me most kindly; then, when there was a moment's interruption in the work of the chamber, he introduced me to it as one who had been a member of the Constituent Assembly and asked if they wished to admit me to the session in the benches reserved for distinguished foreigners. This question being assented to, the Speaker invited me to sit down. My American heart was indeed proud and touched by this honor.

When the session was over I went with my two shipboard companions to see the house that is being built for the

President, but before going far I noticed, in a rapidly approaching coach, two men greatly agitated. Goynard, endowed with better vision than I, told me the two persons looked as though they were waving to me.

Much concerned, I stopped; the carriage came nearer; in a few seconds it drew up beside us. One of the two jumped to the ground and clasped me in his arms. It was Beaumetz![2] The other, descending less nimbly, was Talleyrand![3]

They had arrived together from England! What joy! What happiness! What multiplied embraces! After this first rapturous meeting they urged me to come and have dinner with them. I returned immediately to my lodgings to share my joy with all who were dear to me, then betook myself to the rendezvous.

A French newspaper had announced on April 29 their plan to go with many other Frenchmen, in the preceding month of February, to the United States, but I was ignorant

[2]Bon Albert Briois de Beaumetz (1759–1800?), president of the *Conseil provincial* of Artois, was deputy for the nobility of that province in the National Assembly and at one time president of the *Constituante*. At the beginning of the Reign of Terror he escaped from France, thanks to aid given him by Talleyrand, sought refuge in England and thence passed to America in 1794. He and Talleyrand were constant companions during their sojourn in America and were partners in a land enterprise in Maine and in a cargo shipped to India. Beaumetz left Philadelphia on May 27, 1796, for Calcutta and according to Talleyrand (*Memoirs*, I, 246–247) died there.

[3]Charles Maurice de Talleyrand-Périgord (1754–1838), Foreign Minister of France under the Directory from July, 1797, to July, 1799, and under Bonaparte from December, 1799, to the summer of 1807. In 1803 he conducted with Monroe and Livingston the negotiations that resulted in the sale by Bonaparte to the United States of the Louisiana Territory (Louisiana, Mississippi and East and West Florida), for sixty million francs or about fifteen million dollars—one of the greatest real estate bargains of all time. Although Talleyrand was a master of diplomacy and won many diplomatic victories for France, he was thoroughly venal and corrupt, and accepted millions of francs in bribes. Bonaparte, at their last meeting in 1814, gave him a violent dressing down—"You are a coward, a traitor, a thief. You do not even believe in God. You have

of this notice and my surprise was complete. What a dinner! How many things to tell one another after two and a half years! What a wealth of detail to hear and to communicate! It was indeed the *infandum, regina, jubes.*

After dinner we went together to see Blaçon, Count de Noailles, and Talon. Fresh surprise! Fresh pleasures! During our reunion there was a hailstorm and frightful thunder, as though Heaven wished once again to remind us of the misfortunes we had escaped.

Later I went to pay several visits and embraced La Colombe[4] and Cadignan. You may imagine the questions about Lafayette! I ended my errands with a visit to the Public Library, for which one is indebted to Benjamin Franklin.

It was on this day that I learned from Talleyrand that for more than three weeks after August 10 he had driven in broad daylight in an open cabriolet, first with Louis Narbonne,[5] then with Beaumetz. They had changed their sleeping place every night, and no one ever said anything to them. Narbonne had left France with a Swedish passport; Beaumetz after the arrests from which he saved himself by assuming a family name, Briois, escaped from Bolbec where Lacroix de Chartres, a member of the Convention, helped him to disguise himself as a sutler; and, after driving his cart for two weeks, he escaped from France and reached England.

Talleyrand also told me that on the day he went to the residence of Danton, Minister of Justice, to get a passport, someone came there at the same moment to say that M. de

---

betrayed and deceived everybody. You would even sell your own father." Frédéric Loliée writes interestingly of him in *Prince Talleyrand and His Times* (Knopf), and Joseph McCabe in *Talleyrand, a Biographical Study.* He, his beautiful niece and his château at Valençay are described briefly in *Captain Caution.*

[4]Lafayette's aide-de-camp in the American Revolution and nominated by him to fill one of the posts of aides-majors in the National Guard. La Colombe made his escape from France to Rotterdam, thence to England and to America, arriving in New York at the beginning of May, 1794.

[5]Comte Louis de Narbonne Lara (1755–1814).

Montmorin de Fontainebleau[6] had been acquitted by the Revolutionary tribunal, but had been put back in prison by the people. Some men from the Battalion of the Abbey then entered the Minister's house and said to him:

"The jurymen have had the infamy to acquit Montmorin, and the judges found themselves forced to uphold the verdict. But we are not willing to tolerate this crime. We know Montmorin is guilty and we have taken him back to prison. We have come to ask you for an order that will hold him there."

"You are sure," said Danton, "that he is guilty? Ah well, he must be! The voice of the people never accuses a man in vain."

Then Danton turned to a secretary and said, "Draw up an order of imprisonment."

As these men were leaving, one of them, in vest and cap, with a great red feather, held out his right arm. "Citizen Minister, I have a word to say to you!"

"Speak!"

"I know a great general who lives in the Rue des Gravilliers and is called Monneron. He has beaten Brunswick many times; shouldn't use be made of him?"

Danton advanced toward the speaker with flashing eye. "You are a bad citizen! You know a great general. . . . You know that he has beaten Brunswick. You know that Brunswick defiles the soil of France, yet you do not speak. Is it only by chance that you are now informing the Minister of Justice?"

Everyone present said to the man, "He is right. . . . Why didn't you say it? . . . Why didn't you give the information?"

Danton said: "Yes, I repeat, you are an execrable citizen—

[6]For an account of a most interesting trial before the Revolutionary courts at this time, see *The Reign of Terror: a Collection of Authentic Narratives of the Horrors Committed by the Revolutionary Government of France under Marat and Robespierre*, I, 35–36.

but tonight bring General Monneron to the door of the Council and we'll see whether we can use him. . . ."

The group left, overjoyed to see that one of its members had pointed out a great general, and must take him that night to the door of the Council.

I learned also from Colombe that he had escaped from the prisons of Antwerp. He had just been playing whist. After the rubber he showed noticeably bad temper toward the Governor, his partner; then excused himself on the pretext that he had a fever, and said he was going to bed.

He went to his room, dressed himself as a Dutch priest, a pistol in one hand, a dagger in the other. His servant, who had made a reconnaissance at a very early hour, had given him complete information. The servant warned the other prisoners that Colombe was about to escape, as his master had told him to. They regretted not having adopted Colombe's idea of escaping all together, swearing to wait for each other or die. Many among them were inclined at this moment to imitate Colombe's example, but they lacked courage. Pillet, the former commandant of the Basoche, and aide-de-camp to Lafayette, was the only one who escaped, but unarmed.

La Colombe, after having walked for a long time, was worn out and lay down in the road. All of a sudden he heard a noise and fearing for the twelve louis that he had, when someone was close to him, he took his dagger in his right hand, his pistol in his left, and cried, "Who goes there?" "It is I," someone replied. He recognized the voice of Pillet, to whom he gave his pistol, and they went on their way together.

Arrived at Berg-op-zoom, they were stopped by the guard. Pretending to be priests persecuted in France, they were passed, greatly pitied by officer and soldiers.

From Rotterdam, Colombe went to England in 1792. He embarked at Bristol and arrived at New York early in May, 1794.

May 23. I called on Colonel Parker, Marcel, Longuemare, Georges, Dr. Rush, Terrier, Dr. Rittenhouse.

Several persons of color came to see us.

May 24. We left Philadelphia for New York at one o'clock in the morning.

ROUTE BETWEEN PHILADELPHIA
AND NEW YORK

(Which I have traveled four times, going and coming, from May 24, 1794, to the following October 14)

MAY *24, 1794.* In the two cities of Philadelphia and New York there are quite a considerable number of stages whose only business is to take travelers from one city to the other. Travelers may register for the trip in books maintained for the purpose in various offices. The stages leave from eight in the morning until three in the afternoon; and during the long days some start at one in the morning and arrive the same night at New York.

These stages are usually drawn by four horses and have nine or twelve places, on benches without backs, three people to each bench. The space is hardly ever sufficient for three. From the elbow height of a seated person to the top, the carriages have leather curtains on three sides, fastened to studs by buttonholes in leather straps. The front is open, because the driver always sits on the first bench. It is through the front that one gets into the back of the carriage, by stepping over the benches.

One will never make a European understand that in a country where people travel so readily from one place to another, and where it is a disgrace for anyone to travel on foot, there should be no other means of transport than these carriages in which the passengers are crowded in together, unable to stretch their legs because their baggage is placed beneath the benches.

The carriages are very high, long and narrow, and the

drivers, who are almost always slightly drunk, drive so fast that accidents are excessively common.

When one leaves Philadelphia for New York, one leaves by the northern end. In proportion as one gets farther into the Northern Liberties, which are really its northern suburb, the character of the city disappears more and more. Finally reaching the end of North First Street, one turns a little to the east, then one goes over a stone bridge, before entering Kensington, which is a more remote suburb of Philadelphia, with several houses bordering the highroad.

Kensington has shipyards, rope factories and all the characteristics of a naval establishment. The soil is sandy.

After an hour one reaches Frankfort, where a stop is made to water the horses. The name of this town shows clearly that it is inhabited by Germans. Situated six miles from Philadelphia and twelve hundred toises from the Delaware, it has forty-seven houses, and an English Episcopal place of worship as well as a German. It has a situation made pleasing by the waters of Frankfort Creek, whose winding course and waterfall are a pleasant prospect for travelers. Frankfort is, so to speak, divided into unequal parts by the creek which turns the mills. As the town is made up, one might say, of only one street, which is the road itself, it is almost two miles long, with pretty little houses, mostly stone, ornamented with doors and windows generally painted green, with blinds of the same color or gray. Little gardens and stretches of lawn give a sylvan air to this colony. The two churches are also stone.

Three miles beyond Frankfort is a large hotel whose signboard depicts General Washington. The house is of stone, and the stages sometimes planned their route to make it an overnight stop. This hotel is fairly good.

Four miles after the General Washington comes the Red Lion, another tavern, or rather wineshop, where the horses are again watered, which is always done without requiring the travelers to get out of the carriage.

For the entire thirteen miles between Philadelphia and the Red Lion the view is delightful. The road is wide, there are frequent groves of trees, particularly before reaching the General Washington tavern, and through the glades and meadows one frequently has glimpses of the Delaware, from which one gets farther away as one leaves Philadelphia.

Everything bespeaks the vicinity and the outskirts of a large city. Pleasantly located houses are much more numerous. Farms and gardens are more varied; there are more stages; more wagons hitched in different ways, an increased atmosphere of wealth and activity, noticeable even in the carts and in those who guide them, the carriages of the city, cabriolets, phaetons, which ladies sometimes drive themselves, saddle horses, steeds which obey a pretty female hand. One is less offended by the tiresome sight of the fences because so much verdure seems to make one forget them.

Animals of various kinds, moving about in different sections; the curious who stare at passers-by from the doors and windows; young children who are bound for school or returning from it, giving vent to a turbulence which is sometimes joyous and sometimes malicious; the men on horseback who urge on the slow-footed cattle or the timid sheep toward the place where they must be slaughtered; the cries from two stages as they pass each other—everything in this section is full of life.

However, between the General Washington and the Red Lion, the country is less pleasing, more stony, more uneven, but the very change catches one's attention, and when at the foot of a hill one comes upon a brook which the stage crosses by a bridge, one finds that the somberness of the region, the accompanying silence which is scarcely disturbed by the murmur of the brook, also has its charm.

The construction of the houses which one sees between

Frankfort and the Red Lion still retains some flavor of the German character, which is reflected particularly in the spacious barns, built of stone like the houses.

In the thirteen miles beyond Philadelphia one counts nine stone bridges which do not manifest great solidity. Their copings are covered with pieces of flimsy wood painted a harsh red to conserve it, whereas it would be simpler and more economical to make the coping of flat rocks, such as are used in the construction of the bridges themselves.

After having left the Red Lion, where in the month of August there is a celebrated Melon Frolic which brings together all the neighboring people to eat watermelons and dance, one comes to a less fertile section, the intervening space less agreeable to the eye than that which one has left and even marshy in certain places, four long miles before reaching a creek called Neshaming, quite large, and filled with fresh-water turtles which always show signs of fright at the approach of a carriage.

One crosses the creek by a wooden bridge like the one at the Schuylkill and sometimes in equally poor condition. This bridge belongs to two people whose lands abut upon it. To reimburse themselves and pay for its upkeep they demand a toll which is a forty-fifth part of a dollar, a little more than two sous a person on foot, one eighth of a dollar or thirteen sous and a half for a cabriolet with one horse, accompanied by a mounted servant. Other tariffs are based on a similar scale.

The toll is paid on the side of the bridge to which one comes first, and it belongs to the proprietor who collects it. The stages aren't obliged to stop for this formality, for they pay a fixed sum which covers all tolls on the routes they frequent.

After crossing the bridge, it is three miles to Bristol. This part of the route is not interesting. The soil is dry, and if it weren't for a few pretty houses and an occasional picturesque vista, monotony would rule over this region.

Bristol, situated on the right bank of the Delaware, twenty miles from Philadelphia (eight and a half leagues) has about sixty houses spread over a great extent, because, like those at Frankfort, they front on the main road, so that the town has the appearance of a broad and winding street. And besides, since the houses almost all have out-buildings which separate them from each other, Bristol is truly long. The town is well shaded and in a position that is enlivened by the river.

Across the river from Bristol is Burlington, a town in New Jersey, of about two hundred houses (one hundred and sixty of which are on an island) and an academy or educational institution. The island has a population of one thousand whites and one hundred slaves.

Quakers are the most numerous of Bristol's population, and it is this circumstance that is supposed to be responsible for the depressing atmosphere that reigns over this place.

A ferry-boat is the means of communication between Bristol and Burlington; and packets or barges pass continually from both places to Philadelphia.

If one stops at Bristol one finds many hotels that are not bad. At this point the Delaware is about a mile wide.

Leaving Bristol, where a great many people come to spend the summer, one proceeds toward Trenton, which is ten miles away. From time to time the route is through pleasant woods, which gives the road the appearance of a wide sandy *allée*. One often sees the river and is even sometimes beside it. All the ground is level, the route is beautiful. One comes upon lovely sites, pleasing houses, taverns, farms. If it weren't for some stretches of poor and barren soil, and for the fences, this whole long landscape would be delightful.

One here observes the progressive steps in the labor and surroundings of an American farmer. First he makes a small hut of heavy plank or even of logs. This is his sole dwelling.

If he prospers, he builds a second house of clapboards at least twice as large as the first, which becomes his kitchen. Finally he builds a third, even taller and larger, often of stone. Then the second becomes the kitchen, and the first a cow-barn.

At the point at which one reaches the Delaware to cross to Trenton the crossing had to be made by ferry in 1794. This ferry has been replaced by a stone bridge with sidewalks. On the left is the small but beautiful country home of M. Morris of Philadelphia.

Around this house is Morrisville, a settlement founded by M. Robert Morris, as the name clearly indicates. In front of Morrisville in the Delaware is a little island on which he has established iron works.

North of the river, one can distinguish Trenton and see on the highest point near the river the State House and a splendid private home embellished by a private driveway. Farther down than Trenton, and on the same side, is Lamberton.

At ordinary times the Delaware, where the route crosses it, is a rather inconsiderable stream. Its bottom is rocky, as is the part of its bed which is exposed at low tide. This point is the limit beyond which boats cannot go because it becomes stony, and the rise and fall of the tide is hardly noticeable.

Above this point go flat-bottomed craft, but they in turn cannot clear the stony obstacle of which I was speaking, so that it forms a boundary between these two kinds of navigation.

Two ferry-boats are in service for crossing the Delaware. A stage can be taken aboard a ferry without the passengers being obliged to get out, though such a precaution is usually wise because the slightest movement of a skittish horse can cause an accident, and these are by no means unknown. There was also something to be feared from the horses if

one got too near them. On the Trenton ferry-boat we saw
a mare step on the bare foot of a ferryman and make blood
spurt from three of his toes, which were almost ground off.
In spite of this unfortunate person's courage, this accident
delayed us over a quarter of an hour in reaching the other
side.

But the bridge has remedied all that. The passage is swiftly
made, and no longer prolongs the two-hour journey from
Bristol to the water's edge.

Reaching Trenton by this route, one enters the state of
New Jersey, of which this town is the capital. Including the
thirty houses in Lamberton which adjoin those of Trenton,
there are two hundred houses, many of which are of brick
and attractive. The public buildings are a place where the
state legislature meets, a Court of Justice, a market and four
churches, one for Episcopalians, one for Presbyterians, one
for Quakers and one for Methodists.

The ground rises rapidly coming from the river, and one
crosses a picturesque stone bridge.

Trenton is a pleasant place. The most important houses
are along the road, which give the town an appearance of
length. It has given asylum to many unfortunate colonists,
whom one finds everywhere in Bristol, Burlington and Lamberton. These communities have charming country houses.

There are many inns for travelers, and each one strives to
stand well with the stagecoach drivers, in order to obtain
their patronage in case overnight stops should be necessary,
or daylight halts.

One leaves Trenton for Princeton by a road that passes
through a country devoted to the cultivation of wheat and
flax.

Halfway between Trenton and Princeton, on the left of
the road, is Maidenhead, consisting of several houses and a
church. The horses are watered here.

After Maidenhead and before reaching Princeton, one

finds himself at a place where the view takes in on the right a stretch of some ten to twelve leagues. In it are woods, farms, valleys, hill slopes, and in the far distance low mountains, but high enough to form a pleasant crown for the whole scene.

From this place where the eye is so gladdened, one descends to the bottom of a vale where there is a stream called Stony Brook. There is a bridge over it; and on its parapet, facing toward the Delaware, the traveler reads:

Stony Brook
1792
40 miles from Philadelphia
56 miles from New York

In the vicinity of the bridge, on the opposite slope, are several tanneries. Two miles more, in which space there was once a camp of General Rochambeau, and one reaches Princeton, having traveled twelve miles, fifteen leagues, from Trenton in two hours and a quarter.

Princeton has the same characteristics as the places already mentioned since our departure from Philadelphia, namely, it consists almost entirely of houses that border the road. There might be about eighty, and for the most part they are of brick.

In this town is a Presbyterian church and a college. The latter demands that we pause to speak of it, as we did to visit it.

This stone edifice, which is one hundred and seventy French feet long and about forty wide, has three floors, if one wishes to count the ground floor as the first floor. This ground floor is nevertheless seven to eight feet above the ground-line, which leaves space for cellars. At the top of all is an attic, which causes the Americans to say that the building has four floors.

The central part of the façade protrudes. There are ten windows on each side of it, and below the pediment there are six other windows on the façade. All in all, this building has an impressive appearance for America. Before it is a huge front yard set off from the street by a brick wall, and at intervals along the wall are pilasters supporting wooden urns painted gray. This front yard is untidy, covered with the droppings of animals who come there to graze. In its center is an old iron cannon, a four-pounder, without a carriage. This cannon, the dilapidated condition of the encircling wall, the number of decorative urns that have fallen to the ground, everything bears the imprint of negligence, and one reaches the building grieved that the pupils have such an unpleasant example before their eyes.

One enters the college, which is called Nassau Hall, by three equal-sized doors, one being in the middle of the façade and the two others on the sides. One walks up wooden stairs without banisters.

Each of the two floors is divided into dormitories separated by a corridor which extends the length of the building. There are forty-two rooms designed to accommodate three scholars each. On the floor below there is a chapel, a refectory, a library of about two thousand volumes, and the justly celebrated planetarium built by Dr. David Rittenhouse, at the moment president of the Philosophical Society of Philadelphia. He was born in Pennsylvania.

On the first floor, facing the central entrance door but at the back, is a huge hall furnished with benches, as is any other classroom. Entering, one sees on the right a painting about eight feet high of General Washington on foot. He holds his sword in his right hand in an attitude of command; and his left hand, resting on his hip, holds his hat. Behind him and in the left background is General Mercer lying down but leaning on his left elbow. Behind the general to the right of the picture are his two aides-de-camp, and in the distance one sees the battle of Princeton.

While the painting of this picture may not be without

merit, three things are open to criticism. The first is that General Washington should hold his hat in his hand and strike a formal pose at a moment when he is actually in command of a battle. The second is that General Mercer, who died of the wound he received in this battle of Princeton in the month of January, 1777, has no appearance of suffering. The third is that such an ambiguous attitude has been given to the two aides-de-camp that they seem to have no interest in the dying general.

Behind the college there is an extremely large courtyard. It is dirty and uncultivated, and everything in it is evidence of neglect. Although one hundred and twenty scholars can be lodged in this house, as a rule there are only about eighty, mostly from Virginia and the two Carolinas.

It would be indeed pleasant to be able to speak highly of the curriculum of this institution; but when one has not been brought up in the American way, praise is difficult. Any system that, due to the heedlessness of its masters, fails to impose any restraints on its youths, and indulges them in the customary indolence of Americans, cannot but produce vicious results. These effects are visible at Princeton College, where sport and licentious habits are said to absorb the pupils more than study.

The college fee is one hundred dollars a year (five hundred and fifty francs). Laundry is a gourde a month.

[On Saturday, March 6, 1802, at one in the afternoon, a fire broke out in the steeple of the college. A violent wind destroyed it completely in six hours. The three thousand volumes in the library were burned. The directors made an appeal to the generosity of the public to rebuild the college. The new term was fixed for May 3, 1803. The scholars were lodged in Princeton and the fee from May 3 to the end of September was set at one hundred dollars.][1]

Princeton enjoys a reputation for healthfulness which it

[1]Moreau interpolated this passage after returning to France.

merits, and the college records verify this; for only an infinitesimal number of pupils (five or six) have been lost since its foundation. This may be the reason why so many San Domingo colonists have come to Princeton.

There are many inns in Princeton, in particular the Washington Tavern, where General Rochambeau lodged on his march from Rhode Island to Virginia. It is run at present by David Hamilton.

One sees very beautiful catalpas in front of all the houses. These are the Badaminier of the Moluccas, according to Bomare. The wide spread of this great tree affords an agreeable shade; and its large leaves, handsome flowers and pods attract attention. However, it is said to be extremely poisonous, and even the emanations from its cold leaves are enough to cause dizziness. If this assertion, which I have not verified and which I do not find recorded by the botanists, is true, one would lament that nature could have given such a deceptive exterior to this beautiful tree. Bomare says that in the Indies its fruits are eaten.

Leaving Princeton, which is eighteen leagues northeast of Philadelphia and twenty-two leagues southwest of New York, one continues for some time along the plateau on which it is situated, when one notices that the land declines as it had risen from Stony Brook to Princeton. During this entire interval one notices gracious sites, and fresh and cultivated vales.

At the foot of the descent is Millstone Creek, whose waters turn a sawmill and whose small dam makes a sort of cascade. This spot is quite picturesque.

After having passed Millstone Creek, which is three miles from Princeton, one laboriously climbs a rough, steep hill to reach Kingston, situated on the height with fifteen houses which border the road. One is an inn bearing the sign of a mermaid, which was established there by its present master in 1744. The water which the people drink and use for other domestic needs comes entirely from an extremely deep well dug about forty years ago. If the innkeeper can be believed, the well cost seven hundred dollars (four thousand francs) to build. There is no other water in the vicinity, unless one goes to Millstone Creek for it; and to carry water such a distance would be extremely difficult.

Kingston passed, one is almost tempted to regret the first part of the ascent which had brought us here, since it was necessary to follow its route by Rock Hill, which is aptly named. The joltings are violent and the driver walks the whole distance, letting the carriage take care of itself. The travelers also get out and walk, unless mud prevents them from using the sides of the road.

The quality of the fields is like that of the road, and one sees almost everywhere stone in layers like slate, but crumbly and with indications of iron. To make the road firm these same stones are used on the roadway, but they shift and the successive ascents and descents keep them from remaining in place.

When this detestable section has been left behind, one arrives somewhat later at Six Mile Run. If one stops here, one finds in the inn, run by Isaac Shiver, beds with truly white sheets, which is the rarest of all things in every American tavern. Most of them fill Frenchmen with repugnance, for they are expected to sleep between sheets on which traces of previous occupants are encountered with more or less frequency.

It is a pity that the rats of the town hold court in this house, and rob travelers of the rest of which they usually are greatly in need.

Two masters, one servant and two horses can sup and sleep in this inn for less than three dollars (seventeen francs).

From Millstone to Six Mile Run the earth is a reddish color, hard and clay-like, which is to say it is similar to that already cited in speaking of Rock Hill, which is a part of this stretch.

One leaves Six Mile Run for Brunswick, sometimes after having already changed stages once since Trenton. These changes are disagreeable, since they necessitate getting down from one coach and up onto another, which is highly uncomfortable in cold or rainy weather; and it is seldom that one's luggage, which must also be transferred from stage to stage, can be put in the same place in the new as in the other. There is always the risk of finding the new coach more uncomfortable than the old. Each traveler occupies a place corresponding to the one he left—a corresponding bench and the same position on it. Ordinarily these changes do not take more than five minutes.

The land along the route to New York is well cultivated, although the soil seems mediocre. There are beautiful orchards filled with splendid apple trees, which in general are very common in New Jersey. Small fields of flax also brighten the outlook. The earth, which always has a ferruginous appearance, is by nature hard and clayey, as is shown by some brickyards.

Although it is said to be seven miles from Six Mile Run to Brunswick, one is more than ready to call this figure exaggerated when from the road one is able to see the point of the Brunswick steeple toward which the route is leading. But a long time elapses from the moment when the steeple is glimpsed to the time when Brunswick is wholly seen, and one reaches the inns which stand at the river's edge.

This is the Raritan River, and Brunswick occupies the right bank. The town has more than two hundred houses, mostly of wood and only one story high, and more than fifteen hundred inhabitants. Its situation is peculiar in that many of the houses are in a low part along the river, while the others are on the rising ground of a nearby hill. It is this falling away of the ground in one part which makes the steeple visible two miles before one can see the town, which is only visible when a traveler is about to enter it. The lower part of the town is in a damp location. The roads are paved with small stones.

In Brunswick there is a large barracks made of stone where United States soldiers are housed. Here also are placards promising eight gourdes (forty-four francs) to whoever will enlist, along with the usual glowing promises employed in such matters.

Brunswick has increased so rapidly that a third of its houses weren't in existence ten years ago, particularly the best-looking ones; and in that time rents have doubled. It has direct communication with New York by the Raritan River. This is accomplished by boats that sometimes make the trip in less than four hours, and the cost per passenger is three eighths of a dollar (forty sous).

There are many very good inns in Brunswick; and since slavery has full scope in this state, these have so many Negroes in service that one is served well and promptly. One dines wonderfully for one third of a dollar a head (thirty-six sous). We had a good meal here.

One changes stages at Brunswick, and immediately crosses the Raritan by ferry-boat when the tide is high (at which time there are nine feet of water) or by fording when it is low (when there are only two feet of water).

In 1792 a bridge was started over this river, with eleven arches on stone piers; but bad construction made it collapse at several points, causing a loss of five thousand dollars, or more than forty-two thousand francs. Work was started again with a better plan and the bridge will cost fifteen thousand dollars, eighty-two thousand francs, by the time it is finished. Carriages will continue to pay what they gave ordinarily to the ferry, and this toll will defray the cost of the maintenance. This bridge should be finished in the summer of 1795. [And so it was.]

Across the Raritan, about two miles above Brunswick, is

a wooden bridge built at the expense of the two counties which border the shores. In the neighborhood of the bridge the Raritan has a width of only about thirty-six French feet.

After crossing the Raritan, one proceeds toward Woodbridge, eleven miles from Brunswick. About halfway of this distance is Willington, made up of a dozen houses separated one from the other. There the horses are refreshed with a large pail of water. From this point also the eye takes in a maritime scene, discovering Staten Island, Amboy and all the arms of the sea that encircle these points.

The picture which opens out and draws closer as one nears Woodbridge is not helped by the sight of the land that one passes, because from Brunswick it is barren and made up almost always of dry, uncultivated fields; and the few fences that one sees do not enclose farmland. One can hardly take a step without seeing mullein, which is a sign of sterility and with which New Jersey is, unfortunately, well supplied. One sees also sumac, of which no use is made. Woodbridge is very extensive, but again as regards length only, because the houses, built along the road with large gaps between them, give one the impression that it is just a long ribbon of a town.

Woodbridge has a college intended for the education of about eighty children, but masters are often lacking for their instruction. All the pupils are day pupils, who pay four gourdes (twenty-two francs ten sous) quarterly. Each day a stage leaves Woodbridge for New York.

The inn in this place is simple, but sufficiently clean. In order that this last word (clean) might be applied to our reception, the host would have had to free us from the familiar favors of his son, seven or eight years old, who in spite of having a nose that held a high place for extreme snottiness, came and ate with his fingers what was left of the fried eggs that remained in a plate on our table.

Beyond Woodbridge, whose church and cemetery are far

removed from the dwellings at both ends, the route is again not very attractive, but it does not have the same desert air as the road leading to that place. One soon sees a change for the better, and the eye wanders with pleasure as far as Amboy and Raritan Bay on which it is situated. After an hour one reaches Bridgeton or Rahway built on the Rahway River, which empties into the sea and which the stage crosses thrice on the same number of bridges. The winding layout of Rahway gives it an outstanding appearance. It is rich in charming situations, with pretty and diversified gardens and small clean houses that have the double character of town and country houses. There are fruit trees of all kinds; and the elegance of the women corresponds with the light calèches they drive. Everything about the place made us regret leaving, and impressed us unforgettably.

This impression was maintained all along the road to Elizabethtown, which is ten miles from Woodbridge and fifteen miles from New York. This charming town, which has about two hundred houses, is on a creek whose mouth, west of Staten Island, is only a short distance away. Boats constantly cross to New York from this point, and stages also run continuously between Elizabethtown and New York.

Elizabethtown has an academy: that is to say, a house of education. A beautiful new belfry with a well-gilded steeple gives a splendid appearance to one of the houses of worship; and a wooden bridge over the creek, close to which is a mill, adds variety and life.

Elizabethtown society has the reputation of being extremely pleasant and agreeable; and this advantage must have been one of the reasons which has led many colonists to make their residence there.

Since Elizabethtown has connections of every kind with New York, its inhabitants think of themselves as belonging more to the state of New York than to New Jersey, to which they actually belong, both topographically and politically.

One of the first results of this idea is to lead them to reckon money as it is reckoned in New York—which is how money should be reckoned everywhere in the United States, since the divisions of New York's monetary system are the true division of the dollar, which is the universal money of the country. In effect New York assumes eight shillings to a gourde, of which each eighth is, consequently, equal to a shilling.[2]

In Elizabethtown we saw our relative Maupertuis and the wife of M. Trigant, who was lieutenant of the chief magistrate of Port-au-Prince.

It is six leagues from Elizabethtown to New York.

The route from Elizabethtown to Newark, six miles away, is not devoid of charm. The borders of the road disclose pretty farms well kept up, and the country has an atmosphere of easy circumstance which is always pleasant to encounter.

At the end of an hour and a quarter the stage reaches Newark. This place, which is the capital of the county of Essex, has about one hundred and fifty houses, many of them stone or brick, a Court of Justice, a prison and two churches, one Presbyterian and the other Episcopal.

One of these two churches, built recently, has a stone tower, with a tall steeple of wood. The church is one hundred feet long and eighty-eight wide. A double row of windows gives light, and one larger and leaded is at the end behind the pulpit, which is eight feet in front of the window. The tower is two hundred feet high, and attracts one's attention pleasingly from a distance.

The entrance of the church is in Doric style. In general the whole is simple, clean and elegant.

The market is also entirely new.

[2]This is what Moreau says. Actually the San Domingan gourde was a dollar, or five francs, and New York "assumed" four shillings to a gourde: not eight.

In 1791 a large building was started. This was planned as a public school under the name of academy, and it is on the point of being finished.

It is a brick house of two stories. On the first floor are one hundred boy and girl students, indiscriminately crowded in together, though there is talk of putting them in separate rooms.

The second floor is the hall for the Freemasons, who provided part of the money needed for the building. It is reckoned that the undertaking cost seven thousand five hundred dollars (forty thousand francs). Tuition fees are eighty dollars a year (four hundred and forty francs). The dead languages are taught, as well as English and French.

Among these places of instruction is that of Mme. Capron, whose husband, a native of Lille in Flanders and a bass-viol player, is employed by the orchestra of the Comedy at Philadelphia. She has many small or young girls.

For one hundred and thirty-six dollars they learn French and English, writing, geography, drawing and embroidery of all kinds.

The city of Newark is another whose extent seems to be very great because the streets are nothing but the highway, and the houses line its sides; and as the route from Philadelphia to New York makes a turn here, the houses also have this double direction. Besides, large gardens, numerous trees, etc., take up spaces which extend the territory of the city without increasing the buildings. Newark has a large population in relation to the number of its houses. One is not surprised at this when one knows that the shoe factory established here employs three or four hundred workers and turns out sixty thousand pairs a year.

Sixteen miles from Newark is Manufactory City,[3] a place

---

[3]Although no authority has been found for this denomination, Moreau evidently refers here to Paterson, which had been chosen as the site for the establishment of manufactures by an association formed in 1791 at the suggestion of Alexander Hamilton.

where the state of New Jersey has brought together various manufacturing establishments, notably spinning mills. These establishments are supported by the purchase of shares in joint-stock companies, but the shares have already lost much in value, which demonstrates the impossibility of profiting from a business venture when laborers' wages are too high.

Also, ten miles from Newark is a stone quarry where blocks are produced for building.

Newark has many inns. The one at the Sign of the Hunt, kept by Archer Ciftord, is very good and comfortable, with clean and attractive rooms.

Newark cider is generally reputed to be the best in the United States, and although that of Philadelphia is held to be close behind it, the superiority is justly awarded to the former. However, my colleague Michaux (of the Society of Agriculture in Paris) finds it inferior to that of St. Lô, of Coutances and of Bayeux.

Each day a stage sets out from Newark for New York, which is in every respect the metropolis of this section, as I have already said, although politically this section belongs to New Jersey. Such is the powerful influence of commerce.

Leaving Newark, there are houses along the road for a long way, and the small farms close by seem to belong to the town. Then one comes to a barren stretch with marshy, heavy, sticky earth; and a league beyond the great tower of Newark the route dwindles to a narrow, badly kept roadway with a soft and easily rutted surface. This road is so narrow that there is room for only one carriage. Thus when two have to pass one another, the one that is least advanced on the roadway pulls out into one of the semicircular spaces provided at intervals, sometimes on one side of the road and sometimes on the other, and waits until the other carriage passes.

Finally, after six hundred toises of this, one reaches the bank of the Passaic River, which is twenty-five hundred toises from the Newark steeple, the steeple toward which the road runs, and which one can see marvelously from this distance.

Arriving there, we found the ferry-boat was on the other side. It was already night and raining a little, so we were obliged to return to Newark, where we slept at the Sign of the Hunt.

May 25. The next day we set off again for New York and once more reached the Passaic.

We crossed the Passaic in a ferry-boat which has the inconvenience of obliging all the passengers to get out of the stage so it can be put on board. We then found places as best we could; for in general and in almost every country a public carriage and its horses are attended to first, and the passengers it carries receive no consideration whatever.

The two leading horses are always unhitched before the carriage goes on the ferry, and it is hauled off also with only two horses.

The crossing of the Passaic was not long, because the ferry was drawn by means of a cable which went through pulleys on the sides of the boat, and the river at this point was only about one hundred and fifteen toises wide. Sometimes it took only seven minutes to cross the water, not counting the preparations.

A cabriolet, three men and two horses paid two ninths of a dollar, twenty-four sous.

When we had got back into the stage after crossing the ferry we found ourselves on another roadway, larger but as muddy and as exhausting as the first; and after twenty minutes of joltings we reached the shore of the Hackensack River.

There is now a bridge across the Passaic, four hundred and ninety-two feet long, thirty-eight feet wide, with five-foot sidewalks, and one crosses by carriage.

The embankments which abut here are twenty-five hundred feet long, eighteen feet wide, with an elevation of two feet above the ground.

There are cascades in the Passaic about fourteen leagues from Elizabethtown. Above the cascades this river is about seventy-five feet wide and flows rapidly until it reaches a waterfall which crosses its bed and falls about seventy feet perpendicularly in a single sheet of leaf-like thinness.

As one side of the waterfall has no opening, the water jumps out of the other with incredible rapidity, making an acute angle to its first direction, and flows into a large basin. From there it takes a winding course through creeks and spreads over a very considerable bed, the outlet being from four to twelve feet wide.

The spray forms two rainbows, one dimmer than the other, which is a pleasing sight.

This phenomenon of the waterfall is thought to be the result of an earthquake. About six hundred toises from the great waterfall there is another even more beautiful, flowing over layers of rocks two to three feet perpendicular, which again beautifies the scenery.

The Hackensack River, wider than the Passaic, since it is about three hundred toises, also has a more perceptible tide. Here the ferry uses a big sail attached to a mast which is supported by a sternpost at each end. This mast is movable and can be unstepped, for two purposes—one so that carriages may enter and leave freely, and the other so that it can be stepped in the end that becomes the prow without turning the boat in order not to waste time and sometimes to avoid having the tide carry the ferry in the wrong direction. When there was a strong contrary wind, its effect was augmented by the surface presented by the high-standing stage; and since it was necessary to tack, the crossing was both long and disagreeable, and to undertake it at night was a great risk. The shortest crossing took a quarter of an hour.

When the weather was fair, one enjoyed a view of a rather

high hillock, called Snake Hill, which faces you when you are in the middle of the river, a little distance away and above the ferry as the river runs. This hillock received its name, it is said, because of being infested with rattlesnakes which were destroyed by loosing pigs who devoured them. The pigs in turn have multiplied to such a degree that people go wild-pig hunting.

Ordinary travelers (and those not riding in the stage) pay when they leave the second ferry. The fare is one forty-fifth of a dollar per person, two sous, one thirtieth for a horse, three sous.

Here we have seen paid for the same cabriolet, two horses and three men, five sixteenths of a dollar, three sous. Here, too, we were witnesses of a remarkable scene between a passenger and the woman who collected the fares, who was young, pretty and had an expression of angelic sweetness. Having been given in payment one of those copper half-sous coined by the state of Jersey, she refused it obstinately and became furious, declaring with the most expressive words that she didn't give a hoot for the Assembly of New Jersey, whose members were no better than she and couldn't make her take their money.

Recently Hackensack has also built a bridge. It is nine hundred and eighty feet long and has the same width, sidewalks and embankments as that across the Passaic.

These two bridges cost three hundred thousand francs.

When all the annoyances of the ferry had been endured (and they were considerable, particularly if one arrived to take the ferry at the precise moment when it was leaving, loaded with another stage, which could occasion an hour's wait on the Hackensack shore) there were still two leagues to go before reaching New York. The route passes through country that is anything but lovely, and is only endurable because of the hideous roadways of the two preceding rivers. The aspect is marshy, the reeds distress the eye, and one is astounded, after two miles and a half, to find the small settlement of Bergen, which arouses no desire to share its watery neighborhood.

Five hundred toises further, having reached the top of an elevation, one sees New York and the tower of St. Paul's Church, which seems to lie exactly in the center of the road. This pleasing glimpse contrasts strongly with the soil on which one is; and when one finally comes to Paulus Hook, at the edge of the North or Hudson River which must still be crossed in order to reach New York, one is only consoled by the thought that this new embarkation will also be the last.

Since many things can prevent the crossing of the North River or the departure for Newark, a large inn with twenty-five beds has been built at Paulus Hook. Since this inn is unfortunately the only one, the innkeeper does not fear competition, and so gives no thought to his food or beds. One might even think that he was conferring a favor on those whose money he takes. A meal costs half a dollar (fifty-five sous), one fourth (twenty-seven and a half sous) for a servant, the feed for a horse three eighths of a dollar (forty sous), and a bed costs one eighth of a dollar (fourteen sous), including black and dirty sheets.

Sleeping here is much more costly during the warm season, for the mosquitoes do not let one enjoy the slightest repose, and their fatiguing concert is only interrupted during the painful moment when their sharp sting pumps the blood from the unhappy creature whom chance has made their victim.

To cross the North River at a point where it is fifteen hundred toises wide, one formerly embarked on boats large enough to hold two carriages, their horses and twenty-five passengers. These were propelled by sails and had a crew of two men, one of whom held the tiller.

There were three of these boats, two belonging to the city

of New York and the third to Jersey. This last, or rather the right to run it, was leased for six thousand francs a year to an individual who furnished everything himself.

The toll per person was one sixteenth of a dollar (seven sous), one eighth for a horse (fifteen), five sixteenths for a carriage (thirty-six), one fourth for a cabriolet (twenty-eight). This crossing was far from being without danger; and while it is true that accidents were very rare, there was always something to fear when the wind was violent and contrary, and the tide too. During the winter there were times when it was impassable.

If there was need of tacking, the passage took an hour, and during calms it might take twice as long. An excellent crossing took twelve to fifteen minutes. With a northwest wind it has been done in five minutes.

Another disagreeable feature of the crossing was that the horses had difficulty remaining quiet during the crossing, particularly when there was a swell; and I have seen a horse so frightened that it jumped into the river, fortunately so close to shore that it saved itself by swimming.

But for several years steamboats, with one deck, have obviated all these inconveniences.

The crossing is certain, independent and rapid, and takes a quarter of an hour. The steamboat carries up to four hundred persons, and seven or eight carts with horses unharnessed. Under favorable circumstances the passage is a pleasant one because of the extensive view. To the south one can see down the North River as far as Sandy Hook; to the southwest, where the East River enters this river, is Governor's Island with its interesting new fortifications. All sorts of fish and porpoise provide interesting sights; and if the month is August, it is possible that the cruel shark will also be seen among this happy troop, creating disturbances and calling up sad memories. There is only one record, however, of man-killing on their part, and that took place long ago.

To the north the eye follows the river upward, and after examining the rather monotonous Jersey side, sees New York straight ahead, constantly drawing nearer, and filling one with impatience to set foot in the city whose houses and steeples promise well, even from a distance. At the angle of the two rivers is the Battery, more pleasant as a promenade than formidable as a means of defense.

Finally our longings are gratified: we land and each one starts looking for a lodging. We have ended a journey of ninety-five miles, equal to forty leagues of two thousand toises each, happy that all the stage's passengers have arrived cheerful, active and in possession of all their limbs.

	Mile
Philadelphia to Frankfort	6
Frankfort to Red Lion	7
Red Lion to Bristol	7
Bristol to Trenton	10
Trenton to Princeton	12
Princeton to Six Mile Run	10
Six Mile Run to Brunswick	7
Brunswick to Woodbridge	10
Woodbridge to Elizabethtown	11
Elizabethtown to Newark	6
Newark to New York	9
	95 miles

The general direction of this route is from the southwest to the northeast.

Between Philadelphia and New York we saw not a single growing hedge: everywhere our eyes met only those depressing fences.

At different points we observed animals and chickens in the road at such hours that they must spend the night there —an honorable commentary on the security that exists in this country. One also sees animals without shelter inside the fences.

Pennsylvania butter is excellent.

One frequently encounters, even at points distant from all other habitations, public schools to which children come from a great distance to learn to read, write, figure and sing hymns.

When one passes these interesting creatures, one almost always receives a greeting; and one cannot help feeling annoyed when older Americans make no response, showing that politeness, one of the most charming things in society, is regarded as being childish. It wouldn't be so bad if this uncouth manner stopped there; but it doesn't. One soon discovers that people who do not know each other are admitted to the same room in a hotel. Even while one traveler is asleep, another often enters to share his bed. This untidy and even more unhealthy custom is considered perfectly natural; but I cannot help but rebel at the nonsensical belief that such customs are a proof of liberty.

Another sign of this so-called liberty is the refusal of a carriage to inconvenience itself in any way when passing another unless the other is heavier and the lighter gives ground through fearing a collision.

I have spoken frequently of "pretty" country houses in this description; but when one hears this expression, he must not think that it has the same sense here as it has in Europe, particularly in France. In America, a very pretty country house corresponds only to a place moderately kept up on the outskirts of a large French city, and even then one will find in the former neither the good taste which embellishes the European house nor the comforts which make living in it a pleasure.

In America almost everything is sacrificed to the outside view. To accomplish this the fences of the houses are sometimes varied by these six combinations: 1. Planks are laid vertically and close together. 2. Planks are laid the same way, with a space between them. 3. Little narrow boards are laid across without joining. 4. Vertically placed laths are joined. 5. Vertically placed laths are not joined. 6. Laths are placed vertically, but passing alternately on the outside and the inside of cross members. Further elegance is obtained by using different shades of paint on lattices and partitions. Doors are handled in the same way.

A great part of the route has milestones. This helps to occupy the traveler's mind. He can divert himself by reckoning how far he has advanced toward his objective.

I was forgetting to say that when there are women in the stages, they are not obliged to share in the expense incurred for wine, liquors or other spirituous drinks served with a meal. Politeness requires this expense to be borne entirely by the men. I will whisper this: that this courtesy is sometimes extended to courtesans who figure that a stage can be made to serve purposes quite foreign to modesty, a virtue which is neither their charm nor their companion.

To conceal nothing about this journey, I will add here an observation that can be applied to all others: it is a source of never-ending wonderment that there are never any curtains to the beds or the windows in any of the inns; so that during the long days of summer, such as those we had at Newark, the traveler, arriving late and worn out, is awakened at break of day by the sun shining into his room from the first moment when it appears on the horizon.

On the road between Philadelphia and New York, in the autumn, one sees wooded sections, particularly charming near Philadelphia, because the trees then show all colors: green, yellow, and the orange-red of the maples. If the buckwheat has just been cut, the remnants of the stalks cast a purplish color over the field, resulting in a truly ravishing view.

We reached New York at noon, and lodged at the inn of a Frenchman named Bernardy, an acquaintance of the good Goynard.

SOJOURN IN NEW YORK

MAY 26, 1794. I saw M. Guerlain.

We saw colonists, among them my friend Bonamy, at their houses and at ours.

The same story the following day.

May 28. We learned that Jeanne, my mother-in-law's mulatto, was dead.

I presented my compliments to Chancellor Livingston, went to the Custom House for our luggage; and the same day we took lodgings with M. Earl, M. Guerlain's head clerk, in Courtland Street.

After a series of visits I entered upon my duties as clerk to M. Guerlain.

May 31. I took part of our belongings from the Custom House.

June 1–4, 1794. I went with Goynard and my son to visit St. Paul's Church, and we took a walk afterwards. On the second, third and fourth I finished getting the remainder of our things from the Custom House.

In unpacking, I found two hats. One was that of a grenadier of the National Guard of Paris, which I had worn July 30, 1792. The other, of smooth material and almost new, belonged to Arthur Dillon, and he gave it to me when he went to the army as a general in June, 1792.

I placed the two hats on a table, and examined the National Guard hat first. It had an open cut at the top of the crown on the right side, where the Marseillais had dealt me a great sabre blow July 30, 1792. This blow had almost separated the crown of the hat in two. Down the back of the hat there were at least fifteen sabre slashes, several of them crossing each other, but no arm had been strong enough to cut through the fabric.

This examination ended, I replaced the hat on the table, and began to reflect. I said to myself: "You want to save this to show people. But suppose someone else had shown you this, and claimed to have had it on his head when it had been brought to its present state. What opinion would you have had of the speaker?"

I was forced to say to myself, "I should consider him a braggart who was trying to tell a most improbable story."

My decision was to pick up the hat, cut it in many pieces, and throw them out of the window into Courtland Street; and this I instantly did.

As for the second hat, I had just learned that Dillon had been guillotined on April 5. Sorrow for his death, the recollection of our friendship, the reason that had led him to give me the hat, everything made me look upon it with grief.

Since it would always recall his fate and his executioners, I determined to treat it exactly as I had the one on which the Marseillais had spent their fury; so when I had hacked it with the scissors, I threw it likewise into the gutter of Courtland Street, a sacrifice to the Gods of the Lower Regions.

In Portsmouth my son had made me a present of a round hat, and I wore only that; for it recalled to me no sinister occurrences, but just the affection of a beloved child.

June 8. In the evening I visited Trinity Church.

June 12. I sent out my daughter's pianoforte to be repaired of all the damage it had suffered during the crossing in the *Sophie.*

In spite of my age, my unsettled health and my ability, M. Guerlain put me in charge of the outdoor work at his place of business. I had to see to the stowing of barrels of flour, pickled pork, rice, salt beef, soda, potash, etc., aboard the *Columbia,* the *Industry,* the brig *Rachel,* the merchant ships *James* and *Massachusetts*. This was a horrible day, and I shall say more about it later. In my ignorance I sent to my niece Uranie her harp which I had had put in good condition.

June 26. Talleyrand and Beaumetz arrived in New York, hence what joy to my heart!

July 4, 1794. From the house of Talleyrand and Beaumetz at the side of the square facing the house of Governor Clinton in Broadway, we saw the annual fête of American independence. The Governor and the people who accompanied him in this fête were preceded by a long procession of French Jacobins, marching two by two, singing the *Marseillaise* and other republican songs. Both times, going to the fête and bringing the Governor back from it, they interrupted themselves to address invectives to us in the windows where they saw us, Talleyrand, Beaumetz, Cazenove, La Colombe, Baron de la Roche and me. The Minister of France to the United States, Genêt, brother of Mme. Campan, was in the procession, and sang and insulted us like all the others.

We wept for our country and for him!

July 6. Goynard, my son and I went to Long Island. La Colombe, who was living in Brooklyn, had us for lunch, after which we repaired to New Utrecht for dinner.

In the evening I read from my *Description of San Domingo* to Talleyrand, Beaumetz and Cazenove. The first two had consulted that same day with Guerlain about my distressing situation.

I had an understanding with Guerlain as to my salary, my work on the wharfs, and my share in the commission on any business which I might obtain for him, like the sale of cordage, cables, etc.

July 13. I read my *Description of San Domingo* to Bonamy, who came for lunch and dinner with me.

Dauzat, a surgeon from Limonade in San Domingo, whom I knew very well at the home of De Varenne, arrived in New

York and was struck by my thinness, excepting for my legs, which were constantly swelling.

He told me that if I persisted in my custom of never drinking wine my life would be endangered. I took his word for it and began to drink porter.

July 15. Talleyrand and Beaumetz left by the packet *New Haven,* leaving with me a letter for Minister Hamilton.

July 16. I went to Long Island to see Cazenove and Baron de la Roche. They made me flattering offers; and the very next morning we got together and worked out plans for a partnership in a bookstore.

July 21. In the evening I notified Guerlain that I was resigning as his clerk.

Thus it will be seen that I was employed by Goynard, agent for the house of Daniel Merian, from March 8, 1794, the day I disembarked at Norfolk, Virginia, until June 28 when I went to work for M. Guerlain, henceforth charged with Daniel Merian's business, and became his clerk.

What a changed state! During the crossing I had become the friend of Goynard; and considering his esteem for my family and for me, it never occurred to me to think that I would become, as I did, a clerk-shopkeeper.

At M. Guerlain's I was constantly held to my subordinate position. M. Guerlain was a Milliflore from Le Havre and had been educated in England, so that he spoke English perfectly; but he was conceited, and gave himself grand airs which not even the fortune of Daniel Merian (who was only a straw man for the French government) would have made tolerable.

From the beginning he treated me in the most cavalier manner, making me wait for hours on end, only to be so gracious as to tell me afterwards that he had no need for me.

He was such small fry that he feared a conversation with me would degrade him, and he almost never spoke to me.

Whenever he came to the counting house, he always

sought the opportunity to make disagreeable remarks to me —not personal remarks, but remarks about my friends, my connections, and above all about the Constituent Assembly, of which he very well knew I had been a member; and he was always insisting that the members should have been hanged.

Let whoever knows me conceive, if he can, how I was able to endure such impertinences, such self-sufficiency as would have been hard to bear in anybody. On the twelfth of June, to add everything he could to my misfortune, he put the loading and unloading of his ships in my care.

What an occupation for a man such as I, raised in the colonies, a member of a sovereign court, high in public esteem, and almost forty-five years of age!

In bad health and very tall, it was a task indeed to stoop almost to the ground to mark casks of all sorts with the letters DM (Daniel Merian) and with a number, on an East River wharf, exposed to the burning heat of the sun, noting names and numbers in the lading book from six o'clock in the morning until noon, and again from two o'clock until six.

This sort of galley-slave labor gave me plenty of time to dwell on its distressing features; and my morale as well as my body suffered from it.

In this frightful condition, my son suggested that he should help me. I did not have the strength to refuse him. Marking the casks was a sort of game to him. During this time I sought a little rest in the shade; but I did not let him take my place in the hours of greatest heat in a country where the thermometer registers up to 28 degrees Réaumur [95 degrees Fahrenheit] in the shade for three months.

Finally night fell; and at night, at least, sleep lulled a little my sensitive nature and all that it had been forced to bear. But each evening I was obliged to go to Guerlain's house, to give him an account of my work.

Only one thought made that work endurable: all the goods

that I loaded were destined to nourish the unhappy inhabitants of France, overwhelmed by the horrors of famine; for although the vessels were consigned to false destinations, they were in reality for French ports, where fourteen that I had loaded arrived.

At the time of my daily reporting to Guerlain I frequently found him in his shop. The first five days he seemed rather indifferent; but shortly afterwards he appeared wearied at the sight of my son, and with a display of temper he ended by ejecting him from the shop.

At the sight of such treatment my blood boiled and I was about to make M. Guerlain pay for his behavior. I do not know what angel stopped me, but before it was too late I reflected that I had no other bread to eat than that which he gave me, poisoned though it was! Only on the wharf was my son a clerk; and there, because of his filial love and intelligence, he was treated kindly by teamsters and sailors.

Ah, Guerlain! You may thank Heaven . . . or rather it is for me to thank you; for if I had taken vengeance upon you, what merchant would thereafter have employed a clerk who was capable of thinking that a being reduced to my condition should dare to show passion.

Oh, my wife and my children! I provided you with bread, but how bitter it was for me! May I never again taste any like it!

Despite my just resentment, I was weak enough to continue loading the *Favorite*, which I completed on the twenty-fifth.

July 23. I took Gauvain to Baron de la Roche's house on Long Island.

July 25. I visited the college, the hospital, the asylum for the French, and Dr. Burn, senior.

I went to a concert at the house of Desèze, son of the counselor of Cap François. This interesting young man ran a pension in New York. He was the nephew of the lawyer

Desèze, who had once been so fortunate as to be selected as King's Counsel.

July 27. I went to dinner in Greenwich at the country house of M. Bayard, a New York merchant, situated a little above that town on the left bank of the North or Hudson River.

There I had opportunity to observe that all the customs are servilely copied from those of the English, even to sending the women away from the table at the end of dessert.

M. Bayard is an American. At his house there was another merchant, Le Roy, Bayard's associate in business affairs with Guerlain. Le Roy was made much of in this house, and I had the pleasure of admiring his affectations, right down to the little nets hanging down his silk gaiters which he had put on (like the decorative nets put on horses in tourneys) to keep away flies.

July 29. In the evening I went to hear divine service, the organ and the singing in Trinity Church.

July 30. I took my wife to see Mme. la Baronne de la Roche.

July 31. After having called upon my wife, Baron de la Roche left with his family for Philadelphia, where my bookstore was to be established.

I was more and more struck with the benevolent character of Baron de la Roche, and became strongly attached to him. As a natural result of this feeling, I was interested in finding out everything that I could about him. Because of this, I inquired, every time I saw him, into details of his life; and here is what I gained, bit by bit, up to the end of July, and which is set down, it might almost be said, at his own dictation.

Frederick Frank de la Roche was born at Mayence December 8, 1757. His father, to whom Voltaire used to send his works in manuscript, was the author of several highly praised books, and was First Minister and Vice-Chancellor of the Empire. He died in 1791.

M. de la Roche still has a mother, a woman of rare attainments, who published several books, all dealing with the education of young women. She had been maid of honor to the present Queen of England, with whom she has always kept up an affectionate correspondence.

Mme. de la Roche had been sought by the present Empress of Russia as a governess for her children. M. de la Roche is a baron and colonel of the Empire, a chamberlain of the Emperor, of the King of Prussia, of King Stanislas of Poland, of the Elector of Treves, of the Elector of Saxony, and of the Duke of Zweibrücken.

He was a Knight of the Teutonic order by birth, a Chevalier de St. Louis and a member of the Order of Cincinnatus. He was a captain in the Royal Regiment of Zweibrücken, going from thence to the Royal German Regiment, of which he was captain of the guard in July, 1789. He became major of the Royal German Regiment; then colonel of the Third Regiment of Chasseurs.

He went thrice to the Indies and to China; with M. Bougainville he made a voyage similar to that of Cook's voyage around the world.

At the end of 1786 he was at Cap François, and went from there to St. Eustache and Porto Bello on the frigate *La Fine*.

He knows the whole of Europe, the Isle de France and Batavia.

He was three times sent to the Bastille on the advice of the government to confer with Cardinal Rohan about the affair of the Queen's necklace. He thinks that the Cardinal in all good faith believed that the necklace should be the price of the Queen's favors, he having laid court to her in a most pressing manner when she was still an archduchess in Vienna. The Queen didn't love him and had never forgiven him because, out of resentment at her contemptuous attitude toward him, he did everything possible to prevent her from being Queen of France. At the French court she never spoke to him.

In 1786 M. de la Roche married Mlle. Marcus, daughter of a burgomaster of Amsterdam and widow of M. Lespinasse Langeai, a noble of Auvergne, who for religious reasons had sought refuge in Holland. Mme. de la Roche was born in Holland November 8, 1761.

Her mother, a Dutch patriot, is a refugee in the vicinity of Saintes, where she has a handsome fortune.

M. de la Roche had a magnificent estate in France, between Landau and Strasbourg.

After 1779 M. de la Roche participated in the war in North America.

Frederick the Great, King of Prussia, asked his father for his brother and brought him up.

M. de la Roche has been a great player on the German flute. Frederick the Great went so far as to say he was the only one he had ever found capable of accompanying him. He plays the harp, the pianoforte, and the violin.

He entered the army of the Empire at the age of thirteen, and received permission to transfer into the French army.

He has two sisters of the rarest beauty, and a brother, a Prussian Minister, who, on being modeled, was compared to the Apollo Belvedere.

Between 1791 and 1794 M. de la Roche lost his father, two brothers, a sister and two brothers-in-law.

In 1793 one of his brothers, making a reconnaissance before Mayence with the King of Prussia, had both legs shot off by a cannon ball and died a few hours later.

When a levy is made on the German corps, M. de la Roche, as a member of the Empire, is obliged to supply the equivalent of eight and a half men. Having contributed nothing in the present war, and not having responded to the second call for men, he was sentenced to be banished from the Empire for nine years and his possessions to be put under government seal. He cannot sell any of them because they are entailed forever.

Because of his attachment to royalty and his leanings toward Lafayette, a German-born quartermaster, one of his own retainers, roused his regiment against him on parade, and led the movement by tearing off his uniform and epaulettes. He was beaten and driven out. At great risk he fled to his wife and her mother at Saintonge.

In spite of all that had happened he was named commandant of the National Guard of Saintes, and when he went to the Political Club and showed them his three brevets as chamberlain of the Emperor, of the King of Prussia, and of the Elector of Treves, and also the brevet of chamberlain to Stanislas, he was received with the most cordial approbation. Profiting by this momentary protection, he took his wife and children to Bordeaux, he himself traveling under the name of a Polish nobleman. He embarked with his family for New York on an American vessel and landed in November, 1792.

He was at the siege of Verdun and saw La Bretèche, the commandant there, blow out his brains.

In the Electorate of Treves he has property that yields him one hundred and sixty thousand French livres a year. He built a residence for his own private use, close to that of his father. The building cost only eighty thousand livres; but the furniture, though simple, was valued at more than two hundred thousand livres, since it included all the things M. de la Roche had collected in the countries in which he had traveled.

There were twenty-two master apartments. Water was pumped by a machine into cascades that watered a garden of sixteen acres.

One of his brothers was allied to the Emperor's house through marriage with a member of the house of Nassau.

In 1786, because of the many wounds he had received in the war, he went to the Baths of Bourbonne. There he became acquainted with some creoles, among them Mme. Armand, a twenty-two-year-old creole from San Domingo. He went into business on the American continent, and became a silent partner in the firm of William Louis Sonntag & Company of Philadelphia, whose name he was authorized to sign. Mme. de la Roche has a sixteen-year-old daughter by her first marriage with M. Lespinasse Langeai-Etzy.

M. de la Roche has a six-year-old daughter, Sophie, and a three-year-old son, George.

M. de la Roche's family, through his mother, inherits the title of Knight-by-birth of the Teutonic order. One of his mother's ancestors, while fighting against the infidels, refused to surrender his flag, which bore the image of a saint, and wrapped himself in it. As a reward the Emperor allowed his family to use the flag of the Empire at the head of its coat of arms, and the right of becoming at birth a member of the Teutonic order.

His mother wrote him that she approved his resolution to go into business until the end of his exile and also the end of the calamitous European situation; but his compatriots and above all the canons of Mayence considered that this disgraced him, and never mentioned him before his mother, thinking that it would distress her.

When he was on his way to Philadelphia in 1793, the stage upset and he broke his right arm.

In spite of my strong inclination to believe Baron de la Roche worthy of the deepest affection, and perhaps even because of this inclination, I could not help checking the period about which he himself had told me. When I compared his chronological recital with his age, I found quite a discrepancy. While not distrusting him in the least, I mentioned this discrepancy to him, and he said he had forgotten to make mention of a voyage he had made around the world with M. de Bougainville.

Since I was both curious and interested, I got Bougainville's account of his voyage as soon as I was able. In this account Bougainville noted with the greatest care everyone who accompanied him, even to the lowest sailor. Nowhere in the book did I find the name of Baron de la Roche.

It is impossible for me to conceal the fact that this strange circumstance made a strong impression upon me. This impression increased until my mind was filled with suspicions about the baron. My grateful heart desired to banish these evil thoughts, and he did his foxy best to help me; but they were too strong to be forgotten—or rather, my sensibilities kept me from forgetting them in spite of all he could do.

August 4, 1794. We left our lodging in New York to occupy one which Baron de la Roche procured for us in a part of his Brooklyn house, making the trip in a ship's boat, which made a long voyage of it. On our return, when we crossed the North River, a violent wind came up and placed us in the greatest danger of perishing. We were driven almost to the New York hospital, which is three hundred and fifty toises beyond the regular disembarkation place.

In this crossing, where I instilled the coxswain with courage which had forsaken him, we shipped a wave so large that I arrived at my New York lodging soaked and shivering with cold. I changed my linen, and only put an end to this state by swallowing a large glass of brandy and sassafras beer.

I settled with Guerlain, who did me the favor of paying me at the rate of fifty gourdes a month (less than three hundred francs).[1]

August 21. I left with Baron de la Roche for Philadelphia. In the passage of the North River we encountered contrary winds which delayed us four hours.

[1]Goynard had originally offered him (p. 41) two hundred and forty gourdes or twelve hundred and sixty francs a year.

One of Mme. de la Roche's horses jumped into the river because of restlessness, and reached the Jersey shore by swimming.

August 22. We were obliged to sleep at Paulus Hook, where we were tormented by mosquitoes. We lunched at Newark, dined at Woodbridge and slept at Six Mile Run.

August 23. The next day lunch was at Princeton, dinner at Bristol and we slept at Philadelphia, lodging at the pension of Mlle. Donne on South Street at the corner of Market Street.

August 24. On this day and on the twenty-fifth I paid visits and took tea at the house of M. Sonntag, a partner of Baron de la Roche.

August 26. Same rounds, and in addition I called upon Minister Hamilton with Talleyrand's letter of introduction. I arrived at the house where his office was. A man in a long gray linen jacket, whom I found in the corridor of the ground floor, told me he was not in. I came out again from this house, which had little to recommend it, and went away astounded that the official lodgings of a minister could be so poor.

I had gone only a few feet when I saw a person pass me, who, for some reason unknown to me, I was sure was M. Hamilton. I turned and followed him, and we entered the corridor almost together. The same man was still there. He inserted a key, opened a room where M. Hamilton was (for it was he), and to my pleasure ushered me in.

I had been told to avoid seeming inquisitive, and particularly not to question him; but he showed great trust in me, and spoke to me frankly about France and America.

He advised me to set up my wife as head of a school for young ladies, but I told him of my arrangement with M. de la Roche.

I could not help noticing that the furnishings and equipment of his ministerial office were not worth fifty French livres. His desk was a plain pine table covered with a green cloth. Planks on trestles held records and paper, and at one end was a little imitation Chinese vase and a plate with glasses on it.

His usher, or the man who served him in his office, had, with the gray linen jacket of which I have spoken, trousers of the same material, and his bare legs showed below them. In a word, I felt I saw Spartan customs all about me.

Here are some very important details about M. Hamilton. He was a creole from St. Kitts, one of the English Antilles, and a love child. He went to the North American continent and lived in New York. He was destined for the bar when the first troubles of this country showed themselves. Then he wrote and frequently published his opinions under various fictitious names.

These marks of patriotism caused him to be appointed captain of artillery. Then General Washington, impressed by his opinions, took him as his secretary, made him a colonel and his first aide-de-camp.

Consumed by ambition, he wished to have it believed that he was the master mind in everything, and this determined Washington to part with him.

Then Hamilton was given a battalion. Endowed with true courage, he served with the grenadiers and the chasseurs of the French army. He commanded this battalion in the attack at Yorktown; but dissatisfied because he was not given all the glory for the capture of a redoubt, he retired and took up the practice of law in New York.

When the independence of the Americans was recognized, each state regarded itself as independent and wished to proceed according to its own particular interest. Trouble promptly developed everywhere. Acts of violence even started a civil war,[2] whereupon several people had the idea of announcing publicly that business would be destroyed if

[2]Shays' Rebellion.

each state persisted in obstructing and burdening it. It was then wisely suggested that each state should send commissioners to decide on ways to obviate such a disaster, and New York was designated as the most central meeting place.

Among the number of the zealots for the common good was Hamilton, who had married General Schuyler's daughter and thus had acquired the support and help of his brothers-in-law, Renslaer and Church,[3] members of the Commons of England, and their families.

The commissioners declared that it would be absurd to consider any general rule for business, without some central authority to see that the rules were executed.

As a result they planned to authorize the organization of a central power capable of forcing each state to obey.

This authority was obtained, whereupon they produced the federal Constitution, of which Hamilton is known to have been one of the greatest apostles.

Washington remembered him and made him Minister. For the second time Hamilton in 1794 (the period when I knew him) wished everyone to think that in him alone lay the salvation of America, and for the second time Washington replied by dismissing him.

Hamilton, who had never known anything but the American continent, and who judged Europe from books, was, I repeat, enamored of the kind of great power which makes itself obeyed without argument. Civil war did not frighten him because he was a man of great courage with a natural military talent, and because he believed and said that America could only have a real and stable government after it had been created and consolidated by internal dissensions.

Rather than succeed Washington immediately in the presidency, Hamilton groomed Jay for the position. His reasons were that the very name of Washington had given too great

[3]The French version says "fathers-in-law" instead of "brothers-in-law," and "Munstaert" instead of "Renslaer." See note on p. 145.

a delicacy to the scales in which his successors would be weighed, and that Jefferson's party, which would be displeased to see him, Hamilton, President, would make Jay regret his success, because he lacked character, and therefore Jay would not have a prolonged presidency.

But it was John Adams who succeeded Washington. When the question of a successor to this second President arose, the electors put up Jefferson and Burr. The first became President, and the second Vice-President.

When it came time to elect a successor to Jefferson, the resulting political quarrel agitated the entire United States. This gave rise to a duel between Burr and Hamilton, in which the latter was killed. Thus Hamilton's ambition was ended.

He was small, with an extremely composed bearing, unusually small eyes, and something a little furtive in his glance. He spoke French, but quite incorrectly. He had a great deal of ready wit, kept a close watch over himself, and was, I repeat, extremely brave. He had no desire for private gain, but was eaten up with ambition, and ardently admired the laws and government of England, and its financial system. Personally he was very much of an autocrat, and an ardent guardian of the prerogatives of the Executive.

The death of Hamilton aroused widespread regrets, and it can be said that he was one of the most outstanding statesmen which the United States of America had developed.

August 28. After we had settled many points about our new bookshop with Sonntag, M. de la Roche and I left for New York and slept at Bristol.

August 29. We dined at Kingston, where, due to a jest on the part of Baron de la Roche, we saw a trait of American character.

We were served by the two daughters of our host. M. de la Roche informed them that he was a bachelor, whereas I confessed that I was married. Immediately all attention was centered on him, and I barely received my money's worth as a traveler.

Such is the predilection for those who are considered marriageable.

We slept at Brunswick, lunched the next day at Elizabethtown, and arrived at our own home in Brooklyn at an early hour in the afternoon. I felt very tired and disturbed.

August 31. The following day likewise. Goynard brought his son to call on me.

September 5, 1794. M. de la Roche gave me a letter of credit in these terms:

M. William Louis Sonntag & Co., Philadelphia:

You will be so kind, Monsieur, as to pay to Monsieur Moreau de St. Méry, whose signature you will find below, to the extent of 3000 *piastres fortes*,[4] which you will please deduct from my personal account.

(Signed) FR. FRANK DE LA ROCHE

New York, September 5, 1794.

This credit was then worth about eighteen thousand francs.

September 8. Relying upon the obliging offers of M. de la Roche, I wrote to my sister and to Baudry to come and live in Philadelphia.

The senior Dupuy had already left New York for Martinique.

September 9. Some time before, M. Olive had arrived in New York from St. Malo. The fact that he was from St. Malo filled me with eagerness to see him, more particularly since he lodged at the home of M. Dessoti, whom I frequently visited. Olive was with his wife, now Mme. la Marquise de Cubières.

While on my way to Destourelles' house, I met him. We spoke, according to our custom, of St. Malo, of the imprisonment of my dear De Varenne. and of the horrors that were taking place in France.

[4]Dollars.

"I have just received some newspapers," he told me, "would you like to see them, then return them to me?"

We parted, and I opened the pages and began to read a passage about sentences passed by the Revolutionary tribunal. There, Good God!!! were the names of De Varenne and Mme. de Lys, his sister, and an account of their execution!

I do not know what happened to me. At first I was so shocked that I was conscious of nothing. I re-read the page. Finally a tear came to my eye, and a torrent of weeping ensued.

I went to M. Olive's house, and he wept with me. Dear De Varenne! You are no more! The hand of the butcher has cut the thread of your life! What a fate! How could Heaven permit it!

Oh, what courage is needed to smother the blasphemy, and to feel that virtue itself commands the avoidance of reproach!

I do not know what I did or what I said throughout that horrible day. I returned to my home in Brooklyn with the expression of face that the death of my friend had stamped upon me, even if for the nonce it had not killed me.

My daughter burst into sobs, as did my son, even though since morning he had suffered from a painful diarrhea and fever.

Dear and virtuous De Varenne! The executioners, in the refinement of their cruelty, added to your sorrows the dreadful one of having to see die before your eyes the sister whom you loved the most, and who idolized you.

And what was your crime! That of loving your country too well! And of that crime you could not be absolved!

Incomparable friend! My sorrow at your loss increases each day! It is in response to your wishes and to fulfill my promise to you that I am writing my life. It is this pledge that leads me to speak of your death and the supreme loss of your friendship.

I say here, for the benefit of those who did not know him,

that De Varenne was born at St. Malo in 1739. He belonged
to the noble and rich Fournier family, made up of the Fourniers of Bois-marin, the Fourniers of Bellevue, the Fourniers
of Varenne and the Fourniers of La Chapelle, a family allied
to the Castellanes, the Du Ludes, the Princes of Berg, etc.

De Varenne was educated by the Jesuits at the College of
La Flèche, where he developed marked talents. I recall that
he often told me that his rector had the singular habit of
never passing through a door without moving back for several steps, bowing and removing his skullcap. When asked the
reason for this salutation, he replied that he was paying respectful homage to his guardian angel for allowing him to
enter first, but his homage came more from the Jesuit's self-
esteem than from any feeling of humility toward the guardian angel upon whom he had imposed the particular task of
watching over him.

De Varenne was sent by his relatives to the School for
Naval Cadets at Rochefort. There he specialized in artillery,
and on graduation was appointed second lieutenant for San
Domingo.

He went there in 1759, in the fleet of M. de Blénac, together with M. de la Courcière, a creole from San Domingo,
who was joining the Swiss regiment at that time. I saw them
as they passed Fort Royale, my own native place. De Varenne
resigned from the artillery to make a home for his family in
the Roucou canton of the parish of Limonade, where he
joined the militia. He married Mlle. Fournier of Bellevue, his
first cousin.

My dear De Varenne was five and a half feet tall and
grossly fat. He was very nearsighted and usually used a small
quizzing glass for everything.

He was good, amiable, a trifle shy, extremely gay, but
with the naïve gaiety of a child, and a child's laugh, too,
which always makes the most serious men laugh. His sensitive
soul needed to pour itself out; he loved with unchanging

constancy, and in his own mind he always ranked himself below his friends.

Brave and capable only of what was worthy and honorable, he unconsciously and involuntarily exercised a gentle influence over all those about him.

Not only was he endowed with a wise and cultivated mind; he was discerning to a remarkable degree. Relatives, friends, servants, strangers—everybody honored him, loved him and were proud as long as they lived of the marks of affection and kindness they had received from him.

He was an enlightened philanthropist, and a strong believer in the adage *Homo sum: Nil humani a me alienum puto.* He was not content to practice virtue; he made it a model for others and for himself.

He was a member of the Cap François Chamber of Agriculture, an intimate friend of the Marquis de Gabriac, who was always disposed to honor those to whom he was attached.

De Varenne never had any children. He was little inclined for love, and always preferred friendship.

He paid great attention to the Spanish troops when they came to San Domingo, which flattered and gave pleasure to the officers and soldiers. Count de Galvez, their commander, had a strong affection for De Varenne; and France, in recognition of his efforts in behalf of the sick of their ally, gave visible proof of it by conferring upon him the Cross of St. Louis.

De Varenne idolized his mother and accorded her the deference of a most obedient son. He cherished his sisters with great tenderness, and most of all Mme. de Lys, whom he always esteemed a little more than anyone else.

When he lost his mother his heart was most cruelly wounded. He had returned the previous year to join her at St. Malo. From the very start of the Revolution he showed himself and accepted civic duties, even though the general respect in which he was held entitled him to receive a more brilliant position.

After his return to St. Malo, De Varenne was the first deputy from there charged with conveying to the legislative assembly St. Malo's distress over the misfortunes of San Domingo. He became a member of the administrative body, and during the troubles over the federative system, he advocated peace. It was this which resulted in his arrest and subsequently led him to the scaffold.

He was unusually moderate in his tastes and extremely content with his lot, but he had domestic sorrows, the cause of which made him unhappy, but which he combated valiantly.

We often discussed together the question as to who loved the other the more, and we never altered our views, I always insisting that I received more friendship from him than I gave. But one day, having been led by a certain occurrence to say that he would like to perform the finest act in the world and have it attributed to me, I said to him, "My friend, you are a better man than I; for I should like to have done this deed, and have it imputed to us in common."

But if he loved me the more, I am fated to love him longer, for I shall do so until my last breath.

September 10. M. de la Roche, his family and La Colombe left for Albany.

September 12. I saw Dr. Valentin of Norfolk in New York. He had been a physician at Cap François.

As though to keep alive my melancholy sadness at the death of De Varenne, my son was seriously ill with diarrhea, which did not subside until the twentieth.

September 20. The use of *kina,* an astringent, failed to benefit him, since it only acted as a purgative. I suspect that the first cause of this diarrhea was an excess of fruit, particularly peaches, of which fifty could be purchased in Brooklyn for less than forty sous.

September 21. Today we had news of the beheading of Robespierre. It produced a universal sensation in the United

States, quite different among some than among others.

The Jacobins who were there were profoundly grieved, as at the loss of their father, their leader, their best friend. All those not Jacobins, and likewise all true patriots, all sincere friends of liberty, saw the event only as a blessing from Heaven, unfortunately conferred too late.

As for Americans of all classes and all conditions, they expressed sincere sorrow for Robespierre and were filled with consternation at his loss. This was their reason why:

Robespierre made France uninhabitable for all the French. Every man, every gold piece, escaped at the earliest moment, and both took refuge with us, who are in need of men, of money, of industry. Consider, therefore, how the death of such a one will harm us!

I heard this view uttered a hundred times with a frankness which never made it any easier to tolerate.

For a long time the Jacobins maintained that the news was false. I wagered two gourdes (a large amount for me) against one that it was true.

Oh! I would have given all I possessed if my dear De Varenne could have escaped this monster, on whom posterity can never heap the number of curses that his foul memory deserves! Who did not hold him accountable for the life of a father, a mother, a son, a daughter, some relative, friend, compatriot, a fellow citizen, someone more or less dear! . . .

September 22. I received from Albany a letter from the Marquis de Gouvernet, who had taken refuge there with his adorable wife.

September 23. The good Hunter, bookseller at Norfolk and so friendly toward me, dined with me.

September 29. Yellow fever, with its usual speed, carried off the younger De Leysser.

September 30. We had Dr. Mitchell, the celebrated New York chemist, for dinner. We went together to see a horse race at Jamaica, a place in Long Island.

When I brought him back in the evening to New York, the strong, cold wind blew us almost to Sandy Hook.

October 9, 1794. Talleyrand and Beaumetz left for Albany. I was just about to go to them to read my *Description of San Domingo* when I received this from Talleyrand:

> An arrangement proposed by Colonel Smith to show us an establishment on the North River in which we are interested prevents us from waiting for you this morning, *cher Maître.* We will see you in a month's time in Philadelphia. Until then we are going to be traveling. Adieu, health and prosperity to you and yours.
>
> A letter which we received last night from M. Vaughan (a merchant of Philadelphia) brings it about that we shall not have occasion to use the very good letters which you have given us until a month from now.

I was almost forced to accept an invitation to dinner at the house of M. Guerlain, whose attitude toward me has changed greatly since I ceased to be his clerk.

October 12. We went to sleep at Goynard's house, as we planned to leave the next morning for Philadelphia.

October 13. According to my custom, therefore, this is the place to set down some details about New York.

NOTE:

The obscure and meaningless original of the passage on p. 137—"Hamilton, who had married General Schuyler's daughter and thus had acquired the support and help of his fathers-in-law, Munstaert and Church"—was interpreted by Miss Marie Becker, reference librarian of the New York Historical Society. Miss Becker, working with Mr. R. W. G. Vail, director of the Society, and Miss Dorothy Barck, librarian of the Society, arrived at the following conclusions:

John Barker Church, an extremely wealthy member of Parliament and an intimate of the Prince of Wales, came to America, married Angelica Schuyler (the sister of Hamilton's wife Elizabeth) in 1777, and lived in grand style in New York. Another of Hamilton's brothers-in-law was Stephen Van Rensselaer, 8th Patroon, and a member of the New York State Senate. Moreau, like other visiting Frenchmen, had trouble spelling American names, and was baffled by Dutch names. He therefore wrote the second brother-in-law as "Renslaer," and the copyist further confused matters by writing it "Munstaert." What Moreau should have said was that Hamilton, by marrying General Schuyler's daughter Elizabeth, had acquired the support and help of his brothers-in-law John Barker Church and Stephen Van Rensselaer.

NEW YORK[1]

OCTOBER, *1794.* New York is less citified than Philadelphia, but the bustle of trade is far greater.

New York has beautiful houses. They are almost never built by contract, but by the day. The workmen supply only their tools.

The varied direction of the streets makes the topography of this town difficult to follow. Not all the streets are paved.

Many of the streets, and their sidewalks too, are narrow; while others have no sidewalks at all. The openings to the cellars, which protrude into the sidewalks, greatly diminish their width. The cellars are poorly built, very damp; and when the weather is unduly rainy, or there are extremely high tides, many are filled with water. The custom of placing the kitchens in the cellars is less common than in Philadelphia.

The streets are not particularly clean, and it is not unusual to see animals of all sorts wandering about, chiefly cows and pigs. Although windowpanes and sidewalks are washed on Saturday, nobody bothers to remove the dead dogs, cats and rats from the streets.

Before every door two small benches are placed at right angles with the house, facing each other. In summer these serve as places on which to sit and take the air.

The business district is on the East River.

New York, situated on an island, is less warm than Phila-

[1]An excellent map of New York City in 1797 may be found in *The Memorial History of the City of New York*, III, 130, by the aid of which it is easy to follow Moreau's survey of the city in 1794. The corresponding modern names of old streets may be found in J. J. Post, *Old Streets, Roads, Lanes, Piers and Wharves of New-York.*

delphia, first because it is not so far inland, and again because the currents of the North and East rivers and the changing tides keep the air stirring. The climate is variable, as it is everywhere else on the continent. On August 6, 1794, the thermometer rose to 91 degrees Fahrenheit, but on the seventh it fell to 70 degrees. On the first of the following October fires were kindled everywhere.

The view, at the entrance to the port, is charming.

The streets slope steeply.

Trees are planted along some streets.

Many houses have tiled roofs.

The panes of the windows are badly set, and only the lower part of the windows is movable. These are what we call sliding windows; none are French windows.

There is a singular custom of making crescent-shaped openings in the shutters, so that daylight can come into the interior of the house; but there are no shutters except on the ground floor.

On my arrival in New York people were drinking excellent spring water called tea-water, because it made admirable tea. It was distributed to all houses by twenty-four horse-drawn carts, and cost only one ninety-sixth of a dollar per bucket.

The owner of this spring leased the spring enclosure and the pump which raised the water for one thousand dollars a year (six thousand francs). The pump was operated by two horses driven by a child. The cart drivers in turn bought the water for one sixteenth of a dollar a barrel. Ships could refill their water casks for five sixteenths of a dollar.

Since that time the Manhattan Company, formed by an act of legislature on April 2, 1799, to furnish good water to the city of New York, has prospered well.

This other water that I have been speaking about is drawn up by pumps worked by horses from an elevation placed behind the debtors' prison.

A reservoir, also located on an elevated spot nearby, distributes the water to different parts of the city through pipes made of hollowed-out stones.

The principal streets have aqueducts three feet below the pavements. Lead pipes carry the water from the aqueducts into private houses for a moderate price.

The water, in passing from the reservoir to kitchen or tub, loses its extreme coldness. Thus there has never been a single casualty, whereas formerly many people, while hot during the summer, died each year from drinking it fresh from the spring.

Great care is taken at the places of embarkation and debarkation, which are made accessible by means of ramps or sloping wooden platforms with triangular footholds across them. These ramps are placed along the face of the wharfs, parallel to them, and slope toward the water at an angle of only forty-five degrees. At the end of each street that runs to the water there is a recess for small boats, such as barges and schooners. This is made by the sides of the two adjoining wharfs or quays, and the boats can go into it and be sheltered. These recesses are called slips. However, the wharfs are built haphazard and are made according to the whims of the owners. The approaches to them are narrow, cluttered, muddy, and are a source of regret everywhere in America because they cut off a general view of the city.

It is safe to anchor anywhere in New York Harbor once Governor's Island has been passed; but only the North River can take ships of all sizes.

The present population of New York is forty thousand free people and twenty-five hundred slaves.

In the East River the tide rises five hours, and ebbs seven. Nowhere is there a constant depth.

Porpoises are often seen in the East and North rivers, and during the hottest months of the summer there are sharks, but not as many in the East River as in the North.

New York has numerous inns and pensions, many of them operated by French people.

In this city extremely fat people are seen frequently. They are usually people of color, and for the most part women, and generally mulattoes.

Buildings and Public Monuments

1. New York has twenty-two churches or houses of worship. Four are Presbyterian, three Dutch Reformed, three Episcopal, two German Lutheran, two Quaker, two Baptist, two Methodist, one French Protestant, one Moravian, one Roman Catholic, one Jewish synagogue. I will speak only of two.

(1) St. Paul's Church is the loveliest. It is furnished with benches. On the right against the wall there is a bench for members of Congress, and on the left a corresponding one for the Governor.

There are also two benches in this church for foreigners of the Anglican Communion. The benches are sold by private contract by the churchwardens. The galleries are open to the public, and people of color mix with the whites. The organ is good, and as in the singing of hymns the registers are separated naturally into two parts, one composed of tenors and second tenors, the other of voices with a deeper tone. The effect is extremely pleasing.

In the cemetery behind the church is a steeple, the tallest in New York, and its height and its gilding make it noticeable from a great distance. The bishop and the rector, in addition to their surplice fees, are paid a salary out of church revenues, which come from many landed properties.

In the front part of this church is a monument to the memory of General Montgomery. This monument, recessed into the wall of the church, is made up of an outward-curving pedestal of black marble and a square black marble platform which acts as a canopy for the tablet below, which is flanked on each side by carved supports. Above the platform rises a pyramidal shaft of veined marble, and in front of the shaft is a column topped by a golden cinerary urn.

The face of the tablet bears a carved inscription, arranged and worded as follows:

> This monument is erected by the order of Congress 25th
> Jany 1776 to transmit to posterity a grateful remembrance of
> the patriotism, conduct, integrity and perseverance
> of Major General
> Richard Montgomery
> Who after a series of successes amidst the most discouraging
> difficulties fell in the attack on Quebec 31st Dec^{ber} 1775
> aged 37 years.

Against the right of the column leans the club of Hercules, a Liberty cap and a cluster of palms. Against its left are sculptured the symbols of war—a helmet, a sword, a Roman pike, some flags and cypress trees.

It is regrettable that this interesting monument should be so hidden by the porch of the church that on days when the church is closed the monument can only be viewed through a grill.

(2) Trinity Episcopal Church has a lofty wooden steeple, but the building itself is in no way remarkable. At its entrance there are wooden pilasters which have the polish and hardness of marble. It is pleasant to attend Sunday prayer meeting, which is held there at half past seven in the evening, following which hymns are sung to the accompaniment of an extremely well-played organ. At that time the church is lighted by one hundred and sixty-two candles placed in chandeliers or on brackets.

2. The Governor's House is at the lower end of Broadway, which is seventy feet wide, and on which St. Paul's Church and Trinity Church also stand. This building, which is large and fronts on Broadway, has a projecting part that is deco-

rated by pilasters. It is raised several feet above the ground, which lends it a certain charm. What really embellishes this place is an enclosed bowling green, surrounded by an iron railing in front of the house. One can walk around this railing, in the middle of which is a pedestal formerly supporting a statue of the King of England.[2] No historical monument could possibly portray more sublimely America's transition from monarchy to republic, and it is an impressive sight in the eyes of all those who know why the statue disappeared.

The back of Government House enjoys the most interesting and entertaining view of the port, one of the happiest that the town of New York has to offer.

From here one sees Long Island, Staten Island, Governor's Island and the Jersey shore.

At the upper end of Broadway, when one turns to the right on Chatham Road,[3] he finds on his left a square or enclosure encircled by a railing, destined to become a public promenade.

On the north side of the road which borders this square on the north there are several groups of buildings extending its entire length.

3. The most easterly[4] is the prison, surmounted by a small bell tower in which a guard is stationed at night to ring a bell if he sees a fire anywhere in the city. Close to the prison is a sort of dove-cote, which is where prisoners are hanged.

4. The building in the center is the Poor House, also called the City Hospital. In it the sick are cared for and treated gratis. There are usually from sixty to a hundred and twenty patients, and its death rate is estimated at fifty a year.

Foundlings are also cared for in this same building. At present there are about two hundred of them. They are

[2] A description of the destruction of this statue on July 9, 1776, may be found in *The Memorial History of the City of New York*, II, 496–497, and a cut of same, p. 498.

[3] Chatham Row, now Park Row. The enclosure became City Hall Square.

[4] The building was the jail, later the Hall of Registry.

brought up at the expense of the city. They do not wear any particular dress, because the City Fathers not only wanted to spare them the humiliation that might come from knowing their state, but also did not wish them to look regimented. These children should not be confused with those of both sexes who are seen dressed in blue every Sunday at Trinity Anglican Episcopal Church. The latter belong to the less fortunate parents of that congregation, and a corporation formed for the purpose educates and clothes them. This essentially English custom has no connection with the city government of New York, which is averse to the formation of corporations in the belief that they would tend to destroy civic unity.

5. Finally the building that forms the west corner is the Bridewell or House of Correction. It houses convicts and slaves who are being punished. These prisoners are employed on different types of work for the profit of the city.

6. In addition to the hospital of which I have spoken, there is another located farther up Broadway on the left side.[5] This one does not belong to the city, having been built and maintained by private subscriptions. The subscribers, among whom are many Quakers, appoint two directors from their number. As a rule this hospital has fifty or sixty patients of both sexes. The sexes are separated. The death rate is one in twenty. The building is made up of a ground floor and an upper story. Each patient has a wooden bed, a mattress and sheets. Negroes are put in wards by themselves.

Patients pay two dollars a week if they are able to do so. Four physicians give their services each quarter.

A surgeon is attached to the hospital. In all it has twenty-four employees.

The annual expense of the hospital is reckoned to be between two and three thousand dollars.

[5]This stood in a large space bounded by Barley (now Duane) and Catherine (now Worth) streets, Broadway and Church Street. It was opened to patients January 23, 1791.

The kitchens and the laundry are down in the cellars.

There are four small rooms for lunatics, only one of which is occupied.

There is a yard where patients are allowed to walk, and plans call for planting trees in it.

A vegetable garden takes up part of the grounds, and some flowers are grown in it.

There has been some criticism of this hospital, and if it had any foundation, it would be truly serious. This is the charge that it refuses to accept sick persons if they have no money, particularly those afflicted with chronic diseases. It is further charged that such unfortunates go to the City Hospital and die there.

7. There is also a college in New York.[6] The principal building, which is of stone, has a ground floor and two upper stories. There are several classes with about one hundred pupils, all of them day scholars. The president and four of his professors live in the college, which is excellently situated on a spacious and airy site. There are fourteen professors, some of whom have a fixed salary, and all of whom receive fees from the scholars. Zeal is not particularly noticeable at the college. In medicine, for example, the number of students hardly equals that of the college inspectors.

On Vesey Street there is a house where, when French refugees came here from San Domingo, the Americans placed three hundred of them. In July, 1794, one hundred refugees were still living there, and being fed, clothed, shod, etc.

8. The building called City Hall, which was where Congress assembled when it sat in New York, is at the upper end of Broad Street and faces on it. It has columns supporting a pediment on which is an American eagle. The New York legislature, which meets alternately at Albany and New York, uses this hall for its meetings. The Senate room is

[6]Columbia. It was on a large farm, corresponding to the area bounded today by Murray and Barclay streets, Church Street and College Place.

extremely beautiful; that of the House of Representatives less so. Below is:

9. The room of the Court of Justice. In the committee room, at the right as you enter, is a portrait of General Washington. Its background is the evacuation of New York by the British forces and the pedestal I mentioned on page 151, so that the effect is expressive and beautiful.

Facing this portrait is one of Governor Clinton with a background of the capture of Fort Montgomery and a burning frigate.

It is easy to see that the same artist painted the two pieces.

A third portrait, not yet completed, is of Colonel Hamilton, Minister of Finance, his hand on a ledger.

They are all painted standing and in magnificent frames.

There is a Public Library in the same building, but placed in too small a room. It may contain about five thousand volumes, most of them badly bound.

10. The Play House is on John Street. There is nothing remarkable about it. It is planned to have another under the same management, fronting on Chatham Road in such a position that it will look out on the square in front of the Bridewell, which would give it spacious and beautiful approaches.

During the summer months there are boats on the North River arranged for cold-water bathing. Some of them are for men, others for women.

11. The Custom House is in the southeast part of the city. There is nothing noteworthy about it.

12. At the foot of Wall Street, near the North River, there is a café where merchants gather. They make it a rendezvous where news of all kinds can be exchanged.

In the upper part of the northern section of the city there is a factory for making glue from sheep's feet.

On Broadway, farther out than the House of Correction, are brickyards.

13. There are four markets. The principal one, called Fly

Market,[7] is divided into two sections, one for meat, the other for fish.

In New York meat is cut in such a manner that it is always round in shape; but for quality it is inferior to that of Philadelphia.

The same thing cannot be said of the fish, for they are excellent, of all sorts, in great quantities, and at extremely reasonable prices. For people not favored by fortune, they are treasures.

In the market you can get sixty-three sorts of fish, as well as oysters, lobsters, sea and fresh-water crabs, crawfish, fresh- and salt-water prawns, eight other sorts of shellfish, turtles. There are fifty-two varieties of animals, game, kid, bear, opossum, hare, rabbit, etc.

The vegetable dealers are alongside the markets and their surroundings are not as clean as they might be.

The name of the second most important market is Oswego, the third the Bear, the fourth St. Catherine.

Chains are stretched across the roads on the big market days, which are Wednesdays and Saturdays, to keep carriages from getting in the way of buyers and sellers.

You can buy ice cream in New York. It is made by the French.

Meat and fish can be sold in the markets on Sunday, but only until nine o'clock.

The difficulty of getting domestics in New York is very great, and they are lazy, demanding and capricious. Somebody had the bright idea of setting up an office in Maiden Lane where the names of those looking for a place and of those wishing servants could be registered; but this enterprise didn't result in placing more than half a dozen servants a year. The fee for making an application is three sixteenths of a dollar.

Slaves save many people from the discomfort of having

[7] At the foot of Maiden Lane. Mr. Mims thinks that the word "Fly" may come from the Dutch "Vly," a swamp.

no servants, and it's even possible to say that they lessen it for everyone, because without them the scarcity would be more apparent.

It doesn't necessarily follow, however, that slaves are better treated on this account.

I have seen in the streets a little Negro who was wearing an iron chain around his neck in punishment for absenting himself from his master's house.

I saw an apothecary at 43 Courtland Street whip at great length and repeatedly a little mulatto who was chained by a wrist in an attic. The apothecary fed him there on bread and water, claiming that he had stolen several drugs.

The population of New York has a physiognomy of its own, due to its descent from the ancient Dutch and the ancient English. But since its wealthier elements are English, the whole feeling and behavior of the town seems to be English. People without property, on the contrary, despise these same English.

One would hardly think that in a city like New York, so recently sprung into being, morals would already show one mark of the vilest corruption. In many parts of the city whole sections of streets are given over to street-walkers for the plying of their profession; there are many houses of debauchery in a locality which for some reason unknown to me is called "Holy Ground" by the irreligious; and in addition women of every color can be found in the streets, particularly after ten o'clock at night, soliciting men and proudly flaunting their licentiousness in the most shameless manner.

The temperature of New York is not as hot as that of Philadelphia, but in winter it suffers from violent winds.

Mackerel appear here early in May; green peas around the same time; strawberries by the middle of May; new potatoes in June; small cucumbers in June; beets, apples, pears early in July; pullets in July; excellent white eggplant by the second of October.

Flies have begun to sting by June 10.

Here are prices for the principal things:

Milk (which is abundant) costs 1/16 of a dollar a pint.

Cider costs 1/16 of a dollar a pint.

A pound of meat 1/10 of a dollar a pound if one picks it out, 1/16 of a dollar not selected.

Mutton ¾ of a dollar for a hindquarter.

Veal is scarce, and costs 1/12 of a dollar a pound.

A sucking pig ½ dollar.

Eggs from ⅛ of a dollar to 3/16 for a dozen.

Green peas ⅛ of a dollar a bushel.

Butter 3/16 of a dollar the pound or ¼ of a dollar.

Vinegar 1/16 of a dollar the pint.

Potatoes ½ dollar a bushel, down to 5/32.

Sweet potatoes from a dollar a bushel down to 3/16 of a dollar.

Lard 1/6 of a dollar a pound.

French bread 1/16 of a dollar for 10 American ounces.

Candles, 5 pounds for a dollar.

Men's shoes, 2 dollars a pair.

Short boots, 5 dollars a pair.

Boots 7 dollars a pair; with double vamps 8 dollars.

A workman by the day, in 1792, ½ dollar; at the end of 1792, 9/16 of a dollar; in 1793, ⅝ of a dollar, then 11/16; in June, 1794, ¾ of a dollar.

Between 1792 and 1794 a workman's pay went from 1 dollar to 5/4 of a dollar.

A sailor 1 dollar and ¾ a day.

People paid by the day worked from six in the morning to eight; from nine to noon and from two to six.

In June, 1794, the cargo of a brig of 190 tons was made up of 900 barrels of prime pork, 600 barrels of beef, 478 barrels of flour, all valued at 25,443½ dollars. Prime pork at that time was worth 17½ dollars a barrel; prime beef 10½ dollars; superfine flour 6¾ dollars.

The charge for carting a barrel of beef or lard to a store costs 1/24 of a dollar. From the store to shipboard 1/24 of a dollar.

A cooper's wage for packing and putting brine on the bacon and beef, 1/96 of a dollar.

Storage for a barrel a month 1/32 of a dollar.

Cartage to the store for 8 barrels flour 3/16 of a dollar.

From the store to shipboard, 8 barrels 3/16 of a dollar.

Storage by the month for a barrel 1/16 of a dollar.

Cooperage, per barrel, 1/24 of a dollar.

There are inspectors for flour and for salt meat. They mark flour superfine, fine and ordinary. And salt beef prime, mess and cargo.

Half the cost of this inspection, which is a little more than ⅛ of a dollar a barrel, is paid by the buyer.

A trip by cart 3/16 of a dollar.

If it is very far ¼ of a dollar.

Cherries 1/32 of a dollar a pound.

Red- and white-heart cherries ⅛ of a dollar.

Ham ⅛ of a dollar.

A thousand pounds of staves for salt pork and beef barrels, 12¼ dollars; for flour barrels, 2½ dollars to 3 dollars a thousand.

Five hundred pounds of ship's bread, 4½ dollars.

An empty flour barrel ¼ dollar.

Empty bacon or beef barrel, ⅞.

Rum keg, 1 dollar.

An empty water cask, hooped with wood, 3 dollars.

Parasols of 28 English inches in radius and less are sold wholesale at ⅛ of a dollar an inch; larger than 28 inches ¼ of a dollar an inch.

A fine ship of 300 tons costs 11,000 dollars. The *Massachusetts*, 240 tons, eight years old, was sold in July, 1794, for 5000 dollars. It cost 10,000 new.

The same boat, built in France, would have been fifteen years in depreciating to that extent.

Freight for a barrel of flour, from New York to Isle de France, 1 dollar 2/9 and 10 per cent damage.

In June, 1794, 3d proof Bordeaux brandy 1½ dollars a gallon; 4th proof, 1 dollar ⅜.

A cask of Bordeaux wine (50 imperial gallons), 40 to 50 dollars.

Wine in a case, ½ dollar a bottle.

First-class potash, 17½ dollars for 112 pounds.

A good city cart horse, 72 to 75 dollars. His food 5/16 of a dollar a day in the summer; 7/16 in winter.

French wine vinegar ½ dollar a bottle; country cider vinegar, 1/10 of a dollar.

Storage for a barrel of potash and pearlash [purified potash], 5/96 of a dollar a month.

Cartage for same, 5/96 of a dollar.

Brokerage charges for same, 1/96 of a dollar a barrel.

A quintal of rice, 2¾ dollars to 3⅛ dollars.

Early cucumbers 1/96 of a dollar; later, 8 for ⅛ of a dollar.

A dozen oranges from the West Indies, 1 dollar.

A cedar-wood bucket, 26 inches in diameter, 2⅜ dollars; 22 inches in diameter, 1⅞ dollars; 15 inches in diameter 1 11/16.

A bucket with an iron handle and hoops, for drawing water, 10 inches high and 12 inches in diameter, 11/16 of a dollar.

A barrel of mackerel, 2½ dollars.

Sea bass 1/24 of a dollar or 1/32 a pound.

Eels, 2 or 3 for 1/16 of a dollar.

Salt-water crabs, ⅛ of a dollar.

Four large beets for ⅛ of a dollar.

A live pig at the rate of 5/96 of a dollar a pound; a dead one, 9/96.

A packet of clover 1/16 of a dollar.

Good peaches ⅜ of a dollar a hundred and even less.

Sixteen ears of corn, raw, in August, for ⅛ of a dollar.

Twelve cooked ears, the same.

A watermelon in August, 15/96 of a dollar.

A beautiful French watermelon, ⅛ of a dollar.

Prime hen chickens, ¼ of a dollar.

Fowl, 15/96 of a dollar.

Coffee at retail, 1/16 of a dollar a pound.

A laundress or a person to iron costs ½ dollar a day.

They must be given coffee and butter for breakfast, rum with dinner, and tea, butter and cheese for supper.

Thirty superb Dean's pears or Lammas pears cost ¼ of a dollar, or 1/96 of a dollar for 1, 3 for 1/48.

Ordinary peaches up to 5 for 1/96 of a dollar.

Beautiful peach apricots 2 for 1/96 of a dollar.

A confinement, 12½ dollars.

White cord to bind up trunks and boxes, 3/16 of a dollar a pound. Eleven pounds make 60 fathoms.

The same rope, tarred, ⅛ of a dollar a pound.

French beans, 1/16 of a dollar a half peck.

Onions 3/32 the package. White ones are a little more expensive.

Pension and lodging from 2½ to 9 dollars a week.

A frying pan, 1⅛ dollars.

A griddle, 1 dollar.

A bellows, 1⅞ dollars.

Common shovel and tongs, 1⅛ dollars.

A candlestick with snuffers, 1½ dollars.

A large kettle for kitchen use, 1⅝ dollars.

Chairs, 1 dollar each.

A mill for grinding coffee, 1⅛ dollars.

A pair of flatirons, 1¾ dollars.

Commerce

New York trades with the entire American continent, with Europe, with the Antilles, with the Indies.

Her port has the advantage of being the easiest to make. Ships have shelter as soon as they have arrived at her shores, because it only takes three or four hours to go from Sandy Hook to the wharves; and the same length of time lets them reach the open sea. On the other hand, however, New York is more exposed to outrages and attacks in time of war than any other port in the United States.

The freight for cargo salt beef is 5/4 of a dollar; for mess beef 11/8; prime beef 1½ dollars.

A person who sells rice is obligated to sell it packed in such a manner that it can be weighed. After it has been weighed it is at the buyer's risk.

A seller of flour must deliver it in condition to be shipped. The same thing is true of potash and pearlash.

A tierce of rice weighs from 520 to 720 pounds.

Sometimes ship captains receive a percentage of their cargo instead of wages. This may be as much as 7½ per cent.

Inspectors have been appointed by law for potash and pearlash. Anyone is free to make potash and pearlash, but they must be placed in depots run by these inspectors, who pay cartage and cooperage costs in advance. For this there is a charge of 1/16 of a dollar a quintal, half being charged to the seller and half to the buyer.

When this merchandise is sold, the custom is for the seller to add his half of the cost of inspection to the price he charges the buyer; then from the total he deducts the entire amount of the inspector's bill, which includes cost of inspection, cartage, cooperage, etc.

There are inspectors for flour and salt meat.

The tare on a barrel of potash is 14 pounds and up.

That of rice is accepted as it is marked on the barrels in Georgia and the Carolinas. If no mark can be seen, it stands at 10 or 12 pounds.

The standard weight for heavy merchandise is the quintal

of 112 English pounds, divided into four quarters of 28 pounds. Transactions are considerably complicated by these weights.

Cart drivers own their carts and horses.

Only one trip is necessary to transport 100 barrels of flour. Not less than 5 barrels of salt pork will be carried on any one trip.

To make brine in New York they use 2 bushels of Portuguese salt to 100 gallons of water.

The person who sells the salt meat pays for the pickling; the cooper furnishes the materials. They have large empty barrels for this purpose.

The word "provisions" applies strictly to salt pork and salt beef.

The cart drivers are quick-tempered and given to mistreating their horses. The horses, particularly the chestnuts, are extremely handsome.

A cart horse is good for ten years when well cared for, but only five when badly treated.

A chopine[8] of rum may retail as low as 2/96 of a dollar and as high as 9/32 of a dollar.

The proprietor of a wharf makes the following charges for the use of a wharf:

Nine sixteenths of a dollar per day for a ship of less than 100 tons, ¾ of a dollar, for one of more than 100 tons, and still more if it is larger. A ship that lies alongside another vessel, so that access to the wharf can only be had by crossing, pays half the charge. A third likewise pays a half.

The salt meat barrels which hold 200 pounds have 12 hoops, 6 at each end, divided 3 by 3. Sometimes a beef barrel has 9 hoops at each end.

A flour barrel, which weighs about 200 English pounds, has 10 hoops, 3 at the rim of each end and 2 on each side of the middle. In making the barrels, several nails are put

[8]An old measure, nearly an English pint.

in the end hoops, and little wooden pegs in the second hoop from the end.

Rice barrels have 8 hoops, 2 by 2. These are the worst built barrels.

In New York there are 24 public porters, pushing that number of barrows. These men wear a copper neckpiece stamped with their initials and a number.

Staves are sold in the following way: 120 are reckoned as 100, 1200 are reckoned as 1000 wholesale. Staves for large barrels are 2 feet 6 inches long, 4 inches wide and from 8 to 15 lines thick.

When a charter party contracts that a boat will load so many tons, a ton is reckoned to be 8 barrels of pork or beef or 10 of flour, 6 tierces of rice, 4 barrels of rice, 4 casks of wine.

Pearlash is white and dry. Potash is blackish and greasy. There is no difference in price between the two; but there is a difference in price of the three qualities of potash and pearlash. Barrels of pearlash and potash weigh from 250 to 500 pounds. The tariff on a barrel of potash is: first grade, 3¾ dollars; second grade, 4¾ dollars; third grade, 5¾ dollars.

There are small barrels, called firkins, which are filled with lard and weigh from 50 to 70 pounds.

Mackerel barrels are smaller than those for flour and weigh 200 pounds. They come from New England.

For mess beef there are half barrels weighing 100 pounds.

A cask of rum holds 110 to 125 gallons.

Three days of grace are allowed for payment.

Big sales of merchandise are paid for after three to six months; sometimes after six to nine months.

Business in New York is extremely involved, because of the participation of shipowner, warehouse owner, shopkeeper, etc. Thus transactions are uncertain.

Commercial paper is not negotiated for more than sixty

days, for the banks have agreed among themselves not to discount it for a longer time.

There is a Charleston packet which makes trips exclusively between that city and New York. It is a three-masted ship of about 180 tons. It has 16 mahogany sleeping places and some conveniences in the English taste.

The price for the passage is 20 gourdes (110 francs) for a master, ten for a servant. Each passenger supplies his own food.

The New York Militia are uniformed and well armed. It has two flags, all one color, without stripes. It fires salvos in a well-synchronized manner.

After the review, two men not in uniform carry away the two flags on their shoulders, and the guns are also taken back to barracks.

At the Fourth of July ceremony in 1794, there was a procession in which Genêt took part. Frenchmen and Americans marched in pairs, sometimes singing English songs, sometimes patriotic French airs.

I have spoken elsewhere of the untidiness of the streets. It is also a New York custom to carry on in the center of the city certain businesses which always give rise to evil odors. This is particularly true of fur businesses. They are carried on in damp cellars which exude fumes so noxious, especially during the great heat of summer, as to suffocate passers-by on the sidewalks. The stench of corruption that comes from such places may be the reason for the many fatal illnesses that prevail in New York, among them yellow fever.

Most astonishing of all is the New York custom of choosing the month of August to clean out the sewer which carries away, along the length of certain wharfs and slips, the stinking street filth which the weather has washed into it.

In 1791 the sewage around the wharfs was thought to

have caused the epidemic of yellow fever at that time.

The first victim was Colonel Marcombi, who had amused himself by watching this performance closely. There were fifteen other victims. The disease was limited to Water Street.

The surroundings of New York City are as agreeable as they are varied. There are rope walks, brickyards, beautiful small country estates, a nursery; and particular mention should be made of the charming Greenwich home of Messrs. LeRoy and Bayard, whose surroundings are cheerful and cool, and whose charm is enhanced by its delightful view of the North River.

The inhabitants of New York are, generally speaking, refined and amiable; and it cannot be denied that New York is the pleasantest of all places in the United States in which to live.

A strange habit of New Yorkers is their mania for moving on May 1, if they do not own a house. This moving must be seen to be believed. No one was able to tell me the reason for it.

New York's population increases rapidly. In 1814 it has reached 60,000 persons.

Communication with Long Island, and with Jersey by the North River, is now by means of steamboats, which make these trips more certain and speedy. New York prisons, during November, 1801, supplied food for 315 persons at a cost of:

	Dollars	Cents
For breakfast of rice, coffee, bread	5	7
For dinner of soup and potatoes	9	51
For supper of molasses and bread	3	55
For fire		8
	18	21

or less than six centimes a head.

According to Rumford's[9] calculations, kitchen wood for 125 people formerly cost 2¾ dollars a day; at present, for 315, 2½ dollars.

The number of crimes is greater in the city of New York than elsewhere in the state. In the city there is one crime for every 129 persons. In the state one for every 2633. Therefore, there are twenty-two times more in the city.

1. Almost ¾ of the criminals are foreigners.

2. Slaves make up almost ⅓ of the criminals, in spite of the fact that they are only 1/28 of the population of the state. Only ⅛ of the guilty number are women, of whom 4/5 are Negresses. These details were published in the *American Review,* New York, 1802.

New York is 95 miles northeast of Philadelphia (40 leagues); 252 miles from Boston (107 leagues); 197 miles from Baltimore (88 leagues); 373 miles from Richmond (158 leagues); 913 from Charleston (390 leagues); 1032 from Savannah (780 leagues).

Its latitude is 40 degrees 42 minutes north, and its longitude 1 degree 17 minutes east of Philadelphia.

Long Island

The city of New York derives countless benefits from its proximity to Long Island.

The first and most valuable is that Long Island assures an anchorage and a sheltered harbor in the East River—whose name is derived not only from its situation east of New York, but because some of the waters of the North or Hudson River, in forming the island on which New York is situated, pass east of it.

From Long Island, New York gets cattle, chickens, pigs, sheep, game, a great quantity of fruit, many vegetables, an

[9]Benjamin Thompson, Count Rumford, whose life in America and England was described at some length in *Oliver Wiswell.*

abundance of grain, and particularly Indian corn, eggs, fish and oysters. To assure regular crossings, which both places must have, a ferry runs from a wharf at the end of the Fly Market to the nearest spot in Brooklyn.

This ferry uses four small longboats and four whaleboats. They are owned by four persons who lease ferry rights from the corporation of the city of New York for 1125 gourdes a year (6650 francs).

Sixty years ago the ferry, together with a large and small house belonging to it, were all leased for 250 dollars (1500 francs). In 1798, the same facilities yielded 1500 dollars. The four lessees take in turn a week's income. This simple procedure put an end to distrust and saves bookkeeping.

The lease did not bind a lessee any longer than he wished to be bound. He only had to give notice, a certain length of time before quitting.

The eight boats employed sixteen men who were lodged, fed, and paid ten gourdes (sixty francs) a month. Most of them were Irishmen.

These boats used sails when possible. At other times they were rowed. At such times the two sailors wielded the oars and a passenger held the tiller.

These boats had one mast and carried sail unexpectedly well, yet mishaps were not unknown. Perhaps, too, it is only surprising that they were not frequent, because the sailors were often drunk, and their dislike of rowing led them to use the sail when a sail was dangerous.

Each person paid one forty-eighth of a dollar for the trip, or in kind. People transporting eggs paid their fare with eggs—two eggs out of each hundred they carried. The four large boats carried vehicles and animals, which was frequently a source of annoyance to those who woke up to the fact that they were traveling with beasts.

Favorable trips took two and a half minutes for the mile crossing. The pleasantest were those when the wind was favorable and the tide not strong. These took ten or twelve minutes. In a calm and with a strong tide the crossing sometimes took more than an hour.

There is a long-standing lawsuit between Brooklyn and New York, the former claiming that it has the original right to lease for its profit the ferry from its side to New York. But the very length of the suit shows what its end will be. New York is a great city and powerful, Brooklyn is only a village. Anyone can guess the answer.

The trip from New York to Brooklyn is now made by steamboats, of which I have spoken in connection with the crossing of the North River. It takes eight minutes.

Brooklyn has about one hundred houses, most of them only one story high. Some are stone or brick; the others are wood, and mediocre. The street that leads to the ferry is fairly straight and runs east-northeast. At the top it turns south-southeast along the highway. Most of the houses are chiefly along the shore, or scattered without regular plan.

Almost the entire population of this village is made up of Tories, or people favorably disposed toward England.

One of its residents is an old Quaker named Doughty whose devotion to liberty was such that he was driven out of Brooklyn during the War of Independence. Since then he has been a member of the New York State Legislature. He speaks well, and he is held in such general esteem that in Brooklyn and other sections of Long Island he is regarded as the best adviser obtainable. People frequently consult him.

The streets in Brooklyn, or rather the highway which forms its principal street, is bad, heavy and unpaved, so that the smallest amount of rain makes Brooklyn muddy.

Brooklyn has three churches, a Dutch Presbyterian, an Anglican Episcopal, a Methodist. Moreover, the Anabaptists meet in a building which is used as a school during the week.

At the northern end of Brooklyn and so close to the edge of the river that part of it is on pilings, is a rope-walk belonging to Sand Brothers, who own a large part of the real estate in Brooklyn.

This rope-walk, established in 1791, is 1175 French feet long, 24 feet wide at the south or entrance end, and 18 feet wide at the other end. It employs forty people, who as a rule are paid three fourths of a dollar a day.

Even farther north than the rope works, but on the crest of a rise near the river, is a powder magazine where New York's powder supply is kept.

This building, some 30 feet long and 12 feet wide, is enclosed by a brick wall 1 foot thick in which there are slantwise openings. The floor and ceiling are made of planks, and there are six wooden shelves, holding about two thousand barrels of powder. The loft above and at the end of this warehouse has an opening in each end.

When the guard of this powder magazine is on duty, he allows anyone who wishes to enter.

Powder is everywhere on the ground where everybody walks; it is given to the children to play with, and to make firecrackers. What a country!

The air of Brooklyn is unusually healthy. Its water is not too good, but is better than that of New York—barring the tea-water.

To supply oneself with provisions, one goes at dawn to the ferry to buy from those carrying supplies to New York. This arrangement is highly satisfactory, the only thing against it being the inconvenience of the hour.

So that the transport of provisions from Long Island to New York can be made easier, all ferry-boats, barring one, spend the night in Brooklyn. This remains in New York on the chance that something important might have to be taken across during the night.

During six months the trips end at eight o'clock; during the other six at nine o'clock.

Just south of Brooklyn and overlooking the river is a small chain of hills, on which are the country houses of many wealthy New Yorkers. Its proximity to New York leads New Yorkers to rent the houses and send their families there during the hot season. The men go to New York in the morning, and return to Brooklyn after the Stock Exchange closes.

The elevated situation of these country residences, in addition to being healthy, gives them the advantage of a charming view which includes New York and the nearby islands, principally Governor's Island, and is constantly enlivened by the passing of the boats which ply on both rivers.

One of the houses, one story high with eight large rooms, a piazza, and a stable with six acres of land, rents for three hundred dollars a year (eighteen hundred francs). The proximity of New York daily increases the value of property in Brooklyn as well as those elsewhere on Long Island. There are, however, pensions in Brooklyn where one can be well lodged and fed for four gourdes (twenty-four francs or four dollars) a week.

Brooklyn is the point of departure for all roads to different settlements on Long Island. For example, the highway to the southern part of the island goes through Brooklyn at right angles, always ascending. There are several houses in the Dutch style on the highest part of the slope. There the soil is fine sand, extremely light and loose.

At the end of five miles (two and a half leagues) one reaches Flatbush which has about one hundred and fifty houses, a school called an academy, a Court House, and a

Dutch church built of stone. The road which leads there is about thirty feet wide and not particularly good.

At the end of another four miles is New Utrecht, where there are some thirty scattered houses, almost all of them pensions for children.

These children are day scholars at the college or academy, which is distinguished by a small steeple. It is under the direction of M. Tot, and has twenty-one boarders and forty-five day scholars. To serve all these there is one Negro, a Negress, her two children and a young white domestic.

The academy supposedly teaches Greek, Latin, French, arithmetic and mathematics, and it is all done by M. Tot and a canon of St. Geneviève.

It pains one to go into such an establishment and see the system of education in force, and the sort of order and policy it produces.

A child learns only what he wishes, and the master takes no pride in him or the school. The responsibility for this peculiar state of affairs rests with the fathers and mothers. They are only interested in the cost of the schooling, and in being relieved of the burden of taking care of their children.

Every six months the students are allowed to go home. If at home they find less freedom and diversion than they had at college, they long to go back, whence the conclusion that the school is excellent; for if the child complains and says he wants no part of it, then, without further investigation, he is sent to another.

This is the masters' rule of thumb, and it makes children already spoiled become bad—then become men without talents.

New Utrecht is on the seashore and overlooks the mouth of the New York River. Some time ago a house for sea bathing was built close to the water's edge. As it was also planned as a pleasure resort, it has a dining room forty-five feet long by eighteen feet wide, in which one can dine for half a gourde a person. The owner makes his greatest profits from certain picnics at which the palm is awarded to the one who drinks the most.

In front of the house, on the river side, is a projecting garden; but those who built it forgot to place the center of it opposite the front door of the house. It is about eleven miles (eighty-five hundred toises) from the Sandy Hook lighthouse.

Sandy Hook is thirty miles (twelve leagues) from New York. It has a small anchorage on the east side, but not a safe one. There are ten fathoms[10] of water at high tide and only two and a half at low tide.

One road from New Utrecht to the upper part of Brooklyn skirts the western shore of Long Island. It is not always beautiful; but there is something singularly picturesque about seeing a large city on one side and truly rural sections on the other. This road is thickly bordered with cherry trees, and passers-by are customarily permitted to pick the fruit which hangs over the road.

The soil of Long Island is poor, sandy, stony and shallow. Because of this, luzerne,[11] which has long roots, doesn't thrive there.

This land, however, is high-priced, because the nearness of New York assures a market for all farm products, and because the Dutch families who form such a large part of the population refuse to sell their holdings.

It is planted to crops of Indian corn, wheat, flax, many fruit trees and vegetables. One finds acacias and weeping willows. Among the plants are superb castor-oil plants (*Palma christi*). Although this annual plant, which is both useful and native, flourishes before the very eyes of the Americans, they prefer to pay high prices for castor oil that

[10]Moreau reckons in French fathoms, which are eight inches shorter than English.
[11]The old name for alfalfa.

is imported in insufficient quantities from the Antilles rather than make their own.

It is said to be excellent for dysentery, for lotions, for enemas, as a purgative and as a vermifuge.

Beginning November 30, horse races are held for three days in Jamaica, a pretty little town on Long Island. All New York attends, and the ferries do a rushing business. Among the spectators are many of the habitués of the houses of ill fame which debauchery has multiplied in New York. A carriage with two horses and a driver and seats for four ordinarily costs four dollars for a day; but during the races it costs more.

In Brooklyn there are many such carriages for hire with seats for one, two or four. They are entrusted, with no investigation, to anyone who wishes to hire them. They can be used for any length of time agreed upon.

New York's greatest amusement is to drive to Long Island on Sunday. On Sunday afternoons, moreover, thousands of people from New York go for walks in Brooklyn, where they eat and destroy all the fruit, even green, that they can reach. The owners don't dare to stop them, and the waste is deplorable. Everyone carries away as much as he wishes.

At one time the ferries on Sunday carried on every trip and in both directions as many persons as could be loaded aboard.

Bedford, a small place adjoining Brooklyn, has nothing to recommend it.

There is granite in more or less great quantity along the entire length of Long Island, but always in heaps. Some of these heaps show that they have shifted their position, because the impressions made on the stones by moving water indicate two distinctly different directions.

On Long Island there are green frogs on the trees.

There are great numbers of mosquitoes on the south side of Long Island.

Eels are taken to New York from a distance of twenty-four miles (fifteen leagues) ; other fish from sixty miles.

In many places on Long Island old fortifications built during the American War of Independence may still be seen. The traces of these ruins do not mar the soil which is cultivated by men who have won their independence.

There are many more things to be told about New York, but since they also apply to Philadelphia, I shall insert them in my account of the latter.

SOJOURN IN PHILADELPHIA

OCTOBER *13, 1794.* We left New York at half past eight in the morning, reached Paulus Hook twenty minutes later, and at ten o'clock lunched at Newark. On leaving Newark for Brunswick we experienced a delay rarely encountered on this route. M. Loutherbourg, son of the celebrated painter and himself a portrait painter, was traveling with us in the stage. He had with him a highly intelligent green parrot, and when he let the parrot out of his cage, the bird went and perched high up in one of the trees that bordered the road. The stage willingly stopped at the request of the grief-stricken M. Loutherbourg, who got out, called the parrot and showed him the cage, whereupon the deserter again imprisoned himself.

We dined in Brunswick and slept at Princeton.

October 14. The next day we stopped at Trenton for breakfast. We were in Philadelphia at half past one in the afternoon, where the good Sonntag received us.

October 18. We settled our family in the lodgings which Sonntag had engaged for us.

October 19. I attended services in the German Lutheran church.

October 21. I received from M. le Baron de la Roche a letter filled with expressions of friendship for me and mine.

De Combatz suggested that he be my clerk for six months for a hundred and fifty dollars. He had been employed in the bookshop in Geneva, and had had a fine shop in Cap François. I accepted his offer the next day.

November 8, 1794. There was a fire in Spruce Street a little before two o'clock in the morning.

November 11. I saw Pillet, aide-de-camp to Lafayette, rescued from Antwerp with La Colombe.

November 16. Talleyrand came to see me.

I went to see Washington open Congress and hear his opening address. How wholly simple and natural it was. But this was Washington! This was the gathering of representatives of a nation that has won its liberty! What vast and great ideals in a group so united! How these republican forms appeal to the soul and stir the heart. What a destiny they foretell for this part of the world!

M. de Liancourt arrived from London in Philadelphia on the ship *Pigeon.*[1]

I went to see Talleyrand.

I hastened to go and embrace Terrier, senior, arriving from Bordeaux.

My beautiful signboard was placed on my shop.

Moreau de St. Méry and Co. Bookseller
Printer and Stationner
nº 84 First Street
Moreau de St. Méry et Comp. Libraire.
Imprimeur et Papetier
nº 84 1ère Rue

My printing, stationery and book shop was on the south side of First Street at the corner of Walnut. I should say at this time there are artisans in Philadelphia who make a specialty of painting remarkably beautiful signboards with backgrounds of different colors, speckled with gold or silver.

December 3, 1794. If the signboard has the slightest mistake in spelling, no matter in what way, or if there is any question that the lettering isn't exactly what was ordered,

---

[1] François Alexandre Frédéric La Rochefoucauld, Duc de Liancourt (1747–1827). His celebrated but supremely dull eight-volume *Voyage dans les Etats-Unis d'Amérique* was begun five months after he reached Philadelphia. In spite of the help Moreau gave him, as shown in succeeding pages, no mention whatever of Moreau or of Talleyrand was made in Liancourt's book.

the workman is obliged to re-do it at his own expense. What a difference from France, where even in Paris there are signboards which have the most lamentable mistakes in language. In America children might take spelling lessons from the signboards.

M. Guerlain did me the honor of calling on me.

December 10. M. de la Roche wrote, asking me to stop at his house tomorrow to draw up our deed of partnership.

This, however, was not done until the sixteenth. Gauvain and Sonntag witnessed our agreement with their personal seals.

I opened my shop the same day.

December 26. Fire broke out in the German Lutheran church and destroyed that beautiful house of worship.

December 30. A distressing thing happened to me today. I met a lady who addressed me as though we were friends, but since I could recall nothing whatever about her, I was forced to ask her who she was. She proved to be—though I never would have recognized her—the once attractive Mlle. Popote Boudier, a neighbor of ours in Cap François, whom I had long admired when I lived in San Domingo. Oh, how ashamed and confused I was! How can anyone make amends for the commission of such an unfortunate act, which is equally embarrassing to her who suffers from it.

Alas, I have repeatedly been guilty of this unfortunate forgetfulness, and expect to be guilty of it many times more.

December 31. I did not wish to deprive my business of a profitable item, the lack of which in hot climates would not, I think, be without danger. Consequently, when my old colleague and friend, Barrister Geanty, a refugee from Cap François in Baltimore, who had a wide knowledge of medical supplies, offered me a stock of certain small contrivances— ingenious things said to have been suggested by the stork— I agreed. I wish to say that I carried a complete assortment of them for four years; and while they were primarily intended for the use of French colonials, they were in great demand among Americans, in spite of the false shame so prevalent among the latter. Thus the use of this medium on the vast American continent dates from this time.[2] People from San Domingo as well as from other colonies had frequent recourse to our stock.

January 2, 1795. I was accepted as a resident member of the Philosophical Society of Philadelphia.

January 13. Talleyrand wrote me:

If you were a man inclined to dine with us two days in succession I would say to you come both today and tomorrow. But I know your customary reply to such a proposition. In spite of that, know that tomorrow General Knox dines with us, and that General Knox has long had business dealings here with bookshops and is interested in your success. He told me a fortnight ago he wished to talk to you to tell you how he thinks you can best prosper. Knowing all this, will you decide to come both days, or do you prefer tomorrow or today?

Always yours.

Tuesday   TAL.

Talleyrand and Beaumetz lived together on South Second Street at the corner of Spruce, but they both ate at Cazenove's house, in Market Street. Thus the expression "to dine at our house" meant dining at Cazenove's.

I went to dine at Cazenove's with M. Law, and I also went on the following day with General Knox.

January 14. In the evening I paid my respects to Mme. General Knox, whose husband lavished upon me the marks of his warm esteem.

January 16. I took part in the meeting of the Philosophical Society, and exhibited many American curiosities, among them wooden locks made of mahogany from San Domingo.

January 22. I took from the consulate general an affidavit

[2]Whether Moreau de St. Méry should have a statue erected to him in Philadelphia in gratitude for this contribution to American culture is debatable.

for myself and my family, a precaution I never neglected at any time during my stay in the United States. I always sent these affidavits to France.

January 23. Today the winter cold was down to 6 degrees.

February 3, 1795. A gentleman who called himself Count de Beaufort, and claimed to have escaped from the siege and the misfortunes of Lyons sought me out and suggested that I buy from him some articles for my bookshop, and do business with him.

I found it impossible to comply, but took him to call on M. Sonntag in the hope that he might be able to do business with him.

I dined at M. de la Roche's with Talleyrand and Beaumetz.

February 4. Sonntag gave a dinner for the Count de Beaufort and me.

February 5. M. de la Roche had the Count de Beaufort and me for dinner.

I went with Talleyrand to Minister Hamilton's house.

February 10. I went to Count de Beaufort's house, then to M. de Liancourt's. He read me the manuscript of his work on the prisons of Philadelphia.[3]

I also went to see Minister Hamilton.

February 19. I attended services at the Irish Catholic church.

I viewed the Swedish church and saw its philosopher and philanthropist pastor, Dr. Collins, my colleague at the Philosophical Society of Philadelphia.

February 23. A ball was given, as it had been for some years, to celebrate Washington's birthday. It was on that occasion that I had a scene with John Vaughan.[4]

[3] La Rochefoucauld Liancourt's work here referred to appeared at the beginning of 1796, in English, under the title, *On the Prisons of Philadelphia. By an European,* and, in French, under that of *Des prisons de Philadelphia. Par un Européen.* Both editions bore the press-mark of "Moreau de St. Méry, Printer and Bookseller," Philadelphia.

[4] See p. 333.

March 1, 1795. I published a catalogue of the goods in my shop.

At this time I received new marks of friendship from my colleague in the Cap François Council, M. St. Martin.

March 2. I had M. Martial La Roque of Montreal, Canada, to dinner, and gave him my eulogy of Turc de Castelveyre to give to the Grey Sisters of Montreal. How interesting I found him! How many things he was able to tell me about the country in which he has so long lived, about the condition and sentiments of the French Canadians. What an interesting day for me, spiritually and emotionally!

March 3. Since it seemed to me that M. le Baron de la Roche was insincere and a busybody in his behavior toward me, I reproached him sharply during a passage I had with him.

March 12. I visited with pleasure the museum of M. Peale, my colleague in the Philosophical Society.

March 13. I went to see Talleyrand and welcomed my dear Demeunier[5] who arrived from New York on the *Diana* of Boston, on the tenth.

March 22. I presented my compliments to Mme. Vaudbreckt, whose husband had been the Dutch Minister in Philadelphia.

March 23. I visited the Philadelphia prisons with Messrs. Liancourt and Demeunier.

A watchmaker persuaded me (contrary to the advice of my dear Messier) to let him clean my perfect spy glass, made by Dollin[6] Nairne and Company. He stole it, and disappeared from Philadelphia. How much I regret this loss!

April 1, 1795. We heard that Holland has been conquered.

April 4. The press ordered from London arrived by the American ship *Adrienne.*

[5] Jean Nicolas Demeunier (1715–1814) was deputy in Estates General in 1789 and later president of the *Constituante.* He remained in this country only about eight months. Several interesting entries are made in the diary in regard to him.

[6] Dolland.

April 12. I read some of my *Description of San Domingo* to Cazenove, Talleyrand, Beaumetz and Demeunier.

I received another proof of the friendship of my former colleague, M. de St. Martin, head of the Council of Cap François, who had retired to Wilmington on the Delaware.

April 23. I had M. Nancrède, a Frenchman, to dinner. He is a bookseller in Boston, and my correspondent there. He already showed a strong and habitual satisfaction with his own ideas, and did not cease to do so up to the time when I saw him in France in 1813.

April 24. In the evening I read my article on the *Danse*[7] from my collection of colonial information to Talleyrand, M. de Liancourt and M. Guillemard, an Englishman. The same day I had a long talk with General Ricard, who has just been made Governor of Santa Lucia.

Talleyrand, Beaumetz and Demeunier went to New York.

April 29. M. de la Roche wrote me *in his own handwriting:*

Philadelphia, April 29, 1795.

In response to your letter, Monsieur, we have the honor to call your attention to the fact that M. Frank de la Roche has requested us to credit you with the quarterly allowance due you for house rent. This sum is therefore at your disposal. As he has not given us any other instructions, will you kindly acknowledge this to him personally.

We are very faithfully, Monsieur,

Your very humble servants

WILLIAM LOUIS SONNTAG & Co.

(Business signature of Baron de la Roche)

May 3, 1795. I promised M. de la Roche to remove the words "and Company" from my signboard. I do not know what value he put on this sacrifice.

May 21. Letter from Talleyrand:

New York, May 21, 1795.

CHER MAÎTRE:

Your M. de la Barre's right name is La Bigore. Instead of living on Broadway, his address is White Hall. His Buffon, which you

[7]Later published under the title, *The Dance*, Philadelphia, 1797.

mention as being for sale, was sold two months ago. Beaumetz is so fortunate as to be able to spend several days with you. He will rejoice with you that Barère[8] and Collot d'Herbois are still alive. The two great patriots made a fine defense. I have had all kinds of trouble getting a little house in Stone Street, where I hope to see you on your way to Boston. Adieu, sell high and often. When you think of your friends, I would like a good share of your thoughts.

June 2, 1795. I received the following letter:

Philadelphia, June 2, 1795.
I send greetings to M. Moreau de St. Méry and beg that he will return by the bearer the notes I gave him concerning the siege of Lyons, and oblige his servant

COUNT DE BEAUFORT

June 3. I replied the next day, as follows:

The notes which I received from M. de Beaufort, I did not know were copied almost word for word from a printed book which I have since received from England. The notes bear remarks in my own handwriting, made when I read them with him; so he should not take it amiss if I keep what I have done for myself as well as what he did for me. I am his servant. As the work is in print, M. de Beaufort can easily procure for himself the passage that he took the trouble to abstract from it.

To further explain my reply, I should add that after Count de Beaufort delivered his notes to me, and discovered that I was in no hurry to buy his property at the price he put upon it, he ceased to call upon me. Then I read in a newspaper a frightful denunciation of his infamous conduct at the siege of Lyons where, while acting as engineer for the besieged forces, he betrayed their confidence. Around the

[8]Barère and Collot d'Herbois and Billaud-Varennes had been arrested on March 2, 1795, and then brought to trial on the charges of participation in the Reign of Terror. After a brief interruption of the trial by a popular demonstration in their favor, the three were condemned to deportation to Cayenne on April 1. It was not until May 22 that the decree was enforced against Collot d'Herbois and Billaud-Varennes, Barère escaping to Bordeaux (see Barère *Memoirs*, III, 1). The date of Talleyrand's letter is only the day before the enforcement of the decree.

same time, Count de Beaufort expressed himself in very insolent terms regarding me, and said to everybody that he would kill me.

When he received my note, he sent me a reply by his servant, a small mulatto:

Referring to your notification that you have received from England a book containing a passage similar to the notes I sent you, you can copy your notes from my notes into the book, and erase your notes from my notes. I assure you that I should take it extremely amiss if you did not return my notes to me. I fully intend to have them back, no matter what the means I am forced to employ. I am your servant,

Philadelphia, June 3, 1795.

COUNT DE BEAUFORT

I was at dinner when this reached me, and I replied to the count's mulatto (the count, incidentally, had been wearing the uniform of a colonel with two great gold epaulettes for several days) that I would give him an answer without delay.

In fact, after I had eaten barely enough to keep my family from being alarmed, I left the table on the pretext of having pressing business. I hunted up Gauvain, my wife's first cousin, a person tried and true, and told him I wanted him as a witness of my colloquy with Count de Beaufort. We went to Gauvain's house for a good pair of pistols and their accessories, then went down North Second Street to the inn where the count took his meals.

We were told he was at dinner. I sent word to him to step outside on urgent business. He came.

I said to him: "Sir, you have behaved in a most ungentlemanly manner in speaking of me. This offends me.

"You have written to me in a way I cannot permit. And since you wish to kill me, I suppose you'd like to do it in my presence, so I am here with a second and pistols to ask you when and where you wish me to meet you."

The count's manner and color instantly changed, and, as one says in vulgar French, he wet his pants. Thereupon Gauvain wished to make clear to him what he thought of him, but I said:

"Gauvain! I brought you here to be my second in case Monsieur wished to fight me. Monsieur refuses the challenge, therefore you have no further role to play."

"But, Monsieur," I said to the count, "what do you have against me? If it's my poverty you envy, there is plenty for two. So then, I am leaving you. However, do me a favor. You have said everywhere that you wish to kill me. All right! Now let me repeat everywhere that you are permitting me to live."

And we left.

The same evening at a ball where the count was dancing, young Bousquet of Lyons gathered several Frenchmen together and said to them, "You know Count de Beaufort, who swore to kill St. Méry, has decided to permit him to live."

This jesting drove the count from the ball, and shortly afterwards from Philadelphia, whence he once again returned to San Domingo.

That very same night Beaumetz, who had learned of my dramatic passage with Beaufort, came and took me seriously to task because I had not picked him as my second. I had the utmost difficulty in proving to him that Gauvain, as my near relative, had a better right to be chosen, and I only appeased him by assuring him that next time it would be his turn. This should not be far off.

June 11. Baron de la Roche wrote me:

Philadelphia, June 11, 1795.

I had intended to give myself the pleasure of calling upon you today to discuss business; but several letters which I must write oblige me to put this off until tomorrow.

As we can have more privacy in M. Sonntag's house, I ask you to come there tomorrow morning at the hour most convenient for

you. In case you prefer another meeting place, would you be so
kind as to tell M. Sonntag. Otherwise I will be there without fail.
You must feel as well as I that it is absolutely necessary for us to
make arrangements for the future, so there can be no continua-
tion of our unfortunate misunderstanding, which has occurred
through no fault of mine. You should be convinced, Monsieur, that
I am and always will be the man I was when M. de la Colombe
introduced you to me. It was I who first proposed, until something better turned up, to finance you in the venture at whose
head you now are—and which I believe will succeed perfectly. I
will always do everything in my power to contribute to its success; but my means are limited, and the interest of my family,
and my obligations to many relatives and old friends who have
lost everything in the late unhappy revolutions make it, in spite of
my affection for you, a pressing necessity for me to exercise the
greatest prudence and care in all pecuniary matters.

We have received letters from Hamburg, dated April 14, in
which I am told the orders given for your house will be executed.
I am told the same thing by Amsterdam. I hope soon to receive the
same news from London concerning the articles ordered for the
printing house, and I am momentarily awaiting the shipment
ordered from Bordeaux, which should in great part be drawn on
Paris. As I shall ask M. Sonntag to assist as a friend at our meeting, you will wish to bring a friend of yours. He ought to be a business man, so that any necessary changes can be made on the spot
without referring them to somebody else.

Yours always

Fr. Frank de la Roche

June 12. A meeting took place between M. de la Roche
and myself in the presence of Sonntag and Gauvain.

June 13. Adet, Minister of France, arrived in Philadelphia
and was received on the sixteenth by the government.

June 15. I went to pay my respects to Adet, French Minister to the United States of America. In this legation was
Mozard, advocate to the Council of Paris.

June 19. Champion des Roches, coming from Jérémie,
came to live at our house.

June 24. I was much surprised to see on the day of St.

John, patron of Freemasons, a public procession of the members of this society, carrying all the symbols and decorations of the order.

They made a magnificent appearance and the people of both sexes who were packed along their route showed their approval by a respectful silence. The same thing happens in England.

I received news from London that they are sending the type for my printing house.

June 26. I read with great interest a letter from Beaumetz from New York. It included, among other things, an account of a new play in which I was made the leading character. Beaumetz, out of friendship for me, went to see it performed the night before in New York. It has also been produced in London.

New York, June 26, 1795.

Mlle. Patterson,[9] who is a sublimely beautiful girl, brought me your brochure on the peace. When I opened the package, I had to reward her for her trouble by loaning her the book, so I

[9]Elizabeth Patterson, as Beaumetz aptly remarked, was *une grande fille bien fraiche.* Shortly after this letter was written, Bonaparte's brother, Jerome, fell in love with her and married her, which so annoyed Napoleon that when Jerome brought his wife to Europe in 1805, she was excluded from his states by the Emperor's special order. She is described in Margaret Bayard Smith's *The First Forty Years of Washington Society* (letter of Monday, January 23, 1804): "She has made a great noise here, and mobs of boys have crowded round her splendid equipage to see what I hope will not often be seen in this country, an almost naked woman. An elegant and select party was given to her by Mrs. Robt. Smith; her appearance was such that it threw all the company into confusion, and no one dar'd to look at her but by stealth; the window shutters being left open, a crowd assembled round the windows to get a look at this beautiful little creature, for every one allows she is extremely beautiful. Her dress was the thinnest sarcenet and white crepe without the least stiffening in it, made without a single plait in the skirt, the width at the bottom being made of gores; there was scarcely any waist to it and no sleeves; her back, her bosom, part of her waist and her arms were uncover'd and the rest of her form visible. She was engaged the next evening at Madam P's, Mrs. R. Smith and several other ladies sent her word, if she wished to meet them there, she must promise to have more clothes on." Truly *une grande fille bien fraiche!*

haven't been able to begin reading it myself until this moment. I regretted the delay because of the fact that it was by Mme. de Staël. The little I have seen of it seems to me to be worthy of her talent and heart, though I have scarcely read enough to express an opinion.

Yesterday it cost me a dollar to go to see you. I wouldn't have begrudged it if you had been better represented, nor would I have begrudged it at all if I could have seen you yourself.

The play opens with two women who come on the stage talking about their fears, emotions and hopes. When they discuss the great events that have occurred that day, there are shouts of Hurrah from a mob off stage.

Scene II. The lover of the younger of the two women (a person named Henry DuBois, I think) joins her. He tells her he is fighting for country, liberty and honor; for her; for his father who is a prisoner in the Bastille. He wishes to know whether he can possibly disregard such duties. His mistress is generous and patriotic. She encourages him and quits the scene to make way for the entrance of the mob.

Scene III. Five or six men in the dress of the National Guard: a mob of people: cries of Hurrah. One of the men in the dress of the National Guard, naked sword in hand, seems to command the others and to be the leader of the uprising. He orates on the causes of the Revolution, the tyranny of the court, its perfidy, its designs against Paris, the misery of the people, its oppression, the need to establish equality, the rights of man to destroy an arrogant nobility and a superstitious clergy. Then Henry DuBois proposes that they take the Bastille and free the prisoners. "Glorious thought," cries Moreau. "We will take it, by God!" His troops assemble joyously in the Champ de Mars—off they go to seize it, singing the *Marseillaise* in chorus!

Act II. The troops march off carrying banners emblazoned with such slogans as: Long live Liberty! Long live the Nation! The Rights of Man! Long live the Republic!

Scene II. Interior of the Bastille. Launay is with Major Pujet. The first receives an order, signed Louis, to lure the citizens into a trap by lowering the drawbridge, raising a flag of truce, allowing as many citizens to enter as can be packed into the courtyard: then to close the doors upon them and massacre them. Launay says this vile plan causes him pain, but since orders are orders, he can only obey.

Scene III. Attack on the Bastille. Launay, parleying, lowers the bridge according to orders. . . .

At the cries of the wretches who are betrayed and are being slaughtered, Moreau is transported with indignation. He sounds the assault and at the head of his troops carries the fort, sword in hand.

Act III. Interior of the captured Bastille. Moreau confronts the Governor face to face in one of the rooms of his stronghold, and while the rest of the Parisian army is winning victory, he fights Launay on the stage, beats him down and with sword at his throat forces him to surrender.

Having vanquished him, he then interrogates him. "You have fought bravely; why have you behaved treacherously, like a dastard?" "I had orders" (and he shows them). "Not one man more." "How many prisoners have you in the château?" "About three hundred." "Did you torture them?" "Only when I received an order to do so." "From whom did that order come?" "From the King or from the lieutenant of police." "Were you present at the torturing?" "No, it was the lieutenant of police or one of the inspectors."

"I want the keys of the dungeons and prisons." "They are in the hands of the turnkeys." "Get them for us and escort us." "I hope I need not fear for my own or my officers' safety." "No. Give me a list of your officers and the state of your garrison. Your life will be spared; at least, you will not lose it by my consent."

Thereupon you are conducted to the prison, where a couple of wretches are found, untied and freed. This done you turn toward Launay and Pujet inform them (without anyone understanding why you should so suddenly change your mind) that they must perish. They bravely resign themselves and ask for a confessor. They are led away. The dungeons are inspected, and from them are brought a crowd of unfortunate people who can scarcely walk, two skeletons upright in iron cages, an iron mask. Last of all comes an old man who wants to know why they have come for him; is he to be killed or tortured?—No, he is to be freed. "My father," cries Henry DuBois—recognitions—swoonings—the mistress arrives—marriage. During all this, Moreau de St. Méry does nothing but make compassionate gestures.

Scene III. The guard marches out; also Launay and Pujet to the gallows—mournful music—drums muffled in black—pikes reversed. The heads are not cut off on stage; but at the moment when they are supposed to have fallen, three joyous hurrahs are raised. The mob, sated, returns to the stage and Moreau makes a speech which I cannot recall exactly. He felicitates the mob on its victory, declares that he has won liberty for them and perhaps for all the nations of the world—he talks of the rights of man—everybody sings—Moreau is played by Hodgkinson.[10]

Are you getting lazy? Your news is most interesting; keep on with it. We have no news to give you in return; we do not believe the story that ten French ships out of eleven have been captured in the Mediterranean. Tell us what you yourself think. Shortly you will again have a long account of my news. I am waiting for a packet. We'll take pains, too, to give good service, which, as you can see, is yours by right, since frequent and honorable attention must be paid to the President of the Electors and the commandant of the armed forces—yours for life.

It seems to me that you should as rightly be called the Master of Lyons as well as of the Bastille. My respects to your ladies.— Regards to your son.

July 1, 1795. My mother-in-law was living with us and dwelling in my house. My wife, because of it, was overjoyed in a manner difficult to describe. This expressed itself in her constant care for her beloved mother, who delighted in her daughter's love. My mother-in-law received these attentions not so much as a mother, but as a spoiled child, and yet with a satisfied maternal instinct and a kind of religious deference.

How sweet a picture this made! How touching! But happiness, alas, is not permitted to mortals; for if it were, their lot would be preferred by those perfect Beings who surround the heavenly throne!

[10]From *Annals of the New York Stage* . . . (Columbia University Press, 1927): "Mr. and Mrs. (William) King had another night on June 25th (1795)—King Apparently, having failed on the 5th; they gave The Young Quaker and the pantomime, The Bastile, or Liberty Triumphant, for which Ireland now provides a cast including (John) Hodgkinson as M. Mereau de St. Merry (with the Marseilles Hymn), (Lewis) Hallam (the younger) as Le Braint, (William) King as Henry DuBois, (John) Fawcett as Delaney, (John) Martin as Leontine, Mrs. Wilson as Sophia, and Mrs. Pownall (Mrs. Wrighten) as Matilda."

On the first of the month she was attacked by fever and a cough, the intensity of which threatened pneumonia.

July 3. The illness seemed to subside. Mamma dressed herself and spent the entire day out of bed, sitting up and talking.

Almost immediately the doctor became apprehensive. Her pulse weakened; she had difficulty in breathing; and this condition became worse and worse. On the seventh she seemed in danger. Blistering plasters were applied in the evening, her condition became alarming and she spent an extremely restless night.

At four o'clock on the morning of the eighth the unexpected symptoms diminished, but at eight o'clock she had a paroxysm. As it increased, she grew weaker, and at half past ten without effort, without agony, she expired, having been unconscious for about an hour.

My mother-in-law who, when well, heard the very mention of death with abhorrence and found the idea of dying on the continent of the United States insupportable, showed great courage and resignation during her illness.

She seemed to know that her hour had come and only took medicine because of a desire to please her children.

Mme. Milhet was very good, compassionate and filled with the greatest tenderness for the children. Lacking force in the ordinary things of life, she had rare energy when confronted by unusual circumstances. Her mind was not a cultivated one, but she had unusual rectitude and judgment, and her sweetness and resignation were unvarying.

Her frequent illnesses probably had their origin in a catarrhal inflammation to which she had been a prey for seventeen years. All her later sufferings combined to ruin her health, to burden her with sorrows that were accentuated because of the necessity of concealing them, and to cause her death. Among them were her expatriation from Louisiana, her native country; the causes responsible for it; the tragic events that followed; the dangers to which her three sons-in-law and her two nephews Gauvain and Milhet were exposed during the Revolution; the death of the latter, killed at Cap François on June 21, 1793; the necessity of fleeing her country of adoption without resources, and of abandoning life-long habits accentuated by age; the grievous state of her children on the continent; the lack of news of M. Arthaud; the conviction that she would never return to Cap François.

Her funeral clearly showed the veneration which her virtues inspired, yet Catholic priests refused to bury her.

In order that their motives may be better judged, I should explain that there was in Philadelphia at that time a little French priest, a fugitive from Angers, who not only followed his profession but was a teacher besides. His latter calling gave him frequent occasion to come to my shop, and I always did everything in my power for him.

Toward mid-June, 1795, I was talking with someone on political matters when this little priestling named Houdet intruded himself into the conversation to express the most violent hatred of everyone who had taken part in the Revolution, particularly those who had been members of the Constituent Assembly. When I gave him my reasons for thinking he was wrong, he made the most atrocious misstatements, and behaved in every way like an ignoramus and a fanatic. In spite of this he continued to come to my shop.

He came there the morning of the eighth of July, and after I had asked him where he lived and when I could find him there, I told him that we would probably have need of him soon, since my mother-in-law's condition had been so alarming during the night.

When he said that we should not wait, I said to him:

"Abbé, if anyone called you for me, I would receive you with pleasure. Mamma has her two daughters beside her and a Catholic doctor. At the first word I will seek you, as I sought a priest from the German Roman church for one of my nieces, when she was very ill last October."

The abbé left. Half an hour later my mother-in-law lost consciousness, and she died about an hour after my meeting with the abbé; but when I begged him to come to my house to arrange for the funeral, he replied that since my mother-in-law died unconfessed, she could not be buried in Holy Ground.

When I made a similar request of the German church, Abbé Houdet had already gone there and influenced the pastor, and he also persuaded the Irish church to refuse me.

July 9. So I turned to the Anglican bishop, and my mother-in-law was buried on the evening of July 9, in St. Peter's Episcopal Church, at the corner of Pine and South Third streets.

M. l'Abbé Mangin, who had a pension in Philadelphia, went the same day to inform the Irish priests that M. Marquès de l'Artibonite, who lodged with him, was very ill, whereupon one of the priests began to lecture him about the reluctance of the French to call a confessor, adding that burial would be refused to those who died under such circumstances.

"And where have you come by such rules?" Abbé Mangin asked.

"In the Canons," the priest replied.

"The Canons say that when a man refuses the Sacraments, burial will be denied him because he thus excommunicates himself. But you would refuse burial because a dying man doesn't call in a confessor, being too optimistic to admit the seriousness of his condition, or because his weeping family has similarly deceived itself, or feared to frighten him by suggesting confession! I also am a priest. I also know the Canons. If, when I held a position of authority among the clergy of France, a priest had acted as you have, I would have reprimanded him severely.

"And you, who are a priest and should be a model of piety, what assurance have you that you will not some day be mistaken concerning your own sickness? Can you guarantee that you will know enough to call in a confessor when you are dying?

"Do you know what your error has done? I assisted at the burial of the estimable woman whom you refused, and all around me people were blessing the Revolution that had freed France from the insupportable yoke of priests!

"You saw fit to refuse burial to the venerated mother of a family, a woman of the highest merit, who practiced all the duties of her religion in your own church, accompanied there by her children and all those over whom she had any authority! You have tried to besmirch an esteemed and highly regarded family that belongs to our faith and had called a confessor on another occasion. Your behavior has been most unfortunate and I greatly fear that you are the only ones who have failed in your duty, and who have created a scandal!"

We mourned for this venerated mother, who died in her sixtieth year. We mourned also this combination of all virtues, this model of mothers, this example of wifely love, this brave woman whom misfortune burdened but never changed. Ah! it matters not in what ground your mortal remains have had to be laid, for the Sovereign Being will receive your soul in the halls of his glory!

My grief for Mamma's loss was accompanied by extreme anxiety resulting from a letter from De la Haye, senior, who informed me that he had shipped my boxes, which had been at his establishment, by the ship *Columbus*. This letter of the twentieth of April reached me on July 4, and from then to July 16 there was no sign of the *Columbus*! So long as I had thought of my boxes as being in Le Havre, I was undisturbed; but the moment I learned that they had been shipped—and had been so long delayed—I was terrified.

At the Philadelphia Stock Exchange there is an intelligent young man who receives salary and expenses from the traders to go every day as far as Newcastle, or even farther down the Delaware, to get news of the ships which come in, or which ships may know of other vessels out of the ports of Europe or the colonies, and to find out the details relative to their voyages. Having acquired this information, he returns to Philadelphia and writes it in a register at the Exchange.

July 17. I had asked him to make careful inquiries about the *Columbus;* and on the seventeenth, as he passed by my home, he told me that the *Columbus* was in the river. At that my gloomy sadness gave way to intense joy.

July 21. At the Custom House I fulfilled the formalities which were necessary in order to have my boxes; and on July 23 I had the happiness of again setting eyes on these materials, which had cost me so much expense, worry, weariness and trouble. Of all the pleasant experiences of my life, this was one that I enjoyed the most.

I call to witness all authors, of whatever kind they may be.

As I have said, my friend De la Haye's letter of April 20 did not reach me until July 16, and that of May 12 on the fourth. By the letter of May 12, I learned of the death of Arthaud, my brother-in-law, the result of sickness in the hospital of Metz, the first of the same month of May. I also had two letters of the month of July, but these too were very late in arriving, the second not reaching me until November 2.

July 25. I was worn out and tormented by all these vexations, especially by everything Baron de la Roche had done. He had even come into my house to peer at, scrutinize, pry into and meddle with the private affairs of my household. His final offense was his refusal to deliver to me the printing press which had been purchased for me and had arrived, and I resolved to put an end to this unbearable state of affairs.

Before six o'clock in the morning I called upon the baron, who then lived in Dock Street not far from my house. There

I said to him: "Sir, I have suffered your caprices and your whims far longer than I thought myself capable of enduring them. But at last there must be an end to everything. I have come to announce to you in the most positive manner that I wish this to end and that above all I wish to have the printing press that has come from England for our company."

"Sir," M. de la Roche replied, "I am far from knowing French as you do, but I have sufficient command of it to understand you remarkably well. I am not a man to whom one may say 'Je veux,'[11] if the demand which is made is not to my liking."

Having thus spoken, he turned quickly to a large cupboard concealed in the paneling of the room on the Dock Street side of the house, and I saw him take from it something that I thought was a pistol.

I had followed the baron as far as the cupboard, and finding myself near the door of the apartment opening onto the main hallway, I turned the key which was in the lock, put my hand in my coat pocket, and took out one of the two pistols I had brought.

To the baron I said, "Come!" and with my other hand motioned to him to place himself in the other corner of the room, while I remained in the corner by the door.

Instead of doing so he came to me, and opened what he held in his hand. I then saw it to be a large black wooden case. From it he took a toothpick, and said to me:

"M. de St. Méry, I have tried to do you a favor, because I have felt for you a great affection which your family had increased, and yet you wish to ignore it?"

"And why do you ignore it yourself?" I asked him. "Why don't you carry out the promises that you so freely, so generously, so nobly made?"

[11]The words "Je veux" have already been used by Moreau to the baron. Although they can be translated "I wish," they are infinitely stronger than that, and would be regarded by any Frenchman as an insult.

"Your attitude toward me has changed," the baron said. "You have shown me defiance. You have slandered me and my character. You have even said I am not a baron."

"You have imagined all this," I said, "and this very fact has frightening and hidden possibilities. If it will add to your pleasure, I will even call you prince. But I do not wish that today's scene should be repeated! Let us end it! Give me the printing press and let us have peace on both sides."

"We have friends," the baron said, "who can be our judges, and see that both of us fulfill our obligations!"

"Good, I accept," I said, "but once more, let's have an end to it!" Then I left the baron.

Gauvain went once more in my behalf to speak to Baron de la Roche about the printing press.

August 8, 1795. I read from my manuscript to M. Le Chevalier, a former resident of that place, my description of the parish of the Trou of the northern part of San Domingo.

I did the same thing with my entire *Description of San Domingo* to residents of each place mentioned, and everyone assured me of three things which I found flattering. The first, that truth had always directed my pen; the second, that I had given them details and explanations of which they had hitherto been ignorant and which they now learned for the first time; the third, that I had been unusually careful to give praise where praise was due and that I had either avoided or at least toned down offensive matters that couldn't be passed over in silence.

August 10. Gauvain told me about a letter that the baron had written him on the sixth about our affairs. I sent him the reply which it called for:

Philadelphia, August 17, 1795.
On the tenth of this month, my dear Gauvain, I received M. Frank de la Roche's letter of the sixth, which you were kind enough to communicate to me. I read it attentively before yielding to the conviction that M. de la Roche has completely forgotten

all that took place between him and me since August 18, 1794. At that time he approached me and welcomed me in a manner that indicated anything but changeable feelings toward me. Weighing the proposals in this letter, anyone would think that they were addressed to somebody who, having entered into a contract which he found troublesome and burdensome, would consider himself lucky to be freed of it, no matter what the cost. In short, this is almost a decree from victor to vanquished, softened toward the end by a few polite bits of formal letter writing.

It would be, my dear Gauvain, long, tiresome and useless to set forth in detail at this moment the reasons why I cannot and will not accept such proposals, so I shall only base my refusal on the following sketchy remarks.

Our partnership agreement places me, in relation to M. de la Roche, in a situation which he cannot have considered. This partnership empowers me to market the stock of goods which is entrusted to me, without having to contract any debts except those whose payment would be assured by the success of the business itself. It was because of the advantages which this business offered me, and because of the certainty that it would yield me a profit at least sufficient to support me and my family, that I consented to devote myself exclusively to a project of this nature.

Instead of that, M. de la Roche now wishes to force me to be a bookseller, and wants me, who have been able to get along without creditors all my life, to go into debt. He forgets that I am entirely free, if political conditions continue to improve, to carry out the wish and the hope which never leave the heart of a true Frenchman, that is, to return to my country. He proposes that I buy, partly at interest and partly almost for cash, the books which he himself has chosen to clear out of his own library, and those which were bought secondhand in order to launch the business and make the firm name known to the public. He thinks that I should regard, as a suitable figure for a given object, the cost quoted by London merchants whose honesty is known to me, but who, being unfamiliar with transactions of this kind, have had to rely on agents who consider it proper to pocket the trade discount granted by the manufacturers from whom they buy.

M. de la Roche wants me to adopt, as profitable to myself, all the measures which he took on his own initiative, and over which I had no influence except to adapt them to a large-scale enterprise such as his display of wealth had given me to anticipate—measures which would be out of place in a small partnership, and unquestionably ruinous to a bookseller of small resources; and in addition he thinks that such a bookseller is able to bear the costs of running a business in which the outlay has been large. Finally, M. de la Roche acts and speaks as if I were not in possession of two letters which he wrote me on April 29 and June 11 last, and as if a lack of personal agreement between two associates, of whom one was never to be more than a sleeping partner, annulled a mutually obligatory contract.

I repeat, therefore, that I refuse absolutely to accept proposals which, in effect, cause me to renounce all my advantages, and first of all my peace of mind, for the pleasure of buying what was at first only consigned to me to be sold at a profit. Indeed, these proposals would put me in an entirely new class of purchaser; for according to the conditions which M. de la Roche lays down, I could not take another partner (if I had not already learned my lesson), and I would not be free to dispose of what had become my property, without being obliged to render him the homage of my preference.

But, since matters have come to the point where the termination of this partnership is presented to me as a real pleasure, whereas I am henceforth obliged to regard the partnership purely from the business point of view, I hereby offer my own proposals, without any intention of abandoning, unless these proposals are accepted, all the rights which I have, and which I reserve the freedom to insist upon in the opposite hypothesis.

1. M. de la Roche will withdraw in kind from the partnership all objects which he has put into it in kind, such as the books from his library, his maps and plans, his telescope, etc.

2. M. de la Roche will also withdraw in kind all the articles of stationery which he bought in London through Messrs. Hertel and Company, and which are no longer acceptable to me, since they are no longer destined, as they were in September 1794 (when he had me obtain a note from M. Allen, bookseller in New York), to constitute part of a large investment by him in the firm. The proposal that I should make a deal on this material with the house of Sonntag and Co. (of which M. de la Roche is half owner) is a mockery, especially when he spoke of it to me for the first time after the arrival of this stationery in Philadelphia.

3. M. de la Roche will likewise take back in kind all the books

which he had me buy from M. Allen of New York, which consequently are secondhand.

4. M. de la Roche will take these articles at the figure at which they have been carried for his account in his share of the partnership.

5. As to the articles which are covered in the first three clauses and which have been sold, and as to M. de la Roche's surplus investment in money, articles for my personal use, and other merchandise, I will pay him interest on these, counting from the day they were furnished to me, at a rate of six per cent, every six months, until December 31, 1797, the day set for the expiration of our partnership and the term at which I agree to pay the capital.

6. It will be optional for me to repay this capital to M. de la Roche sooner, in whole or in part, if I judge it convenient, without his being able to refuse a payment on my part as long as it is not less than one hundred dollars.

7. As for the type which arrived on the ship *Adrienne* July 4 last, and over the delivery of which M. de la Roche raised difficulties, I offer to buy it at the invoice price, after checking the type against the detailed order which I gave, payable February 15 and May 15, 1795, giving my notes for these two terms, leaving M. de la Roche free to make any arrangements he likes with M. Sonntag in case the price of this type belongs to the House of Sonntag and Co.—it being simpler for me not to come upon M. de la Roche twice in the same transaction. There, my dear Gauvain, is all that I can do and wish to do to dissolve my partnership, and my heart assures me that it is enough.

If you think it worth while that M. de la Roche should know what I think in this regard, be good enough to add this new burden to those which these disputes have already given you— disputes that you surely did not expect any more than I did, in view of the facts of which you were a witness in New York and Brooklyn last year.

However, as these disputes have already lasted all too long, and as they are a source of grief, the unhappiness of which, exceeding the power of man to bear, has afflicted me for the last six weeks, they are becoming wearisome, unbearable. If M. de la Roche does not accept my proposals; if, in rejecting them, he does not regard it as strict justice to consider the type as being included in our partnership; if he does not take into consideration that this type has been awaited for more than five months, for orders which are dependent on it and whose loss can only be charged to him; then be good enough to ask him to choose a referee immediately, to judge our differences according to the terms of Article 16 of our agreement, and tell him that I have chosen you as my referee.

He cannot refuse this last amicable means, which will doubtless recall both of us to what is our duty. I cannot believe that the courts or the public should ever be concerned with this pitiable affair. But if, against my wish, my inclination, my hope, it were otherwise, I hope to make the affair so clear that the reproach of frivolity, or at least of inconstancy, which is sometimes leveled at the French, will not fall upon me. I shall expose my conduct with such well-substantiated detail that I can have no doubt of a success which I still find a personal satisfaction in not desiring. If M. de la Roche is still willing to take the word of one who, whatever he may say, is older than he in experience as in age, he will believe, for his tranquillity and for mine, for his interest and for mine, for the interest of his other business, and even for public decency, to which we always have a debt, that the best procedure is to put into the partnership all that he has ordered for it, all he has promised it, all that his friends and mine have heard him repeat that he intended for it, and to keep going a business which according to his own words was to be chiefly of the nature of a benefaction, the first characteristic of which is that it be not a subject of reproach.

You know, my dear Gauvain, my unfailing friendship for you.

August 21. The next day Gauvain delivered my letter to the baron, who replied to him on the twenty-first.

Fairy Hill, August 21, 1795

Monsieur,

Since this bad weather and our fine bad roads are depriving me of the pleasure of going to see you today, I write and beg you to be so good as to communicate, without delay, the contents of my letter to M. Moreau de St. Méry; I have read with care, which the subject demanded, the letter which he has written me and which you have had the kindness to deliver to me. I don't want to discuss this very long letter—about which, however, I could say a great many things—and I will confine myself simply to saying

positively that I accept the proposals that M. de St. Méry has made
to me through you, namely:

1. I consider our partnership dissolved the moment the contents of this letter are known to him.

2. I agree to take back in kind all the different articles which I
furnished to him from my library, and which he has not sold and

3. All those which he still has from the shipment of M. Allen
of New York,

4. As well as everything still remaining in his shop from the
shipment made by M. Hertel of London on the *Molly.*

5. The sale of these various articles must cease immediately;
and after an exact list has been made of them, M. de St. Méry will
deliver them to me.

6. I agree to take M. Moreau de St. Méry's notes for the amount
of the different sums which I have furnished him and the amount
of the proceeds from the different sales which he has made, M. de
St. Méry binding himself to pay me interest every six months at
the rate of six per cent until these sums have been repaid in full.
Payment cannot be deferred beyond the dates set in his letter.

7. I shall always accept whatever sum he may wish and find
convenient to pay me in advance.

As for the press from London which arrived on the *Adrienne,*
I will sell it to M. Moreau de St. Méry as it stands for what it cost
me, although I should be able to sell it for cash and at a good advance; so I can only do it for sixty- or ninety-day notes that I
can have discounted. M. de St. Méry would give me pleasure if—
as he must be able to do—he would give me a co-maker on his
note for the balance he owes me. Then I could more easily use it
advantageously if a profitable occasion arose. I deeply regret,
Monsieur, that you should have been put to so much trouble over
a quarrel for which I was not primarily responsible. With my most
sincere thanks and high regard I have the honor of being, Monsieur, your

(Signed) FRANK DE LA ROCHE

August 22. I received also from New York a letter of the
twentieth from Talleyrand, a part of which also referred to
my association with La Roche:

New York, August 20, 1795

Your letters are distributed, *mon cher Maître;* the packages
have gone to M. de Liancourt; I have an Indian bow and some

arrows which M. de Liancourt sends to your child and which will be taken to him at the first opportunity that I shall find. Your partner is now insufferable; but does your agreement with him prevent you from going to law? He once told Cazenove about his troubles; and Cazenove said to him: "Suggest dissolving the partnership on condition that Moreau pays the regular rate of interest on all funds invested by you for as long a time as may be agreed."

He seemed to find this proposition agreeable and it seems to me to be equally good for you. It would leave you the wherewithal with which to conduct your business, and there would be no further occasion for dealing with the said baron.

If this proposition were renewed by a third person, I am convinced it would end favorably. You see by this counsel I do not see the possibility of letting you have the thousand dollars. I have spoken about it with M. Goynard who does not think so any more than I. Cazenove, instead of lending or investing money, is gathering together all that he has in order to leave next May. Here the best houses borrow money at two and a half to three per cent a month.

I am writing at Demeunier's desire to ask you to send him the laws of Congress at the first opportunity, and he wants you to write him whether you have sold M. Divernois's pamphlets. He puts his commissions in my letter because he finds postage ruinous. L'Hercule, as you have read in the papers, contradicts positively the news of a naval battle published in the Philadelphia papers. Here we know nothing about France. All our news comes from your house. The warm weather is beginning again and one is roasting to death. *Adieu, mon cher Maître.* Always yours.

Beaumetz will not come for another three weeks or a month.

Because of this the agreement to dissolve the partnership was drawn up, corrected and signed.

August 26. I had another letter from Talleyrand written from New York the twenty-sixth.

New York, August 26, 1795

This morning, *cher Maître,* I have given to a Frenchman named Dupuis a letter of introduction to you. He comes from Paris and brings with him the new constitution. It is the only copy in America; you can make money by printing it.

As a translator you have at your hand M. Nugent, whose address at the Comedy Theater you know. Above all you ought to publish Boissy's speech,[12] which is sensible and most excellently written. You will find two hundred items worthy of note in the constitution, and the great word "Amnesty" pronounced in the speech.

Adieu. Always yours,

I have turned over to M. Law a bow that Liancourt is sending to your child. M. Law left this morning and will lodge in Mulberry Street, at the corner of North Fourth. Please inquire of M. Gauvain at Vaughan's house for my guns, hats and money.

At the very moment I was congratulating myself at having had no relations with M. the German Baron Frank de la Roche since August 26, he, through M. de Combatz, my clerk, took back all his possessions. As a crowning act he transferred his favor from me to Combatz and opened up a bookstore in partnership with him in Philadelphia.

I shall speak again about this gentleman.

September 4, 1795. I dined with General Collot, who had returned from Guadeloupe.

September 9. Talleyrand's name was removed from the list of *émigrés*.

I dismissed Combatz from my service—regretfully, because of his knowledge of the details of my business, which long experience had given him to a superior degree. But his plans were too ambitious and I couldn't tolerate them. He had long counseled me to put up with Baron de la Roche's behavior; and I too strongly suspected him of stirring up the baron's fractious spirit for his own ends, to want to keep with me the inheritor of his confidence. I was soon confirmed in this belief, and facts proved me right.

September 11. I took as head workman in my printing shop La Grange, a Parisian who had been a printer in Paris and gone from there to Cap François to follow his trade. The fire

[12]Talleyrand is referring probably to Boissy d'Anglas's eloquent discourse of March 11, 1795, entitled, *Motion d'ordre contre les Terroristes et les Royalistes faite a la Convention Nationale le 21 ventôse an III* and ordered printed by the Convention.

and the disasters brought him to Philadelphia. I also took
Despioux, a young compositor from Bordeaux, driven from
Cap François for the same reasons.

Another letter from Talleyrand:

New York, September 12, 1795

I give you a great deal of trouble, *mon cher Maître*, with all my
little commissions. However, I would not make a pretense of
thanking you if you had read the letter of Baron de Bruziene,
which you sent me. It would have paid you for all your pains, considering that he asks me to get for him "a jawb in bizness becuz
he's good in evvy kinda aggiculchuh," and further he assures me
that he speaks and writes English as well as he does French. Send
my guns by water, but by a captain who is known so that they
won't be harmed, and so no one will spend too much time squat-
ting on my hats. Get a receipt from the captain and send everything to me at M. Seton's address. M. Sonntag will certainly know
all the captains who make this sort of voyage. Around November
I shall turn my steps toward Front Street. Beaumetz returns from
his journey tomorrow or the day after. You are fortunate indeed
that your partnership has been dissolved, because the new boarder
whom I've sent you would have very much upset the baron, who
would have undoubtedly asked you to pay for the amount of milk
he drinks. *Adieu, mon cher Maître.* Always yours.

M. Law through haste has left at his house the bow for your
son which, nevertheless, is a poor effort (I speak of the bow).

I sent for it last night, and as soon as Governor Mifflin will
allow the quarantine to be lifted from our goods and our residences, you will receive it.

Demeunier has left for Connecticut and Boston. Thanks for
the Collet. Not a word of news.

September 23. De la Haye brought me the stone from the
Bastille which Galloy gave me. From that moment many
Americans came to see it, up to the time when I left for
France.

September 29. Demeunier writes me from New York:

My friend, we are all being invited to return to France. My
own case comes under the decree which permits those to return
who left after May 30, 1793. My mind is made up, and since one

must bury one's self again, I prefer, whatever may happen, to do so in the Department of the Jura rather than anywhere else.

I am told there is a cartel ship in Philadelphia.

Talleyrand and Beaumetz are in Boston. I met them in New York because I have just come from the Eastern States.

I am told Lafayette's son is here. Last night I hunted for La Colombe, but I didn't find him.

September 30. The following day another letter from Demeunier from the same place, again telling me about the cartel ship. He says the yellow fever is diminishing:

Your establishment will succeed. As for you, you have with you your entire family, and you would do well to keep on here and even relinquish Europe if you can find it in your heart to do so. My position is different. A country which I do not care for in any way cannot offer me, and never will, any suitable employment. What do dangers matter to me? I shall devote myself anew to the good Cause if it is necessary. I will go back in spite of Jove and all his thunders. If all is forever lost, I will bury myself in a corner. I only left in November, 1793, and after Dumas in the examination of the Queen had brutally marked me out as a victim and asked if I had not declared myself for the King in June, 1789. That was the fifth occasion on which the tigers of the revolutionary tribunal had called me by all those lovely epithets with which you are familiar, and by that time everyone knew that I couldn't possibly save my head if I remained in France.

And it may be insane, but I am curious to see what they will have to say to me. The storms of the future, the return of barbarity; these I have foreseen, and they don't stop me.

Lafayette's son is really here with his teacher. They came to see me yesterday. They are going to take a turn around the country while waiting for the chiefs to decree what line they must take. Meanwhile if anyone should mention them to us, we must play the idiot boy.

You know that our friends are in Boston. Talleyrand won't return until the fifteenth of next month. I see with regret that his brother's regiment is among those that landed at Quiberon, and I believe that the colonel is captured. [No, he was still living in 1815.]

La Colombe came to tell me that I have done well to inform you about the young man.

Governor J. has received the young man coldly. Hamilton, who conducted our young friend, went out of his way to teach the old man his manners.

October 1, 1795. By the nineteenth of September, 1793, Gatereau of San Domingo had begun the publication in Philadelphia of a newspaper called *The Courier of France and Her Colonies,* issued on a single quarto-sized sheet every Tuesday, Thursday and Saturday.[13]

This newspaper was published until March 17, 1794, when it stopped because of lack of subscribers. It started again in 1795 with the title of *Courier of France and the Colonies.* I published an advertisement of it on October 1, and the first number appeared on the fifteenth, also in four pages, but in quarto. I printed it on my press until March 14, 1796, when Gatereau gave it up.

October 11. Volney arrived.

October 12. Demeunier gave me to understand that Talleyrand has returned from Boston, but because of fear of the yellow fever is remaining at Cazenove's house in Brooklyn.

And then on the fourteenth I heard from Talleyrand:

You think rightly, my friend, that it would give me extreme pleasure to embrace Volney, and that I would have many things to tell him, and to ask him about. Is he coming with the idea of living here? Give him my love and ask him whether he still has some affection for me.

---

[13]Persistent search has proved fruitless to find a file of this most interesting paper during the first period of its existence. The library of the Boston Athenaeum, however, contains a complete file of the second and last period, extending from October 15, 1795, to March 14, 1796. During this period the paper appeared daily, except Sunday, and was published in French at the press of Moreau de St. Méry. Gatereau, its editor, was an avowed aristocrat and, according to his own confession, had "a personal interest in the restoration of the monarchy." The one hundred and twenty-nine numbers of 1795–1796 reflect in a most interesting way the important events in France and in the French West Indies and reveal many phases of the life of the large band of French *émigrés* at Philadelphia.

November 1, 1795. Demeunier arrived and had dinner with us.

November 2. We went together to see Volney. I began printing my *Description of the Spanish Part of San Domingo.*

November 3. I received a letter from Talleyrand which gave me great pleasure. Here it is. . . .

New York, November 2, 1795

I thank you, *mon cher Maître,* for the newspaper which you sent me and from which I learn I am no longer an *émigré.* By the last boats I have received many letters from France, the last dated from Paris on August 18. Here is what sticks in my mind after reading them carefully. Public opinion is wiser than the government and seems to dominate it for good, just as it so often forced us to evil. Liberty exists, and there is peace for reasonable men, but I don't yet see that there is any guarantee that this condition will continue. However, the influence of the land-owners seems to increase each day, and with their help we ought to be able to struggle along for some time. The Chouans,[14] since the peace with Spain,[15] don't bother anyone, and everyone is confident that they will be crushed. I shall doubtless visit you at the end of the month and shall spend several months with you. Our excellent friend Demeunier is leaving. I hope he will arrive at a good time that will let him settle himself and look about without being disturbed. After fifteen days on French soil he ought to know pretty well how he stands, and the first letters we get from him will be an excellent guide for all of us—Beaumetz has not returned—Adieu. Your friend for life.

November 11. M. de Liancourt returned from his journey to Maine.

November 12. The following day Demeunier left for Newcastle, whence he started for Le Havre on the fourteenth, writing me as follows:

You have heaped attentions and friendship upon me during my stay in Philadelphia, and I have used and abused your kind-

[14]Name given to the Breton rebels. The *émigrés* had planned, in the so-called Quiberon expedition, an alliance with them in the hopes of conquering Brittany. This expedition had been defeated by Hoche on July 20 preceding.

[15]The treaty with Spain had been signed on July 22.

ness without discretion. Mme. Moreau has been perfection in the welcome she was so kind as to extend to me, and I beg her to accept my most affectionate gratitude.

Adieu, my friend, for the last time. I most ardently hope that you will all have good fortune, and if ever I should be able to contribute toward it, it would give me the greatest pleasure. I would curse Fate, if it should deprive me of the privilege of some day embracing you in France.

General Ricard pays you a thousand compliments with all the cordiality which you have already observed in him.

November 15. I had another severe attack of nerves, like those to which I have been subject since before my fourteenth year.

November 28. I worked industriously on the map of San Domingo, which I wanted at that time.

November 30. I gave a dinner for M. de Liancourt.

It was in this same month that Talleyrand wrote to the Minister of Foreign Affairs in the following terms about the decree of the preceding third of September, which had released him from the status of *émigré*.

November, 1795

Citizen Minister,

After three years of exile, of libels and persecutions of every kind, I have finally been freed of charges which their authors themselves have never seriously believed. My conscience is clear, so that I can savor to the full all the sweetness of this act of justice. My prayers have ever been for France, for her liberty, for her happiness. Only in the accounts of her victories, only because of my association with the glory of her independence, have I been able to find patience in exile, courage in adversity. Deprived of the right to serve liberty, at least I was suffering for such a worthy cause.

When navigation is resumed in the spring I shall return to the bosom of a country made dearer to me by my absence and with new obligations imposed upon me by her honorable decisions. I place in your hands, Citizen Minister, this expression of my respect, my gratitude and my fidelity, and I ask you to transmit it to the proper authorities of the Republic.

December 5, 1795. Talleyrand and Beaumetz reached Philadelphia from New York.

Congress opened, and Washington spoke before it the next day.

D'Orléans escaped from the prisons of Marseille. Montpensier, in attempting to follow his example, broke his leg.

December 25. Demeunier gave me news of his arrival at Le Havre. In the evening Talleyrand received a long letter from him, which said, among other things, that an unsigned letter from me had been read by the municipal government of Le Havre.

I received the same news from General Ricard, who returned to France with Demeunier.

In my letter written in Philadelphia and received at Le Havre I had told De la Haye, among other details, that I was employing all my ingenuity [*m'ingéniais*] to find means of existence for myself and my family.

This word *m'ingénier* led the municipality to think that I had become an engineer [*ingénieur*], doubtless against the interests of France. Obsessed by this idea, they had sent for my friend and questioned him in a thousand ways. Finally satisfied by the sincerity of his replies, they showed him my letter. When he explained the word *ingénier,* they returned the letter to him, but recommended that he advise me against using equivocal expressions. What vast knowledge one finds in municipal governments!

December 31. I ended the year by dining at Sonntag's house with M. de Liancourt, Talleyrand and Beaumetz. It was at this time that Dr. Morse sent the Rev. Dr. Read to me to ask for several notes which I had promised to write for the colonial parts of his geography. I fulfilled my promises.

January 9, 1796. Gatereau was publishing a gazette in Philadelphia which I was printing. In No. 8 of January 9 I put in an article of my own about death by guillotine.

This was in answer to the views of M. Sue, who had said

in print that the guillotine was an atrocious form of death. He based his reasoning on what happened at the execution of Charlotte Corday, celebrated because she assassinated Marat, when the executioner, by slapping her after she had been guillotined, supposedly made her cheeks red—something that couldn't happen to the cheeks of a corpse. This had given rise to a widespread belief that Charlotte Corday was not dead, even though her head had been separated from her body. . . . Therefore . . . Therefore . . . I held that the case cited by Sue was caused by response to stimulation, a purely mechanical effect. In support of my theory I instanced similar contractions in frogs and reptiles; the contraction of a human muscle that had been removed from the body to which it belonged. I further reproached M. Sue for suggesting that hanging should replace the guillotine. I do not pretend that my article showed any great knowledge of either anatomy or physiology, but I expressed my opinion in support of a mild philosophy, and argued against the art of inventing physical pain which is supposed to survive us, and to which groundless arguments, which reason and the facts reject, attribute existence.

January 15. M. de Liancourt and M. de Grandprey were elected members of the Philosophical Society of Philadelphia, and I had the pleasure of voting for them.

January 19. Talleyrand wrote me:

I am informed that today is the nineteenth, and consequently I must this day remit to the bank the payment due tomorrow, the twentieth. What do you know about a ship that has made the passage from Bristol in fifty-six days? Read what the English papers have to say about Mme. de Staël. Is it true that she has fled? If so, there would be reason to draw some sad conclusions. Good night.

January 27. Beaumetz left us to get married. We tried to advise him against this union with a widow who has many children and no fortune, but he was in no mood to listen to our arguments. He got married, and for his sake we agreed that his future wife should have our interest and affection.

This month I finished printing Cobbett's two-volume English translation of my *Description of the Spanish Part of San Domingo*, and brought it out.

This work brought me into close relations with Cobbett, who is a man of wit and talent. I have never known any Englishman to be so violently attached to his native country as is Cobbett. He is a genuine fanatic; and fanaticism, being a passion, is always wrong-headed. He sees nothing comparable to the English. He despises the Irish beyond words, and completely scorns Americans.

He has published several books on the United States. He was a bookseller here, and his views, which he has altered considerably since he returned to London, show a wholly different Cobbett[16] from the one who was known in America.

February 6, 1796. General Wayne, returning from his war against the Indians, led a great parade in Philadelphia.

---

[16]Cobbett came to the United States in September, 1792, and taught English for a time to French *émigrés* in Wilmington, Delaware, among them Talleyrand. According to Cobbett, Talleyrand spoke English, and only hired him to be free from Cobbett's attacks. Cobbett made his first literary sensation by his *Observations on the Emigration of a Martyr to the Cause of Liberty,* a biting reply to Dr. Priestley's complaints of treatment received in England. This pamphlet was followed by papers signed "Peter Porcupine"—*Prospect from the Congress Gallery,* the *Political Censor* and the *Porcupine's Gazette.* In the spring of 1796 he quarreled with his publisher and went into business in Philadelphia as bookseller and publisher of his own works. On the day of opening, he filled his windows with prints of the most violent French Revolutionists alongside those of the founders of the American Republic, George III, the British ministers, and others obnoxious to the people. He persistently eulogized Great Britain, scoffed at American institutions and cudgeled the French party. He was abused and threatened, and in August, 1797, the Spanish Ambassador prosecuted him for attacking Spain. Then he was sued for libeling American statesmen; and he was prosecuted a third time for saying that Dr. Benjamin Rush, an advocate of blood-letting, killed nearly all his patients. On this charge he was fined five thousand dollars. After this last misfortune he edited a newspaper called the *Rushlight;* but in June, 1800, he sailed for England, where he was held to be a champion of order and monarchy.

There were also big fireworks in celebration of peace between France, Holland, Spain, Prussia and Sweden.

February 8. I went delightedly to see Bolman, who had tried to help Lafayette escape from prison.

February 15. Talleyrand wrote me this note:

I'm going to send you a piece for tomorrow's issue of your paper (that of Gatereau, which I was printing)—two pages which are pretty piquant. Save a place for them. It's badly written, because your pens aren't sharp.

Good day—what's new?

Send me one of your young men in an hour to get my scrawl.

February 17. I dined at Talleyrand's with M. and Mme. de Beaumetz.

February 19. Dr. Priestley came to the meeting of the Philosophical Society.

February 25. I put on sale my first volume of the *Description of the Spanish Part of San Domingo*. In this description (Tome 2, page 9), I have expressed a truly ardent vow from my heart:

The most valuable thing we could have—if the Spanish character permitted it, which it doesn't—is the archives of the Council of the Indies, which should contain the most accurate and authentic proofs of everything that has happened in the Spanish possessions in America since the discovery of this part of the world. It is there that history's most useful secrets are hidden, and in all likelihood there has never been a repository that was at the same time so valuable and so useless.

I know that this Council of the Indies has an historian who is even obliged to prove each year that his title is not an empty one, but who is doubtless convinced of the small fruit which is likely to result from his labor, and content to show no enterprise in a task that he knows to be little desired or that he knows must be as forgotten as everything else connected with the Spanish government. And how can history be written under the prying scrutiny of the very people whose administration would be instantly exposed? How can a person be a truthful narrator of facts, when those facts would perhaps accuse or condemn his censors? History must have, as its companions, Truth and Liberty;

and unless it has this sublime escort, it is nothing but deception or base adulation.

The archives of the Council are in charge of one of the counselors, and they contain what is brought there successively by two secretaries, both of whom, in order that the labor may be equalized, handle the documents dealing with one half of the different sections of America.

In Spain, independent of the Council of the Indies, there is a Minister for the Indies who, although in the same department as the Council, is subordinate to it. In a way he seems to be merely a commissioner, unless the King, desiring to consult his six ministers, summons them in council.

February 28. I went to pay my respects to M. Adams, who had become Vice-President of the United States of America.

March 13, 1796. Talleyrand and I went together to the house of the Minister of France, Adet.

March 24. M. de Liancourt left Philadelphia to visit Charleston. Being extremely desirous of publishing also my *Description of the French Part of San Domingo,* I suggested to M. Adet that he help me, but he was unable to do so.

April 10, 1796. Fire broke out at the end of Spruce Street. My son and I went there at half past twelve at night.

April 14. I received a proof of my map of San Domingo by Valence.

April 17. I was summoned before the Circuit Court of the United States in the district of Pennsylvania to testify in the affair of Mme. Goux and M. Esprit Gautier. On the nineteenth I was questioned concerning colonial regulations, and particularly concerning the legal rate of interest in San Domingo, where the affair took place.

April 20. I went to see Mme. Beaumetz. The same day I had the pleasure of embracing Lafayette's son, as I did again on the twenty-ninth.

April 24. Fire broke out between Walnut and Chestnut streets.

May 8, 1796. I saw the Chinese brought by M. Van Braam.

May 9. Talleyrand returned from Washington, the federal city, which he had been to visit.

May 17. At Talleyrand's recommendation I paid a call on M. Van Braam, a Dutchman coming from Canton in China. I agreed with M. Van Braam to edit his account of his voyage as Dutch Ambassador to Canton and Pekin, and to print and publish it.

May 27. It was with the greatest regret that I saw Beaumetz embark for Calcutta on the ship *Asia*. I foresaw all that could result from this voyage, offspring of necessity, and forced upon him by his unfortunate situation.

June 9, 1796. Cazenove left for New York.

June 10. I took Volney to M. Van Braam's house to see the many curious objects he had brought from China.

June 11. I dined at Richardet's house with Talleyrand, and we worked all night.

June 12. The next day Talleyrand dined with us, and left our home on the thirteenth, bound for Hamburg on the brig *Den Née Prove*.

June 13. Behold me, then, robbed of one of my greatest pleasures. In no way can I possibly give a true picture of the nature of my relationship with Talleyrand. After I had lost my dear De Varenne, he was the friend who most nearly replaced him in my affections. Every day that he was in Philadelphia, after we had been reunited, from October, 1795, up to the present time, he came to my private office at eight o'clock in the evening. There alone and without interruption (except when Beaumetz, Talon, Blaçon, Noailles, Volney, Payen de Boisneuf, Demeunier, Boislandry, were with us all together or separately) we opened our hearts to one another, we poured out our feelings; and each of us knew the other's most intimate thoughts.

In these delightful confidences we spent all the time until someone came to tell us supper was being served.

Talleyrand took no supper, while I had a little rice with milk cooked in the oven of the stove in my bookshop.

But when we were with my family, Blaçon, Beaumetz, La Colombe often joined us at supper most cheerfully. I had some excellent Madeira which Talleyrand found extremely pleasing and which he drank at supper. Gaiety reigned constantly at our reunions, where we often amused ourselves by playing jokes, particularly when Blaçon jestingly "Monseigneured" Talleyrand,[17] who revenged himself by cuffing him.

When the hour for leaving finally arrived, my wife would have to urge the boisterous company to go home to bed.

How many times Talleyrand, having got as far as the little yard at the foot of my stairs, would steal back up them to prolong the party! He would finally yield when my wife said to him: "Tomorrow you will play the sluggard in your bed until noon; but promptly at seven o'clock in the morning your friend must get up and open his shop."

At other times, in the bookshop, Talleyrand, Beaumetz, Blaçon and M. de Liancourt continued their uproar even until daybreak, regardless of my observation that they were driving away my customers, since Americans never came into a shop where they heard a disturbance. They stopped only when they were quite tired out, as was often the case when M. de Liancourt and my son wrestled with each other like two schoolboys.

On every night we were together, without a single exception, Talleyrand and I discussed the condition of France in the past, her present lot, and finally what would happen to her in the future.

The last part of the picture always made us think of Louisiana, and we found many reasons to make us wish to

---

[17]Talleyrand had studied for the priesthood, and had become Bishop—Monseigneur—of Autun on March 15, 1789. He was, however, anticlerical, favored the confiscation of church lands by the nation, and openly advocated that the state, not the Pope, should have authority over the church. He resigned the See of Autun in January, 1791, and in March was officially un-Monseigneured when the Pope placed him under the ban of the church.

have a home there for ourselves. Then we would determine to devote all our thoughts and energies in this direction, and Talleyrand would decide that we would wind up by becoming its governors.

Agreed on this project, agreed too that the day must come when we would never be separated, Talleyrand and I ended each one of our talks, when we were called to supper, by clasping hands and vowing that we would be as one throughout the remainder of our lives—in our affections, our interests, our successes of every kind, even in that of our fortunes.

As can be imagined, the intimacy of our association was such that everything which interested one of us was of interest to the other.

For example, at the beginning of 1796, when I was printing, from my colonial collection, the article *Danse,* which I had written and which my son, whom I had taught to be an excellent compositor, had set up in type, Talleyrand asked to be allowed to correct the proofs of this piece, which he called a lovely picture by Albane.

At all times and in every respect our affectionate agreement was unvarying. In short, never did the vulgar expression "joined like two fingers of a hand" apply more perfectly to anything than to my association with Talleyrand.[18]

[18]Of this "strange, redoubtable and important personage," Charles Maurice de Talleyrand-Périgord, Victor Hugo wrote: "He was of noble descent, like Machiavelli, a priest like Gondi, unfrocked like Fouché, witty like Voltaire, and lame like the devil. It might be averred that everything in him was lame like himself,—the nobility which he had placed at the service of the Republic, the priesthood which he had dragged through the parade-ground, then cast into the gutter, the marriage which he had broken off through a score of exposures and a voluntary separation, the understanding which he disgraced by acts of baseness.

"This man, nevertheless, had grandeur; the splendours of the two *régimes* were united in him: he was Prince de Vaux in the Kingdom of France, and a Prince of the French Empire. During thirty years, from the interior of his palace, from the interior of his thoughts, he had almost controlled Europe. He had permitted himself to be on terms of

He assured me at the time of his departure for Hamburg of his eager desire to take my son beneath his wing, in order that he might care for this affectionate and interesting child. My wife, touched though she was, replied to Talleyrand that the condition of France was so uncertain that she couldn't allow him to burden himself at this time with our son; that circumstances might force him to make port in San Domingo, or even come in contact with a ship from that island, in which case my son's very name might be fatal to him.

But in confidence my wife told me that she feared Talleyrand's intentions for our son, since he would cultivate tastes which we would be unable to gratify, and which might turn him against us.

I postponed a decision on Talleyrand's suggestion, to the great sorrow of Talleyrand. On his ship I placed one hundred copies of my *Description of the Spanish Part of San Domingo* and two hundred copies of my description of the Philadelphia prisons, which Talleyrand hoped to sell for me in Hamburg.

I accompanied Talleyrand to the boat, and my son and I stayed on the shore, watching, until his ship was no longer visible.

June 16. I received a letter from Talleyrand:

Newcastle, June 15, 1796, 9 A.M.
We are sailing at once, my dear friend. The unknown passenger proved to be M. Vidal. Another young man with a large cockade joined us on the way; but no one knows his name. He has arranged with the captain to go to Hamburg. All is well with us. The wind is fair.

---

familiarity with the Revolution, and had smiled upon it,—ironically, it is true, but the Revolution had not perceived this. He had come in contact with, known, observed, penetrated, influenced, set in motion, fathomed, bantered, inspired all the men of his time, all the ideas of his time; and there had been moments in his life, when, holding in his hand the four or five great threads which moved the civilized universe, he had for his puppet Napoleon I, Emperor of the French, King of Italy, Protector of the Confederation of the Rhine, Mediator of the Swiss Confederation. That is the game which was played by this man."

Adieu, my friend, a thousand greetings to all of you. I will write you at sea and again from Hamburg. My respects to all about you. I embrace your child and you with all my heart. Our boat is a bad sailer.

June 27. I attended the funeral of the celebrated Dr. Rittenhouse, American astronomer, whose death was universally and justifiably regretted. He was buried in the ground floor of the observatory which he had built in his own house. How philosophically significant, this union of his perishable ashes with a building dedicated to the observation of the more sublime wonders of nature! What a contrast between man's nothingness and his genius!

June 30. I received a letter from Talleyrand:

> 10:30 A.M. Cape Henry
> Saturday, June 18, 1796
>
> We are here at sea, my dear friend. The wind is light but fair. For several days there has been no sight of a privateer. Adieu. In forty-five days I will write you from the Elbe. Regards, remembrances, affection for all about you.
>
> Everyone aboard is well. Our unknowns are M. Vidal and M. Bérard. You were acquainted with the first one; and the second is a nephew of Bérard, of the Company of the Indies. Our captain is a good sort of man, but he sleeps fifteen hours without waking. Love to Blaçon and to La Colombe.

July 3, 1796. I went with Cazenove to see M. Van Braam at his country house near Bristol. He has named it the Chinese Retreat. Cazenove left me there, and I spent the night. The next day M. Van Braam took me to Bristol to a dinner (federal frolic) to celebrate the anniversary of American independence.

July 15. I had news of Rochambeau. I put the details here:

> Cap François, July 15, 1796
>
> It is true, Citizen, that I didn't write you by Citizen Bournouvelle, but I have been overburdened with business. But it is also true that I sent you a short line by a ship which left this port several days later, and by now you should have received another letter from me from Port de Paix.

I have read with pleasure and interest your work on the Spanish Part, and I promise to let you have any observations of my own which might interest you, once I have learned more about this part of the colony than I know at present.

You depict the dance of the creoles in such pleasing colors that I couldn't resist making a close examination of the different dances which you describe so well. Until now I had never had time to see them during my stormy mission in this part of the world.

Ah, well, as a result of my observations, I wound up in a sort of drunkenness which it was easy to allay. The dance is certainly lively in the tropics!

I have sent word to Roume that you were here.

How right you are in saying that the time is still pregnant with great events, particularly here! You are wise in your decision to philosophize for some time to come at the corner of Walnut Street, and I promise faithfully to send you word if I think a sojourn on this land could be pleasing to you. But no, remain where you are! We'll hope that the troubles of this colony are almost over, but nobody can possibly say for certain.

Do you wish to know in two words how things stand? Here it is: The Men of Color[19] wish to seize the property of the proprietors, and are giving bad advice to the Africans, who are becoming openly defiant. The Africans haven't yet dared to think about wholesale freedom, but they prefer soldiering to farming. The small group of whites not in the army is irritated and humiliated. The colony is still divided among head-men like Rigaud, Beauvais, Villatte, who administer their sections for personal gain, and among those like Toussaint and Laveaux, who work for the Republic. Everything has taken on a military aspect; those who make sugar do so with sabres at their sides and guns on their shoulders.

Do you wish to know where we are going, or rather where we will be going? I know nothing about that, but what I am sure of is that I am in a hellhole!

My affection for you is what you have long known it to be.

(Signed) Dr. ROCHAMBEAU

Ricard, who has already written to me here, asked for news of you.

---

[19]I.e., Negroes with white blood in their veins. Pure-blooded Negroes were called Africans. There was even more enmity between Negroes and Men of Color in San Domingo than between blacks and whites.

July 19. M. de Liancourt returned from his tour of the southern parts of the United States.

August 11, 1796. Dear Grimperel died of a black sickness, and it was my sad duty to go to his funeral the next day.

August 27. Cazenove wrote me from New York:

The friendly little souvenir which you sent me by the blond Blaçon has given me great pleasure, *mon cher Maître,* and I was also pleased to learn that you are all very well, and that you are pleased with the Mandarin [Van Braam] and that, as Lea said, he is "going goot mit China." My health isn't at all what it ought to be. In spite of being settled in an airy apartment overlooking the North River, my gout keeps me perpetually in bed or in an armchair. The pain isn't great, but the fever at night is bad. Since the fever burns up the gout, we have to leave it alone.

I still have no news of M. Liancourt, who is always running away from what rides behind all of us. This business of running around through countless tiresome towns strikes me as a miserable remedy against boredom. But *de gustibus,* etc., and see if you can get me from Paris the fourth volume of Dussault's journal of surgery revised by Bichat, and published by Neufville in the third year of the indivisible and *divided* Republic, both in one volume and in parts. The fourth volume has appeared and is sold separately. This contains a lot of useful things for persons who make those who are taking a walk with them stand on street corners waiting for them.

Nothing new. M. Adet is going to Albany, accompanied by Sweitzer, the torch, and by Flamant, who goes along, I think, only as a torchbearer. My son has been in Paris from the fifteenth to the thirtieth of May, and writes me that everything there is very gay. Twenty-eight shows a day crammed after four o'clock. The Palais Royal looks just as it did in 1786. Restaurants, concerts, balls, hackney coaches, livery coaches, hotels full, gaming houses —nothing has changed; and he went and came by post through Basle just as he used to do before the Assembly of the Notables.[20]

Adieu. My respects to your ladies. Does Hatker improve?

A. CAZENOVE

[20]A French Revolutionary word. Notables were citizens chosen by a commune to superintend proceedings in criminal cases.

September 22. Urbain Domergue[21] sent new assurances of friendship:

Louvre, September 22, 1796

The chimes of La Samaritaine wake me, ushering in the anniversary fête of our Republic with its foot races, horse races, Roman chariot races, songs of victory, and magnificent displays of fireworks. I rise, and to start the year properly I write to my friend.

Anacréon has delivered to me the two copies of *Spanish San Domingo,* and the charming letter which accompanied them. How touched I am by the sentiments with which you have welcomed my few lines, feeble interpreters of the sentiments which I have promised you for life! As for your work, I shall present it in five days at a General Assembly of the Institute, the first to be held since the package arrived.

I have already spoken to several of my colleagues about your intention to return to France, and about what an excellent acquisition you would be to the Institute. There are two places vacant in the history section, that of Reynal, whom death has taken from us, and that of Gaillard, who has become a nonresident member. As soon as the former Bishop of Autun returns, we will put our heads together as to how we can serve you most effectively. He belongs to the class of which the history section is part, and I have many close friends in that class, such as Garat, Guiguéné, Lebreton, Cabanis, Bernardin de St. Pierre, Mercier, Rigeau, Pastoret, Dupont de Nemours, Roederer, Levesque, Buache, Meutelle, etc. The section presents five candidates to the class, the class reduces them to three, and the General Assembly to one, who is proclaimed by the president; but between vacancy and nomination there is a long delay, and I think that it would be very much to your advantage, and that you will be better served, if I wait for Charles Maurice Talleyrand.

Volney is in Philadelphia. Does he know that he is a member of the Legislative Corps and a member of the National Institute? I believe a letter from him to the Directory might enable you to get the necessary funds to publish the *French Part of San Do-*

[21]François Urbain Domergue (1745–1810), a noted grammarian of the period, *membre de l'Institut,* member of special commission for the revision of the *Dictionnaire de l'Académie* and author of many works on the French language.

mingo. What convinces me that he is in high favor with the Directory is that the Directory has declared that even though Volney is not in residence, the Institute should consider him as one of their resident members.

A chair of law in our central schools of Paris would also suit you marvelously. I will work for all this; but I warn you, my dear friend, that a place in the Institute is worth only fifteen hundred livres tournoise,[22] while a professor's chair carries a fixed salary of only three thousand livres and about twelve hundred livres in perquisites and lodgings. It is true that you are qualified for places of much greater importance, and you won't remain becalmed for long without being called there. How sweet the moment will be when I shall clasp you in my arms! We loved each other in happier times, and I feel sure that we shall love each other a thousand times more.

My newspaper had few subscribers and is still suspended, though I swear it wasn't at all my fault. I have abandoned it, but I have no intention of abandoning my grammar. I shall publish it as a book instead of in detached sheets. At the present time I am publishing a work entitled *French Pronunciation Determined by Invariable Signs* in an octavo of 312 pages. At the first opportunity you will receive twenty-five copies, the wholesale price is three livres, retail price four livres tournoise. One copy is a present for you, two others to the charming little printer, one to his cousin, a fourth and fifth to the two young ladies who ornament your home. As for my loved one, I am reserving for her a beautiful surprise on her arrival in France. I dare not offer one to Baudry, in spite of my strong affection for him, for I'm afraid that certain verses that he would find in it might make him refuse the book.

Nevertheless take the risk for me; no matter how the book may offend him, he will nevertheless have the complete regard and complete affection of the author.

If the notices in the public prints, and your own kind words, sell the remaining nineteen copies, you can reimburse me—if you can do so without too much trouble—in rolls of good tobacco, and at every good pinch of snuff I shall say, "The joy that is mine comes to me from my good friends."

This book will be followed in a year by a general grammar simplified and analytical, in an octavo of about 600 pages. Then I propose to do three volumes under this title: *Grammatical*

[22] A livre tournoise was four fifths of the ordinary franc.

Solutions, Taken from the Journal of the French Language. I shall eliminate everything useless from it, and correct all its imperfections. Then, then . . . we shall see. What is certain is I mean to strive to love you all my life.

Our affairs progress well in Italy. We are masters of Italy, of the Tyrol and of Triuli. Vurniser and his last seven thousand men have been cut off. We hope every moment to have news of the capture of the Austrian general. In Germany we are not doing so well, and have pushed our triumphal march too far. Jourdan has fallen back before Prince Charles, whom he has so often put to flight. Five days ago we learned that the Austrians had re-entered Frankfort. All the newspapers said joyfully only yesterday that we had driven them out again. When will this terrible strife end? When will we have peace? The peace which will bring back abundance, the arts, the pleasing brotherhood of mankind, my adopted family? Adieu, my good friends! I embrace you all tenderly, without distinction of age or sex.

In closing, I make a wish, the execution of which is guaranteed by your friendship for me: it is that after you have read my letter, you will all join hands, dance in a circle, place your lips close together and out of the seven resulting kisses make one so loud that its sound will cross the seas to reach me and echo in my heart.

(Signed) DOMERGUE

P. Charles Pougers has written you about your bookselling business. Léger is well. I saw Citizen Talleyrand at the National Institute. The lively interest for you that I expressed to him resulted in a thousand proofs of friendship. We are going to put our heads together to procure for you in Paris the means to live decently and comfortably. . . . Someone is waiting for this letter and hurrying me. I don't know what I'm saying. I know only that I keep you all in my heart.

September 26. I took my children to Peale's Museum, which they visited with great pleasure.

October 14, 1796. I received a letter from Talleyrand:

Hamburg, July 31, 1796

Forty days from continent to continent, no privateers, a short visit from a fleet fifty leagues from Sorlingues, rain every day, an abundance of food, too much wine, and on reaching Hamburg Mme. Moreau's water still was better than that from Hamburg pumps. Except for M. Bérard (whose history you can learn from M. Bousquet) a very good and joyous company. As yet I know nothing about the city. Only one of the Lameths is here. Alexandre, after having returned from England, left to take the waters in Germany. He is living with D'Aiguillon.[23]

The son of M. de Liancourt is at Altona with his beautiful daughter. The *émigrés* are agreeable. I have not yet paid a single call. The cockade is very fashionable, and I put mine on as soon as I arrived. When I know a little better where I am, you'll have a long letter from me. I embrace you, my friend, your son, and send my respects to all about you. Friendly greetings to Messrs. de Liancourt and La Colombe. Yours forever.

I was delighted to know surely that Talleyrand had arrived in Europe.

October 24. Around ten o'clock in the morning M. Cunningham, a neighbor who lived five or six doors away, came to my shop to say that he had a Frenchman in his house who had asked about coming to see me. I asked his name. . . . He said he came from Hamburg on his ship, the *America,* and that he had arrived the evening before. Again and again I asked his name . . . and learned that it was M. d'Orléans.[24] My answer was to hurry quickly after M. Cunningham in search of M. d'Orléans. He received me with a welcome which I couldn't sufficiently praise.

I returned on the same day, as usual, the books I had bor-

---

[23]Charles Malo François, Comte de Lameth (1757–1832), and his brother, Alexandre Théodore Victor, Baron de Lameth (1760–1829), rendered services in the American Revolution which preserve their names from being forgotten by Americans. They were both associated during their exile in Hamburg with the Duc d'Aiguillon in a commercial enterprise.

Armand Désiré Vignerot Duplessis Richelieu, Duc d'Aiguillon (1761–1800), deputy in the Estates General and member of the *Constituante,* was forced to seek shelter in England and afterwards in Hamburg, where he died in 1800.

[24]The future Louis Philippe, King of France, had sailed from Hamburg on September 24 and had just reached Philadelphia. He was joined in February by his two brothers, Duc de Montpensier and Comte de Beaujolais. For their sojourn and travels in America, see G. N. Wright, *Life and Times of Louis Philippe,* pp. 294ff.

rowed from the Philadelphia Public Library, where borrowers have to sign an agreement to bring them back at once or pay a sum far in excess of their value.

October 25. M. Van Braam came to see me at my house.

October 29. The creole refugees, and also the Europeans who had fled from France, could find no church books for the practice of their religion. Therefore they engaged me to print the new Book of Prayers in use in Rome. I finished this in October, a small duodecimo of 290 pages, and the book was well received.

The Calendar is attended to. It was during this same October that I put out a duodecimo volume of 420 pages with the title *General or abridged outline of the sciences and arts for the use of the young, published by* M. L. E. Moreau de St. Méry. I got the idea of an abridged outline of all the sciences for the use of children from M. Formey, who had published one in 1783. I venture to believe that this little book is extremely useful, and my belief has been shared by the public, as I shall show later. It certainly contains some things that I believe to be wholly new.

November 4, 1796. I put on the cockade.

December 10, 1796. I received M. d'Orléans in my house with great satisfaction.

December 16. I took M. Van Braam, at his urgent request, to call on M. d'Orléans.

In the evening the eulogy to Dr. Rittenhouse was read at the Philosophical Society.

January 16, 1797. Here is a plea from Cazenove relative to a translation of Mitterpack.[25]

Sunday, January 15, 1797

Here, *mon cher Maître,* are some notebooks and some details about the extraordinary author Mitterpack. Take care of them. This is the only copy I have of this faulty translation, made hastily with the idea of putting it into good French later. My first aim was

[25]Possibly a reference to the learned Hungarian agriculturist, Ignace Mitterpacher.

to have some ideas. If you think after reading it that it might turn into something you can send back my rough draft and I will make a fair copy with a half margin. Yours.

T. Cazenove

January 20. I dined at M. de Liancourt's house with M. d'Orléans and Volney. There I had a good opportunity to observe the latter's monomania.

I received Messrs. d'Orléans and Liancourt.

This day brought a letter from Talleyrand from Hamburg, which read thus:

Hamburg, August 31, 1796

Today I finish with Hamburg, my dear friend. This evening I shall proceed to Amsterdam, remain five or six days, and from there go straight to Paris.

One of your boxes was sent to M. Mettra, as you wished. I am not at all satisfied with Fauché, with whom I had hoped to do business about your books. In all, Hamburg is not a place for business in books. Bear this in mind for your guidance. I have loaded the copies of your book and M. de Liancourt's on a boat for Dunkirk: from there they will easily get to me in Paris. Fauché will send you the two volumes of the encyclopedia which you lacked. There's no Emilie[26] here.

The business I hoped to do here goes forward very slowly, but I was completely successful in another small matter: you can draw on Cadignan, February 15, 1797, for a thousand dollars. I shall send Cadignan this sum before that time, and I am notifying him to that effect in a letter which I am sending him today. That and two hundred subscriptions ought to enable you to print the *French Part of San Domingo.*

I write nothing to you about France. I will send Liancourt what I was told about our country during my month in Hamburg, and you can get the information from him. In Hamburg the Lameths

---

[26]Emilie, Marquise du Châtelet, was the beautiful and talented mistress of Voltaire. They lived together on Voltaire's farm among the mountains of Cirey-sur-Blaise, and Voltaire addressed many poems to her. Thus it became the fashion among literary-minded Frenchmen to refer to their ladyloves as Emilie, or Emilie of the Mountains. Talleyrand is doubtless referring here to Mme. Grand, who was his mistress for many years, and to whom he was married in 1803 at Bonaparte's insistence. He refers to her again on p. 240.

have been involved in several Orléans plots; but it's a poor tool they're using; and as La Colombe says, their young man uses their intrigues and their backing as a means of getting to America, where positively you will see him three months hence, and his brothers as well.

Damourien is destroying, by some bad books which he prints each week, the respect that circumstances were doing their best to give him.

The *émigrés* are meek: they all want to return; they detest England first, the princes second, and are ready to sacrifice three fourths of their fortunes in order to live beneath the sky of France.

I'll write you from Paris the moment I arrive.

Communication is easy between France and England: all business letters come regularly.

But persons, as well as letters that aren't strictly business, have a more difficult time. I have not yet made any plans for myself: from here I can't clearly visualize what I should do. I imagine that during the winter you will busy yourself printing your *French Part of San Domingo,* and that by spring you will be free. By "free" I shall never mean anything except that you are getting on a ship to come to us. I shall work to that end after my arrival in Paris. I shall conceal my dealings with Veloni, who has much credit and with whom Messieurs the Electors have scarcely any.

Adieu, my friend. Write me via your correspondent in Le Havre who can re-send your letters to the address in Paris which I will give him. My respects to your family. I embrace you and love you.

I received M. Foncin, the engineer, arriving from Cayenne, and took him to M. de Liancourt's house, where we all dined together the next day.

January 26. This day brought me a letter from my friend Champion which I here add:

Paris, September 9, 1796

I take advantage of the opportunity given me by Citizen Cabot to reply to your letter of the first of July, which he just delivered to me.

I shall take great care to see that those enclosed in the package reach their destination.

I thank you for your courtesy in putting me on the list of your subscribers for your descriptive book about the *Spanish Part of San Domingo*, and for the gift of the copy you sent me, as well as for the piece on the Dance. I have already read this pamphlet with pleasure, and I hope to have as much in reading the other.

I do not need these proofs of your friendship to think about you. No day passes that I do not dream of means of obtaining for you a homecoming which would be as profitable to you as I am sure your talents would be to our country. Unfortunately I have no credit, and I am not the sort of person who will have any. I have small inclination for venturing into business, and have no other ambition except to maintain myself in a position which I was on the verge of losing. If I had lost it, I would have lost the only means of subsistence for myself and my family, which, as you know, is rather numerous, although I have no children—but I'm wrong, for I may very well say that my brother's two children have become mine since he is no longer able to provide for their needs. On his arrival in Paris I got him a situation in the same office with myself. He remained there only two months; then, against my wishes, he decided to return to Cap François. He had even obtained his passage and a position as magistrate, but events answered my prayers more favorably than he. Now he congratulates himself that he didn't sail—though he had gone to Rochefort and even boarded the ship. He is now at the home of his brother-in-law at Marqueville, near St. Jean d'Angely. I don't believe his trunk has yet arrived. I will tell him about the shipment which you have made and he will, without doubt, be delighted to have your news.

The lot of Citizeness Regnier has not improved. At present she lives in an extremely small furnished room. I must be truthful and say that Citizeness Baudry continues to give as much aid as is possible, considering that she herself is one of those unfortunate persons of independent means whose income at the moment is paid in bills worth almost nothing. She did not conceal from me that she found Citizeness Regnier hard to get along with, and that rather than take Citizeness Regnier back with her, she prefers to sacrifice herself financially to make it possible for her to exist elsewhere. And in truth I think I recollect that she was proud and exacting. What is certain is that Citizeness Vinet, who has shown the liveliest interest in her, told me that she was very content, that she had given back the apartment she had loaned her, and why? To go and live with her sister, which necessitated a most disagreeable parting. Her brother, on whom she counted, had made her all sorts of fine promises; but he was in Paris for almost three months without asking whether or not she was alive; and when he accidentally ran into her, he soon left the city without saying goodbye to her. When he once more came back, he again didn't deign to go to see her. Finally he was sent to join the army in Italy, and left nothing but debts to be paid by his wife, with whom Citizeness Regnier had quarreled. Now she is reconciled, thank God, in accord with our advice and that of Mlle. Baudry. She said lately to my wife that she had no friends but us; but a moment later I saw her growing angry over remarks I was making to her concerning M. Mony, about whom she had complained. I appreciate that the situation in which she finds herself is enough to make her bad-tempered, so I don't let anything she does upset me. My only regret is that I haven't the means to be as useful to her as I should like.

I shall not fail to call upon M. Talleyrand as soon as I know he is here. Even as you write me that you are an intimate friend of his, the newspapers announce that he is already at Hamburg. I will see if we can put our heads together and work out something to your advantage.

It was not long ago that I saw Pome, who told me about a letter he had received from you, and of something he wished to send you. I suggested that he turn to Citizen de la Haye, senior, at Le Havre. I do not know if he was successful in carrying out his plan.

I believe I wrote you that Clément has lost his son. He is separated from Mlle. Deserts, who remained at Fontainebleau; and he has come to Paris with his brother, Director General of Military Subsistences. M. Darile is quite well, but I haven't seen him for some time. I no longer happen to meet Edmond; but I shall try to arrange a meeting with him on the chance that you will continue your business when peace comes.

My wife refuses to think of you as strangers. She has always shared my feelings for you and your family, and asks me to present her compliments.

I shall take upon myself the duty of obtaining Aménaïde's certificate, until you hear from Urbain Domergue that he has received your package. He has been appointed professor of general grammar to one of the central schools established in Paris in the building of the Four Nations. The position carries with it a salary of six thousand livres in addition to the pension which he has already obtained.

Adieu, my friend! When shall we meet again? May heaven grant that it may be soon! Until then, do not forget me, as I never forget you and all of yours.

P.S. Some days ago I wrote you by way of Le Havre, enclosing in my letter a package from Citizeness Baudry, as is the case with this one.

January 28. All Philadelphia was stunned as the result of a fire in which Mme. Broom, wife of the brilliant librarian so highly esteemed here, was killed. She was buried in the same coffin with her three children. The throng of people attending the funeral was prodigious. A poorly extinguished fire in a stove caused this frightful misfortune.

February 5, 1797. M. de Liancourt gave a dinner for M. Van Braam, and I accompanied him.

March 13, 1797. My friend Sonntag, also annoyed by his partner Baron de la Roche, appealed to his friends to make him behave better:

March 13, 1797

I hope, my dear M. Moreau, that I am not being obtrusive; but knowing that you are favorably disposed toward me, and long-suffering, I'm going to ask you to be so kind as to write for me a letter in the style merited by the man to whom it is addressed. The contents should be as follows.

1. Explain to him the embarrassing situation into which I have been plunged by his delay in settling with me for the amount he owes to our former partnership, and by his failure to explain or even to try to explain what he plans to do about it. He hasn't kept his promises, though I well know he has used funds that were not his to use, and that should have been turned into the general liquidation fund.

2. Ask him to what end he has proposed to the creditors to pay the money that is due them, why he proposed an immediate meeting to agree on terms of payment? I demand satisfaction for the false insinuations which he has made against me and of which I have been told. In spite of past commitments, he changes his mind and aggravates the feelings of our creditors, making them demand

earlier payments than they had agreed to accept if they had not been taken in.

3. Tell him in unequivocal terms for the last time that I demand immediate action from him, unless he wishes me to take all possible steps, however violent and disagreeable they may be, to make him carry out the duties which should be sacred to him—unless, too, he wishes me to make public the baseness of his soul and let it be known everywhere that he is without consideration, which I am in a position to do since I have documents which prove the meanness and vileness of his acts.

Finally, if you think an interview would get more satisfactory results than such a letter, do not write the letter, but propose such a meeting, before witnesses.

A thousand pardons.

Yours

Wᵐ Lᵉˢ SONNTAG

March 21. M. de Liancourt, at whose house I had dined with Gauvain, sent me this note in the morning:

I return your notes, which I have read twice. In them I find many things suitable for my journal, and from which I wish to take many more. Will you let me see them again when you have no further need for them?

Good day. I embrace you.

This Tuesday morning.

I was much flattered at such praise from a man whom I loved, and whose merit and character I was able to appreciate.

March 26. I went with my friend Sonntag and Carpentier of Guadeloupe to visit Robert Morris' greenhouse near Philadelphia. It had very beautiful specimens of orange trees, lemon trees, and pineapples.

May, 1797. It was during 1797 that I decided to have my outline of science translated into English and published in this language.

The translation, in 380 pages, is by Michael Fortune. This edition was quickly exhausted because American schools adopted it for their teaching. It was reprinted under the careful supervision of M. Gouin, a Frenchman, who, with my permission, made a second edition of it. My French edition also was quickly bought up. It is worthy of note that Toussaint L'Ouverture, Governor General of San Domingo, ordered La Grange, my master printer in Philadelphia, to print another edition in Port-au-Prince. I have good reason to say, therefore, that this book has had a success most flattering to my self-esteem, and to my desire to be helpful to the young.

May 25. I wrote an opinion of a plan for public education in the United States which had been proposed by a man of great ability, and submitted in open competition on this matter. In it I found sound and patriotic ideas that were praiseworthy, but not worth the cost.

1. The article dealing with the government as it acts on education fell short of the one concerning the influence of education on the government. 2. The section distinguishing between public morality and religious morality was well done. 3. The director of the bureau was given too much power. 4. Educators of other nations had nothing in common with the staff of the Federal Institute. 5. If the government was so intimately concerned with the actual administration of teaching, it would too greatly influence the selection of teachers, and all students would feel obliged to please it. 6. Honorary members would be ridiculous. 7. Why should professors of the national university have to be naturalized, especially when they have been obliged to renounce their countries? 8. Why should the theory and the practice of medicine fall under different departments? 9. No degrees; they're the playthings of children! Admission or non-admission should be only by examinations. 10. Why should central schools be paid for by the states? Such an arrangement would break the unity of the plan. 11. Professorial groups should be independent on the one hand, and on the other hand be uninfluenced by anything except their own talents. It seems to me that the author has omitted one of the most

important things to be considered in a nation where every citizen may be called to public office: i.e., instruction in the central schools concerning the functions of public servants.

These were the substance of my criticisms on a highly important subject.

June 4, 1797. M. Gallet, councilor of the Superior Council of Cayenne, came to dinner. I was under obligations to him without knowing it; for he had helped to assemble the material I used for the code of that colony. He had been reduced to hunting for ways to support himself, and had become a dancing teacher in Baltimore.

June 16. M. Robineau de Bugon, son of the former Attorney General of the Council of Cap François, received my visit. Misfortune had driven this wise and agreeable septuagenarian to abandon France and seek a more peaceful refuge.

A most delightful pleasure was that of embracing my dear Estève, who, in spite of his eighty years, came from Wilmington, where he was living, on a little excursion to Philadelphia. What happy days the sight of him recalled, and how hideous the misfortunes of San Domingo seemed!

July 1, 1797. Baudry, finding that his business was producing only a trifling profit because of the manner in which English and French vessels were capturing American ships, went to the country with his family and took up his residence near Germantown on an estate belonging to M. Van Braam, and although he was German, he called it Deslozières's Cottage.

July 5. I had a letter from Demeunier, who wrote about Paris in a manner extremely strange to one who left it four or five years ago:

> Paris, July 5, 1797
>
> After a favorable crossing of thirty-five days I have finally reached, my dear Moreau, the blessed shores of our native land.

Never had they appeared so beautiful to me, and from Le Havre to Paris, I seemed to be crossing a magnificent garden. When I got to the *ci-devant* capital of France, I scarcely recognized it, as you might say.

Constitutional Paris has little resemblance to Revolutionary Paris. Balls, spectacles, fireworks have replaced prisons and Revolutionary committees. There is the most elaborate dressing, the rags of Jacobinism, the fops and loose women, the stinking pawns of tyranny and royalism, the fanaticism of liberty carried to license; but let this picture not frighten us, my dear Moreau; there is nothing dangerous about it, for morals and liberty are not in peril.

You know how the women of the court and prostitutes appeared wherever they could show off or find pleasure, drawing in their wake the giddy fools whose only happiness was pleasing fashionable women? Well, that same state of affairs still exists today, but the individuals have changed. The women of the court have disappeared, and have been replaced by the women of the *nouveaux riches;* and in their train, as in the train of the others, are the prostitutes, who fight with them for the wherewithal of luxury and extravagance. Around these dangerous sirens buzzes the wanton swarm of lack-wits formerly called *Petits Maîtres,* today called *Merveilleux,* who talk politics as they dance, and sigh for royalty as they eat ices or yawn at the fireworks.

As for the sensible people, the true friends of liberty, their number has not decreased; but they are not seen at brilliant fêtes, where everyone shines in the splendor of Greek and Roman raiment: they busy themselves with more useful affairs, leaving to the sots the amusements in which they themselves find no interest.

A stranger would make a great mistake to base his opinion of the sentiment of Paris on its assemblages. The thoughts that prevail in the boudoirs of the Phrynes and the Laïses are not those of the people, as one would quickly learn if the advocates of royalty and of liberty assembled beneath their respective banners.

You have seen by the newspapers that some members of the New Third have attacked the Directory. It will doubtless be thought in your delightful country, where our affairs are judged so sanely, that the counter-revolution has taken place; but you need have no anxiety on this point. A vast majority of the Council of Five Hundred are excellent men, in favor of the Republic;

and if a few light-headed members have erupted, you'll have to blame a few hot-heads, or those who have axes to grind, or those who are rebellious because of personal hatred. The quarrels that disturb the Council are not of any consequence outside it. Fledgling members have no experience; they want to use their wings like Papa and Mamma, but they have neither the means nor the strength. They'll learn in time; and what is more, the Council of Ancients permits no nonsense and rejects any resolution that is contrary to the public good with gratifying firmness.

As yet I have not been able to deliver all your letters. I am waiting for a moment when I shall be free of all public affairs, so that I can devote all my time to your commissions. I have, however, seen Talleyrand. I found him very well, and launched into the thick of the constitutional circle. Collot will tell you about this. I gave him everything you sent me for him. All the newspapers are saying he will be a minister, but I do not know whether the Directory will agree with the newspapers. Up to now there have been no signs of it. The Directory not only doesn't seem disposed to give up any of its ministers, but it defends them against the whole world.

Adieu, my dear Moreau. By the next post I will tell you more. A thousand respects to your ladies. I embrace you with all my heart. Tell me your news, and address your letters to me at Rue de la Révolution No. 27. Talleyrand tells me he has written you twenty letters. The negotiations of Lille are going well up to now. Those of Vienna continue daily in spite of the detestable things said in the newspapers.

July 19. I received a letter from Talleyrand, written from Paris.

July 20. The Chevalier d'Irujo, Spanish Minister to the United States, wrote to thank me for defending his country in Parent's gazette:

The Chevalier d'Irujo presents his respects to M. Moreau de St. Méry, and has the honor to thank him for his splendid defense in Parent's gazette. It is a piece worthy of his pen, of his patriotism and of his friendship for Spain.
High Street this Friday morning.

July 29. M. d'Orléans came again to see me.

July 31. The general business depression has also affected mine, and to such a degree that I felt I must decrease my rent, which hitherto has been quite considerable. While I was hunting a new location I was conscious of a fever.

The fever of July 31 turned into a grave illness which lasted until August 13, when the fever left me. During its entire course my evacuations were green.

August 1, 1797. At that moment yellow fever broke out and filled the Americans with profound terror. Twenty thousand residents of Philadelphia, one third of its population, deserted the city and fled to the country. The Board of Health conceived the idea of placing little red flags above the doors of houses where there were cases, and we could count twenty of them within a musket shot of my house.

It was said everywhere that I was stricken with it, but since I am a creole it was highly improper to include me in their number.[27]

M. Baudry, Mme. Baudry, my sister-in-law, and their daughter Eléonore came from the country to see me.

August 23. I engaged lodgings at 259 Callowhill Street, at the corner of Front Street.

August 30. M. de Liancourt, leaving for Hamburg, wrote me his goodbyes:

New York, August 30, 1797

Ever since my arrival here, my dear colleague, I have been on the look-out for your letters for Europe as well as for an account

[27]This is confusing. The word "creole," properly speaking, has no connotation of color. It means a person born in the West Indies of Spanish or French parents, as distinguished from immigrants direct from France or Spain, or from Negroes, mulattoes or aboriginals. So, too, West Indian horses are creole. Moreau on p. 364 speaks of his son having a creole fever. A plant peculiar to the West Indies is creole. Nowhere is there any indication that Moreau had colored blood. Yet only Negroes and Men of Color were supposed to be immune to yellow fever. White creoles were not supposed to be immune. As a matter of fact, not even Negroes are immune. When the Sternberg treatment for yellow fever was being tested, it was administered to 373 yellow-fever victims, 301 of whom were whites and 72 of whom were Negroes, which disposes of the often-made statement that Negroes can't catch yellow fever. Why Moreau should imagine that he was immune just because he was born in the West Indies is a mystery.

of what I owe you. You promised to give me this before I left Philadelphia; then you said you'd send it to me in New York. I would very much like to put this in order and pay it before I leave; and as I leave on Saturday I shall scarcely have time to do so. I trust my debt to you is not very large, since you have received three hundred and thirty-five dollars from me, but nevertheless I greatly desire to know what it is.

I return to you your last three journals, for which I thank you.

That of New York induced me to look again at some of the things you pointed out on the route between New York and Philadelphia, and to give it more space in my journal than I had originally given it. However, since I have not borrowed a single phrase, nor even so much as a single thought from your journal, you needn't be afraid of repetition if you should ever decide to publish your own.

I leave for Hamburg on a good Swedish boat, and in excellent health, and hope shortly to be in France. I flatter myself that I shall find resources in Hamburg; so if you wish to entrust a letter to me, or have any commission you wish me to perform, inform me and you may be sure that it will be faithfully attended to.

Goodbye, my dear Moreau. I embrace you sincerely. A thousand compliments to La Colombe. Come back quickly after you have closed your affairs satisfactorily. Do not let the shameful detention of the unfortunate Van Braam hinder your affairs. Do you believe in the nomination of Talleyrand and Demeunier?

LIANCOURT LA ROCHEFOUCAULD

September 5, 1797. I started moving, a task which took until the ninth, on which day I slept in Callowhill.

September 11. My young and interesting clerk, Jules, born in Paris, and belonging to one of the many families who trusted the wild promises of the Scioto Company[28] and had been driven by poverty to take refuge in Philadelphia, died from yellow fever, although just two days before he had helped me with my moving. He had been with me since January 15, 1796.

---

[28]For an interesting short sketch of the Scioto Land Company, see McMaster, *History of the People of the United States*, II, pp. 146ff. For more extended study see E. C. Dawes, *Scioto Company and its Purchases* (*Ohio Arch. and Hist. Pub.*, III, 107).

It was this same September 11 that a letter came from Talleyrand from Paris, dated February 17, full of interest:

Paris, February 17, 1797

The sale here of your *Spanish Part* has not yet supplied Mlle. Regnier with much of an income, my dear friend. I believe that she can count on getting only about eighty books through Dupont. Books do not sell at all here. Anything larger than a pocket pamphlet remains on the shelves. Everybody who reads spends his time on newspapers, the others read nothing. Keep this in mind when you think of sending anything to France. Nevertheless I have had M. Van Braam's book[29] advertised everywhere. Nobody pays any attention to anything except the elections. No stone is left unturned to influence the legislative elections. People resort to everything, and slander is a favorite weapon. My own opinion, however, is that with the help of the reactionaries and in spite of the anarchists, the elections will turn out well. Your friends, and those whom I call your friends, are utterly and forever devoted to you, had thought of having you named professor of jurisprudence in the central schools of Paris. The position is worth four thousand francs, and the duties are not burdensome. I have taken this up with the jury which, as you know, is composed of Garat, Laplace and a third whom I can't recall at the moment. Laplace and Garat have promised me to vote for you, which is all we need. But the administration has held up the nomination, because it is talking of making changes in this sort of school. The whole thing is still unsettled. Something has been said about giving up the chairs of jurisprudence. This is at the instigation of Guiguéné, who is head of the Department of Public Instruction, but nothing definite has been done about it. I shall keep an eye on this matter; and if the plan has to be abandoned, we'll think of another. My thought is that nothing will happen until after Germinal [March 21 to April 19]. Everything has been postponed until then, in anticipation of great changes in the government; and everyone hopes for it. At that time we shall make a united effort to obtain for you a position which will call you here, and which gives you independence without too much work.

[29]A reference to the work of Van Braam, at that time in preparation and entitled, *Voyage de l'Ambassade de la Compagnie des Indes Orientales vers l'Empereur de la Chine*. It was printed at the press of Moreau de St. Méry at Philadelphia, 1797–1798.

I well know that you were never afraid of too much work; but I am lazy, take great pleasure in being so, and want my friends to have the same opportunity. I deposited here at the end of January a draft on Hamburg for two hundred and twenty-five pounds sterling to be sent to Cadignan, whom I have instructed that you may draw one thousand piastres in February. I have had no news as yet from my man or from Cadignan, but since this is only in the middle of February, the delay is perfectly natural.

Not even the parties have chosen their candidates for the Directory. It seems to me that Cochon is the best supported.[30] His party lends its voice to Bénézech.[31] The others favor Merlin de Douai.[32]

Your city of Paris is not at all revolutionary. You will not recognize it. To occupy the credulity of the Parisians with something, one frightens them with an Orléans faction which is supposed to be extraordinarily dangerous because it is invisible. You hear about it everywhere, but never see any part of it. I am honored by being regarded as one of the heads of this able faction. It seems to me this rumor comes from the priests, who are working hard at politics; but don't think that this amounts to anything.

My opinion about you is that by May we'll be able to write you in such a way that you will be able to make definite plans. Count on me. I will keep you informed. I have made so little progress in getting support for our excellent ideas relative to the colonies that I have given up everything we planned together about that. Present-day diplomats are not at all impressed with the possibilities of Louisiana. It is probable that Demeunier and I shall be deputies. What would prevent it would be the Vendémiairists, who have a great many votes in Paris.

Adieu, my friend. Remember me to Sonntag, to La Colombe

[30]Cochon de Lapparent (1750–1825), called to the *Ministère de la police* on April 3, 1796, had won distinction in discovering the conspiracy of Babeuf and was considered a serious candidate for the Directory. He not only failed of election, but shortly afterwards lost his portfolio.

[31]Pierre Bénézech had been Minister of the Interior under the first Directory. He likewise failed of election.

[32]Merlin de Douai (1754–1838) was at this time Minister of Justice. François de Neufchâteau and he were elected on September 6 to the Directory in place of Carnot and Barthélemy. It is interesting to note with what small success Talleyrand was able to forecast the elections.

and to all our friends. A thousand compliments to Blaçon, whose little magpie of a wife is very well.

A thousand tender regards to you and your family. I love and embrace you. Paris is filled with talk of Emilie Montagne.[33] I have forwarded to Liancourt the plots of the time, and Mme. de Staël's book. You will find it interesting.

September 16. Mme. Tully from Martinique came to see us.

September 17. I went to call upon M. d'Orléans and his two brothers. Orléans came to my house on the nineteenth.

September 24. As relations between France and America were darkening, and acts might occur that would make the sojourn of French people in the United States very disagreeable, my friend Letombe proposed to attach me to the French Legation as a measure of protection for my family and myself. I accepted his proposal thankfully.

Accordingly he gave me this commission:

September 24, 1797

Philippe Joseph Letombe, Consul General of the
    French Republic
       to the United States

By virtue of the powers delegated to me by Citizen Adet, Minister Plenipotentiary, gives and confers on Citizen Médéric Louis Elie Moreau St. Méry the appointment as Examining Commissioner pro tempore, for auditing the receipts and expenditures, not only for the Consulate General but for the Consul personally; wherefore the said Citizen Médéric Louis Elie Moreau St. Méry will work both for the Consulate General and for the Consul personally, in the examination and verification of the said accounts, with the emoluments attached to the said position of Examining and Verifying Commissioner, and will account to me, at stated intervals, the progress and the results of the said examination and verification, made and sealed under the seal of Office of the Consul General at Philadelphia this Third Vendémiaire in the Sixth Year of the French Republic one and indivisible.

LETOMBE

[33]See note, p. 226.

October 6, 1797. The *Leyden Gazette* of this date announces that the first volume of Van Braam's book is on sale in Amsterdam, and that the second will follow shortly.

The beginning of this month my dear Lapaquerie of San Domingo arrived, which was very pleasant for me.

October 8. I went to dine at M. Brunau's country seat at the mouth of the Schuylkill. There I found Letombe, Flamant, General Collot and the Minister of Spain. The location was such that wild ducks contributed their persons to the dinner; and the game of skittles or ninepins, at which General Collot excelled, occupied us all day until dinner, over which we sat until we had to leave to return to the city.

October 15. I went again, as on the eighth, to the mouth of the Schuylkill. There we were joined by the good M. Other, Consul at Norfolk.

October 18. I went to receive the goodbyes of young Lafayette, who had been prevented by the prevalence of yellow fever from coming to Philadelphia. He wrote me as follows:

Wednesday, October 18, 1797

MONSIEUR,

I am off to New York to take passage for France. On leaving Mount Vernon I promised not to set foot in Philadelphia. I must keep my word; but I should reproach myself if, before my departure, I should pass so close to you without seeing my father's oldest and best friend. Consequently, instead of going from Lancaster to Reading, as I had been advised to do, we have preferred to go closer to Philadelphia; and at this moment M. La Colombe, M. Frestel and I are at Middle Ferry on the Schuylkill, where we await you, if your affairs permit you to take advantage at once of the carriage which we are sending for you, and which is to bring us to sleep tonight beyond Frankfort. I do not need to tell you that our pleasure would be complete if your son could come with you, so that we might, before parting, have a rendezvous all together at a common center which would reunite all of us.

I beg you to present my respectful compliments to the ladies, and accept for yourself the sincere assurance of an attachment which will last as long as I live.

(Signed) G. W. MOTIER LAFAYETTE.

October 24. Letombe had me to dinner with General Desfourneaux, in accordance with this note of invitation of the twenty-third:

I have heard nothing spoken of for three days, except San Domingo. Tomorrow I shall have to dinner one of the principal actors, well known for his eloquence and for his love of truth, and that ought to amuse or instruct a good historian. See then, my dear *confrère*, if you can do me the pleasure of coming tomorrow to my house to a family dinner.

You know, my dear *confrère*, the attachment that I have pledged to you.

This Tuesday evening.

LETOMBE

October 25. [Letter from Frestel:]

New York, October 25, 1797

We have just received the French and Spanish passports which M. de Letombe has had the kindness to send us, and we are leaving in two hours. This deprives us of making a return in any way for the favors which he has done for George. Will you be so kind as to thank him in his name and mine. The English Consul has refused to give George a passport, but he has given him a word in writing with his signature and seal to be treated courteously en route if any commandant of a frigate should take the fancy to show him the Tower of London. We have received your package, and shall carry out all your commissions. Your friend M. Rozier has been the soul of kindness; and according to your instructions he had done everything that lay in his power. Say a word to him about this when you write him.

As this is the last scrap we are permitted to write on the American continent, I seize the opportunity to send you once more our goodbyes. George and I beg you to present our compliments to the ladies, and our regards to your son. We shall be waiting for you in the Mother Country.

(Signed) FRESTEL

October 29. Again went to the mouth of the Schuylkill, a visit which has become customary every Sunday.

November 17, 1797. The Chevalier d'Irujo, the Spanish Minister, begged me to make a small English translation for him. I hastened to comply.

Here is his note:

Market Street, Friday, November 17, 1797
Chevalier d'Irujo presents his respects to M. Moreau de St. Méry, and after having asked to be excused for the liberty which he is taking, he sends him here enclosed a couple of sheets of English which he begs him to be so kind as to return to him in French at his leisure. The chevalier is very sorry to give M. de St. Méry this trouble, but the person to whom he had sent this piece for translation made such a bad translation of it that the chevalier is obliged to have recourse to the kindness of M. de St. Méry.

The word "old settler," as M. de St. Méry well knows, is difficult to render into French, but the chevalier takes the liberty of observing that it might perhaps be given all its primitive force by observing in a footnote that the word "settler" also means a person who has contrived or completed something which M. Pickering has never done.

November 24. I went to General Laveau's house with General Collot.

November 25. Another request from the Spanish Minister to translate something for him:

Chevalier d'Irujo presents his compliments to M. Moreau de St. Méry, and has the honor to deliver to him the little work in question, which he has had the kindness to promise to translate.

December 6, 1797. I went again today to call upon M. d'Orléans. It was toward the end of this year that I became very intimate with Aristide Dupetit-houars,[34] to whom I was related. I gathered from him some of the details about

[34]See *Biographie Générale,* Tome 15, for an excellent article on this interesting character. Moreau's exclamation of pity for him was probably added later after he had learned of his death in the naval battle of Aboukir.

his voyage in search of La Pérouse[35] on the schooner *Diligent* of about eighty tons, on which he sailed from Brest, September 6, 1792.

All the French were sent from the Cape Verde Islands to Lisbon in March, 1793. Dupetit-houars left Lisbon for Philadelphia with three men of his crew in August, 1793. He sought a passage to the Western Ocean. On December 17, 1795, he announced at New York that he was returning to France.

After many misfortunes, Dupetit-houars was back in France in February, 1796. The eighteenth of that month of February, he wrote from Paris to Minister of the Navy Fruguet to ask him for employment. "I am back at a time when I can again shed my blood for the Republic in the uneven and glorious struggle which its navy is maintaining against a force which centuries of success and perfidy would render invincible to any others but the French."

Unfortunate Dupetit-houars!

January 1, 1798. I received this note:

Chevalier d'Irujo has the honor to wish M. de St. Méry a Happy New Year, and to send him fifty copies of *Verus*, begging him kindly to accept them and distribute them as he thinks proper. Chevalier d'Irujo at the same time thanks M. de St. Méry for the assistance he has been so kind as to give him in this little book.

Monday, January 1, 1798.

January 2. After receiving an invitation from the same Minister on the second, I went and dined at his house. The

---

[35] Jean François de Galaup, Comte de la Pérouse, sailed from Brest in 1785 in an attempt to discover the Northwest Passage from the Pacific side. He got as far as Mount St. Elias, Alaska, in June, 1786; turned back because of bad weather; he visited Hawaii, Asia, the Philippines, Japan, Korea and the Siberian coast. From Kamchatka he sent his journals, notes, plans and maps back to France by Lesseps; then went to the Samoan Islands. He arrived at Botany Bay in January, 1788, and from there wrote his last letter to the French Ministry of Marine. Nothing more was ever heard of him. In 1826 Captain Peter Dillon found the wreckage of what was believed to be his two vessels on the reefs of Vanikoro, north of New Hebrides.

meal was very gay. At the table he sat between Count Alexandre de Tilley Blaru, just arrived from London, and me. This agreeable count was attended on his way to Philadelphia by a series of erotic adventures which lent an added charm to our conversation.

I remember that during the evening of this day, which was cold, with a great deal of snow, I said that on the eighth of the year 1793 I was stricken with my second attack of gout at Le Havre and that I hoped I should be spared for still a long time.

January 8. But the next day, in the evening, even allowing for the difference of about five hours between the meridian of Le Havre and that of Philadelphia, the gout took possession of my left metatarsus. This time it only stayed with me five days instead of three months, as in 1793.

January 16. I bought, from one to whom Baron de la Roche's assignee, Combatz, had sold it, the debt I owed him.

January 20. I saw General Kosciusko, who had come to Philadelphia. The Americans received him with great demonstrations of joy, unhitching the horses from his carriage and drawing it from the point where he had debarked to the lodging that had been reserved for him.

February 1, 1798. M. Guillemard, an Englishman, who had been a great friend of M. de Liancourt, and whom I had enjoyed meeting at his house, came to see me. This gave me great pleasure, and our friendship is strengthened.

February 27. M. Sharples,[36] an English painter, who had come to Philadelphia to practice his profession, asked permission to do my portrait. I acceded at once to this wish.

February 28. Dubourg, one of the employees whom I had known at the printing house at Cap François, acknowledged

[36]James Sharples, the English portrait painter, had arrived in New York in 1796 and "at once became popular for his small portraits in pastel and his miniatures." His portrait of Moreau is in the Metropolitan Museum of Art, under the title "Portrait of an Unknown Gentleman."

the receipt of several copies of my *Description of San Domingo* and of my *Outline of Science* which he had taken at my request, and which I had sent in charge of my master worker, La Grange, who had gone back to San Domingo.

March 7, 1798. A new proof of Demeunier's friendship reached me on this date. He speaks of the likelihood of a rupture between France and the United States of America:

March 7, 1798

I am extremely distressed, my friend, by the details of your situation which Goynard has given me. I have been unceasingly occupied as to what could be useful to you in the United States, but circumstances have not made it possible for me to get anything for you. It's needless for me to say how sorry I am, and you well know my affectionate interest in your welfare.

If you decide to return to France, you must be sure to get a certificate showing the length of time you lived in Philadelphia; and even though you are not listed as an *émigré,* you must have a passport from the French Consul. People known like you are on the list, who like you have rendered great services to the Republic, and Goynard at my advice, has gone to the department to make sure that no such mistake has been made in your case. He has reported to me that the only law that could affect you—that of the 19th Fructidor—is no bar to your return. Thus it rests entirely with you as to whether or not you can and shall leave your present abode in that infamous country where Frenchmen are rightly discontented, and bring your numerous family back to your country. The damnable treaty between the United States and England is causing trouble that shows no signs of abating. As things are, all your business ventures must suffer unless managed with the greatest prudence and skill, and French republicans who live in Philadelphia can expect nothing but enmity. I well know you can ask nothing better than to leave, but after all your misfortunes, can you afford the trip? You have suffered another loss of which you are ignorant. The American ship which was carrying to France five hundred copies of your printing of Van Braam's *Voyage to China,* has been captured by one of our privateers, and your five hundred copies were not only confiscated with the rest of the cargo, but were sold. Citizen Monneron of Nantes came to me for information about this book, for my library is the only place in Paris that has it. He wanted to see whether it was the same book as the ones that had been purchased at Nantes by the person for whom he was acting as agent. There is no provision in the laws that would make it possible to bring suit against anyone; any attempt to recover would be useless, and I can't be of any help to you in the matter.

If you return to Paris, what useful work can you find to do? I am wholly at a loss to know! You will be distressed, but at least you will have our companionship—which is something you can't have with Americans who act so badly; and you'll have the consolation of knowing that when you die, you will rest on the soil of our beautiful Republic.

France, in spite of all its troubles, is still not only the best country in the world, but by far the pleasantest. As for me, who loved it even when I was driven from it, nothing whatever could make me leave it.

My friend, I know your courage. We have had striking proofs of it, and I don't need to admonish you to hold firm. But I pray your wife to show herself your worthy helpmeet, and your son to look forward to a life less troubled than ours.

P.S. Embrace Dove. I have not forgotten him for an instant. Goynard will write him in detail about his interests. Remember me to our other friends, and warn Olive and Cheriot in New York of the care they must exercise in their transactions in view of the extremely dangerous relations between the United States and the French Republic; but be most guarded in this respect.

March 17. M. Van Braam had shipped the first volume of his *Voyage,* which I had published, to England, but the boat was captured and the edition was sold in France. Garnery published it in two octavo volumes and sold it for six francs. This was recorded in the *Courier of the Legislative Corps* for March 17.

March 18. I again called on General Kosciusko. Seven or eight of us went to see him on the same day. Kosciusko had landed with his head bandaged as though he had been wounded. His knee, too, was bandaged. Those who visited him found him either in bed or stretched out on a couch like a sick man. His lodging was a bedroom with a little antechamber before it; and since his bed and couch left no room for more than two or three people, only two or three of us could see him at a given time. If other visitors happened to call, we had to leave. This was the arrangement that Letombe, General Collot, Flamant and I agreed upon.

March 26. Mme. d'Aiguillon, most interesting in every way, whose society I had cultivated in Le Havre, and to whom I had pledged the greatest devotion because of her misfortunes, her unfailing courage and her obvious gratitude for my admiration of her, wrote me a letter which I received on June 27. It was expressed in these terms:

March 26, 1798

M. de Mourgues is leaving for Philadelphia, and has kindly undertaken, Monsieur, to deliver my letter to you and to remember me to you. He counts on remaining several months near you. He is your compatriot, and is in every way deserving of your interest if he has need of your services. I trust that you will not refuse him, and that you will grant my request to help him in every way you can. I venture to believe that my recommendation has some value with you.

For a long time, Monsieur, you have sent no news of yourself, and everyone who knew you is none the less very often concerned about you: there had been a momentary hope of seeing you again, but all the things that have happened are doubtless reconciling you to remaining in your retreat. Do you ever think of rejoining us? What more can you desire than to be, as you are, tranquil and happy in the bosom of your family? Many envy your lot, but few have any possibility of attaining it. You will now learn from the bearer of my letter how many have lost everything for the second time. He will answer all your questions, just as later he will, I hope, answer mine about you and your charming family.

Nobody who has known them can ever forget them; and whatever you tell me about them will be read with the greatest pleasure. Again I send you my sincerest affection, born in misfortune and undiminished by distance. Nothing would give me greater pleasure than to prove that affection, and be of service to you, so write me with complete confidence. If you think I can serve you in any way, you can depend on my willingness and zeal.

MME. AIGUILLON

April 2, 1798. Gout came back in my left foot and remained until the ninth, so this time I didn't escape with a five-year interval.

April 10. I had a letter from Champion which so delighted me that I was no longer conscious of the gout.

Paris, December 26, 1797

I have received, my dear Moreau, your last two letters, including the one dated August 24, 1797, which was delivered by Citizen Dupont. It was a little late in arriving because Dupont was detained in Le Havre until his passports could be visaed by the Ministry of Police.

I was delighted to learn from Dupont that Citizen Talleyrand, after his promotion to Minister of Foreign Affairs, had written you offering your son a position under him. I went to see him, as I told you in my preceding letter, and expressed to him my hope of seeing the end of the quarrels between the Republic and the United States, so that he could get you a post that would be as useful to you as you to it. He told me that the differences were not so great that they couldn't be adjusted, and that I must remain calm about your lot and remember that he was taking a genuine interest in it. I told him you had so many great problems on your mind that I was afraid they would distract you, and I suggested that if he had an opening in his ministry for which I was qualified, he give it to me so that I could be near him to remind him of a friend who must be as close to his heart as he to yours.

"If the opportunity occurs," he told me, "I'll do this for you with pleasure; but rest assured that I won't forget Moreau; I am too sincerely attached to him as well as to his whole family." Those were his sentiments when I left him, and I won't fail to keep them alive; for in spite of my impatience to have you with us, the present conduct of affairs is such that I think you would do well to stay away a little longer. I am convinced it would be to your advantage to do so, because you can easily return at any time you wish, and meanwhile can be earning additional funds to help you when you do return.

I have told all our friends and acquaintances that you have settled upon next spring for returning, and they have all been as happy as I. Rest assured that you and your family will find our affections unchanged, mine least of all. My only regret is that I am unable to offer you the means of returning sooner. You know

I have lost everything; and even though they speak of re-establishing the Colony, I never expect to see the day when I shall be able to recover my fortune. Meanwhile I have only my position, which is improving, since salaries are now being paid in hard money. I do not know whether I ever told you what my position really is. From being chief of the Bureau of the Criminal Division, I am now chief assistant of the Division of Accounts. My income is forty-five hundred francs a year, which is not much, considering my expenses; but somehow I make both ends meet. Fortunately I have an economical wife. I am not ambitious, and am only concerned to hold onto what I have.

You have doubtless been informed of Mlle. Baudry's marriage and of the death of Mme. Livry. This was a great loss to Mlle. Regnier. I can't give you any news of her; for we live so far apart and I have so few free moments that we haven't seen each other in a long time.

Citizen Dupont told me that you had charged him to note down the addresses of all your old friends. Mine is still the same one you knew, Rue Montmartre No. 52, and will be until after Easter, 1798. Then I shall move to a house opposite the one in which my sister used to live with our aunt, Rue Neuve Egalité, formerly Bourbon Villeneuve No. 342. You can write me there, and when you arrive here I hope you will not fail to come there to receive the embraces of your faithful friend.

P.S. My respects and regards to your wife and all your family. Our two better halves will be the delight of our society. Mine asks me to tell you that she is looking forward to it in advance and begs you to accept her compliments.

April 13. My nervous headache came back on the thirteenth and the fourteenth.

April 29. I attended with great sadness the funeral of M. Aubert, old and virtuous merchant of Cap François, for whom, ever since my arrival in 1775, I had always had the highest regard.

May, 1798. During the whole of this month, I saw frequently and always with renewed pleasure the eldest son of my friend Dupont de Nemours.

June 21, 1798. I have just received a letter from Talleyrand, written March 28, in which he speaks of young Mourgues. This letter is worth quoting:

Paris, March 28, 1798

MY DEAR MOREAU.

Be a little good to the young Mourgues, who is going to America on personal business; he knows Paris well, and will tell you about it; and since he also knows me very well, he will tell you that I love you with all my heart, and I shall be most happy on the day when we are again together, never again to be separated. I think Lafayette has decided to go to America, at least for the trip. Dupont has plans for a huge business; he is more youthful and more romantic than ever. Bureaux de Pusy[37] will accompany Dupont. Liancourt hasn't yet decided what to do. I hold the same position, and am serving the Republic to the best of my ability, but I need a rest. What I would like is to travel for a year or two; but so far this idea exists only in my head, and in the vaguest way. Send me M. Van Braam's plaids. I have written him two letters thanking him for his kind thoughts about us, who are richer in artistic possessions than any other nation, but almost wholly lacking in those of China. Adieu, my friend; embrace for me all who surround you. I love you most tenderly. If you decide to return, and I learn the moment and the port where you will arrive, you will find everything necessary to transport a large family to Paris. I tenderly embrace the excellent La Colombe.

This letter clearly shows what I have elsewhere said about the affection that Talleyrand and I had for one another. He sends word by Mourgues that he loves me with all his heart; that he will rejoice in our reunion, knowing we will no longer be separated; and that when I land in France, I shall receive the means to convey all of us to Paris. There is, however, a clause in his letter which needs explaining. The Chinese collection of M. Van Braam, at the time it was made, had cost him more than a hundred and fifty thousand francs, whereas in France it would be worth a million and a half. M. Van Braam had offered this collection as a gift

[37]Probably a reference to Jean Xavier Bureaux de Pusy (1750–1805), a president of the *Constituante*, who was imprisoned (1792–1795) at Olmütz. In 1797 he went to Hamburg and thence to the United States.

to France, and had written Talleyrand asking that it be accepted, as had I. It was to this that Talleyrand referred.

But the Directory failed to realize the worth of this invaluable collection, and said nothing about it; so finally M. Van Braam sent it to London to be sold. What a glaring and damnable example of French indifference!

June 27. I received a letter from Rozier, the Consul at New York, who said:

June 27, 1798

I am told your departure for France is at hand. I envy your lot, for our own is becoming increasingly difficult. Do me the favor of letting me know the approximate date on which you plan to sail. I had hoped to see you and say goodbye, but I must give that up. This disappointment is an added reason for me to damn all these busybodies, all these rascals, who are trying to throw this country into a turmoil. All those who have no love for Robespierism had better get out and get out quick!

Adieu, always yours

T. A B. R.

This letter shows how disturbed the United States was. In reality the Federalist party (which is the English-loving party of the country) worked for war against us, while the Republican Americans favored the French Republic. People acted as though a French invasion force might land in America at any moment. Everybody was suspicious of everybody else: everywhere one saw murderous glances.

June 28. Mourgues lunched with us.

July 12, 1798. I received a letter from General Hédouville of Cap François, written June 17, in which he acknowledged the receipt of the copy of my *Description of the French Part of San Domingo* which I had sent him.

July 13. I went with Baudry to visit the ship *Adrastes,* which was being made into a cartel ship, and on which we hoped to sail for Bordeaux.

I saw Rouvray. He had returned from San Domingo suffering from a scorbutic diarrhea which did not permit him to leave his bed. He seemed delighted to see me. He spoke bitterly of the falseness of the many people whom he had considered his friends, and regretted that he could have been so mistaken. He longed to return to France, but he died almost immediately.

He was buried in Philadelphia, where his funeral gave rise to quarrels. It was decided that he should be buried wearing his cross of St. Louis, which led several people to refuse to attend a ceremony which, after all, merely indicates the nothingness of man.

July 14. I received a passport for myself, my wife and the children.

Antagonism against the French increased daily.

I was the only person in Philadelphia who continued to wear a French cockade.

Soon thereafter the Republicans, fearing acts of violence on the part of the Federalists, met secretly and took steps to defend themselves. Since I was a party to these meetings, I was given keys to two shelters in which I and my family could take refuge in case my own house should be attacked.

July 18. I engaged passage on the *Adrastes*. Shortly afterwards we learned that M. Adams, the President of the United States, had made a list of French people to be deported, and that the list was headed by Volney, General Collot, myself, etc., etc. I was sufficiently curious to question M. Adams through M. Langdon, senator from New Hampshire, to find out what I was charged with. He replied, "Nothing in particular, but he's too French."

Now M. Adams had often come to my house, to my study and to my shop during his term as Vice-President and we had exchanged our books as gifts. But after he became President I never saw him.

A letter from Cap François from General Hédouville told me that he had received everything that I had sent to him, and assured me that he would give favorable consideration

to Jérome Gauvain and my former servant Phoenix because
of my recommendation.

The British Minister Plenipotentiary, M. Robert Liston,
showed me the utmost deference and supplied me with a
passport for myself and family covering all my belongings,
papers, maps, designs, etc.

August 1, 1798. In order to wind up my connection with
M. Van Braam, I was obliged to have recourse to an arbitra-
tion. This took place.

In this regard, I must quote from a letter which Cazenove
wrote concerning M. Van Braam on July 22. He said he had
been convinced for some time that Van Braam had more
ostentation than true wealth, and that the Americans are
craftier about such things than the Dutch.

August 3. M. Pickering, Minister for Foreign Affairs for
the United States, supplied me with a passport similar to
M. Liston's.

Mme. Beaussan caught up with me in Trenton to ask me
to help her get passports for France.

August 4. I was able to get the Consulate to give them
to her the next day.

August 6. I said goodbyes to my old and kind friend
Cazenove.

August 14. I returned to M. Van Braam everything of his
that I had.

August 17. I had written to M. Guillemard to clear up a
debt which I had contracted through his kindness, and he
replied with this friendly letter:

Solitude, August 7, 1798

I am distressed, my dear Monsieur, that you have given yourself
so much trouble about a paltry debt which doesn't inconvenience
me and which I should never have asked you for. Since I first
knew you, I have held you in respect and esteem, which is all
I need to say. Since I wrote you I have been in Bristol on business;
for the time has come to get ready for emergencies and build up
resources as protection against the spreading storm. I have not

seen M. Blaçon. I live outside the city, which I visit as seldom as possible. In the future I won't go there at all. Our office has been moved a league outside Philadelphia.

When you think of me, remember me as a young man who wishes ill to no one, and is happy to have had an opportunity of showing his good will and gratitude.

With a regard that has never grown less since I first had the honor of knowing you, I remain

Your devoted
GUILLEMARD

P.S. If M. de Blaçon is still in town, I beg that he will come to see a poor creature afflicted with toothache.

August 18. As one can well imagine, M. d'Irujo, the Spanish Minister, also granted me a passport for my return crossing to France.

In the company of Breuil I had my last dinner at the home of my friend Letombe.

August 19. I also had the sorrow of attending the burial of the wife of M. Homassel, the merchant, from whom I had received a thousand marks of affection, and whose friendship I valued highly.

I tried to sell everything that could be turned into money, of which I was very short, since my business was no longer going on. My passage aboard the cartel ship *Adrastes* was gratis; but the expense of moving the quarters of the four of us as well as Baudry, his wife and his daughter from the lower deck to berths opening into the Great Cabin was seventy-two dollars a head, or five hundred and four dollars, which I paid. We also had to buy provisions for the entire crossing, and to have a closed place to put them in.

August 20. Early in the morning I said a number of good-byes; and at nine o'clock my wife, my daughter and I boarded the packet schooner *La Mouche* for Newcastle, where the *Adrastes* had already gone.

Baudry, his family and my son had boarded her the night before.

August 21. We arrived at one in the morning and went aboard at six o'clock.

August 22. I went ashore at Newcastle so that I could go to dinner with Don Francisco Ramirez, a Spanish officer of great merit, who had repeatedly urged me to come to Havana and write a description of that enormous colony.

The captain of the *Adrastes* arrived in the evening, bringing with him a Philadelphia *Gazette* containing the news that Captain Smith, whom I had embraced on the morning of the twentieth when bidding him farewell, had died the same night of yellow fever, though when I left him he was wholly well.

I shall, according to my custom, now speak of Philadelphia, where I lived three years and ten months.

PHILADELPHIA

PHILADELPHIA or *the city of brothers* (named thus by Penn, in memory, they say, of that city in Greece which took its name from the fraternal love of Attalus and Eumènes, and is famous because it was the site of one of the seven churches to which St. John addressed his Revelations) is situated on the right bank of the Delaware at 40 degrees latitude north and at 75 longitude west of London. It has the same latitude as Spain, Italy and Greece. It was probably less cold before the growth was stripped off.

Seen from the river, it has a genuinely lovely appearance, and offers in its form a slightly concave line whose ends round out toward the east.

The length of the city proper is one mile, or eight hundred and sixty toises, and each of its suburbs is about six hundred toises long. Thus the total length of Philadelphia is two thousand toises, and its depth from the Delaware to the Schuylkill River, which is half as wide as the Thames at London and is the city's western boundary, is two thousand toises. The Schuylkill is navigable by boat, for ninety-four miles as far as the city proper.

Philadelphia, capital of Pennsylvania, situated in a plain more than six miles in extent and in the county of the same name, is the most beautiful city of the United States, but only the second in commercial importance, New York being first.

It was founded as a corporation with a charter dated October 28, 1701; and until 1800 it was the seat of the federal government of the United States, an honor which it lost because of its repeated and disastrous epidemics of yellow fever.

In front of Philadelphia, which is fifty leagues from where the Delaware empties into the sea, this river is about a mile wide, and deep enough (they assure you) for a 74-gun ship-of-the-line. The rise of the tide is six feet, and it flows about four miles an hour as far as the falls at Trenton, thirty leagues above Philadelphia. This city is four and a half miles northeast of the junction of the Delaware with the Schuylkill.

Philadelphia is in the form of a long square, with the streets intersecting at right angles. The streets that run north and south are numbered, starting at the Delaware. All streets from First to Thirteenth begin at the Schuylkill. Between the river and Thirteenth Street is Broad Street, the broadest indeed in the city, and it is five streets nearer to the Schuylkill than to the Delaware. This was brought about by the actual elevation of the ground on which Broad Street was built, this being the most elevated point of the town of Philadelphia.

Streets running east and west, from one river to the other, are called by the names of the trees which the first colonists noticed on their arrival—Vine, Sassafras, Mulberry, Chestnut, Walnut, Spruce, Pine, Fir, Cedar.

This arrangement of Philadelphia makes it easy to find streets, since one knows that the High Street or Market Street occupies the middle and that streets crossing this Market Street from east to west are South First Street, South Second Street, and so on.

That leaves only the streets running north and south to learn; and with very little practice one learns them, because one knows at once whether a given street is north or south of Market Street.

There are three hundred and four "squares" or "islets" formed by intersecting streets. Many of the squares are cut again by small streets and by even smaller ones called alleys.

The number of squares entirely constructed, or constructed in part, is about one hundred.

The streets are of different widths. High Street is one hundred feet wide, Broad one hundred and thirteen, Mulberry sixty and the others fifty.

In general, three fifths of the width is paved with cobbles. On each side there is a brick sidewalk. Between the street and the sidewalk there is a gutter, also paved with brick, which carries away the water. Posts ten to twelve feet apart on the outside of the gutter prevent carriages from running up on the sidewalks. In recently paved streets, a curb of flagstones with holes drilled in them has been laid up to the height of the sidewalk.

In addition there is Water Street, which is thirty feet wide and runs parallel to the Delaware. It was originally intended for wharfs and storehouses, but the city has spread out along the Delaware.

This Water Street is in a low and disagreeable section. At Pine Street it juts out eighty feet in an easterly direction, and a street named Penn Street starts from here and goes to Almond Street.

But above this Penn Street there is another street toward the Delaware called Little Water Street, which runs south to a point just beyond the shipbuilding yards. At first this land was intended for a wagon road to serve the wharfs and storehouses which were being built on the bank, but with a few exceptions all the houses are large ones, even up to five stories high. It is a convenient embarkation point, and a busy place, full of work and movement.

The wharves which edge all of Philadelphia along the Delaware are made of squared logs. These are placed one on the other, also in square formation. The interstices are filled with earth and stones, and the top is paved. Oak Street, originally a sort of swamp, then planned for a basin, has been filled in until it is now a beautiful street between ninety and one hundred feet wide. Each Wednesday and Saturday morning there is a horse market at the northeast end. In 1794 poplars were planted there. The lumber yards for firewood are at the Delaware ends of the streets.

At the end of the city, above Fifth Street and beyond Cedar Street, there are no more paved streets, so that when it rains, everything outside these limits is a quagmire. The pavement on Front Street, however, extends beyond Cedar Street.

In the north beyond Vine Street, Third Street is not paved. Neither is Fourth or Fifth. The city ends at Fifth Street. All the northern section beyond the city, beginning with this street, is peopled by Germans.

Six hundred and sixty-two lamps with two branches light the streets at night. They are closed in a glass lantern placed on top of posts along the edge of the sidewalks. They consume annually 30,424 bottles of oil.

The outskirts north of Vine Street are called Northern Liberties;[1] and those south of Cedar Street belong to South-wark, a southern suburb. This plan doesn't follow that of Penn, who wanted Philadelphia to extend from the Delaware to the Schuylkill.

The slope of the streets, especially the ends of those near the Delaware, is far too steep, even though it has recently been decreased.

The highest elevation of the populated section is only forty feet above the Delaware, and is much less in several streets, especially in Water Street, where the storehouses are sometimes damaged by high tides when the wind is strong from the southeast.

[1]"In 1676 Governor Andross patented to Jurian Hartsfelder three hundred and fifty acres on Cohocksink's Creek for three and a half bushels of wheat quit-rent. This was sold ten years afterwards to Daniel Pegg, who gave the name of Pegg's Creek or Run to the stream and this tract formed the Northern Liberties of Philadelphia." Scharf and West-cott, *History of Philadelphia, 1609–1884*, I, 74.

An ordinance of the corporation of the city of Philadelphia of May 4, 1795, forbids the erection of wooden buildings below Tenth Street.

The houses of Philadelphia, more than nine thousand in number, seldom have more than two stories. Usually they have a ground floor, a first floor and an attic. They are covered with clapboards, or painted or tarred shingles. Each house is numbered. In streets which go from north to south, the numbering starts with number 1 on the north side; and then for the south side of Market Street too. That is, on one side of Market Street going north, number 1 is on one side followed by number 3, whereas on the other side of the street it begins 2, 4 and so on through all the even numbers. Going from Market Street south, there is the same system. For the streets going from the Delaware to Broad Street, number 1 is at the left, followed by 3, 5, 7, and so on, whereas the numbers 2, 4, 6, are on the right.

I adopted this system when the houses in the States of Parma had to be numbered. It has since been used in Paris, too.

In Philadelphia one finds the ridiculous custom of using guillotine windows. The result is that they cannot be tightly closed in winter, nor widely opened in summer. Only occasionally are there shutters on the first floor, though they are usual on the ground floor.

A little Greek portico, or one with a triangular top or with a cornice, spoils their appearance. The doors are too narrow. Only stables and coach houses have porte-cocheres.

The houses have a gloomy appearance because of the bricks of which they are built. These bricks are eight inches in depth. An attempt is made to enliven the façades by painting them brick-color, then painting symmetrical white lines in squares, thus seemingly outlining the divisions between the bricks. The window trim is also painted white in imitation of cut stone.

A custom that might be termed extravagant is that of washing doors, sidewalks and window ledges every Wednesday and Saturday morning, even in winter when it's freezing. This lunacy exposes the passers-by to the danger of breaking their necks; and as a matter of fact, falls on the sidewalk are not rare.

The water used by the inhabitants of Philadelphia is taken from the Schuylkill. It is distributed by wooden pumps placed forty toises apart on the outside edge of the sidewalk, as well as forty toises apart, but alternately, on the other side of the street; thus, on one or the other side of each street, there is one of these pumps every twenty toises.

The water from these pumps is used for everything, but especially for drinking. At a convenient height the pumps have an iron piston that serves to draw up the water.

None of the water is particularly good, and it cannot be kept pure for a twenty-four-hour period. Some of the pumps have a better reputation than others, but that is only relative, and in only a few cases.

Everybody is free to use these pumps.

Several streets have trees, usually elms, planted on the outer edge of the sidewalk.

This use of trees was not common, and the streets were not particularly beautified by them. Some persons considered them helpful in hot weather; others believed they prevented the free circulation of air and attracted insects, especially mosquitoes. Since then Italian poplars have been put at both ends of each street, as well as on all sides of the city's principal square on Market Street between the Delaware and the Schuylkill.

After I left Philadelphia a stationary bridge was built over the Schuylkill. This was authorized by an act of the Pennsylvania legislature March 19, 1798. It was begun in 1791 and finished in 1805.

The Schuylkill bridge has three arches, is covered, and has windows like portholes. Carriages pass to the right, following the custom of the United States, to avoid collisions. Each side has a sidewalk for pedestrians. The Schuylkill bridge, at the point where High Street ends, is of stone.

The canal which furnishes water to Philadelphia has its intake between Middle Alley and Gray's.

The canal is vaulted in all parts with a double vault of freestone. A steam machine has been constructed to pump the water so that it flows to all the streets.

It is carried by a subterranean canal running beneath the sidewalks on both sides of each street; and whenever one wishes, the turn of a knob makes it flow from the end of a faucet about two and a half feet high.

This water is excellent for drinking.

It is piped into the homes of private persons who have bought the right of using it.

The wooden bridge at the Gray's Ferry crossing remains unchanged.

The water stored for city use is pumped to a reservoir fifty feet high. This advantage cannot be overestimated. Starting July 12, 1795, Front Street was watered at ten o'clock every morning by watering carts like those which serve the Paris boulevards. But now that the waters of the Schuylkill are collected in a reservoir, it is made to flow in every street. And words cannot express how much good is accomplished by the manner in which it renews and refreshes the air during the extreme heat of summer.

Trees have been planted on both sides of every street, the Italian poplar being the one most in favor.

Almost all Philadelphia houses—and this is also the case with all houses in the United States—have the simplest of furniture, usually consisting of several pieces of mahogany, chairs of the same wood with seats covered with horsehair in the case of wealthy people. Other classes have walnut furniture and wooden chairs painted green like garden furniture in France.

There are no hangings, no upholstery, the walls are all alike and usually painted a grayish-white color. There are no mirrors, no pictures, but they have carpets imported from England, and these are kept laid even during the summer, except in Charleston, where they are unrolled only during the winter and after noon, and kept rolled the rest of the time.

But this decoration of the houses is only to be found in the rooms which a visitor is likely to see in any particular house; for everything that is normally out of sight is very ugly and very little cared for. Self-respect does not exist, because the servant who religiously washes the door and the sidewalk twice a week goes barefoot and makes no point of cleanliness. Just as long as parlor, kitchen, stairs and entrance door are clean, everything else can get along in any old way.

The true character of Americans is mirrored in their homes. They always have broken windowpanes, doors without locks; and leaks are common to every attic. These, the owners coldly insist, are impossible to prevent.

Each house has for a toilet a small room set apart from the house, but it is far away. One often gets wet going to it.

The population of Philadelphia, when I left that city, was estimated to be sixty thousand. Since five or six persons are usually figured to a house, that would make the number of houses nine thousand five hundred.

The population includes many foreigners, especially Germans. Above Third Street in Northern Liberties, as I have said before, there are only Germans. Their peaceful character, their love of work, the similarity of their language to English, which easily lets them understand and be understood—all these things bring them in great numbers to the American continent.

Almost all other foreigners come from Europe because they are discontented with their government. They are upset and unruly, and without property, furious because the government sold to city people the land on which they counted on establishing themselves. They hate cities, and suspect everybody of profiteering, speculation, etc.

The misfortunes existing in the colonies have also brought many French to Philadelphia. Twenty-five thousand are estimated to have sought refuge in the United States.

American men, generally speaking, are tall and thin, especially the Quakers, but they seem to have no strength. They are listless, those in the towns even more than the others. Neither sex can boast a complexion. They are brave, but they lack drive. Indifferent toward almost everything, they sometimes behave in a manner that suggests real energy; then follow it with a "Oh-to-hell-with-it" attitude which shows that they seldom feel genuine enthusiasm.

Their manner of living is always the same. They breakfast at nine o'clock on ham or salt fish, herring, for example, which is accompanied by coffee or tea, and slices of toasted or untoasted bread spread with butter.

At about two o'clock they dine without soup. Their dinner consists of broth, with a main dish of an English roast surrounded by potatoes. Following that are boiled green peas, on which they put butter which the heat melts, or a spicy sauce; then baked or fried eggs, boiled or fried fish, salad which may be thinly sliced cabbage seasoned to each man's taste on his own plate, pastries, sweets to which they are excessively partial and which are insufficiently cooked.

For dessert, they have a little fruit, some cheese and a pudding. The entire meal is washed down with cider, weak or strong beer, then white wine. The entrée is accompanied by Bordeaux or Madeira, which they keep drinking right through dessert, toward the end of which any ladies who are at the dinner leave the table and withdraw by themselves, leaving the men free to drink as much as they please, because then bottles go the round continuously, each man pouring for himself. Toasts are drunk, cigars are lighted, diners run to the corners of the room hunting night tables and vases which will enable them to hold a greater amount of liquor.

Sometimes dinner is prolonged in this manner far into the night, but finally the dinner table is deserted because of boredom, fatigue or drunkenness.

Before dinner and all during dinner, as is the English custom, all the silver one owns is displayed on the sideboard in the dining room.

In the evening, around seven or eight o'clock (on such ordinary days as have not been set aside for formal dinners), tea is served in the evening as in the morning, but without meat. The whole family is united at tea, to which friends, acquaintances and even strangers are invited.

There you have the three meals of the day, because there is no supper. Evening tea is a boring and monotonous ceremony. The mistress of the house serves it and passes it around, and as long as a person has not turned his cup upside down and placed his spoon upon it, just so often will he be brought another cup. You hear a thousand true and false accounts of Frenchmen who, in their ignorance of this peculiar custom, have been so inundated by tea that they have suffered intensely.

Americans have almost a passion for oysters, which they eat at all hours, even in the streets. They are exposed in open containers in their own liquor, and are sold by dozens and hundreds up to ten o'clock at night in the streets, where they are peddled on barrows to the accompaniment of mournful cries.

The temperature of Philadelphia is frigid in winter and stifling in summer. Ordinarily it averages around 8 degrees Réaumur in the first of these seasons, and rises to 24 Réaumur during the four months of summer.

The cold is glacial and extraordinarily piercing because it is accompanied by a northwest wind which cuts through the thickest garments. As for the nights, the temperature is often 23 degrees Réaumur. This is because the houses are constructed of brick eight inches thick, and continued heat saturates the bricks, which in turn hold it and spread it through the rooms, making them fiery hot.

Added to this, the climate is extremely variable, and on a given day there may be great changes in the range of the thermometer, so that one should never risk going to the country without taking along all paraphernalia that will be needed to guard against this atmospheric inconstancy.

The air of north Philadelphia is purer than that in the south.

The character of the Americans of the United States is not uniform in all of this great continent. However, there are some traits which one can call outstanding. In spite of their pretended detestation of the English, they really love them, even though they fear them. In spite of their conceit, they subconsciously feel themselves to be inferior to the English, and this leads them to treat them with adulation. Their tastes, their customs and above all their habits are really the same as those of the English. If the English had courted this leaning by sending them as Ambassador a man of note who was wealthy, ostentatious, a giver of parties, and one who would have flattered the American people, their conquest would have been assured.

But instead of this, the English have openly shown contempt for the United States in everything they have done since the peace of 1783. They proved this by the first man they chose to represent them, M. Temple.[2] He had held a

[2]Sir John Temple, whose father came to America to establish a Scotch-Irish settlement on the Kennebec, was born in Boston in 1732 and educated in England. He was related to the all-powerful Grenville family, and was appointed Surveyor General of North American customs. He later became Lieutenant Governor of New Hampshire. He married the

high position in America before the rupture, and had only inspired feelings of scorn because of his debts and indecorous behavior. M. Hammond,[3] new to diplomacy, was an equally bad choice, because in addition to disliking Americans, his violent nature makes it impossible for him to hold his tongue, and frequently leads him to make mountains out of molehills.

Consul General Bond,[4] though born in America, is full of hatred for the country. His one noteworthy quality was his ability to influence M. Hammond. The fact that Hammond could be thus influenced says nothing for Hammond's ability.

daughter of James Bowdoin of Boston and was a close friend of James Otis and other patriot leaders in Massachusetts. His openly expressed convictions got him in trouble with officials of the crown, who lodged false charges against him and had him recalled. In England he got in trouble because of giving Benjamin Franklin the celebrated "purloined letters" written by Governor Hutchinson of Massachusetts. How Temple got the letters has never been learned. His sympathy for the American rebels led him to be sent to New York in 1778 on a secret mission— which was to persuade the American leaders to agree to peace terms short of complete independence. He was markedly unsuccessful (an excellent account of his mission and its failure can be found in Lewis Einstein's *Divided Loyalties*, Houghton Mifflin, 1933) and went back to England in 1780 to insist frequently and openly that the Americans would never return to English rule, and that British arms could never make them. In 1785 he was made first British Consul General to the United States. Einstein says of him, "He carried out with success an important task . . . became an intimate friend of John Jay. During his residence in New York, where he principally lived, he exercised a bountiful hospitality congenial to his taste and which the other consuls envied. He was known as a man of warm heart, though with an impulsive temper. He died at his post on Nov. 17, 1798."

[3]George Hammond, Oxford graduate, became first British Minister to the United States in 1791 when twenty-eight years old. He married (1793) Margaret, daughter of Andrew Allen of Philadelphia. He was a close friend of Jefferson; at odds with Genêt; left America in 1795 to be undersecretary in Foreign Office; led a distinguished diplomatic career until his death in 1853.

[4]Dr. Phineas Bond was a native of Philadelphia, a Tory. He was arrested in 1777, and signed the parole. He was made British Consul for the Middle States in 1786; but on the outbreak of the War of 1812 he was deported to England, where he died.

The Americans have formed settlements with astounding speed and as far as sixty miles inland. Their mode of life seems exactly adapted to their undertakings; and when their trickiness and their commercialism have been replaced by the virtues that citizens of a great nation ought to have, the country should enjoy perfect tranquillity.

Americans are said to be a sort of blend of Europeans and Indians. It is evident that they have progressed far beyond the Indians and are rapidly becoming more and more like Europeans.

One of the gravest of the Americans' many faults is the contempt of the residents of the Eastern states for those of the Southern states—that is to say, for Virginians, Carolinians and Georgians.

The faint differences between the various states are not at all marked by politeness. They have the same form of government, the same ideas, the same notions—and the residents of each one have the highest opinion of themselves and of their section. The Governor of Philadelphia, while I was there, said that America wouldn't change places with any other country in the world, since in America one could have venison, turtle and wine.

A letter of introduction, in America, is equivalent to a dinner invitation, unless it specifically mentions business.

When one goes to an American home for dinner, one leaves his cane, hat and topcoat on a coat rack in the front hall. If other guests have already arrived, the host takes the stranger by the hand as if he were a member of the family and introduces him successively to everyone, giving his name and at the same time naming to him the person to whom he is presented. This extremely prudent custom could well be made a part of French etiquette; for as things now are in French houses, a guest frequently makes offensive remarks about someone who is there but whom he does not know.

An American has no pride when he needs money. A wealthy Philadelphia merchant sought me at my residence on March 24, 1795, and in the most casual way said: "I need six hundred dollars until tomorrow morning. Don't refuse me! Lend them to me!" I did not have them.

The next day, on meeting me in South Fourth Street near his own home, he said: "You have no money, eh? Well I shall soon have a great deal!"

It is noteworthy that this merchant had only spoken to me once before, and that was when he bought about thirty dollars worth of goods from me on credit.

Where generosity is concerned, there are great incongruities in the American character. Some of their ways suggest the most parsimonious economy. Someone suggested to a senator that he buy an extremely beautiful harp for one of his daughters. "I certainly would buy it," he said, "if the cost of keeping it in strings weren't so enormous."

A Philadelphia widow employed a Frenchman to teach French to her daughter. She reminded him that her daughter would not be able to take lessons on Saturday, and that he would have to make a proportionate reduction in his monthly charges.

One of his socially prominent pupils who was absent once a week paid him for two months with two portuguese[5] on which he lost six francs in exchange.

Love of money sometimes even stifles delicacy. A celebrated Democrat, a business man, learned that the English government had sent a London merchant to America in January, 1796, to buy wheat, and that the Londoner was dealing through an American firm that was a rival of the Democrat's. The Democrat told M. de Talleyrand: "This is a dirty trick because I have enabled that London firm to earn more money than the firm which he chose here." This Democrat was the man who had persuaded the people to

[5] A Portuguese Johannes was worth eight dollars.

burn the commercial treaty between England and America June 25, 1795.[6]

One of my friends, a Guadeloupe merchant, sent fifteen thousand dollars to an American merchant with an order to buy some bank shares. The merchant replied to him, "I have received and executed the orders in your letter."

Three years later the Guadeloupian came to America and asked for his shares. He was told that they had been sold, and that he would be reimbursed with colonial interest.

He refused, and went to see a lawyer, who advised him to settle because if he didn't, he would waste four years in litigation at a cost of six thousand francs.

In the end he got back his original fifteen thousand dollars, and no more.

A merchant consigned to me a piece of goods, and agreed that I could take from it any desired amount, paying an agreed price when the remainder was returned. But when the goods were taken back, he demanded a higher price for the material I had taken.

In Pennsylvania receipts are called *billets de plaisir*. A law of this province says that it is merely an assurance of solvency, not binding if the giver can prove that he has received nothing. There is no certainty in business transactions. It is often necessary to ask a hundred times for one's money before getting it from those to whom it has been entrusted.

Clerks in the Southern states do not have a high reputation for integrity. If not watched, they raise prices, and pocket the amount they have added to the bill.

[6]An allusion to the treaty which Chief Justice John Jay, acting for America, signed with Great Britain late in 1794. Word of it got out in mid-1795, and aroused bitter resentment among the "Democrats," who were also called "Jeffersonians," "Jacobins," "Republicans" and "The French party." These "Democrats" rioted against the treaty, arguing that so many concessions were made in it to England that English merchants were enriched by it. A description of the riots and treaty-burnings in New York, Philadelphia and elsewhere will be found in McMaster's *History of the People of the United States*, II, 218 et seq.

It is almost impossible to persuade an American to undertake anything he has never done or seen done. It was only after innumerable entreaties that I was able to persuade a man to make me some different-sized boxes for wafers.

One of the things which makes the character of the American people so different in many points is that they have come from far lands, and they retain traces of their origins.

Thus, Americans descended from the Dutch combine to a pronounced degree the indolence of Americans with the avarice of the Dutch, thus emphasizing the eagerness for gain that is common to both.

They carry niggardliness so far that it couldn't possibly go farther. They almost starve themselves, and treat their slaves miserably.

Sometimes carelessness seems the outstanding characteristic of Americans, and expressions of friendship or of gentle philanthropy seem wholly alien to them.

Dr. Ross, a Scot living in Philadelphia, said to me on May 29, 1795: "I have lived in Philadelphia more than ten years, am connected with several corporations, and my position as doctor has given me many connections; but there are not two American houses where I can go to dinner unless I have received an invitation."

An attempt was made in Philadelphia to take up a collection for the benefit of American prisoners in Algiers; but it produced only about twelve hundred francs. Actors of the same city gave a performance for the same cause and took in nearly six thousand francs, even though there was no particular desire to attend the performance. Thus it was chiefly actors, needy themselves and English for the most part, who showed the greatest sympathy for unfortunates, who, in going afar to serve the welfare of their country, have left their women and children in misery.

In the winter of 1793, while crowds were skating on the Delaware in Philadelphia, the ice broke and a young man disappeared. There was some screaming; and when, after a few instants, his head came up, he was pulled out and skating began again. A quarter of an hour afterward another skater disappeared and was drowned, but the skaters went right on skating with no show of emotion.

Here is a curious idea they have about drowned persons. Around noon on Sunday, May 31, 1795, the son of General Pierre Muhlenberg was in a canoe on the Delaware, between Philadelphia and a small island. His canoe was overturned by a boat and he was drowned.

The next day around five o'clock in the evening, ten cannon shots were fired from the wharf at the lower end of Walnut Street at one-minute intervals. It was claimed that the explosions would make the body float; but it never appeared.

This belief was so deeply rooted, however, that half an hour later people shouted that the body was appearing, and crowds ran to see it happen. There was no more truth to the report than there is value to the method.

During the winter many people are constantly falling down in the streets, but no one ever goes out to help those who have fallen—barring Frenchmen, whose interest surprises the victims, and doesn't always elicit their thanks.

These same Americans, however, sometimes show sensitivity and generosity.

This is particularly noticeable in their treatment of the French who were driven from the colonies by misfortune. I have already pointed out what has happened in Virginia, New York, Philadelphia, Baltimore, Charleston, where so many moving examples of generosity have been given. On February 4, 1794, Congress voted ninety thousand francs to these unfortunates. This relief has been multiplied many times over in the cases of refugees who have been given private assistance, and their gratitude should be eternal.

Several American sea captains have carried colonials to the United States without charge.

A Maine captain, among others, commanding the brig *Eagle* of Charleston, brought twenty-two French passengers to Charleston in February, 1794, without asking anything of them except that they feed themselves.

Here are some incidents of another sort. An American schooner at San Domingo contracted to carry two military convalescents to Boston. Instead of that it marooned them on Turtle Island with one bottle of water and a few crackers.

Another American delivered to the enemy on the quay at Jean Rebel a few French guardsmen whom he had on board. During the unhappy times in San Domingo, Americans overcharged Frenchmen to take them to the American continent, bought their belongings dirt cheap; then turned the Frenchmen over to privateers from Jamaica, Bermuda and New Providence. Other faithless guardians have denied receiving goods entrusted to them. The bell from the church of Cap François was recognized at Baltimore. But even these traits cannot nullify the kindnesses I have publicly acknowledged.

In New York the Americans have established a refuge where more than one hundred unfortunate French have been fed, dressed and supported. In November, 1798, this refuge still housed fifty old men, women and children. At New York, too, Dr. Romaine helped and cared for the French. Commodore Michelton and his wife took all the responsibility for a family of five persons.

A young woman from Cap François was brought to bed without money or resources. The doctor told M. Michelton's daughter, who went weeping to her mother to repeat the story. The latter provided the necessary help, and the young mother's needs were fully supplied.

In Philadelphia there is widespread compassion for the French.

However I wouldn't be a faithful historian if I silently permitted it to be thought that a true feeling of affection exists between Americans and French colonials or Frenchmen in general.

Any slight political event may alter their relationship, weakening it to such a degree that both parties to it forget that they ever were friends.

France's choice of ministers and envoys to the United States showed little desire to win the friendship of the Americans. M. de la Luzerne was the only one who knew how to please them. M. de Montier's maladroitness was such that when he dined at the home of M. Hamilton, the Minister, he took with him two or three dishes cooked in the French fashion on the pretext of being on a diet. M. de Ternan merely passed through the country. Minister Genêt wanted to burn up everything. If he had been minister another six weeks, he would have been successful, and the President would have been forced to call a session of Congress to declare war on England.

Fauchet was less of a diplomat than a cowardly slave to the Jacobins on the continent.

Adet was wise and gentle, but his home life was such that it attracted no one.

It must be admitted that France, after becoming a republic, never paid her ambassadors to America adequately. The fundamental characteristics of her ambassador should be resolution united with extreme politeness. He must be all that is amiable, see all, hear all, receive everybody without affectation, with tranquillity. In brief he must use his dinner table for diplomatic purposes, astutely attracting to it influential members of the House of Representatives and of the Senate. He must never permit the English Ambassador to serve better Madeira than his own. If he meets with approval in America, he can be of great service to his country.

The behavior of the French Minister must set the best

example to the French. Many Frenchmen have come to every part of the United States with all sorts of opinions and from every rank of society, but the chief impression they have left here is one of the lightness and lack of restraint of the French. They have been contemptuous of all customs unlike those of their own country. Those whom interested and trusting Americans have welcomed into their families as friends have brought to those families only seduction and shame. Those who have taken American wives have abandoned them forever, thus displaying the blackest and most dastardly ingratitude.

The population of Philadelphia is, as we have noted, fifty-five or sixty thousand souls, made up of three different classes,

1. Whites
2. People of Color } of two sexes.
3. And Slaves

Let us examine them in turn.

I. The Whites, as everyone knows, are the dominant class, but they are subdivided, nonetheless, into five classes— 1. white men; 2. white women; 3. white children; 4. white servants; 5. indentured white servants. II. Colored People are divided into men, women and children. III. Slaves into men, women and children.

We shall not speak of the Indians, who are red men and aborigines. Moreover, they inhabit only such places as are set apart for them; and if they appear in cities, even in Philadelphia, it is always for some political reason.

I   *The Whites*

1. White Men.—Everything I have said about the general character of the Americans refers to them. They are made up of English, Scotch, Irish and all the nationalities of Europe;

and Americans born in different provinces of the United States have extremely diversified European ancestors.

Even in 1678, before the arrival of Penn in Philadelphia, Hollanders, Irish and Swedes were already in great number at Upland (the present Chester) at Newcastle and at Haxkills (now Landslin). Many Quakers like Penn were at Shackumaxon (at the present time Kensington), a suburb of Philadelphia.

When the ship *Shield* of Stockton, the first which dared sail as far up the Delaware as Burlington, ran its bowsprit into the trees which bordered the right bank where the city of Philadelphia now stands, someone said: "This would be a beautiful place for a city."

Penn, having left London in August, 1682, arrived at Philadelphia on the ship *Welcome*, Captain Greenway.

He brought with him one hundred of his friends and companions, despised by the English because of their habit of shaking in their churches.

On October 24 Penn landed at Newcastle, whence the joyful Hollanders escorted him to Upland (Chester), their chief seat, and recognized his authority over them.

In the northernmost part of the little village of Kensington, adjoining the city of Philadelphia, and at the most northern shipyard, the tree still stands under which Penn concluded his treaty of acquisition with the Indians.

This tree is the Charter Oak. It is beautiful and majestic. Nothing marks its history except memory based on tradition.

Penn left an enormous estate to his family. His descendants were loyal to England and retired there during the war which ended in 1783.

The government of Pennsylvania confiscated their lands, which an English paper values at five hundred million sterling, from an act of Parliament dated May, 1790.

The government of Pennsylvania has decreed payment to

the Penn family of an annual income of one hundred and fifty thousand pounds or four million two hundred thousand francs.

The first installment was paid in United States paper which was almost worthless. Then the English Parliament in 1790 granted the family a pension of four thousand pounds sterling (one hundred thousand francs).

Penn chose the location of Philadelphia. It was completely covered with trees. Its soil is clayey, and its higher portions have stone, chalk, marble, and coal and iron mines.

In the first year eighty-one houses or rather cabins were built. One of these still stands. It is a tavern at the corner of Front and Dock streets, bearing the signboard of Bostoman and Cull. Another was Penn's home in the city, at present standing in Black Horse Alley, exactly behind Lochlin, so called from the name of one of the proprietor's daughters.

Opposite this last house, in the middle of Market Street, there was for many years a monument of primitive simplicity. This was a wooden jail, seldom occupied except by the jailer.

The first child born in Philadelphia was John Key, who lived eighty-five years.

Edward Drinker, born in a cave under the bank of the Delaware, only died after the Declaration of Independence. Another instance: until recently there was still a widow whose mother came from London when Philadelphia had only three houses.

It was during the War of Independence that houses began to be numbered, and that the royal army made a floating bridge across the Schuylkill.

The city then extended a scant half mile on the west bank of the Delaware. There was a road to the hospital, to the Swedish church in the south, and to Kensington dockyards in the north.

An inhabitant of Philadelphia, who in the beginning saw perhaps three carriages in the entire town, with only two or three vessels arriving from London in the course of a year and only a few small craft sailing to the colonies, has in the course of a lifetime seen the three carriages grow to three hundred, and twelve or fifteen vessels sailing daily for every port of the globe, even for the Antipodes.

Americans, indifferent in love and friendship, cling to nothing, attach themselves to nothing. There is plenty of evidence of this among country dwellers. Four times running they will break land for a new home, abandoning without a thought the house in which they were born, the church where they learned about God, the tombs of their fathers, the friends of their childhood, the companions of their youth, and all the pleasures of their first society. They emigrate, especially from north to south, or toward the outermost western boundary of the United States on the Ohio. Everywhere, even in Philadelphia, which is America's outstanding city, everything is for sale, provided the owner is offered a tempting price. He will part with his house, his carriage, his horse, his dog—anything at all.

Americans are not only smokers, but they chew too. Sometimes they indulge in both, that custom so dear to sailors. But an American of either sex who uses snuff is a sort of phenomenon, and the women never deform or dirty their noses by using this powder so cherished by Europeans.

And in spite of all the pretenses invented by those who have the habit, it is far more contrary to cleanliness than useful to health.

In Philadelphia, as elsewhere in the United States, three meals are eaten each day, as I have already told in detail. Hot drinks are also used immoderately, and tea is served boiling hot. In summer everyone drinks cold and iced water, and makes frequent use of liqueurs, rum, brandy, whiskey. Brandy is mixed with water and called grog.

People consume green fruits, eat seven or eight times as much meat as bread, and lie far too long in feather beds.

Even when houses are repainted, which is usually done at the beginning of autumn almost every year, the Americans continue to live in their apartments without interruption.

Americans are not as good for work and solid character as the Germans who form a great part of the population. The Germans of Pennsylvania and of Philadelphia are less given to drunkenness, and have larger families. They have as many as twelve or fourteen children, while among twenty-seven American families there was only one that had thirteen children and one that had twelve.

The sixty thousand inhabitants of Philadelphia are estimated to consume annually forty thousand pounds of market-meat, or eleven ounces per individual.[7] It is generally agreed that American meat is one eighth less substantial than in France.

The Quakers, who are numerous in Philadelphia, are becoming fewer, because many Quaker children leave the faith. The coquetry of young Quaker women is apparent, and they combine a pretended simplicity with extremely worldly tastes, which must cause many of them to abandon the sect.

It is to the influence and the number of Quakers in Philadelphia that one must attribute the melancholy customs of this city, which has less society than most places.

At this point we stop our references to the white men of Philadelphia, not because there is nothing more to say about them, but because in the rest of our description of the population of this town, they become mixed in with what we are going to say about other groups.

If we dared go out of Philadelphia and glance at those who live far in the country in sections that are remote, though in

---

[7] *"On évalue que les 60 mille habitans de Philadelphie consomment par an 40 milliers de viande poids de Marc à raison de onze onces par individu."*

the same province, we would say that Americans who live there have neither justice nor public security. If a person buys land, one is apt to find that someone has already seized it and established himself upon it. If you try to make him abandon it, a gunshot may stop you, and none will be interested in avenging you.

There is a judge, but he only holds court for form's sake so that the clerk, who is related to him, may earn a livelihood. There is another official called a counselor, who is usually the tavern-keeper.

In the country, when the people are busy plowing and harvesting, they are contented enough with their condition, and pay no attention to what is going on in the cities.

Now let us speak of white women:

2. White Women.—We will begin our observations concerning this beautiful sex with a flattering and happy statement. An American woman, no matter what her rank or where she was born, never—except as a result of an accident —displays one of those faces so common among the lower orders of Europe and even of France: repulsive faces with bloodshot or bleary eyes and offensively deformed features. If one encounters such a face in America, he can safely jump to the conclusion that it was imported from another land: never the product of a soil so favorable to womankind.

American women are pretty, and those of Philadelphia are prettiest of all, and generally acknowledged to be superior to any others on the continent. Philadelphia has thousands of them between the ages of fourteen and eighteen; and proof of this can be had on any fine winter day on the north sidewalk of Market Street between Third and Fifth streets. There one can see four hundred young persons, each of whom would certainly be followed on any Paris promenade. This tempting state of affairs is one which no other city in the world could offer in like degree.

But they soon grow pale, and suffer almost universally

from an inconvenience which is known to be highly destructive to the preservation of a woman's freshness and youth. Their hair is scanty, their teeth bad; and all the little details which adorn beauty, or rather which join to create it, soon fail most of them. In short, while charming and adorable at fifteen, they are faded at twenty-three, old at thirty-five, decrepit at forty or forty-five. They are subject to nervous illnesses and to those which the English call [*quatre mots anglais illisibles*],[8] which is extremely frequent.

Few people live to be a hundred in the United States, and among the gravestones of Philadelphia cemeteries there is only one of a person who lived to be ninety. Most people die between thirty-five and forty-five.

There are exceptions, however. At Preston, Connecticut, Mme. Elizabeth Hericott died September, 1804, at seventy-nine. She had been married sixty-one years. She left nine children, sixty-three grandchildren and nineteen great-grandchildren, a total of ninety-one. At the same time at Brunswick, Maine, M. Thomas Hum died at the age of eighty, leaving five generations of descendants, one hundred and twenty-two persons in all. Seven of his sons were present at his funeral, the youngest being fifty years old.

At Rowley, Mme. Aphen Gage, widow of the late General Thomas Gage, died in August, 1804, aged eighty-eight. She had had two children, twenty-two grandchildren, fifty-two great-grandchildren, and one of the fourth generation, a total of seventy-seven, of whom sixty-four live in Berwick, Maine.

Daniel Belly died in August, 1804, aged eighty-eight. He had sixteen children, one hundred and thirteen grandchildren and seventy-two descendants of these latter, a total of two hundred and one living.

Girls ordinarily mature in Philadelphia at the age of fourteen, and reach that period without unusual symptoms. The

[8]Four illegible English words.

reproductive faculty usually ceases between forty and forty-five; and this period, so dangerous in our climates, has no dangerous consequences in America.

Young girls never appear at social gatherings until they have reached puberty.

As they are usually large for their age, one is struck by the tall and pretty young girls one sees in the streets, going and coming from school. They wear their hair long, and skirts with closed seams. But when nubility has arrived they put up their hair with a comb, and the back of the skirt has a placket. At this time they meet everybody at tea, become their own mistresses, and can go walking alone and have suitors.

They invariably make their own choice of a suitor, and the parents raise no objection because that's the custom of the country. The suitor comes into the house when he wishes; goes on walks with his loved one whenever he desires. On Sunday he often takes her out in a cabriolet, and brings her back in the evening without anyone wanting to know where they went.

Philadelphia women are markedly extravagant in their purchase of ribbons, shoes and negligees of lawn and muslin. However, they still have no gauze or lace, and almost no artificial flowers. They have a habit, which they think is stylish, of letting the men pay for what they buy in the shops, and of forgetting to pay them back.

They are greatly addicted to finery and have a strong desire to display themselves—a desire resulting from and inflamed by their love of adornment. They cannot, however, imitate that elegance of style possessed by Frenchwomen. All except those of the highest position go to market Tuesday and Friday evenings (the evenings before market days) dressed for dancing.

After eighteen years old they lose their charms, and fade. Their breasts, never large, already have vanished. It is true that many of them, because of a notion as harmful as it is ridiculous, flatten and compress those female charms with which the sex has been endowed by Nature.

The women of the Lutheran religion may be distinguished from the others because they wear untrimmed hats with a fold in the back, like those of Quakeresses.

Although in general one is conscious of widespread modesty in Philadelphia, the customs are not particularly pure, and the disregard on the part of some parents for the manner in which their daughters form relationships to which they, the parents, have not given their approval is an encouragement of indiscretions which, however, are not the result of love, since American women are not affectionate.

But they are very ridiculous in their aversion to hearing certain words pronounced; and this scruple is frequently a confession of too much knowledge, rather than of ignorance.

A woman made her brother leave the room while she changed the diaper of her own son, aged five weeks, although women and young girls were present.

The adoption in this city of French styles in dress and manner does not, however, indicate that it has any marked affection for the French nation, and its residents have no hesitation in charging the French higher prices and higher rents than anyone else.

The young ladies commonly stick to their first suitor unless circumstances more or less unavoidable necessitate the absence of the first, which may then result in their making a second choice. The same situation may arise several times, always with the same result.

If the suitor continues to reside in the same place, he is always bound by the same chains unless he is criminally inconstant and, having drained the delights of happiness, flees and laughs at the tears of the loved one he has betrayed.

But if the dastardly deceiver should seduce a married woman, he is universally execrated and watched wherever he may go in the United States; and never, never will he ever be able to obtain in this vast country any situation, any position, not even that of watchman or patroller of the streets.

It is true that virtue is the result of habit or of disposition. A young woman trusts in her suitor's delicacy and charges him with maintaining for her a respect which she is not always able to command. Each day both of them are entrusted to no one but each other. Since the young lady must wait for her servant, who leaves the house as soon as night has arrived and cannot be persuaded to return until eleven-thirty or midnight, her only protection is her suitor. Her father, her mother, her entire family have gone to bed. The suitor and his mistress remain alone; and sometimes, when the servant returns, she finds them asleep and the candle out, such is the frigidity of love in this country.

When a young lady notices that her chosen one is growing cold, she reproaches him most outrageously in public; and if another young lady, either through ignorance or by desire, seeks to supplant her, she tells the latter that she has rights which she has no intention of giving up.

They are cold and without passion, however, and—a thing that is unpermissible except in an uncontrollable delirium—they endure the company of their lovers for whole hours without being sufficiently moved to change their expression. They always act as though everything they do is done for a purpose.

When one considers the unlimited liberty which young ladies enjoy, one is astonished by their universal eagerness to be married, to become wives who will for the most part be nothing but housekeepers of their husbands' homes. But this eagerness is just another exhibition of self-love, inspired by the fear that she who does not marry will be thought to have some fault that disgusted her suitors.

They think, too, that French women have some peculiar talent because of the way in which men of their own nation make efforts to please them, especially by their politeness.

Marriages are all the more easy as sometimes they are made in a hurry, and many of them are secret.

I am going to say something that is almost unbelievable. These women, without real love and without passions, give themselves up at an early age to the enjoyment of themselves; and they are not at all strangers to being willing to seek unnatural pleasures with persons of their own sex.

Among common people, at a tavern-keeper's, for example, or at a small shopkeeper's, the daughter of the house, when no longer a child, sleeps with the servant. That is to say, from her eighth to her tenth year she may have shared the bed of fifty or sixty creatures of whom nothing is known except their names. They may be dirty, unhealthy, subject to a communicable disease of more or less seriousness, and possessors of habits that could be disastrous to young persons.

When a young woman marries, she enters a wholly different existence. She is no longer a giddy young person, a butterfly who denies herself nothing and whose only laws are her whims and her suitor's wish. She now lives only for her husband, and to devote herself without surcease to the care of her household and her home. In short, she is no more than a housekeeper. To put it more correctly, she is often the one and only servant.

American women carve meat with a great deal of elegance, and carving skill that would seem astounding in a French woman is commonplace to them. They also prepare pastries with great success.

At Philadelphia, starting the day after their marriage, a bride serves punch and cold meats for three successive mornings to all her friends and all those who wish to give themselves that title. Then, on the three following days, the bride serves tea in the evening, and her friends and acquaintances attend, each one trying to outdo the other in the elegance of their apparel. The honors are done by her young relatives, or by friends of the bride, who are called bridesmaids. So go the outward rejoicings of the marriage feast. The mistress of the house busies herself with all the details, carving and serving at table.

If she has had the misfortune to lose her chastity, her already altered health finds new dangers in the very pleasures of matrimony. The more her husband is capable of multiplying them, the more her health may suffer, most of all when she has a child; for sometimes while still nursing it, or as soon as it is weaned, she has already conceived another.

The women don't dress warmly, their food is bad, and they make too much use of over-hot tea. On the other hand, false modesty prevents them from admitting infirmities of which the husband has never been told and which become serious.

They also have bad teeth, weak stomachs, minor illnesses which wither or at least tarnish their beauty; sometimes a neglected fault results in skin eruptions.

Women wash their feet with cold water during menstruation, and mothers do not like to teach children why this imprudence is dangerous, because they do not wish, they say, to discuss such things with them.

They take no precaution against changes of climate, not even those which cleanliness seems to require. They wear only one colored skirt which they put on during menstruation, and which serves always in the same capacity until it must be thrown away. Men have given them a disgusting name. They consider French women most reprehensible for having a different custom, and washing the linen thus used.

The American women divide their whole body in two parts; from the top to the waist is stomach; from there to the foot is ankles.

Let us imagine the embarrassment of the doctor who must guess from such a description the nature and especially the location of an illness! He is forbidden the slightest touch; his patient, even at the risk of her life, leaves him in the vaguest doubt.

Here is an example: A young woman was nursing her first child. One of her breasts had a crack. She was suffering dreadfully from it, but only complained to her doctor that she had pains in her stomach, and her trouble continued to grow.

A woman neighbor, seeing this woman fading away, questioned her. She told her the truth, and even went so far as to show her the ailing breast. But when her friend urged her to let the doctor see it, she was refused.

Frightened by the danger, she spoke to me about it. I determined to speak to this woman about her condition, using all the discretion demanded by the most violent prejudice, and tell her of the risk she was running, and of the death with which her condition threatened her much-loved little boy. I argued that she was failing in the most sacred duties of nature and religion; and finally I told her that her obstinacy was truly suicide.

Speaking as a husband and father, I used such eloquence that the patient was convinced, and promised to entrust herself to the enlightened care of the doctor.

She did it and, after long treatment, recovered her health; but with this result: although she knew that she owed me the saving of her life and that of her child, this young mother never spoke to me again and didn't even wish to acknowledge my existence.

In their opinion French women are not clean because they dress in such a way that their chemises can be seen.

I am ashamed to say that it is exactly because American women are so sensitive about these garments, and because they have so few of them and change them so seldom, that they are guilty of not keeping them clean, and of dirtying them with marks of that need to which Nature has subjected every animal.

American women carefully wash their faces and hands, but not their mouths, seldom their feet and even more seldom their bodies.

When a Philadelphia woman bears a child, her husband is never present. He cannot enter the room until an hour after the birth.

During the first week the mother receives only near relations, intimate friends, old women, but never men or young girls.

The second week she receives the rest of her family and acquaintances, but no man.

The third week is for the receiving of ceremonious visits; and occasionally a man who has asked and obtained permission comes in with his wife.

The fourth week everybody is admitted without distinction, and after that the woman takes up her accustomed work. I repeat that in Philadelphia a husband resumes conjugal relations with his nursing wife a month after the birth.

A gentleman gives his arm to young ladies but not to mothers, who, even if he offers, relegate him to the young ladies.

A husband will offer his arm to his wife, but does not bother about other women.

There are no casual runnings in and out, in American homes. Never does one walk into a woman's bedroom.

One frequently sees in the newspapers notices of husbands requesting that no further credit be given to their wives, who have left their bed and board.

One very remarkable and very important thing is the respect in which married women are held, and the virtuous conduct of almost all.

This respect is demonstrated in one particularly praiseworthy manner. I have spoken of the unrestrained life of the young girls. Before their marriage several suitors may possibly have enjoyed a dangerous freedom in their company. But once they have pledged their faith to a husband, no matter how many times they may meet one or all of their former suitors, never will a word which might wound the ears of the wife or make her blush escape from the mouth of one of them. This is perhaps a unique state of affairs: a country in which love is silent where marriage exists.

In spite of conjugal customs which would seem to indicate a state of happiness, they do not produce the happiness which would be expected to result, nor tenderness for children, nor love on the children's part.

This is evidenced by the multiplicity of second marriages, and the manner in which children of different beds live in the same house. The men in particular remarry oftenest; and a delay of six weeks between the loss of a wife and the choice of another is the limit of their outward expression of regret.

The children live with each other with neither affection nor jealousy. They never have to complain about favoritism because none of them ever get it.

Divorce is obtained with scandalous ease. From this alone one can judge the extent of loose habits. The conjugal union is the fountainhead of all family relations; and since it is one of the strongest ties in the social order, it is impossible that these ties and relationships shouldn't be weakened or destroyed by easy divorce.

All American girls or women are fond of dancing, which is one of their greatest pleasures. The men like it almost as much. They indulge in this pleasure, either in the morning, from eight to eleven, or the evening from the end of the day far into the night.

I believe I have already said elsewhere that dancing, for the inhabitants of the United States, is less a matter of self-display than it is of true enjoyment. At the same dance you will see a grandfather, his son and his grandson, but more often still the grandmother, her daughter and her grand-daughter. If a Frenchman comments upon this with surprise, he is told that each one dances for his own amusement, and not because it's the thing to do.

3. White Children.—The character which I have ascribed to Americans shows that it is formed by the examples which have surrounded them, one might say, from birth. They are brought up in the paternal home, and are very willful. In general they are naughty.

Their naughtiness is principally exercised in hitting little Negroes. They throw snowballs at passers-by and even I have not been free of feeling how badly they have been brought up.

Children in the cradle who belong to women who work for a living are rocked without interruption from the time the mother rises until she goes to bed. The cradles are built for rocking, and are moved with the foot and with such vigor that the child must be in a state of continuous dizziness. If there are other women or children in the house, they are put to work at this exercise in relays.

When they are larger, they are sent to school, where they learn to read, write and do arithmetic. These schools have one great advantage in writing, in that all use the same sys-tem. It is almost English and extremely legible, and because of that it doesn't matter on what part of the continent a child learns to write: he is certain to find the same teaching and the same handwriting in every other place.

This is all the more valuable because children are given early, for a certain number of years, into the charge of those who will teach them to be mariners, a profession which re-quires them to know how to write. So when after a crossing a child reaches port, the man whose apprentice he is sends him straight to school.

292 Moreau de St. Méry's American Journey

In almost all cities of the continent, especially in the North, there are superintendents who notify parents when their children have arrived at their seventh year, and order them to be sent to school. If the parents refuse to obey this order, it is repeated and a time limit set, at the expiration of which the superintendent takes the child to school.

Because of this valuable work, it is generally accepted that a man who knows how to read and write somehow doubles his intelligence, in contrast to those who are denied these two benefits; that all Americans of both sexes should know how to write; also that it is an insult to doubt it.

In this connection I remember that when I was employed at ten years of age in the Record Office of the Admiralty of Martinique, where I was in charge of receiving declarations, I boldly presented a pen to American sailors to sign, while the great part of the French sailors didn't know how to write, which was always humiliating to my national pride.

When the children have become bigger they are sent to boarding schools, if their parents are able to stand the expense. There they are taught English, Latin and Greek, because in North America this last language is taught like Latin. But I have mentioned often enough the manner in which lazy and undisciplined children behave in these schools, where masters and instructors think only of retaining them as pupils by displaying toward them the most unfortunate complacency.

Boarding schools for girls are bad too, but in another way. I saw one to which one of my nieces went to learn English. It was directed by an Englishwoman. For punishment the mistress maliciously fastened the scholars' arms back of the chairs. This treatment was even inflicted on girls fifteen or sixteen, as well as on little children.

To get meat in this boarding school, the pupils had to write on a small piece of paper the words beef, veal or mutton, since there could be one of these three kinds on a given day, and each pupil had to pass in her name with this little indication of her preference.

Schools for little boys are rather severe. My nephew, aged eleven, received eighteen strokes in September, 1795. This is because such schools do not fear to lack scholars, which is quite a different state of affairs from the boarding schools.

On June 3, 1795, Matthew Clarkson, Mayor of Philadelphia, deplored in a long proclamation the disorders resulting from bad conduct and intractableness of Philadelphia's children, apprentices and domestics.

Bastards are extremely common in Philadelphia. There are two principal reasons for this. In the first place, the city is full of religious sects, but none of them give their clergymen any authority to enforce obedience. Consequently there is no way of inspiring shame in women who become mothers for no reason except the pleasure they get out of it. In the second place, once an illegitimate child is twelve months old, a mother can disembarrass herself of him by farming him out for twenty-one years. This makes it possible for her to commit the same sin for a second time. It never occurs to her that her child can never know her, and that the whole business is shameful. Needless to say, when mothers have such ideas and are so heartless, abortion is seldom resorted to.

4. White Servants.—It is extremely difficult to have any in Philadelphia; they are almost all indentured servants—that is to say, persons brought over from Europe.

The custom of importing indentured servants has long obtained and is still common in America, and began with its earliest settlements. Even the legislatures of some states have authorized it, and this is the case in Pennsylvania.

As a rule, the captain who brings the indentured persons is obliged to declare the name, age and profession of all passengers, because if he brings in persons convicted of crime, or those with infirmities that would make them state charges, he would be obliged to pay a fine and to give surety for their future good conduct. A judge is supposed to go aboard to check and verify the facts. Indentures have to be made before the Mayor.

The length of a person's servitude may vary, since it depends on the arrangements that the servant has made with the captain as to the expense of the passage, as well as on the sort of service that he is able to render.

If a person doesn't wish to sign a contract, he can be forced to. Children are indentured until twenty-one years of age in return for the payment of their passage or of that of a parent who may have died during the voyage. A husband and wife can also be indentured for the same motive. By an act of 1700, anyone who has reached his majority can be indentured for only four years. Every passenger who offers to pay for his passage can free himself. If he cannot do so, the captain of the ship has thirty days in which to dispose of him. After that time, the passenger is considered in the light of an ordinary debtor, and can then make a declaration of insolvency.

An indentured servant receives his clothing each year, and by a law of 1700 receives two complete suits at the end of his term. Those are the general principles. Here is what happens.

One who takes an indentured servant on his arrival at the port pays his passage, takes charge of him for the length of time agreed upon, and employs him according to his needs, either for work in the country, or domestic service, in city or country houses. The same is true for both sexes.

Americans are never bound out.

The master takes care of the indentured servant in health or in sickness, feeds him, and at the end of the specified time allows him the clothes he possesses, and in addition gives him one new outfit, including shoes and a hat.

The people from the Palatinate are the most highly sought because of their faithfulness and intelligence.

Before the Revolution, because of the great numbers of scalawags and prostitutes who were coming from London, Franklin put an open letter to the King of England in his Philadelphia *Gazette,* January 13, 1763, saying that in return he was sending the King an equivalent present of several rattlesnakes with which to stock his gardens. And after the peace of 1783 a whole shipload of condemned criminals were sent over by the English, and promptly sent back to England.

There is no prejudice against an indentured servant who has worked out his time; and never does he sell himself a second time. Manual labor is too well paid in the United States for any man to think that he wouldn't find it more profitable to be free. The children of an indentured servant are born free.

Bondwomen or bond girls have the right to charge their masters with seduction if the occasion arises.

The only proof they need, as in the case of any other woman, is their own legal statement. If the case is proved, the master is liable for the support of the child and has to pay a fine for fornication or adultery—unless the servant yielded to him of her own free will, in which case she has no more claim against him than any other woman.

These unfortunates are usually so unhappy as indentured servants that they never draw a happy breath until they know the joy of being their own masters.

For example, the Germans employed by M. Richelet of Maryland in his foundry are indentured for seven years.

According to the law of 1700 and of 1771, an indentured servant who runs away must, if retaken and convicted by a justice of the peace, serve five days for each day of absence, and in addition be subject to any other fine the judge may wish to impose.

A master has the constant right to insist upon the work to which he is entitled by law.

If a master is dissatisfied, he can demand that the justice of the peace put the indentured servant in prison. The latter has the right of appeal to a superior court, which can revoke the indenture if the master has taken advantage of it. Such prison sentences, inflicted as corrective measures, cannot exceed thirty days.

The law does not take a hand in other forms of punishment, which must be the same as fathers exercise over their own children.

If an indentured servant is sentenced to prison, he is subject to the general rule which makes prisoners earn their keep by working. If the indentured servant was a citizen before being jailed, he keeps all citizenship rights. Unless he is a minor, he can go to law in his own name—if a woman, unless she is under marital authority—and provided further that indentured servants of both sexes have done nothing to injure the rights of the master.

An indentured servant cannot marry without the consent of his master. If he does so, he must serve an additional year beyond the agreed term. If an indentured servant marries a free person, the latter must pay the master an indemnity of twelve punchs (one hundred and ninety-two francs) if the indentured servant is a man, but only six if a woman, in addition to the extra year of service.

Marriage, even though the master gives consent, does not alter the contract, which can only be dissolved by mutual consent.

One of these indentured servants, who had been guilty of gross malingering, was given twenty-five lashes of the whip for the slightest fault.

The services of an indentured servant can be sold, just as can any commodity, but the master must guarantee that he will not steal, a promise which is not always without risk.

It is not unusual for indentured servants to run away. In such cases their names are published as fugitives in the papers.

An indentured servant whose time has expired is anxious not to be confused with those who are still in service.

This is one of the reasons why servants are hard to find or keep, especially female indentured servants who have been freed.

There is nothing more singular than their aversion to having anyone think that they are still *boundées*,[9] an English expression which signifies "bound." Even though one of them may have long been a servant, all the other servants in the same house urge her to leave so that she won't be considered an indenture.

They hate to do errands on the ground that they may become servants of the persons to whose houses they are sent. If they are sent to buy something, and the purchase is unsatisfactory, they refuse to undertake such errands in the future. As a rule they are immoral and there is hardly an indentured servant in Philadelphia who can't be had for very little money.

Ordinarily they have but one chemise, and some not even that. These reach only to their waists. They wash their chemises on Saturday. During menstruation the only protection of indentured servants is a skirt of bunting which they wear next to the skin, and which they use until its old age forces them to take another.

They do not like to serve Frenchwomen, on the ground that they want too many errands done and that the French wash their feet too often and it's too much trouble to prepare water for them.

They love to dress up for their evening promenade, which lasts from nine until eleven and, it's said, leads them to places where they traffic in their charms. On Sundays it is difficult to distinguish mistresses from servants. Some are barefoot, and at the same time wear hats with large ribbons.

At the slightest whim they leave the house where they

[9]Hence the expression "bounder," still considered uncomplimentary.

serve, sometimes in the middle of a meal. They get drunk. All servants, no matter what their sex or color, insist on having coffee, sugar and soft bread.

Both indentured and free servants, men and women alike, have similar faults and vices.

If an indentured servant who has been freed has enough ability to be a farm hand, he can earn one hundred dollars a year (six hundred francs), can have coffee and sugar every morning, tea and sugar every night.

He will drop whatever he is doing to talk politics for an hour at a time with any passing acquaintance.

He borrows the sleigh, picks up girls, and doesn't come back for three or four days.

He spends an hour or two at the table over his tea with his wife. He expects his wife to serve him, and he takes twelve or fifteen cups with lots of sugar.

On Sundays the two of them do nothing whatever. On that day a Negro has to milk the cow to get for them the milk which they insist on having in their coffee and tea.

The woman, whenever she wishes, spends two or three days at her mother's or a relative's.

Since I have gone into such detail, I may as well add that at harvest time the farm hand finds it necessary to go to his neighbors and, after speaking of many indifferent things, say: "By the way, neighbor, I hope that you will want to help me in about a quarter of an hour or half an hour." The neighbor answers by promising this favor, for which he is paid a dollar a day in addition to food and grog whenever he wants it.

In spite of the independence of the servants, it is not always their fault if they behave as they do, because their masters treat them personally with a haughtiness which verges on contempt.

One singular American custom as compared with our own is that no traveler gives tips to servants in hotels. I knew of the wife of a Philadelphia lodging-house keeper who violently beat the female servant of a woman who lodged in his house on the ground that the servant had accepted a small gold ring from a male lodger—and this in spite of the protests of the master and mistress of the servant, who were astounded, and rightly, by such furious behavior.

5. White Indentured Servants.—All that can be said about them has already been included in the chapter on white servants. Philadelphia receives every year four or five thousand white indentured servants. A Philadelphia paper for December, 1798, carried the following:

"In three trips one Irish boat has brought a sufficient number of white indentured servants to this city to earn 10,000 pounds sterling (250,000 f.) for the shipowners."

In a year thirteen thousand white indentured servants have entered the country. They were sold at an average of ten pounds sterling apiece, a total of three million two hundred and fifty thousand francs. It is not, therefore, the good quality of the soil or the excellence of the laws which are responsible for the growth of the population of the United States, but the traffic in Europeans who have been poured into it. This emigration brings to Pennsylvania alone a yearly average of eight thousand white indentured servants. No wonder it grows so astonishingly.

Mittelberger,[10] who was in Philadelphia in 1751, 1752 and 1753, said that he witnessed the arrival of more than twenty-five thousand of his compatriots, all of whom were sold. Children from nine to twelve brought from a hundred and fifty to two hundred francs; men above eighteen brought from three hundred to three hundred and forty-five francs.

In the six years before the Americans seceded from the English, the northern and central United States received

[10]Gottlieb Mittelberger's *Journey to Pennsylvania in the Year 1750 and Return to Germany in the Year 1754* (translated from the German by Carl Theo. Eben) contains a most interesting account of the life in Pennsylvania of the German immigrant.

more than sixty thousand indentured servants purchased in Germany. This emigration was so much felt that the Palatinate, Swabia, Bavaria and the Ecclesiastical Electorates[11] passed stringent laws forbidding these indentures. Americans then turned to Switzerland for recruits. Ireland never stopped furnishing them with indentured servants, and still continues to do so.

In 1774 Pennsylvania had a population of 350,000 inhabitants, divided as follows:

	30,000	Blacks
	100,000	Germans
	90,000	Irish
	45,000	Hessians
	10,000	Free English
	275,000	Foreigners, all bought,
leaving	75,000	Americans
Total	350,000	

By an act of Congress, an indentured servant who flees from one state to another must be given back with the product of his work.

In 1786, Claude Byron, born at Lyons, France, arrived in America as an indentured servant, presented a petition to the magistrates of Philadelphia. It represented that when he found himself crushed by poverty in London, he had stated that he was an upholsterer, and had agreed to pay for his passage to America out of his earnings, but that he is now about to be sold, and asks for protection. His petition was without effect.

When a French privateer captured a shipload of Irish who were on their way to America as indentured servants, all of them were given their liberty by the French consul in New York.

[11]Mainz, Treves and Cologne.

Here is an article published in a Philadelphia newspaper while I was living there:

"The ship *Sally*, Captain Hernes, arrived from Londonderry in forty-five days with eighty-three passengers, all well and having received good treatment. Captain Hernes announces that a ship sailed three weeks before him with five hundred and fifty passengers for Philadelphia. The *Adolphe* sailed for the same place two weeks before him, with the same number. Just before he sailed, the *William* and the *Harwick* had left with two hundred and eighty, the *Eliza* was ready to sail and the ship *Union*, both loaded with passengers, left shortly afterwards for Philadelphia."

Here is an announcement I found in the Philadelphia newspaper published by Porcupine, the well-known Cobbett, on January 25, 1798:

"A number of German passengers, principally young people, some of them women, others persons of middle age, have just arrived in this city from Hamburg. Their passages from Hamburg will be paid by persons who take them into service for a certain time. Among them are carpenters, turners, makers of musical instruments, calico printers, farmers, butchers, tobacco makers, candle makers, goldsmiths, watchmakers, teachers of different languages, coachmen, horse trainers, servants, café waiters, etc. They are living at the Swan Hotel, where they can be seen and contracted for."

I don't believe anything gives a better picture of a slave market.

When a white apprentice escapes, a notice containing his description is put in the newspaper.

II *Colored People of all Ages and both Sexes*

Under this heading I include all persons not white, but free and descended from the African race. The people of color live entirely among themselves without distinguishing between mulattoes, griffes, Negroes and quadroons, who are extremely rare.

All the colored women of Philadelphia dress well on Sunday, and wear chignons of white people's false hair.

Old Negresses have white kid gloves and parasols.

Negresses wear pale pink.

Nearly all colored people are poor and unhappy, and obliged to work as servants.

A white servant, no matter who, would consider it a dishonor to eat with colored people.

In the Philadelphia prisons and among condemned criminals, colored people and whites do not eat together.

There is a cemetery exclusively for them in Philadelphia. In the same city there is an African church, as if there were an African religion and an African God, and the Anglican faith is professed in this church. In other churches, they are separated from the whites. The protection which the Quakers pretend to grant them is, like all the acts of this sect, an ostentatious display of humility. It is a form of condescension which many business men use to their own advantage.

The congregation of the Irish Catholic church, on South Sixth Street, does not allow colored persons to be buried in its cemetery.

In South Carolina they are subject to a poll tax from their sixteenth to their fiftieth years, and pay two dollars (twelve francs) a head.

Colored burials are extremely decent.

All I have said of the faults, vices and customs of indentured servants applies to colored people as well.

Women, those of color especially, seduce young white girls and sell them to houses used for corrupt practices. The price for such a transaction is ordinarily thirty dollars (one hundred and eighty francs), of which the purveyor keeps the better part. It is thus that colored people partly avenge themselves for the shocking contempt with which they are treated in Philadelphia.

Ordinarily they are badly dressed.

White children strike colored children.

When it snows, any colored man who passes is sure to be showered with snowballs by white children.

Workmen do not want to accept them, or to let them be apprentices.

There are societies in the United States for the abolition of slavery. They are composed of whites and are called Conventions. The one in Philadelphia on January 6, 1796, published a notice to Africans and to free people of color in the United States. It recommended that they turn to the various religions, learn reading, writing and arithmetic, bring up their children properly; that they frequently study the Holy Scripture, that monument to the fundamental equality and parenthood of the human race, which has only one father; that they encourage their children to learn useful trades, to be faithful to their duties as fathers, mothers, husbands and wives; that they abstain from strong liquor, avoid intemperance and dangerous pleasures, enter only into legal marriages. Finally the Convention commended them to the care of the Supreme Being.

III *Slaves*

Every state has had or still has slaves, but their conditions are more or less severe in some and more or less mild in others.

Since the misfortunes of the French colonies, it has been the habit in France to praise the attitude of the United States toward slaves. Let us examine the actual truth about this.

The New Hampshire constitution says nothing about Negro slavery, and its last census reports only one hundred and fifty-seven slaves in the state. They are more burdensome than profitable.

In Massachusetts and Rhode Island, slavery has been entirely abolished.

In Connecticut every child born of a slave after 1784 will be free when it reaches the age of twenty-one. Children born before that year must be freed on January 1, 1816.

Universal freedom has had no bad effect in Massachusetts. Crime has not increased. Some slaves have become workmen, but only a few of them. Their total has greatly diminished. None of them, however, has felt obliged to become a slave in another state, nor has he died of want. This is the testimony of M. de Liancourt in the truthful and instructive *Voyage* that he published on the United States.

The slaves of Carolina number nineteen thousand. There are next to none in Rhode Island, which has less than a thousand of them. Thus in Northern states, slavery has almost abolished itself because of the nature of the climate. Some families of Dutch descent who live in the state of New York own whole families of slaves, all of them born on their estates. From time to time they free a few.

The state of Delaware possesses about nine thousand slaves, and its constitution says: "Hereafter no person imported from Africa into this state shall be held in slavery under any pretext. No Indian, Negro or mulatto shall be brought into this state from any part of the world for the purpose of selling him."

This law was not retroactive for those who were slaves when it was passed, and while there was considerable manumission as a result of the zeal of the Quakers, those who did not wish to follow their example were not forced to do so.

It is certain that there is universal prejudice all over the United States against people not white. They are excluded from all elections.

Even though an article in the Delaware constitution says

that no preferential treatment shall be given to any religious denomination in preference to another, every member of the legislative chamber and every state official is nevertheless obliged to take the following oath:

"I (name) declare that I believe in God the father, in Jesus Christ his only son, and in the Holy Ghost; and I recognize the Holy Scriptures of the Old and New Testament as having been given by divine inspiration."

We shall return to Pennsylvania.

Let us pass to the Southern states, which insist that Negro slaves are necessary to their agricultural prosperity. The legislature of Maryland has rejected a proposal to abolish slavery gradually. The most beautiful plantations of Virginia have no more than two hundred to two hundred and fifty Negroes, and some landlords have two or three plantations of this sort. Beverley, who lives on the Rappahannock, a large navigable river of Virginia, inherited three hundred and thirty Negroes from his father in 1768. He has bought forty, and given more than that number to his children, and in 1794 he had seven hundred and fifty. In Virginia Negroes, if well treated, double in sixteen years. The big proprietors treat them badly, but the little landowners treat them well.

In several parts of Virginia mulattoes are extremely common. Negroes, like whites, are judged before juries composed of white property holders. They are not allowed to testify against whites. He who kills a Negro in Virginia is guilty of murder.

They are allowed one fourth of a bushel of corn meal a week, no matter what their age.

A surgeon is called for them only in unusual cases and in acute illnesses. They are given a little ground to farm for their own profit.

The white overseers overwork them detestably, because they get a percentage of the produce: one fourth share on plantations employing under twenty Negroes, one eighth on those under forty, one tenth for those under one hundred. There are also general managers who have several white overseers under their orders.

Each winter a Negro is given two shirts, one jacket, one pair of trousers, two pairs of stockings, one pair of shoes and a hat. In the country the jacket and trousers, or the skirt and short jacket, are made of a very common white cotton; in the town a less coarse green cloth. In the summer he receives jacket and trousers of unbleached cloth.

The Negroes work from sunrise to eleven o'clock, when they go to lunch and dinner for an hour—perhaps a little longer if they came far. Then they resume work until sunset, when they have their second meal.

They always have Sunday for themselves, and ordinarily spend it working for their own account. They keep poultry and pigs. They are also given three days vacation at Christmas and the same amount at Easter.

They are baptized, but not married. Almost all are Anabaptists or Methodists.

An act of the Virginia legislature, 1784, reads that no slave shall henceforth be imported into that state, or sold or bought, under pain of a fine of ten thousand francs against the importer and five thousand francs on the seller or buyer.

There are nineteen thousand slaves in North Carolina. In South Carolina there are fifty thousand, regulated by the law of May 10, 1740. This black code is a little shady.

M. Bligh, who lives in England, has several plantations in South Carolina, and twelve or fifteen hundred Negroes. He produces from thirty-five to forty-five hundred barrels of rice annually.

A law of 1788 in that state forbade the importation of Negroes prior to 1793. This was because the debt for the purchase of slaves was already too large. The law was advanced two years. In 1794 it was again advanced to January 1, 1797.

When the indigo of Carolina ceased to be in demand, the more remote plantations planted Indian corn.

Formerly in North Carolina, when a white killed a Negro, he merely paid a fine; but since 1792 the same law obtained for North Carolina as for Virginia. Nothing was said in the law against slavery; public officials had to be of the Protestant religion. In Maryland they had to be Christians.

In South Carolina a white who kills a Negro is only fined two hundred dollars. There is no law against slavery, and public officials must publicly profess Protestantism.

At Charleston a Mme. P——— had a Negress who was nursing a six-months-old child. When this Negress appeared wearing a rather clean skirt, the mistress questioned her on this new acquisition. She made an answer at which the mistress was so angry that she threw herself on her and beat her. Afterwards she had her taken to prison by a constable, and there she was given ten lashes of a whip every day. At the end of six days, the mistress allowed herself to be moved by the entreaties of several persons and had this woman released from jail. The unhappy creature, whose breasts, grown big with milk, had caused her severe pain, hastened to empty them so that they would fill with a more recent milk. Then, having washed them, she nursed her child, whom the mistress had made drunk with Madeira wine in order to stop the infant's cries during the six days of the mother's detention.

In the Carolinas, iron collars are used on slaves.

The Carolinians say their Negroes are happier than those who are free, but the fact remains that a husband and wife, fathers, mothers and children can be separated and sold.

The field slaves are only a third of the total number of Negroes on the plantations. Each Negro cultivating rice in 1796 brought in to his master annually 257 dollars (1542 francs). His cost to the master is about 13 dollars (78 francs) a year.

During three years at the port of Charleston, South Carolina, the commerce in Negroes resulted in the entry, in 1804, of 5658 slaves; in 1805, of 6727 slaves; in 1806, of 8804 slaves, a total of 21,189. Several shiploads are not included, since they had not yet been verified.

The legislature of South Carolina rejected by a large majority the abolition of slavery and of the traffic in blacks.

In Georgia one can be neither an elector nor an elected official if one is not free and white, and if one does not also profess the Protestant religion.

In Virginia wheat, tobacco and cotton have supplanted indigo.

Since there has been an end of the importation of Negroes, they are better treated. Before that they were treated with extreme severity.

On good plantations, the birth rate runs as high as six per cent. The average rate for the entire state is reckoned at three per cent.

In South Carolina, slaves of every age pay one dollar a head poll tax.

The treatment of slaves was made extremely bad as a result of fires which unexpectedly broke out in several places. A letter from the Minister of War to the Governor of Georgia, dated September 7, 1798, approved the rigorous measures taken to deport colored people arriving from Port-au-Prince, and added that all Southern states should take steps to keep them out.

Charleston newspapers in March, 1800, offered a five-hundred-dollar reward for the identification of a band of incendiaries who had recently made several attempts to destroy the city.

On June 14, 1795, at three o'clock in the afternoon, fire broke out in Charleston and lasted until three o'clock in the morning. It destroyed all the houses of Queen Street from the bay to the corner of Church Street, all but two houses between Broad Street and St. Philip's Church, Chalmer and Barresford Avenues, Kimlock's tower, the north side of Broad Street, from the State House to four doors below Church House, five houses of the Bay at the corner of Queen Street.

In Philadelphia on December 18, 1799, fire consumed Oeller's Hotel, a magnificent building, the most beautiful and most comfortable inn in the United States.[12]

In Richmond, Virginia, fire consumed the theater on December 27, 1811. Sixty-two persons died, among them the Governor and his wife.

Now let us come back to Philadelphia.

The color prejudice is more deeply rooted in Philadelphia and in Pennsylvania than in the other states of the union, and among the Quakers more than any other sect. In general the Negroes have poor clothing. When one goes to a shop to buy something for a slave, one is shown only the coarsest and ugliest material; and if one asks for something better, he is told that it is good enough for Negroes. White children beat little slaves and if grown-up slaves try to interfere, adult whites beat them in turn.

A white woman who drives a cabriolet in the streets of Philadelphia has a young Negress sitting on the carriage step, her feet on a lower step outside, to hold the whip when the mistress can no longer endure its weight.

What we have said up to now concerning the condition of slaves in the United States is fittingly climaxed by that which follows.

These states seem to wish to make everyone believe that great inconveniences will arise from freeing slaves employed in agriculture, as they are in the Southern part of the United States, where two million slaves cultivate cotton, indigo, rice, tobacco, etc.

When America separated from England, Washington said

[12]Scharf and Westcott, *History of Philadelphia*, shows that up to this time Oeller's Hotel had served for a long time as a popular rendezvous for banquets and reunions.

in the Constitution[13] that universal freedom would be pro-claimed in 1800. Nearly twenty years passed between then and the specified date.

During this space of time that part of Southern United States which can be considered as absolutely colonial be-cause of its products and its slaves, made plans to separate from the Northern states in case universal freedom should be proclaimed.

Congress did not ignore its resolution, and to avoid civil war it proclaimed nothing in 1800. Two more years passed after that.

In 1802, a judge sitting in Savannah, Georgia, instructed the inhabitants to ask that the Constitution be lived up to. Somebody shot at him. A jury convicted him and put him in prison. Congress was informed of the fact and contented itself with returning him to his duties and throwing the accused out of court.

Nothing more was done about it.

And for fourteen years more the Constitution has re-mained ineffectual on this point, because the American peo-ple, so excited about their own liberty, don't consider the liberty of others unless it suits their political convenience.

Doesn't this imply that it would have been better for the people in slavery if liberty had never been mentioned?

Another oddity: A savage from an Indian nation in Louisi-ana has a plantation in the northern part of Mississippi. He has his Negroes, and is well served by them. He retains all his native customs and goes nude, but he nevertheless owns his plantation and cultivates it.

[13]Nothing whatever was said in the Constitution about the "proclama-tion of universal freedom." By the Thirteenth Amendment, passed January 31, 1865, slavery and involuntary servitude were abolished. Article 1, Section 9, of the Constitution, reads: "The migration or importation of such persons as any of the States now existing shall think proper to admit shall not be prohibited by the Congress prior to the year 1808, but a tax or duty may be imposed on such importation, not exceeding ten dollars for each such person."

When the savages of French Guiana learned that France had freed her Negroes, they were extremely distressed by it.

I must add here that French colored women live in the most obnoxious luxury in Philadelphia, and since this luxury can only be provided by the French and by former French colonials, the contrast of their condition with the misery of the mass of their compatriots is revolting.

Americans ordinarily will not rent houses to colored prostitutes. In Philadelphia they are lodged for the most part on the outskirts of town or in alleys or small side streets.

After having partly reviewed the different classes which make up the population of Philadelphia, I repeat that morals in this city, as elsewhere in the United States, are not pure, although they pretend to be virtuous. I have given some examples. Here are others.

In Philadelphia I knew a rich man's widow in whose home a Frenchman lodged. This woman, who had a most modest demeanor and was highly regarded in the city, was thirty-two years old. She gave every privilege to this Frenchman, who knew her weakness for porcelains. Her eldest daughter, thirteen years old, gave herself to the same man for a quarter of a dollar. A girl of eight years allowed every sort of indecency for twelve and a half cents. Her young Negro servant, seventeen years old, succumbed to the charms of pleasure, but took no pay for fear her mistress would suspect her.

In this family there were also two boys, the elder ten years old. Together they stole knife blades from a shopkeeper; a thirty-franc note which they sewed in the lining of the garment of one of them; a hat which they hid for three weeks in a cellar and sold when search for it had ceased. One of them, who had been shut in by the mother for stealing, set fire to the house. There is no law providing for the punishment of children.

In the "Back Countries" and more remote sections, young

girls accede almost without hesitation to all caresses of men whom they have seen that day for the first time, and whom they will never see again. When Vaustable's squadron was in Hampton Roads (at which time I was also in Virginia) Frenchmen found that in outlying country districts young girls allowed and conceded everything except the final favor for thirty sous (quarter of a dollar).

On the evening of October 16, 1793, a mob formed in St. Paul Place in New York. The house of Mother Carey, public procuress, was wrecked and torn down, and the furniture broken. Another house of the same sort, run by Mother Giles, suffered the same fate. People who were stationed in the first to defend it fired on the assailants and wounded three, one dangerously. The Mayor was insulted and threatened when he attempted to make the mob disperse.

At Portsmouth, Virginia, there are prostitutes gifted with all the allurements which men find attractive, but they want only to drink liquor. They only wash themselves in very hot water.

Sailors' wives sold themselves, preferably to Frenchmen.

Such customs go hand in hand with peculiarly superstitious ideas. Philadelphia hairdressers united and petitioned the Mayor to forbid hairdressing on Sunday. This was in 1793. The French and American hairdressers signed, but three Spanish barbers of soldiers at the port failed to give the unanimity which the Mayor had demanded and one continued to hairdress on Sunday.

When a Quakeress feels lecherous impulses, she notifies her husband of it, and does her best to make him share her torment.

The daughters of Quakers are extremely imprudent, and frequently get into trouble.

Quaker youths are frequent visitors in the houses of ill fame, which have multiplied in Philadelphia and are frequented at all hours. There is even a certain well-known gentleman who leaves his horse tied to the post outside one of these houses, so that everyone knows when he is there and exactly how long he stays.

There are streetwalkers of every color.

When a Quakeress violates the conjugal bond—which is only in rare cases—it is, she says, the evil spirit which is acting; and if she adds that she repents, the fault is supposed to be effaced. American women would not perhaps be very badly represented by the portrait that Jean Jacques drew of Mme. de Varens.[14]

In Virginia women visit each other in their homes for long periods, even when they live only short distances apart—sometimes in the same town.

Since 1806 there are streetwalkers of a new sort in Philadelphia. These are very young and very pretty girls, elegantly dressed, who promenade two by two, arm in arm and walking very rapidly, at an hour which indicates that they aren't just out for a stroll. They are found most commonly on the south side of Market Street beginning at Fourth Street and coming up this street. Anyone who accosts them is taken to their home. They pretend to be small dressmakers. They fulfill every desire for two dollars, half of which is supposed to pay for the use of the room.

Another sort is also becoming quite common. Women, usually well along in age, are known to be procuresses. Anyone taken to their houses by a reliable friend asks permission to visit them sometime. If these duennas are alone, they are asked to use their influence to obtain a friend who is free, and the girl is chosen by them. Sometimes the duennas themselves suggest a desirable companion.

[14] Jean Jacques Rousseau was the acknowledged lover of Mme. de Varens. The portrait that Rousseau drew of her is in the *Confessions,* and pictures a good-natured, sentimental, fairly intelligent woman given to taking her pleasures wherever she found them. Saintsbury calls her "nominally a converted protestant . . . in reality, as many women of her time were, a kind of deist, with a theory of noble sentiment and a practice of libertinism tempered by good nature."

The duennas contact the desired person and report as to whether or not there is any hope. They arrange for women or young girls whom they debauch in this manner to come to their house for the meeting, and such meetings can be repeated as often as desired. If the patron wants a different woman, the duenna provides her with equal complaisance.

On each occasion of this sort, the lady who dispenses the favors is paid three dollars, and she in turn gives the procuress a dollar for her trouble.

If one's desires run to a beautiful person of high rank, or one more difficult to persuade, or one supposed to be a novice at love, higher prices must be paid, either in money or in gifts.

During the entire diversion, the innocent young thing perpetually and in cold blood demands a larger gift, on the ground that the duenna will require from her a much heavier reward for keeping silent. This is the only language her tenderness speaks.

But never during your voluptuous ecstasy should you allow yourself to enthuse over the treasures you are receiving, because you will get a reply you don't expect—that she never dreamed when she yielded to your desires that she would be treated like an unchaste person; and your pocketbook would again have to be used to dry the flood of tears brought on by such truly virginal modesty.

You would encounter a greater and more dangerous peril if you should meet your sweet friend anywhere except at the place of assignation, and give any signs of knowing her. She would maintain an imperturbable sang-froid, and if you insisted on molesting her, especially on the street, everybody would rush to her assistance and only flight would save you from being assaulted.

It is in a country such as this that syringes, when first imported by French colonists, seemed a hideous object. Later they were put on sale by American apothecaries. The

Quakers were responsible for this change, and were the first adopters of this custom.

There is a house in New York where a woman had found the detestable secret of attracting young persons of the fair sex. She diligently avoided letting Frenchmen be admitted. One of the latter, having learned from a wealthy merchant all the details of this house of corruption, presented himself there, posing as a foreigner from a country whose language he spoke marvelously.[15]

So well did he play his role that he was promised a tender beauty, provided he would swear eternal silence. Everything was discussed and agreed upon. The young innocent arrived. Imagine the amazement of the young man when he recognized the daughter of the home to which he had brought a letter of introduction, the celestial Venus with whom he had dined!

What was he to do? Already the matter had gone too far to retreat, and so the final step was taken and happiness put a seal upon his lips.

To conclude from what I have reported that there are not, in the United States, any individuals who are in every respect virtuous and worthy of the veneration of all would be to understand me badly and would be a false interpretation.

But I say that the customs which prevail there are not the most estimable, and here is proof of it:

When Europeans first came to live in the United States, their customs were so respectable that lovers were permitted a wrapping-up or engagement.[16] A young suitor, whose conduct had been carefully observed, received from the parents of his loved one occasional permission over a period of as long as ten years to share the bed of her whom he cherished. In spite of this long trial, no virtue was lost, and

[15]I.e., he pretended he wasn't a Frenchman.
[16]Bundling.

the suitor was rewarded for his devotion and delicacy by receiving in marriage the one he had so religiously respected. The loving fiancée became the honored and faithful wife of a husband whom she had thus nursed along to a condition of complete happiness. But this custom, which is not exactly suited to our French ways, has grown more and more rare, and is no longer encountered except in the uttermost confines of Northern states, where it only exists as a freak.

Forty years ago some Frenchmen who traveled through these Northern provinces during the war were permitted as a matter of course to share beds where innocence alone reposed, and I have heard some of them say that it was not for their cold bedfellow that the ordeal had been so difficult. But one word of accusation from a young girl, if they had ventured on any indiscretion, could have endangered their lives.

For the feeding of her inhabitants Philadelphia has three markets, one in the center, and one in each north and south suburb.

For beef, veal and mutton the big market of Philadelphia is only second to that of London-hall, and for fish it only yields to that of New York. All sorts of provisions and manufactured articles are also sold there. It is built on the long ridge of Market Street from First and Front streets to the west end of Fourth Street. It is built of brick with three hundred posts, in such a way that air circulates freely in all directions. Along both sides of the building are spacious streets for the passage of provision carts, and the entire length of Second and Third streets is left open for public traffic.

The provisions always have an attractive appearance. The meat is sawed in round and appetizing shapes.

During the summer the flies must be continually driven away, and the provisions are kept fresh with wet or sprinkled cloths.

The market of the south suburb is smaller and at right

angles to the direction of the big market, but it is equally clean.

The market of the north suburb is in Callowhill Street, between First and Second streets, and is made up of four buildings erected two by two, running in the same direction as the big market.

On Sunday, in all three markets, nothing but bread and milk can be bought, and only until nine o'clock, and besides, in the summer, meat. Not only is each market built like the big one, but each is broken by a street running through its center. Every Tuesday and Friday evening a bell in City Hall rings from dark to nine o'clock to give notice that the market will be open on the following morning. This custom is said to have originated in the days when the city was just taking shape and when the roads were so poor that marketmen approaching the city in the evening needed something to show them the way to the market.

It wouldn't have been a bad idea to abandon this custom when it ceased to have any value.

Taverns and boardinghouses, French boardinghouses included, have greatly increased in number in Philadelphia. Some cost from eighteen to seventy-two francs a week. There are eighty of these. These boardinghouses are the sole means of existence of American men and American women who have no other way of earning a living. Their inefficiency obliges them to demand payment in advance from the boarders, and they never fail to ask payment for anything not a part of the ordinary supplies which the boarders may desire.

In spite of the low standing of this trade, a boardinghouse keeper considers himself as a personage entitled to consideration from his boarders, and seldom thinks of giving his boarders any of the consideration that he expects from them.

In some families, the heads only eat at table with the

boarders; sometimes the eldest-born eats there too; but usually everyone in the house lives on what the boarders leave.

There are also thirty-five taverns where people go to drink wine, beer of every sort, grog, liqueurs of different kinds, whiskey (brandy made from rye). These taverns or cafés do not sell tea or coffee by the cup, but only whole teapots or coffee pots which hold a dozen cups and cost a dollar.

There are twenty more places that sell only beer, cider and brandy, and ten others that sell only beer and cider.

Some of these taverns have a great reputation for beefsteaks; and people go there to have steaks with oysters, and to drink good wines.

There is considerable selling, in Philadelphia, of unripe fruits, whose extreme greenness must cause untold havoc among the Americans who eat them and let their children eat them. In France there isn't a village where the police would allow such a state of affairs. All along the wharves are small boats loaded with green or rotten fruit which people buy and eat greedily.

Peaches are extremely abundant in Philadelphia, but their size and flavor show the prevailing mania for picking them before they are ripe, a mania which may be caused by the boldness with which fruit is stolen by the first comer, especially in the neighborhood of cities.

Moreover the peach tree has been damaged all over the United States by a pest which is thought to be a sort of sucking insect. In its first volume the Agricultural Society of New York published a report on this misfortune, which has increased since 1776. Of all European fruits, the peach tree succeeded best in the United States.

The markets of Philadelphia also sell vegetables such as cabbage, asparagus, onions, beans, carrots, turnip, leeks, potatoes, sweet potatoes. Philadelphia also has game. You can find excellent sausage for 24 sous a pound, four calves' feet for 22½ sous. One pair of beautiful chickens costs from 6 francs to 7 francs 10 sous. A live turkey is 6 francs. In the rivers of Pennsylvania and particularly in the Delaware they catch a turtle called snapper. It is small, with claws on the toes of its four feet, and a tail which, in a foot-long turtle, is about eight inches in length. This tail is like that of an armadillo or lizard. This animal is extremely hideous and is sold for 15 sous. Sweet potatoes cost 15 francs a pound. Beef in Philadelphia is worth from 8½ to 11 sous a pound, veal the same, mutton 8 to 9 sous, a pint of milk 7½ sous, a dozen eggs 30 sous, a baked apple pie 3 francs. A little horn lantern 6 francs. Feed per year for a horse costs 600 francs.

On the Rivers and More Particularly on the Temperature and the Climate

In Pennsylvania the air has a very high degree of dryness in spite of violent changes of wind.

Winters are longer and colder than in England; the springs are short; autumns long and mild.

But the winters are more serene, more agreeable and healthier than those of England. The contrary is true in summer because of the intense heat and sudden changes which cause dysentery, slow and putrid fevers, and other dangerous sicknesses.

The prevailing winds of winter are northwest. At all seasons this wind brings cold and a cloudless sky. Southwest winds are hot and the sky is overcast. East winds bring fogs and rain clouds. Spring comes a month later in Pennsylvania than in England; and yet the harvest is a month earlier than in England.

Sudden storms accompanied by rain and wind are common during the hot season, and bring cold if they are followed by the northwest wind. There is a great deal of snow and frost.

A river like the Delaware freezes over in one night. The older a person is, the less he is able to endure these sudden temperature changes. In one evening at the end of December we had such mild weather in Philadelphia that during supper at my house we left the north window open. The next day when I awoke I found eight inches of snow. By three o'clock in the afternoon the thermometer registered 3½ degrees below zero Réaumur.

Temperatures in Charleston and Boston may vary 15 degrees. The feeling of the air on the body is often quite different from what might be expected by looking at the thermometer.

Water freezes at 2 degrees below zero Réaumur and does not melt at zero. Pennsylvania is a composite of all climates. One has the humidity of Great Britain in spring, the suffocating heat of Africa in summer, the temperature of Italy in June, the sky of Egypt in autumn, the cold and snow of Norway and the ice of Holland in winter, the storms of the Antilles at all seasons; and during each month of the year the changeable weather and winds of England. And just as there are all climates, so are there all sicknesses.

On January 1, 1800, two feet of snow fell in Savannah. The summer and autumn of 1804 were the mildest and the most temperate within the memory of anyone in the United States. In Virginia, South Carolina and Georgia the heat was extreme. The summer of 1805 was scorching. Winters in the state of Virginia may be as rigorous as those of Canada. On November 27, 1798, there had already been eighteen inches of snow in Albany in five days. Stages crossed the river on the ice and it was frozen as far as Hudson.

The winter of 1801 was so mild at New York that before the end of February, 1801, bluebirds, blackbirds, blue heron had arrived on Long Island from their winter retreats: that is to say, three weeks earlier than usual. The ice on the Hudson River broke up on February 28, and on March 3 a boat came from Albany (sixty-six leagues north of New York) in twenty-six hours. Ordinarily this takes place on Saint Patrick's Day, March 17.

South Carolina has a rainfall of 110 to 118 inches a year.

In the United States and in Philadelphia for example, the barometer rises rapidly and suddenly when the weather is going to be bad; then afterwards it descends gradually. The greatest cold, at least in unusual years, is 10 to 12 below,[17] Réaumur, at Philadelphia, and the greatest heat from 26 to 28 degrees. The greatest recorded height of the barometer was 29 inches 4 lines. But it often reaches 29 inches 2 and 3 lines Réaumur. One very remarkable thing is that when the thermometer is at this point, which indicates that the air has more elasticity in the United States than in France, a sudden rise of two to three lines is as much an indication of imminent rain as when it (the barometer) goes down the same amount below 28 inches.

In an ordinary year there are:

> 15 days of thunder
> 75 days of rain
> 12 days of snow
> 5 days of storms
> 258 fine days
> ———
> 365

There are thirty-five inches of water annually. The sky is rarely cloudy three days in succession.

Violent thunder is often heard, but thanks to the remedy recommended by the immortal Franklin, Philadelphia is preserved from the misfortunes resulting from it. On the other hand, also, it seems to be a greater threat to houses

[17]Twelve below zero Réaumur is 5 above zero Fahrenheit. Twenty-eight above Réaumur is 95 above Fahrenheit.

where this preservative is neglected. Wednesday, March 27, 1782, lightning struck the house of the Minister of France in three places. It knocked down M. le Chevalier de la Luzerne's chimney to the level of the roof, broke the cast-iron stove which closed the opening of the chimney, broke all adjacent plaster, smashed furniture and windowpanes. It started a fire on the roof, set the curtains ablaze, entered the dining room, split two mahogany sideboards, and broke all the porcelain. Papers were burned in another room. Lastly it wounded M. de Meaux, officer of French artillery, breaking his left arm and burning the lower part of his belly and his genital organs, so that he died of it the seventh day afterwards.

Wheat is harvested from the eighth to the twenty-second of July.

The Ohio froze in 1787, which is very rare. The Réaumur thermometer went down to 32 degrees and even broke in the month of February. The cold at that time was 16 degrees in Philadelphia.

The United States have iron, lead, copper and silver.

In the winter of 1779 the Delaware was frozen almost three months. The ice near the city was from sixteen to nineteen inches thick, and inland from four to five feet thick. Many plants were destroyed by the cold. Old cattle and the feet of the pigs that weren't sheltered were frozen. Partridges were found dead near farms. In the month of February the thermometer descended to the mercury, stayed several hours below 16 degrees 4 lines of Réaumur, and except for one day of this month it did not get up to the freezing point. The summer of 1779 averaged 28 degrees.

The greatest heat of the summer days usually occurs between two and three o'clock in the afternoon; the coolest part of the day is at dawn.

Evening dews are extremely abundant, and wet the garments.

Great downpours occur in autumn and cause floods.

In view of what I say about the intense and enduring heat, it is no wonder that Americans have a fondness for ice cream and sherbets.

In Philadelphia ice cream is made by M. Collot, a creole from San Domingo, son of M. Collot, former president of the High Council of Cap François, and former officer in the Orléans Dragoons. Like so many other colonists, he has been reduced to earning his living by his labors. His talent for the violin, which he studied for his own amusement, has made him first violinist at the Philadelphia theater. The ice cream he makes will bear comparison with that of the cellar of the Palais Royal in Paris. It costs twenty sous.

On Market Street above Eighth Street, at Carré's, ice cream can be bought for fifteen sous.

At the Comedy M. Mercier, a Frenchman, makes some too, the dearest but the most mediocre of all. It is true that he must pay the director of the theater eight hundred dollars a year for the exclusive right to sell it there.

Many people ride in sleighs in the United States, and sleigh-riding is much enjoyed in the streets of Philadelphia.

During hot weather thirst is so widespread and irresistible in all American cities that several persons die each year from drinking cold pump water when hot. Some die very suddenly. Sometimes in Philadelphia two men will die on the same day.

Printed handbills are distributed each summer to warn people of these dangers. Strangers especially are warned either to drink grog, or to add a little wine or some other spirituous liquor to their water. People are urged to throw cold water on the faces of those suffering from water-drinking, and bleeding is also suggested, etc.

Sometimes notices are placed on the pumps with these words: *Death to him who drinks quickly*. But all these teachings are ignored, and even Death threatens in vain.

The hot season in Philadelphia is so debilitating that it deprives people of all energy and makes the slightest movement painful. Even when one feels the need to eat, one must argue with himself to make himself go into the neighboring room to take the food that is waiting there. As Talleyrand said, "At each inhaling of air, one worries about the next one."

Water left standing in a house is boiling hot at the end of a half or quarter hour, so that whenever one wishes to drink, one must get more at the pump, usually in a very small varnished tin jug, and one puts in a goblet some fresh water. The temperature of this water is so glacial that it fogs the glass but becomes intolerably warm in a few minutes.

In spite of this hellish existence, one must bathe. A Frenchman named Glaise, in June, 1795, installed seven bathtubs in his house at 120 South Front Street. The bathtubs were sheet iron. One subscribes at the rate of three baths for one dollar; for a month, eight dollars, for just one bath, one half dollar. They were much frequented by the French.

Another veritable torture during Philadelphia's hot season is the innumerable flies which constantly light on face and hands, stinging everywhere and turning everything black because of the filth they leave wherever they light. Rooms must be kept closed unless one wishes to be tormented in his bed at the break of day, and this need of keeping everything shut makes the heat of the night even more unbearable and sleep more difficult.

And so the heat of the day makes one long for bedtime because of weariness, and a single fly which has gained entrance to your room in spite of all precautions drives you from your bed.

I say one fly because many among them are a sort of blisterfly, and once they have attacked you, you can have no peace until they are killed. If one writes, the paper is spotted with flyspecks. If a woman is dressed in white her dress is in like manner soiled, especially her fichu. The uphol-stery and bellpulls are sticky.

At table and above all at dessert they light upon and befoul all food, all drinks. They taste everything they see. One's eyes are revolted by them; one's appetite destroyed. When a rather large room, hitherto closed, is suddenly opened in the summer, a noise is produced there which imitates that of the sea roaring in the distance; it is the flies who are escaping and cover you as they pass. It is because of this frightful inconvenience that the custom arose of going without hangings, and repainting apartments every autumn.

In many of the houses people make a sort of chandelier or garland of very white paper to attract flies. This paper must be changed often; for it quickly becomes black and disgusting. Other persons use saucers filled with vitriol; all the flies which pass its poisoned atmosphere perish, but in a state of eroticism which forces them, before they die, to taste the irritations of love's delights. In large stores the dead flies must be swept up at least four times a day. They are gathered by bushels. Poultry like to eat them, and appar-ently do so without the slightest inconvenience.

Bedbugs harass the entire continent in hot weather, and in Philadelphia even daylight doesn't prevent them from showing themselves. The universal use of feather beds helps this vermin to multiply.

Elder-flower powder is thought to be the best insecticide. It kills ants, weevils, moths of different kinds. It is being tried on preserves, wheat, rice, sheets and so on.

In Virginia and South Carolina the fleas are enormous and innumerable. Mosquitoes torment the whole city of Philadelphia.

In Philadelphia very beautiful Northern Lights are seen. On July 24, 1796, in that city, there was a circle of pris-matic colors around the sun. There was a second circle around the inner, twice as large as the first, and between the two there was a part of a third circle. The second circle was white; the third milky. They appeared between nine forty-five and eleven o'clock.

On March 27, 1796, high tide in the Delaware in front of Philadelphia was two feet lower than the lowest recorded low tide. This occurrence was attributed to a violent wind from west-northwest, which drove back the rising tide.

Summer goes at last and the season arrives when people have to warm themselves. An open fire is a truly rare luxury, and indeed something of a magnificence. Ordinarily rooms are heated by cast-iron stoves, or stoves of sheet iron called Prussian. This sort grows fewer every day, however, and is being replaced by the stoves perfected by Franklin, because of which they are called Franklin stoves.

They stand on the floor of a room in front of the fireplace opening. The back of the stove is a piece of iron which slants forward to make an acute angle at the top of the fireplace. The smoke escapes by way of this angle. The wood is placed on andirons in the open stove. It can thus be placed far out in the room. On the bottom of the stove is placed a layer of four or five large sticks; above them as many layers, each with one less piece of wood than the last, as the stove can hold. Since the sticks are rounded and touch only at spots, the fire can pass between them and they all burn together.

This instantly makes a hot fire which can be kept up by adding a small amount of wood at long intervals. Thus the heat remains strong and constant until bedtime, and at least six or eight persons can sit around the fire, since it protrudes into the room.

Good carpeting tends to concentrate the heat, which is an advantage in a country where, as I have said, rooms are drafty.

In Philadelphia they burn black spruce logs, which shoot out sparks like chestnut; chestnut, which is bad; large acacia logs, which are good for back logs because they burn slowly.

But the best woods are sugar maple, birch, live oak, white oak and, best of all, Northern walnut or hickory. Nothing can be compared to hickory. It costs half as much again as the next best wood; but even at that price it is preferable to the others. It gives out great heat, its coals are compact and lasting, and it burns a long time. Hickory logs keep their shape until wholly consumed. Like chestnut, it burns with loud crackling noises, and shoots out burning splinters, which necessitates the use of fire screens.

The American climate has a marked influence on the character of animals in the United States. They are gentler than in Europe. This is particularly noticeable in the horses, cattle, cats and dogs.

The horse has less vigor, the bull less violence than he ordinarily shows in his loves and his battles. As for the dog, his temper is greatly changed. Not only is he less courageous and less hardy, but he lacks the usual canine nobleness of spirit. Big dogs bite little dogs. What is even more astonishing, males bite and fight females.

One sees dogs resulting from intercourse between a wolf and a bitch. To obtain these, one takes a bitch in heat to a wood and ties her there. If a she-wolf happens by, she strangles the bitch; if a male comes along, he copulates and produces little ones whose features are wolfish, principally around the head and ears. They can also be recognized by their muteness (because they never bay), by their lust, and by their incurable determination to attack and kill sheep and ewes.

The dogs of the United States are subject to attacks of syphilis.

The domestic cat is astoundingly tamed. At any time it can be seen in the streets, going from one house to another. It is not frightened either by noise or by the approach of man. The she-cat even allows herself to be touched or caressed, always provided that one is not accompanied by a dog, or that one isn't wearing garments impregnated by doggy odors. In such cases the cat's maternal instincts incite her to rage and to biting people.

This climate so influences men as to deprive them of much of their energy and makes them indolent.

But this does not stop them from being quarrelsome, and quarrels end in the action known as boxing. Here again the English origin of the Americans is shown. Boxing has its rules and regulations. The two athletes settle on a site for the fight. They strip to their shirts, and roll up the sleeves to the elbows. Then at a given signal they run at each other and swing on chest, head, face and bellies blows whose noise can only be realized by those who have been present at such a spectacle.

At each new clash, they draw back, and start again from the mark. If one of the two has fallen in one of these attacks, his adversary cannot touch him as long as he is on the ground; but if he makes the slightest movement to get up, the other has the right to hit him again and force him to remain on the ground. Nobody interferes to separate the combatants: a ring is made around them, and the spectators urge on their favorite.

So long as one of the two does not admit that he is conquered, the other showers him with fist blows the moment he tries to get up. When he at last admits defeat, he gets up, dresses himself, is free to withdraw, but can again challenge his conquerer, if he dares to do so.

At the end of the fight the boxers are bruised, disfigured, and covered with blood, which they spit out, vomit out or drip from the nose. Teeth are broken, eyes are swollen shut, and sometimes sight is completely obliterated. Boxing matches are always held in the late evening, by the light of the moon, unless the participants belong to the lowest orders or are drunk, in which case they fight in broad daylight where anyone can see.

So you see once more how similar the Americans are to the English when they find in a contest between two boxers an opportunity for gratifying their passion for betting!

The commonest form of betting is on cock fights, which take place every day. Some men devote all their time and efforts to the training of fighting cocks. In order to make them pugnacious, nothing is neglected. They are subjected to a diet which excites them, and even to the use of strong drinks. They are armed with iron spurs, their combs are cut to offer less of a hold to the enemy; they are urged on by cries and placed in an enclosure from which they cannot escape. The fight rages amidst a crowd that seems to be wholly made up of Englishmen, but which is composed of their descendants, and the unfortunate cocks tear each other to pieces and die in order to decide their bets. The public houses benefit, too, by making sure that the atrocious winners—the men, that is—drink up their winnings in the company of the vanquished—men again. If death hasn't been the reward of the actual winner, never fear! It is only delayed a little.

I shall not speak of duels with pistols except to say that this English sport becomes daily more popular with Americans.

Lilies from bulbs flower in Philadelphia early in April; hyacinths by April 20. Cherries come on the market late in May and cost 1 sou each and on May 28 they cost ¼ of a piastre a pound. By the end of June they cost 1/16 of a piastre. The red- and white-heart cherry arrived May 20, 1795, and sold for a sou apiece; on May 28 they sold for ¼ of a piastre a pound; on June 20 1/16 piastre. Strawberries arrived late in May and a small basket cost ½ piastre on June 6. Apricots can be eaten July 20.

Fresh corn, good to eat in milk, appears in Philadelphia around mid-July.

During the summer small boats arrived in Philadelphia

from Nassau, loaded with bananas, fig bananas and pineapples. They do not always arrive in good condition. A pineapple is sold for ¼ of a piastre. I have eaten some excellent ones.

A banana or a fig banana is sold for 1/16 of a piastre. The bananas are eight or nine inches long and are excellent. The fig bananas are unusually beautiful.

Green peas appear in Philadelphia May 20, and by June 16 are selling at 1/16 piastre for half a peck.

Asparagus appears April 20. It is superb. In the month of June it costs 20 sous a bunch.

One gets a plate of spinach for 15 sous.

All fruits are inferior to those of France. The walnut is small and easily becomes rancid. The chestnut is small and does not keep at all.

After having spoken of the climate and of the temperature, one should add that the cities of the United States, especially Philadelphia, have a method of knowing the state of the weather at every hour during the night.

This is accomplished through watchmen who vigilantly patrol the streets from ten in the evening until five in the morning, between September 10 and March 10, and from eleven to four in the morning thereafter, and cry out, each hour, what the hour is and what the weather looks like.

Thus everyone is told whether the weather is beautiful, rainy, snowy or overcast—a delightful thing to know, for example, when one is good and warm in bed while the weather outside is terribly cold.

This service is also of use to travelers. The watchman will awaken anyone at the precise moment he has been ordered to do so.

These watchmen also give warning of fires as soon as they discover them. They circumvent thieves in their plots and thefts, and make certain that houses are locked after a certain hour has passed.

In spite of all efforts to prevent fire, they occur frequently all over the United States, and particularly in
Philadelphia, and usually take place at night, despite the
revocation of a law which imposed a fine on the person whose
house took fire, and which has now been wisely replaced
by another that fines anyone who fails to give immediate
warning on discovering a fire.

People frequently shout "Haro!" and sometimes without indicating in what part of the city the fire is.

Although the insurance company gives a bonus to the
first fire engine to arrive at a fire, there is always a wait of
one quarter hour before it gets there. The zeal and eagerness with which all Americans fight fires are admirable,
but at the same time there are so many willing helpers and
there is so little order that they do more harm than good.

Their help consists of throwing water. The pumps are
nozzled and you point with the hose, which makes it very
easy to direct the full force of the water on any given point,
and necessitates changing the position of the pump more
frequently.

Over and above the water from neighboring wells and
from the river, if it is near, every house is supposed to keep
a certain number of buckets hanging in the corridor where
passers-by can get them when needed. They are filled and
passed from hand to hand to the pumps by a line of robust
men, and they are passed back empty by a line made up of
those who are less strong or who are wearied by the long
duration of the fire (which, in spite of everything, is always
rapid, especially at night and when there is wind).

When the house is well started, the water from the
pumps is turned to steam by the intense heat when it
reaches the desired point, and this only serves to make the
fire burn more fiercely. In the daytime a fire is sometimes
extinguished; but what hope is there at night, considering
that the houses are covered with painted or tarred shingles,

best of all foods for the flames!!! All that can be done is to sprinkle adjoining houses and those on the other side of the street, in the hope of preserving them.

It is noticeable that in general the workers have too good a time, that the buckets are left in the streets after the fire, and that hoodlums amuse themselves with them.

There are companies that insure against fire and against the loss of what the houses contain. Houses surrounded by trees pay a heavier premium, and the insurers come to the fires to encourage those who are fighting it.

From October 14, 1794, when I established myself in Philadelphia, until the following December 26, there were six fires. The last one of these started in the German Lutheran church around seven o'clock in the evening. The weather was overcast and at times slightly rainy. Toward nine o'clock everyone thought the fire was out, the pumps ceased, and only idlers were left. At nine forty-five it blazed up violently, by eleven forty-five the entire roof had burned, and the building was lost.

From December 26, 1794, to November 29, 1795, there were ten more or less serious fires in Philadelphia. And from this last date to the time of my departure in August, 1798, there were thirty others.

I have lived in two houses at street corners in Philadelphia during my stay of five years, with houses close to those in which I was living, or in the immediate neighborhood. Judge, then, of my anxiety when fires broke out since my stock in trade was equally susceptible to water and fire, and more especially since I had my colonial collection with me.

Occasionally people had no time to escape from their houses, and died in the flames. Witness the case of printer Brown, who was burned to death with his family and an apprentice.

June 14, 1795, Charleston underwent a fire that destroyed the buildings on two hundred and fifty-three pieces of land.

The loss was three million francs on the buildings, as much again in furniture and effects, and three hundred families were ruined.

On November 1, 1798, a fire in the city of Wilmington, North Carolina, destroyed all but twelve houses.

In February, 1804, a fire destroyed most of a city in Virginia. The loss was estimated at two million francs.

There is a great deal of snobbery in Philadelphia, where classes are sharply divided. This is particularly noticeable at balls. There are some balls where no one is admitted unless his professional standing is up to a certain mark. At one ball a scene degenerated into fisticuffs because of the insults that passed between the wife of a small jeweler and the wife of a hairdresser.

At one of the balls held on February 23, 1795, to celebrate the birthday of Washington, I begged Mr. Vaughan, my near neighbor, and my colleague in the Philosophical Society, to buy me one of the tickets of admission. But he replied that since I was a *storekeeper* I could not aspire to this honor. . . .

And what did I say to him? "Don't you know that I have never been more your equal than now, when I am nothing?" I got no tickets, and did not see the ball.

One day Swannick, a merchant and member of the House of Representatives, was in my store and I was chatting familiarly with him. The bookseller, Matthew Carey, a man of parts, but an American born in the United States, took me aside and with a worried expression said, "Do you know that you are speaking to Mr. Swannick?"

"Yes."

"And you are not addressing him as 'Your Excellency,' as is due to a member of the lower house of Congress?"

"When Mr. Swannick, who knows I have been a member of the Constituent Assembly, worth at least ten times as much as your Congress, addresses me as 'Excellency,' I will also render it to him, but not before."

Their self-admiration is very noticeable and their manner contemptuous, but they kowtow to the English. The workmen are proud and unbearably haughty. They never have all the tools they need, and they pretend to do everything without a ladder which they should have brought.

At Philadelphia a shoemaker for men would consider himself debased if he worked for children. The captain of the ship *Columbia* of New York told me his mate never ate with him, because eating together necessitates conversation, and conversation leads to familiarity.

However Baron Steuben admitted to his school a son of M. John Adams, Vice-President of the United States, and a son of a bankrupt tailor, giving both of them the same education. They are both lawyers in New York, and the son of the tailor has more sagacity.[18]

But to the mind of Americans, that which without exception denotes the greatest superiority is the possession of a carriage. Women especially desire them to a degree that approaches delirium; and a woman who owns one is very certain that no other woman who lacks a carriage will ever be considered, or ever become, her equal.

Private carriages are numerous enough, but not comfortable, because most of them are open in front, like the stages.

In Philadelphia there are estimated to be six hundred carriages with two wheels, cabriolets or solos, and four hundred with four wheels. In addition there are three hundred carts and five hundred four-wheeled wagons for carrying goods.

Americans—and more so in Philadelphia than anywhere else—pride themselves on their cleverness and knowledge; and this, like everything else in America, is based on nothing. A prescription written in Latin by the French Dr. Grassy was taken to every apothecary in the city, and only one

[18]No foundation for the statement made by Moreau can be found either in F. Kapp, *Life of Steuben,* or in any of the numerous published papers and documents relating to John Adams and his family.

druggist could be found who was able to put himself in a class with Stahl, Briker, Rouelle, Lavoisier by being able to read it. Almost all are merely druggists, and their ignorance, and especially their lazy inattention, results in frequent blunders. They more often than not fail to weigh the drugs for medicines, but only measure them by hand or eye. They even take it into their heads, sometimes, to use their own judgment in replacing one drug with another, when they do not have the one prescribed.

I saw one of them in Philadelphia thus replace juice of cress with spirits of cockleshells, and condemn to horrible suffering an unfortunate who contracted a scurvy-like consumption that stripped all the skin from his stomach.

As yet there is no class of American society deserving of the name of men of letters. Americans agree that Europeans must not only supply them with calico, faïence, mirrors, etc., but with arts and literature as well.

Their outstanding men are lawyers, whose profession is even more lucrative than in England. Their salaries are excessive. There are some who make around three thousand louis a year.

People are not very hospitable in America, between Massachusetts and Maryland. Inns are numerous and the travel is very heavy.

From Maryland to South Carolina, inns are scarcer and more expensive. People in this section are hospitable even to generosity.

Dr. Peale complained bitterly in the news sheet *Aurora* of Philadelphia, on June 27, 1801, of the neglect into which his interesting museum has been allowed to fall.

The arts in general are poorly supported and not at all encouraged.

However Dr. Rittenhouse, an American of Pennsylvania, at the age of twenty, made a cast-iron reflecting telescope which is said to be the first made in America. In 1767 he built

a planetarium. This piece of mechanics brought great honor
to its originator, who in 1792 became Director of the Mint.

He died on June 26, 1796, and his funeral eulogy was delivered on the following December 17 in the Presbyterian
Church on the south side of Market Street opposite the
Philosophical Society of Philadelphia, of which the doctor
was a member, by Dr. Benjamin Rush, our colleague in the
same society, in the presence of President Adams, of Congress and of ministers of religion. I was present.

But M. Pope, watchmaker of Boston, who through native
ability and meditation had developed great skill at his trade,
has spent ten years perfecting a planetarium. He needed a
modest subscription of three hundred piastres (eighteen
hundred francs) in order to complete it, but was not able to
raise it. He has gone to England.

A clock belonging to Queen Marie Antoinette was bought
by Ambassador Morris and sent to his father, Robert Morris,
in Philadelphia. No American watchmaker was ever able to
repair it, but it was easy for a Frenchman.

Americans in Philadelphia have few days on which they
meet at the call of gaiety and pleasure.

The anniversary of their independence is always celebrated
on July 4. Cannon are fired; then at noon about fifty in-
fantrymen in arms, as many members of the Society of the
Cincinnati, who wear their medal on that day only, and
about thirty cavalrymen parade through two streets. They
call upon the President to greet him, and they pass in line to
compliment him. More than three fourths of the stores remain open. There are no signs of gaiety.

The first of May, which seems to permeate all creatures
with a delicious joy inspired by the freshening of all nature,
is, to be sure, marked in Philadelphia by a few exterior signs,
but they are almost all confined to the lower orders, to children and young persons. Groups of Americans occasionally
gather in taverns on that day for a picnic dinner. Working-

men fix deer tails to their hats in place of cockades. Children go to the homes of their grandparents and have their hands filled with toys. A teamster with a small howitzer mounted on his cart goes along the wharf and fires several shots. The cart is decorated with a light blue silk flag on which is painted a cart.

However, the city of Philadelphia has public establishments, to wit: (1) 33 churches or houses of worship; (2) 22 cemeteries; (3) 2 theaters; (4) the Pennsylvania House of Representatives, House of Congress, and public garden; (5) 1 meeting place for the Philosophical Society; (6) 1 museum; (7) 1 Public Library; (8) 1 prison; (9) 1 City Tavern; (10) 3 markets; (11) ———— hospitals; (12) 1 Poor House; (13) ———— schools; (14) 1 university, 1 fish market; (15) 1 house destined for the President of the United States; (16) the Mint; (17) City Hall; (18) 3 banks; (19) 3 insurance companies; (20) 1 powder magazine.

(1) *Churches or Houses of Worship*

There are 33 places consecrated to worship; 5 for Quakers, 6 for Presbyterians and dissidents, 4 for Episcopalians, 3 for Roman Catholics, 3 for German Lutherans, 3 for Methodists, 1 for German Calvinists, 1 for Swedish Lutherans (this is the oldest church in the city), 2 for Moravians, 1 for Baptists, 1 for Universalists, 1 for Africans, 2 Jewish synagogues: total 33.

The first thought which this list suggests to every good and philosophical man is that this plurality of cults is permitted in Philadelphia, and that everyone enjoys the most precious of all liberties, that of worshiping the Supreme Being according to his heart and as he likes, without any attempt to place obstacles between him and his God, who, being infinite, must necessarily be good. The government has no preference for any of these cults, nor does it pay a subsidy to any of them. All dissenters are citizens; and the law treats them as citizens, protecting them if they are good and virtuous, and punishing them if they are wicked and enemies of the public welfare.

There are no quarrels over religion, and anyone is privileged to believe his own the best so long as he does not try to force anyone else to adopt it. This liberty of conscience is even pushed so far that it is not beyond the bounds of fancy to say that a mother and a father who have twelve children might go out together from their home at the hour set by all churches for their services, and each might go to one of the thirteen different churches without one of them ever asking the other why he goes to another church than his. It is considered perfectly natural for everyone to choose his own cult and follow his own beliefs.

This picture is admirable, and should be brought home to all ministers of all religions throughout the entire world—a sublime lesson from the Sovereign of Beings to all men to show them that the most gratifying gifts they can offer Him are tolerance and the love of one's neighbor.

An even more striking thing, especially to Roman Catholics, is that when a funeral is held in a family of sufficient means, the parents of the dead person ask their minister to invite the ministers of other faiths to attend the funeral. Thus he is surrounded by ministers of different beliefs who willingly ignore their differences—except for Roman Catholic priests, who remain aloof.

When the bier is about to be lowered into the grave, the dead man's minister preaches a sermon to which the other ministers listen without impatience, even when he expresses opinions contrary to their own—opinions that will be refuted whenever one of the listeners has a similar chance.

All the sects are united against atheism, on the ground that it is anti-social, and because they are sure that atheists cannot be depended on to conduct themselves properly toward other men.

Everybody knows, of course, that Quakers have no ministers; and that anyone, man or woman, who believes himself or herself inspired by the Holy Spirit has the privilege of speaking, and even has the sacred right of abusing it.

In general the churches of Philadelphia are severely simple. The German Lutheran church, rebuilt after the fire that destroyed it December 26, 1794, is one of the most beautiful. Its value is thought to be two hundred and forty thousand francs. Divine service was celebrated there December 27, 1795. It has a fine organ and a beautiful steeple.

The Church of Christ, in the Gothic style, has a moderately beautiful set of chimes. The Presbyterian church is also remarkable for its spire. The Episcopal and Roman Catholic churches have organs.

What I have said about the harmony which reigns among representatives of the different faiths in no way applies to the Roman Catholics. As I have said, they have three churches in Philadelphia. One, called simply The Chapel, is located interiorly between Walnut Street and a small alley and between South Third and Fourth streets. It was the first church of this faith in Philadelphia. It is merely a sort of oratory where low masses are said and where, for the convenience of priests who live in that neighborhood, the sacraments can be administered.

In the choir, on the Epistle side of the altar, is a small oil painting about one and a half feet wide by two feet high, representing a brig with a shattered foremast; the Virgin is in the sky, with her Son near her, and seems to be protecting the vessel.

On one of the sides of the picture on the canvas itself one reads *Ex Voto* and at the bottom of the canvas "Made the 1st of November 1791 by the passengers of the brig *Minerva,* coming from Cap François to Philadelphia."

The priests of this chapel are Irish and consequently fanatics. They have charge of the parochial duties of the Church of St. Mary of the Irish on South Fourth Street. This church is only an ordinary house with a large door in front and another on the side. Above the altar as altar screen is a representation of the crucifixion of Christ. The pulpit almost touches the altar on the Epistle side. Moreover it has benches and pews and a small organ, as in Protestant churches, and sermons are in English.

The third church is the German Catholic, on the north corner of Spruce and Sixth. Its members withdrew from the Church of St. Mary because Irish domination prevailed there, and because the priests are the real administrators of it. The German church is newly built and is prettier than the other, if such a word can be applied to either. The pulpit is on the Gospel side of the altar, but too near the choir. Preaching is in German. The altar screen is a frightful daub purporting to show Jesus Christ ascending to heaven and being received by His Father, who holds in His right hand a monstrance with the host. It has benches and a small organ. The custom of Rome is followed in these churches at divine service, but services in the German church are more like those in the churches of the French colonies, which follow the same custom.

The two churches use the cemetery which surrounds St. Mary's, but each church uses a separate portion of the ground. Because of its distance from the German church, the clergy, preceded by the Cross, conduct the corpse to the cemetery after saying prayers for the dead.

The Roman churches are the only ones that display any form of ceremony publicly and in the streets.

The priests of the German church are considered moderates because they are not like the Irish, who will not perform the marriage ceremony unless both parties provide proof of confession, or bury those who have not confessed. Both churches acknowledge the authority of the Roman archbishop, M. Carroll, born in Baltimore.

The Catholic cemetery, like those of other faiths in Philadelphia, is full of monuments and inscriptions no more interesting than were the insignificant humans whose deaths occasioned them.

During the War of American Independence, four Frenchmen were buried there, and marble slabs placed over their graves; but as nobody expected to see any more Frenchmen, these tombstones were taken and used to form the top of the flight of stairs by which people from the German church enter the cemetery from Eighth Street.

On March 5, 1797, the German Catholic church was deprived of its rights by an injunction of M. Carroll, pronounced in the Irish Catholic Church of St. Mary.

The pretended reason for this interdiction was that the parish priest was seizing all surplice fees, even when his vicar did his work, whereupon the churchwardens proposed that he limit himself to the fees he himself could collect, plus half of those that his vicar received, but he refused and was discharged.

The Irish priests of St. Mary made a capital affair out of all this, because the churchwardens of the German church had separated from St. Mary's on the ground that the Irish priests had usurped too much temporal administration.

The only effect of the interdiction was to attract more people to the German church.

Another church, of which I have already spoken, paints American peculiarities with bold strokes. It is the one which the intolerance of the whites has caused to be built on the west side of South Fifth Street between Walnut and Spruce; it is of brick, and has this inscription:

> The African church
> MDCCXCIII
> The people that walked in
> darkness have seen a
> great light

And so there is a special God for black men!

In September, 1795, an Anglican bishop ordained a Negro as minister of this church. This representative of the black God was present with all the white ministers of all faiths at the ceremony when Dr. Rittenhouse's funeral oration was delivered.

In the Anglican cemetery on Mulberry Street between Fourth and Fifth streets is the tomb of Franklin and his wife. This tomb is five feet eight inches long, and its width is three feet sixteen inches three lines. A stone covers it with this inscription:

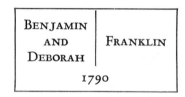

BENJAMIN AND DEBORAH	FRANKLIN
1790	

Franklin himself composed the following epitaph, forty years before his death:

The Body
of
Benjamin Franklin
Printer
(Like the cover of an old book
Its contents torn out
And stript of its lettering and gilding)
Lies here, food for worms.
But the work shall not be lost
For it will appear once more
In a new and more elegant edition
Revised and corrected
by
The Author.

Franklin died April 17, 1790. It pains me that no mention of his philosophical ideas has been made on his monument. Free people of color are Episcopalians.

Lutherans are more numerous in Philadelphia than the members of any other church.

(2) *Cemeteries*

Philadelphia has 22 cemeteries. I published an account of these places of man's last repose in a letter dated April 15, 1798, under the title "Letter of a French Traveler to a Friend in France." In it I showed that the cemeteries of Philadelphia occupy one twenty-fifth of the area of this great city. This enormous amount of land will allow fifteen hundred corpses to be buried annually for forty years without the necessity of using any of the graves a second time. And why should these cemeteries be placed in the center of a city? Above each grave is a stone or a monument three feet high, two feet wide and one or two inches thick, placed vertically, and all the members of a given family are united beneath it.

Coffins in Philadelphia are made of very durable wood and the ground is clayey, reasons which make cemeteries more dangerous. Neighboring buildings prevent the circulation of air in the cemeteries; mists are frequent in them; and in rainy weather the seepage from the cemeteries drains into the water that is pumped up for drinking.

Moreover lime and water-of-lime are seldom if ever used in burials, although this method surely and easily renders them less dangerous!

I declared that this neighborliness of cemeteries had one moral advantage: that of freeing children from the fright of imaginary ghosts. But I am not attracted by the frequency with which children go to these cemeteries to play, thus trampling upon the ashes of those who gave them life. Such a custom can lead to an insensibility concerning objects which nature makes dear to us.

I proposed that there should be only one cemetery in Philadelphia: the Potter's Field at the corner of Sixth and

Walnut. Its large extent would require no re-using of plots for ten years, since it occupies an entire square and was used only for the burial of foreigners or poor who belong to no church. I did not know that after the winter of 1794 a row of Lombardy poplars was planted along each of its sides, and that plans had been made to turn it into a public promenade. I was slightly consoled by its future destination and by reflecting that the emanations from this cemetery were blown over the lawns and gardens of Congress by the southwest winds which prevail in warm weather.

I added that there should be, in some remote part of the city itself, a depot where the dead could remain until the next day at daybreak, when they could be carried to the cemetery.

I advocated having graves made deeper and the coffins made of thin wood; using lime lavishly; doing away with tombstones, except in memory of great names, outstanding virtues, noteworthy benefits rendered. Finally I advised planting low-growing shrubs which could be cut down often, rather than trees whose roots vie for the ground and which hinder the air from circulating. I said that after a cemetery had been filled and abandoned for twenty-five years it should become a public possession and be used as a reservoir that would be helpful against fires, and be put in the care of men trained to make them more healthful.

And what resulted from my philanthropic advice? Only that trees have been planted in cemeteries since 1802. This happened first in the Quaker cemetery at the southwest corner of Mulberry Street and North Fourth Street, and then in the cemetery of the Irish Catholics of the Church of St. Mary, which runs between Fourth and South Fifth streets.

They were planted to cypresses, with weeping willows at the four corners.

This is the place, at the end of the part about cemeteries,

to put in a word on burials. They are extremely extravagant everywhere in the United States.

If it is the funeral procession of a married person, the married persons walk at the head, two by two, then the persons of the sex of the dead person, two by two, and finally the other sex, two by two.

If it is a boy or a girl, the persons of the sex of the dead person go two by two and the other sex, always two by two.

The coffins are of pine, cherry, walnut or mahogany boards that are more or less large, and they are more or less decorated with gilt or silvered metal bands, manufactured in England, which bind the edges of the coffin. Sometimes the name and age of the dead person are carved on it.

The coffin is carried on the shoulders of four bearers. There are eight bearers, because they change at each street corner.

The priest walks in front, except in the case of Roman Catholic burials.

Husbands go to the funerals of their wives, and wives to those of their husbands, if they have the strength to endure this heartbreaking ordeal. Funeral processions are numerous, and inspire respect and grief. Because of a custom that I cannot sufficiently praise, fathers and mothers wear mourning for their children. And what loss could be more deplorable! And what unhappiness it engenders!

(3) *Plays*

Philadelphia has two theaters. The first, called the Old, is at the corner of Cedar and Fourth streets, and thus on the outskirts of the city. It is abandoned.

The New Hall, on the northwest corner of Chestnut and Fourth streets, has nothing on its brick façade to indicate that it is a public building. The entrance is shabby and differs in no wise from that of an ordinary house. The interior is pretty, and three tiers of boxes are pleasingly arranged in a semi-ellipse. There are fifteen boxes in each tier. Of these fifteen the five opposite the stage have seven rows of rising benches so arranged that each box holds thirty-five persons. The ten boxes on either side have two rows of benches, each bench holding four persons. Each tier of boxes thus can accommodate two hundred and fifty-five persons, a total of seven hundred and fifty-five. The seats in the pit descend in amphitheater from the bottom tier of boxes to the orchestra. There are thirteen rows of benches, holding thirty persons each, which makes about four hundred persons.

The hall is painted gray with gilded scrolls and carvings. The upper tier of boxes has small gilded balustrades which are quite elegant. The boxes are separated in the front by small columns which interfere with the view. They are papered with red paper in extremely bad taste.

The theater is lighted by small four-branched chandeliers placed on every second box, beginning at the middle of the second box on each side, starting at the stage. Thus there are seven of them on the upper exterior of each tier of boxes. They are supported by gilded iron S's. The orchestra holds thirty musicians in two rows facing each other. The front stage is huge. Its wings represent portions of façades of beautiful houses, but they project too far onto the stage and hide the rear of the stage, as well as the row of side wings, from spectators in boxes nearest the stage.

The stage, which is large, is lighted by oil lamps, as in France. These can be changed from high to low for night scenes and those that require dimness. The wings have illumination lamps.

The acoustics are adequate, and the view is good from all points except the back of the boxes of the second tier. In these the sloping ceiling of the third tier is so low that one has difficulty in seeing the curtain at the rear of the stage. From other points of the theater it is hard to recognize persons seated at the rear of the boxes which have seven rows of benches.

The price of seats in the boxes of the first and second tier, and in those with eight places on the sides of the second tier, is the same: a piastre per person. A seat in the pit costs three fourths of a piastre, and only half a piastre in that part of the third gallery corresponding to the five boxes with seven rows of benches in the first and second. The corridors are roomy and comfortable. In the upper part of the wall of each box, a little sash window opens into the corridors, so that air can be admitted without the necessity of opening the doors.

Women go in the pit like men; but these are not women of any social standing. The upper gallery admits women and colored people who can't sit anywhere else.

The decorations are colorful and skillfully painted. They are shifted easily enough.

This playhouse, called the New Hall, was built by a stock company which rents it to the management. The companies which play there are road companies, and also play in Baltimore. The shares yield six per cent interest.

The actors are of a bearable mediocrity from the English point of view. The performance is boisterous, and the interludes are even indecent. It is not unusual to hear such words as Goddamn, Bastard, Rascal, Son of a Bitch. Women turn their backs to the performance during the interludes.

The actors are well enough dressed; the style of the plays, which are English and in the English taste, is extremely coarse and full of pleasantries highly repugnant to the French taste.

There are dancers whom Nicolet would have been able to claim. People eat and drink in the pit. The refreshments, of which there is a store in a pretty little shop in the lobby behind the first boxes, cost fifty per cent more than in the city, which is the natural result of the rental cost of the shop.

Most of the musicians of the orchestra are Frenchmen, enabled to exist by this means.

Philadelphia also has two circuses where coryphees from England often exercise their talents and amuse people with equestrian exercises. Among them I saw M. Ricketts and M. Lailson. Ricketts' circus is opposite the new theater in Chestnut Street; the other stands at the corner of Thirteenth and Market streets.[19]

(4) *The House of Representatives of Pennsylvania of the Assembly of Congress and Its Garden*

The House of Representatives of Pennsylvania (for each province has its own legislature to deal with everything outside the jurisdiction of the Congress, which is an assembly of representatives from all the United States) is situated on the south side of Chestnut Street between Fifth and Sixth streets, and was built in 1753. Its architecture is good for that period. Its front extends from Chestnut to Walnut Street, thus occupying an entire square. It is built around a garden. In the rear, framed by the walls and buildings of Chestnut Street, is a garden with many rows of trees, intersected and surrounded by gravel walks—a pleasant place for promenading.

The State House is one hundred and fifty feet long, and proportionately wide. It is divided according to the object for which it was planned. Its upper side is a terrace with a balcony running all around. On each side of this building there is a lower one used for offices.

In 1787 there was built on the northwest corner of the square another structure intended for a court house, but

[19]Ricketts, a Scotch equestrian, opened a circus on April 12, 1793, at Twelfth and Market streets and met with such success that he built an amphitheater at Sixth and Chestnut. The latter was burned down on December 17, 1799, and led to Ricketts' ruin. His efforts with Lailson to recuperate his fortunes proved vain. See Scharf and Westcott, II, 952–953.

later converted into the House of Congress. This added to the beauty of the north façade. On the lower floor is the Chamber of Representatives, above it the place where the Senate assembles.

Congress held its sessions there from the time when it left New York, until 1800, when it moved to the federal city, called Washington.

A building parallel and similar to that of the Congress is the new Court House. In it the Court of Errors and Appeals meets in January every year, with power to adjourn when it sees fit to do so. The Supreme Court for the county meets on the first Monday in January, April and September. There are four sessions of a Court of Common Pleas in March, June, September and December. The federal Supreme Court meets in February and August, the Circuit Court in April, and the District Court in February, May, August and November.

All these buildings are built of brick, and their interiors are simple in the extreme.

I shall say a word about the ceremony which takes place at the opening of the sessions of Congress.

When both chambers have the number of members required by the Constitution, they inform the President of this fact and he specifies a day when he will come there.

On that date both chambers assemble in the Chamber of Representatives; the president of the Senate on the right, the Speaker of the House of Representatives on the left.

The Senate attends in a body, and it is then that the Chamber of Representatives becomes the Congress. The members of the Senate occupy armchairs in the center of the gathering.

When the Senate arrives, the members of the House rise, and the herald at arms bearing his mace leads the senators from the door of the chamber to their seats.

Promptly at noon on the nineteenth of September, 1794, Washington arrived alone in a carriage drawn by four horses.

His three servants and his coachman wear white liveries with red collars and cuffs.

Seven high constables with white wands walked before the carriage, and in front of them were fourteen constables.

When the President enters, everyone rises. He seats himself in the chair ordinarily occupied by the Speaker of the House; then, a moment later, he rises, steps forward to a position between the two presidents of the Senate and the Chamber, but on a step above them. Then he bows, and delivers his speech standing, the whole Congress also standing.

The ambassadors are in chairs on Washington's right but on the floor of the room. They remain seated during the speech.

At the end of his speech, Washington presents a copy of it to each of the two presidents; then leaves and returns to his house escorted as he came.

Washington was dressed in black, his hair in a bag, a turned-up hat, and a sword. He did not wear his hat, nor did anyone else. There was no applause on the President's arrival or departure.

The silence which reigns in the galleries of Congress deserves the highest praise.

What a pity that Congress does not always preserve its self-respect! In the month of May, 1800, two members of the Chamber of Representatives reviled each other, and even came to blows in their assembly hall. This deplorable scene grieved all Americans who truly loved their country. On May 13 Congress decided to assemble on the third Monday of the following September.

(5) *The Meeting Place of the Philosophical Society*

This Society occupies several rooms on the first floor of a building south of the Court House. The room for meetings has a long table on the south side of which the president sits alone in a shabby armchair which Franklin had long used as a desk chair, and which he himself had occupied when president of the Society. On the wall behind the president is an oil painting of this venerable philosopher who worked to such good advantage for his country's liberty and prosperity.

The other members are seated along the north, east and west sides of the table. The rooms are furnished with glass-fronted cupboards in which are kept the Society's books, instruments and papers.

The American Philosophical Society was formed January 2, 1769, by the amalgamation of two older literary societies. It was incorporated March 15, 1800, with the privileges and the necessary powers to fulfill its purposes and to assure it of funds equal in value to that of ten thousand bushels of wheat. The number of members is not limited, and at present is around 450.

The Society has already published three quarto volumes of its minutes. They are justly esteemed, and each day necessarily adds to the Society's usefulness and reputation as the century progresses. The first of these volumes was issued in 1771, the second in 1786, the third in 1793.

The College of Physicians meets in the hall of the Philosophical Society on the first Wednesday of each month.

(6) *Museum*

The ground floor of the Philosophical Society's building has been given by the Society to M. Peale, one of its members devoted to the natural history of sciences and arts, for use as a museum.

You cannot expect it to be like the museums of Paris, nor should one insist that Philadelphia must resemble the capital of Europe. But M. Peale, an American, has gathered together there all that his slender resources have allowed, and everything is native to the United States.

His interesting children help him in this estimable work, and share in the gratitude which it inevitably evokes daily.

(7) *The Philadelphia Library*

This is situated opposite the Philosophical Society and adds to the beauty of the square on which it fronts. It was incorporated in 1747, and was originally established by subscription in 1731. It has fifteen thousand volumes. It is open to the public daily except Sunday. Books are borrowed by leaving a sum of money as a guarantee of their return, and to replace them when they are worn out.

In 1792 a decree added to this Library the rare and valuable collection bequeathed to the public by Dr. James Logan. The structure of this Library is well designed. One enters by a door which opens on a circular staircase built as a ramp.

The Library is on the ground floor and is divided into two parts. The first contains ten thousand volumes and is restricted to the six hundred subscribers. The second, which has about five thousand volumes, is open to the public. This is the legacy of Dr. Logan, whose portrait hangs here, as well as that of Penn.

In a niche on the front of the building, above the entrance, is a statue of Benjamin Franklin a little larger than life size. He wears a Roman robe, and his left arm rests on several books piled on top of a column. At the base of the white marble statue is this inscription:

This statue of
Dr. Benjamin Franklin
was presented by
William Bingham Esqre
MDCCXCIII

(8) *Prison*

In the square south of the court of Congress is the public prison, which is built of stone.

It has a half story on the ground floor and then a first and second story are vaulted in arches against fire. It is a square building with a hundred-foot front, the largest of its kind in the United States. A Work House is attached to this prison. The sexes are segregated, and debtors are not put with the criminals. Recently a new building was erected for criminals condemned to solitary confinement, in accordance with a new penal code which has almost abolished the death penalty.

The jail yard extends to the south side of Spruce Street, and is enclosed by a high stone wall.

Of the 4860 debtors and 4000 criminals confined in the past ten years, only 10 persons have died, and no criminal who was released has been convicted again.

The law forbids that their faults be held against them when they have been pardoned, and the good conduct of more than one condemned person has regained the esteem which was formerly his. In a case where a guilty person has been condemned to the gallows, if the President pardons him, the people cut down the gallows and cheer this act of clemency. When on June 17, 1795, however, he pardoned two men who had been sentenced to be hanged as a result of troubles in the western part of Pennsylvania, the people cut the gallows according to custom, but without any hurrahing.

The details of this prison can be found in M. de Liancourt's work, and sensitive souls can learn that mankind was improved there, and that the death penalty can be spared in most cases.

In this House of Correction (bettering house) each sick man cost thirty-two cents a day. In Philadelphia there are debtor-prisoners who frequently consume in one month's time food that has a higher value than the debt for which they were arrested. The prisoners are not under much restraint, and do not have to be locked in their cells until nine o'clock at night.

The jailer is responsible for the debts of those who escape, but the prisoners make it a point of honor not to subject him to this. Some are even allowed to have keys, and to unlock and lock the doors for those entering or leaving the prison.

What, then, is honesty?

(9) *City Tavern or the Tavern of the City*

This is the name which the merchants give to a house which they maintain in Second Street near the corner of Walnut as a sort of exchange; and there they gather at two o'clock every day to find out about market prices, to learn about ship movements, the records of which are kept in a register, and to hear the news. Each day an officer goes from there to the lower part of the river at least as far as Newcastle, depending on the weather and the season, to find what vessels are expected or which are preparing to sail from Newcastle. All this is paid for by assessment levied on the merchants. In addition the man in charge of the house sells refreshments and punch, and the patrons treat one another and sometimes even dine in private rooms on the first floor. On the whole, City Tavern is an extremely useful establishment.

(10) *Markets*

I have already spoken about the three markets.

(11) *The Hospitals*

The largest of these, called the Pennsylvania, is for the sick in mind and body. It is on Eighth Street between Spruce and Pine. It was incorporated in 1750, and is under the direction of twelve persons, six of whom are directors and six the most capable doctors of the city. Two directors and two doctors come every Friday and Saturday at eleven o'clock in the morning to receive and discharge the patients, and the doctor prescribes medicines for the patients. This hospital was built in 1756. Up to March 5, 1795, nine thousand patients had been admitted, of which almost five thousand were cured, 120 declared incurable and 1150 died. There are generally from thirty to forty lunatics, most of them as a result of love, and it might be remarked in passing that the great majority of Americans are to be congratulated that this is something they don't need to worry about.

The medical students of the university pay a hundred louis to be attached to this hospital, which also receives maternity cases and children.

Plans are on foot to enlarge this asylum for suffering humanity.

There is also a large building on Spruce Street, between Tenth and Eleventh, where the poor of the city and of neighboring towns may find employment in the manufacture of rough articles when in need of help to reduce their expenses.

The Philadelphia dispensary was founded April 12, 1786, to furnish the indigent sick with needed remedies. This establishment is maintained entirely through the generosity of individual subscribers who, by donating one louis a year, can provide care for two patients. Sixteen months after its establishment 800 patients had been treated; and in December this number had risen to 1892, of whom 1578 had been cured. Twelve directors are chosen each year from among the subscribers, six members at a time. Four consulting doctors and one apothecary give their services free. The dispensary's annual expenses are twelve thousand five hundred francs.

There is a house of charity supported by Quakers on Walnut Street between Third and Fourth and managed by a committee of Quakers. It has apartments or rooms for Quakers who have been reduced to poverty. It has a large garden which supplies the city with medicinal plants.

Christ Church Hospital is on the north side of Mulberry Street between Third and Fourth. This is a small two-story building. A white marble slab between the ground floor and the first floor, and in the middle, bears this inscription in black letters: Christ Church Hospital.

Dr. John Kearsley the elder was a distinguished doctor of the city, and after him the institution was greatly enlarged by a donation from M. Delbens.

This hospital includes twelve widows who are cared for and supported. Such women of the same communion who cannot be accommodated in the hospital are lodged in different parts of the city, and their expenses are paid.

(12) *The Poor House*

(13 and 14) *The University, the Academies, the Schools and Everything That Bears on Public Instruction*

Prior to 1791 the city contained an old college, an academy and some charitable schools founded in 1779. In 1791 the university was incorporated by the Pennsylvania legislature, and these older institutions were assigned to it.

The university is situated on the west side of Fourth Street, between Market and Mulberry. At present it is directed by a governing body of twenty-four trustees, the Governor of the state always being president. Its capital is about sixty thousand francs and it has 510 students of whom 25 receive degrees annually. It has a library and a physics laboratory.

The College of Physicians, established in 1787 and incorporated in 1789, was formed to encourage knowledge in medicine, anatomy and chemistry, and to render the practice of medicine more uniform.

Almost every religious sect has under its immediate direction one or more schools where children of both sexes belonging to that church can learn to read and write, and are supplied with books and everything necessary for their instruction.

There are private academies to teach young girls all sorts of excellent knowledge. The public attitude toward these academies is one of interest and pride. Many have Frenchwomen as principals.

One astonishing thing is the fact that there are schools called African, designed for the education of colored children.

Besides the establishments I have mentioned, Philadelphia has many others.

One organization is working to bring about the abolition of slavery, but it makes little progress, and public opinion is opposed rather than favorable to it. A society to better the condition of unfortunate prisoners has already produced good results. One for the encouragement of arts and manufactures dates from 1787. Each member pays twelve francs admission fee, and annual dues of twelve francs.

There is an Agricultural Society, an Irish Relief Society, a German Relief Society, a Charitable Society for the relief of widows and families of Presbyterian clergymen, a Mariners' Society made up of ship captains, a Charitable Society of St. George and St. Andrew, the Franklin Society with a membership of printers, a Society of Carpenters, and the Philadelphian Society to Investigate and Assist Emigrants to America, founded in 1794.

It is impossible to deny that since independence, many useful organizations have been formed in America and especially in Philadelphia, but their beginnings have been meager and the progress insignificant.

To tell the truth, circumstances have not always been favorable; and any attempt to arouse interest in public welfare has too often been impeded by the sluggishness and the heedlessness natural to Americans. It is to be hoped that with time these obstacles will lessen.

(15) *The House Destined for the President of the United States*

This house, situated on the west side of Ninth Street and between Market and Chestnut streets, was well designed. It is entered through a courtyard; and the apartment intended for the President is reached by a staircase with two curving ramps. This was under construction in 1798, but I think that the transfer of the federal government to the federal city, Washington, will cause this building to be abandoned, so that it will be used for a different purpose.[20]

(16) *The Mint*

There is one of these in Philadelphia, but it is not busy, because the chief money is piastre gourdes.[21] There are still

---

[20]"In 1791 the Legislature of Pennsylvania purchased the property extending from Chestnut to Market streets, and from Ninth Street west one hundred and fifty-two feet, and proceeded to erect thereon a house for the President of the United States. . . . By the time the spacious and substantial edifice was completed, at a cost of nearly one hundred thousand dollars, Mr. Adams had become President. When the building was finished it was tendered by Governor Mifflin, by direction of the Legislature, to President Adams at a fair rental. Mr. Adams declined the offer, and the State was left with the property on its hands. In 1800 the property was offered at public sale . . . and was purchased by the University for the sum of forty-one thousand six hundred and fifty dollars, less than half its original cost." It was later sold to the United States Government for five hundred thousand dollars for the site of the new post office in 1874. Scharf and Westcott, III, 1939.

[21]A piastre gourde was a San Domingan coin worth one dollar. A writer once advanced the theory that the word "shin-plaster" came from the habit, in colonial days, of protecting the legs from the heat of open fires by wrapping the shins with Continental bills. Actually "plaster" came from "piastre"; "shin" came from "chien": dog money.

only a very few eagles worth ten gourdes, half eagles worth only five, and quarter eagles worth only two and a half. Thus the Mint, as one might say, is merely a curiosity.

(17) *City Hall*

The city was incorporated in 1701, as I have said. The heads were chosen by themselves. After a new charter in 1789, the members were elected by the tax-paying inhabitants.

Now it is governed by a Mayor, a clerk of court, fifteen aldermen, fifteen sheriffs and a City Council made up of thirty persons.

The Mayor is elected each year by the aldermen from their body. The clerk of court is elected for seven years by the Mayor, and the aldermen are chosen by the citizens.

Aldermen are elected by property owners every other April. The City Council is elected every third year, also in April, by the voters qualified to vote for the members of the State Assembly.

The Mayor, the clerk of court, eight aldermen and sixteen members of the City Council make the laws and regulations for the government of the city. The Mayor, clerk of court and aldermen are justices of the peace.

They meet four times a year to consider debt cases and crimes committed in the city. Two aldermen are appointed by the Mayor and the clerk of court to hold court each Monday and Wednesday morning on cases which come within the jurisdiction of the Court of the Justice of the Peace.

(18) *Banks*

Philadelphia has three banks. 1. The Bank of North America was incorporated in 1781. It is directed by one president and eleven directors, chosen annually. Its capital is four and a half million francs and can be increased to six million. 2. The Bank of the United States was incorporated in 1791 to run until 1811, its president and twenty-four directors to be chosen each year. The capital was sixty million francs divided into twenty-five thousand shares.

When the United States refused to renew the bank's charter at its expiration, it ceased to exist. This caused great distress to its officials and employees, and they attempted to sell the bank's property to Philadelphia.

As Americans have an exaggerated idea of everything that belongs to them, they put the extravagant value of more than a million and a half francs upon it. This was in line with the absurd claim that this bank building was one of the eight Wonders of the World, a wonder so flimsy that its portico was destroyed by rats. Everyone has been to see the place.

When Stephen Girard, a Frenchman and a merchant in Philadelphia, offered to buy it at a reasonable valuation, the price was reduced to nine hundred thousand francs, which he paid. He announced that he intended to carry on the bank, and raised a capital of twenty-four million francs in dollars. After March, 1812, his bank took the place of the Bank of the United States, paying only four per cent interest instead of the six per cent which the Bank gave.

3. The Bank of Philadelphia[22] was incorporated in 1792 for a term of twenty years. It is governed by a president and twenty-four directors. Six of the directors are chosen by the State Assembly; eighteen by the shareholders. Its capital is twelve million divided into five thousand shares. It has a marble portico.

The banks of the United States were formed by speculator merchants, who can, when they wish, make business

[22]Moreau has confused names. The first mentioned should be the Bank of Pennsylvania, incorporated in 1792, and the second, the Bank of Philadelphia, founded in 1803 and incorporated in 1804.

difficult for other merchants. By refusing to discount bills, they can control all purchases and all sales, or at least embarrass the merchants seriously by obliging them to borrow money at a high rate.

There is a fourth bank, the second Bank of Philadelphia, on Chestnut Street opposite the Bank of North America.

(19) *Insurance Companies*

In Philadelphia there are six marine insurance companies and two fire insurance companies.

(20) *The Powder Magazine*

This was formerly situated on North Seventh Street between Sassafras and Vine. Now it is farther south, on Achilon Street, and holds over fifty thousand barrels of powder.

Besides the things we have mentioned in detail, Philadelphia also has, in the city and its suburbs, ten rope-walks using one hundred tons of hemp annually, thirteen breweries which consume over fifty thousand bushels of barley a year, six sugar refineries, seven powder factories for making powder, two rummeries and one distillery, three playing-card factories, fifteen potteries, six for making chocolate, three for mustard, three factories for cut nails and one for uncut, one for nitric acid, one for sal ammoniac, one for sulphate of soda, one for oil color, eleven for brushes, two for buttons, one for Morocco leather, one for parchment. There are also cannon foundries, coppersmiths, hatmakers, tinsmiths, etc., etc.

There are many brickyards all around Philadelphia.

Pennsylvania has many paper mills.

The city of Philadelphia has thirty-one printing houses, three type foundries and fourteen newspapers, of which one is French and one German.

Good ink is made in Germantown, two leagues away, and also in Philadelphia. There is paper for engraving, and skilled engravers of maps, landscapes and portraits, of business forms and letterheads; engravers on wood and on metal; engravers and printers on copper-plate.

The commerce of Philadelphia is considerable and increases daily. In 1795 she sent fifteen ships to the Indies and to China, but her chief trade is with England and the colonies. In 1794 she exported four hundred thousand barrels of flour.

In 1794 her exports were valued at forty-seven million francs, and during the same year fifteen hundred vessels arrived at the port, and her yearly receipts are six million weight of sugar, three million gallons of molasses, and two million of rum.

Goods of all sorts are transported on the Delaware by one hundred and twenty small boats from Philadelphia.

To cross the Delaware to Jersey by ferry, a trip of a mile, one person pays two French sous; a horse, nine French sous; a carriage, fourteen French sous. Vessels built in Philadelphia are usually ships with three masts, while the Northern states run more to brigs and snows, and Virginia to schooners.

The figureheads of the vessels built in Philadelphia deserve high praise. They are executed with extraordinary skill and with great care. Many are portraits, and they are strikingly lifelike.

The wood in the United States is not on a par with that of Europe, particularly that of the northern countries. Vessels built of North American oak do not last half as long as those built with European oak.

It has been proposed in England to give rewards for the preservation of North American woods that are shipped to Europe for shipbuilding. One builder proposed that they be allowed to season in huge reservoirs, but this long and costly process was not considered feasible.

American oak grows in moist locations. It rots easily, and is attacked by worms which devour the sap in an instant; and in addition the heart does not endure as in European climates, which have no worms to fear, other than those terrible boring insects imported from the New World.

Besides, the populated sections, and those adjoining navigable rivers, have already been stripped of wood, so that it is as rare and expensive as in Europe. Coal is already used in many towns and factories, and the government has been forced to get building wood from Georgia and Louisiana. The destruction of forests is widespread and cannot be prevented, 1, because the government has no means of stopping it; 2, because anyone can buy unlimited quantities of timberland in the back countries; 3, because sawmills are speculative enterprises and have stripped river banks of all wood as far as a hundred and twenty leagues from their mouth; 4, because the government never made any plans for reforestation.

Only a few houses in Philadelphia deviate from the regulation shape and size that characterize all of them, but some are much larger; and some, even, are decorated with marble. Such for example, was one that Robert Morris was building when imprisoned for debt.[23]

But these edifices which Americans build for ostentatious display are not sufficiently beautiful to merit the name of mansions. Never can marble columns, even though that marble be Carrara, beautify the gloom of a brick structure. Pride can make an effort in this respect, but good taste will always nullify it.[24]

[23]Compare Isaac Weld, *Travels through North America*, I, 8, and see T. Westcott, *Historic Mansions of Philadelphia*, pp. 359ff. on "Morris' Folly."

[24]Moreau wasn't familiar with the beautiful architectural effects attained in Williamsburg, Charleston, and on the Eastern Shore of Maryland by the combination of "gloomy" brick and "marble" columns.

RETURN JOURNEY

AUGUST 23, 1798. Now I shall take up the details of our crossing from Philadelphia to France.

We sailed from Newcastle at midnight on Thursday, August 23, and dropped our pilot at eleven the next morning.

August 24. On that very day my son came down with a fever that caused us great anxiety, in spite of ourselves and even though it was a creole fever. We were anxious first because yellow fever had been raging in Philadelphia, which we had just left; and second because one of our passengers who had remained on board in the port of Philadelphia had died there.

The fever was still with my son on the twenty-fifth. On Sunday the twenty-sixth I gave him ipecac, which helped him, and his improvement seemed to cheer everyone on board.

But on the twenty-seventh there was another death—the married daughter of a certain Pepin, a Canadian, who had embarked with his wife and family. Then the brother of the dead girl fell sick, as did another young passenger called Sallèles, a resident of Bordeaux.

Young Pepin recovered, but Sallèles, in the fullness of youth, only lived until the thirtieth. On the evening of the twenty-ninth there had been a storm which aggravated his condition; and on the thirtieth, in spite of the rain and the fact that he was in agony, he was carried up onto the forward part of the main deck. I was asked about his condition, and as to whether there was any hope for his recovery. I wouldn't swear that in the general panic they were hardly willing to wait for his actual death before throwing him overboard. What a disgusting beast man can be in certain circumstances!

August 31. Then another misfortune overtook us!

M. Bénard from St. Malo, a man of good birth and education, an excellent violinist, had embarked with us, but with neither victuals nor resources. Filled with pity for his unhappy circumstances, I invited him to our table. Our son, though convalescent, was unable to eat, so that M. Bénard had an excuse for eating with us.

In the night Bénard had an attack of apoplexy. Next morning I gave him a full dose of emetic. But his apoplexy —as I found later by observing the inroads he had made on our supply of liquor—was alcoholic. M. Bénard lived only a few hours, and his death made us regret our own kindness toward him. So there already we had four deaths on the *Adrastes.*

The same day we spoke the brig *Le Levrier,* out of Cadiz, by which I sent a letter to my dear sister.

September 1. We made soundings on the Banks of Newfoundland.

September 2, 1798. Another night yellow fever carried off M. Gepory, a colonial from San Domingo.

At noon they threw overboard another of Pepin's daughters—the blind one.

The entire ship's company was in a turmoil.

At high noon M. Neblon died of the same disease.

My success in the matter of my son's cure made them regard me as a real physician. Nevertheless I had no medicine, no purgatives, no vesicator. Hence I could do nothing, though in these terrible circumstances I would have tried to do something if I had possessed the means. It wasn't long before I again regretted my helplessness. A pretty young girl of eighteen, one of the daughters of M. Vieillot, the ornithologist, was stricken with the fever. Mlle. Euphrosine coughed dreadfully, had spasmodic convulsions like those of rabies, and died in frightful agony. On the twentieth her younger sister, Virginia, was carried off, leaving the parents childless.

What a scene! Where to flee? Death horribly was everywhere in the narrow confines in which we were imprisoned.

September 22. To windward we sighted thirteen French war vessels.

September 24. We spoke two vessels out of Bordeaux. The next morning at eight o'clock we were boarded by the English frigate, *Phaeton,* of 36 guns. Her curiosity was not of long duration; for as soon as yellow fever was mentioned, their officer flung himself back into his boat and made off.

September 26. We sighted land at 3:30 A.M. At nine o'clock a pilot came on board and we dropped our anchor at Verdon at 5 P.M.

We learned of the misfortunes of the army of Aboukir and particularly those of my good friend Aristide Dupetit-houars.

September 27. We reached the breakwater a little above Bec d'Ambec, and at seven the following evening were at Bordeaux.

The next day all the passengers of the *Adrastes* were conducted to the central bureau of the municipality; but as soon as we declared our eight deaths, we were sent back on board.

September 30. In the morning the *Adrastes* was moved to Lormont, where a second inspection took place. That evening the Marine Commissary sent to ask whether I had any packages for the Ministry of Marine and the Ministry of Foreign Affairs. These I gave to a naval policeman.

On October 1 my family and I left the *Adrastes* at Lormont in the gig of Captain Chevillard and reached Bordeaux. We put up at the hotel.

October 2, 1798. I went to the Central Bureau. To my great joy I saw my good friends Jolimon and Desbarrières.

October 5. My dear Aménaïde suffered severe indigestion from eating Bavarian cream, but it did not prevent her from accompanying Eléonore and me to the theater.

October 7. I went to see my things through the customs.

The younger Mourgues, who was about to embark for Philadelphia, gave me a letter from Talleyrand dated September 8.

Paris, 8 Sept. 1798

The Cartel ship is now at Bordeaux. My friend should have arrived on it with all his family. He has not come. I have no letter from him. Why this delay? I hope that you have found us entirely sympathetic toward the United States. We surely had the right to suppose that the United States Government only wanted the semblance of an agreement with us, and was actually making a treaty with England; we hesitated to believe this. Won't the thinking men of the country do their utmost to check the follies committed by the President through vanity? I hope that all my correspondence has been published in America. Undoubtedly nothing could be more loyal or clear than the desire of the French government. To side with America now, as we sided with her up to the declaration of peace, can hardly be called a barbarous proposition. Volney has arrived and is about to publish something. Liancourt's book is being printed. Four volumes are already in print. The work will be published in its entirety. A note of yours was brought me and I will pay it. Liancourt is in Holland. Dupont has delayed his departure. Your cousin Regnier has found you a very comfortable apartment. So come along. What is the news of your Indian? Adieu, my friend. I embrace you and love you. A thousand greetings.

Moreover the younger Mourgues loaned me fifty louis, which, as I gathered from Talleyrand's letter, I thought I had a right to expect of him. I had to reserve and pay for six seats on the coach for Baudry's family and my own, and another seat for my son in a light carriage to which I sometimes relegated him.

October 8. We left Bordeaux for Paris at 5 A.M., dined at St. André de Cubsac, slept at Jouvenceau.

October 9. Dinner at Barbesieux. Supper at Angoulême where we took a walk and left again at 10 P.M.

October 10. Lunch at Ruffec. Supped at Poitiers, where happily I met with no incivility at the customs.

October 11. Dined at Chatellerault, where the noise of the knife factory drove us almost crazy. Slept at St. Maure, where there was a remarkable occurrence.

We were served at supper with the coach passengers from Paris. At table my wife, contrary to her usual prudent conduct, looked at the gentleman opposite her at table and said to me aloud, "How that gentleman resembles M. Talon!"

The gentleman looked worried, retired to another room, sent for me and complained about my wife's indiscreet remark.

It actually was Talon, and I assured him that my wife would never have mentioned his name had she really recognized him.

October 12. We had to push on again at 3 A.M. We dined at Tours. After leaving Tours my son developed fever. I therefore gave him my place in the coach and took his in the carriage. We arrived thus at Blois.

October 13. St. Méry had fever all night, and it proved to be smallpox.

We left Blois at 3 A.M., dined at Orléans, and proceeded to Angeville to sleep.

October 14. Breakfast at Harpajon and so to Paris at 2 P.M.

We went to the lodging which Mlle. Regnier had secured for us near her own, on Rue de l'Université near the pump and the Palace of the Legislature.

I called upon Talleyrand and we embraced with warm affection.

October 15. I reported at the Central Bureau and next day dined with Talleyrand.

October 17. I also went to my own municipality and returned there the following day.

October 18. In the evening I went to see the Directors Treilhard and Barras. The first received me with open friendship. The second, who only knew me through Mirande, made me highly welcome.

At Treilhard's I received a warm reception from everybody there, and Baroness de Staël, whom I met again with great pleasure, paid me special attention.

October 20. I received from Mme. Côte, née Levous, widow of one of my colleagues on the Council of San Domingo, and a fellow passenger on the *Adrastes,* a request that I should send her passport to Bordeaux, whither she was going.

From Citizen Grannet I received a daily pass to the Bureau of Marine.

October 23. As had been arranged with Heurtault La Merville, member of the Council of Five Hundred, he and I called on the Directors Rewbell and Revellière-Lépeaux, but were unable to see them. We then called on Director Merlin, who received us. We found him in front of his fireplace. Observing that his reception of me was somewhat chilly, I said to him:

"Citizen Director, your reception of me leads me to believe that you do not know who I am."

"On the contrary, it is because I do know who you are that I have received you in this manner. You are Moreau de St. Méry, and you are an *émigré!* And if I did my duty," he added, indicating the door and planting himself before me, between the door of the apartment and of the antechamber, "I would have you shot by that sentry!"

On hearing these words, I advanced upon Merlin, forcing him to re-enter the apartment, and said to him: "No. I am not an *émigré,* and you know it!"

He went and got the first volume of my *Description of the Spanish Part of San Domingo* and read me paragraph three of my account.

The order to yield my head to the ax was changed into a permit to return to San Domingo by way of the United States; and when one of Robespierre's agents, warned doubtless that I was about to escape him, came to Le Havre with a special warrant for my arrest in spite of the legal passports that I held, the vessel bearing all that was most dear to me in the world had been at sea for barely thirty-six hours.

"So you see," Merlin said, "that you *are* an *émigré!*"

At this point Heurtault La Merville, pale and trembling, said: "Citizen Director, I did not know that Moreau de St. Méry was an *émigré* when I undertook to present him to you."

I replied indignantly to Heurtault La Merville: "Don't be anxious! Mine is the head that will pay. Yours is in no danger."

To Merlin I repeated, "No, I am no *émigré,* and what you have just read from my circular printed in Philadelphia proves on the contrary that I left France with my passport in good order. Moreover on the nineteenth I saw Citizens Treilhard and Barras, and they welcomed me."

"Very well," Merlin said. "If you are not an *émigré,* I will receive you as I ought to."

I then withdrew, leaving Merlin with Heurtault La Merville, to whom Merlin said: "He would certainly have been guillotined if he had stayed in France!"

From Merlin's house I went immediately to the Minister of Finance, Ramel. My name was announced. He asked me to wait. While seated in the waiting room, I saw a mounted messenger enter. When he came out, I was shown in. Ramel received me as a former colleague and asked what I wished of him.

I told him what had just taken place between me and

Merlin and said I would like a certification that I was not on any list of *émigrés*. Upon which he read me the letter he had just received from the mounted messenger that Merlin had sent. In a tone admitting of no doubt, Merlin demanded proof of the fact that I was an *émigré*.

"And what did you reply?"

He read me his answer to Merlin. It certified that I was on no list and that on the contrary every document in his office relating to myself made me out a good citizen.

At full speed I went to Talleyrand, and told him all that had happened. He told me to get hold of Heurtault La Merville again and to return with him immediately to Merlin's.

I went to the Palace of the Five Hundred, saw Heurtault La Merville, who made excuses for not coming with me to Merlin's. But Talleyrand, learning of this treachery, went himself to Merlin and told him all I had learned from Ramel.

October 24. Once more I went to Heurtault La Merville and again received no satisfaction. I then went to Ramel to obtain a certification that I was not an *émigré*.

Bretel, to whom I had written on my arrival in Paris, wrote me from Chartres telling me that Mme. Bretel's sister, Mme. Girault, had married Berlize and had lost her daughter. His joy at my return equaled my own.

An amiable letter from Mlle. de Maulde asked me to help Blaçon, her brother-in-law, in his project of returning to France. Mme. de Maulde, her mother, asked the same service of me.

October 29. I went to see the Spanish Minister, the Chevalier d'Azava, and found him kindly disposed toward me because of Talleyrand's recommendation.

October 30. I was called to the public session of the Free Society of Arts and Sciences and was seated next to Merlin. As I learned soon after, he had insisted that his colleagues, the directors, should put me on the list of *émigrés*. But Barras and Treilhard refused, and Rewbell and Revellière-

Lépeaux refused to lend themselves to it. That is how I escaped the fury of this cowardly scoundrel.

November 3, 1798. I dined with M. Schemelpenmak and his interesting family. This I owed to Talleyrand's touching friendship for me.

November 4. It was not without surprise that I received from M. Mourgues, senior, a request for twelve hundred francs which his son had loaned me on behalf of Talleyrand, at Bordeaux.

November 7. I began working at the offices of the Bureau of Marine.

November 11. I was most impatient to receive, and pained at not receiving, the identity cards which my family and I needed in order to reside in Paris. Many inquiries on my part had shown me that I had a powerful obstacle to overcome, and Merlin evidently had a finger in the pie.

On the eleventh the Minister of Police informed me that he had sent the necessary documents to the municipality of the 10th Arrondissement.

My baggage, sent from Bordeaux on October 18, arrived in Paris the eleventh of November and I paid three hundred sixteen francs seventeen sous.

M. Mourgues informed me of the death of his son, Eugène.

November 21. When I saw Talleyrand in the morning, as was my daily habit, he asked whether I would care to dine with Volney. I replied that it was for Volney to decide whether he wished to meet me. He said Volney had expressed a desire to do so, and that consequently he would expect me at dinner with Palissot Bauvois. And indeed Volney advanced to embrace me as soon as he perceived me.

November 22. The Minister of Marine took another fifty copies of my books on San Domingo.

From Milan, Sivry wrote me of his pleasure at my return and his extreme grief at the insanity of his son.

November 23. I visited the curious collection of natural

history specimens made by my friend Palissot Bauvois. There I met Director Merlin, his wife and family. I had a much more pleasant and agreeable time dining with Saisseval, whose friendship I had cultivated ever since the courses I took with Sigaud de Lafond and Bricquet in 1772 and at whose house Mme. Saisseval displayed the most admirable graces. Talleyrand dined there also.

November 24. I took Sivry's son to the asylum. In spite of his condition, he had moments of lucidity and memories reminiscent of days when he was in full possession of his faculties. Although one sees heart-rending sights on such a visit, I was profoundly impressed at the evident control of the Mother Superior of the Grey Sisters over the other sisters, nurses and patients. Even the insane who gave way to cries, turmoil and distressing scenes seemed to recognize the Mother Superior, for at sight of her they ceased their clamor as if fearing to displease her.

How powerful and far-reaching are the influences of well-doing and virtue! How venerated is a Grey Sister! What a vocation to sacrifice one's whole life to the care of these unfortunates! What a heaven-sent mission!

All that day I was troubled, but I must admit that the thoughts that the day inspired in me induced the gentlest philosophy.

That evening I was admitted as a member by the Free Society of Sciences, Letters and Arts, affiliated to the Musée de Paris.

November 26. I took my daughter to the house of my friend, the painter Houel. He showed her his studio and gave her advice.

Bonamy congratulated me from Copenhagen on my arrival.

November 27. The Institute did me the honor of accepting copies of my description of San Domingo, both the

French and Spanish parts. Bishop Gregoire and M. de Fleu-
rien were made commissioners.

December 1, 1798. I went to dine with my good friend
Desaudry.

December 6. Sivry again begged me to help his unfortunate son.

I had the opportunity that evening to speak on yellow
fever before the Institute.

I was received by the Free Society of Agriculture and
went to the Republican Lycée.

December 7. Another subject of rejoicing: I was made a
member of the Lycée of Arts and Sciences.

December 10. I dined with my dear Parmentier.

December 17. Went to Talleyrand's with Hédouville.

December 19. And to Chouly's with Caille.

December 20. I received my baggage from Bordeaux. It
cost me seven hundred and forty-six francs in charges.

My friend M. Regnaud de Villevert, to whom I had sent
all my books on San Domingo, thanked me and spoke to me
of the right that I had to the gratitude of the colonists, and
renewed his expressions of friendship. My son took fever.

December 26. I made him take ipecac, and the fever left
him the next day.

December 28. Today M. de Montesquiou was buried. He
was a member of the Constituent Assembly, and for twenty-
eight years we had been friends as a result of an amorous
adventure in which he played the leading part and of which
a happy accident had made me a witness at the Opera Ball
in 1770.

It was in this year that I published Volume II of the
journey of Van Braam of the Dutch Embassy.

INDEX

INDEX

Abolitionist conventions and societies, 303, 357
Abortion, 293
Acadian settlement (Frenchtown, Md.), 84
Actes de la Commune de Paris pendant la Révolution (Lacroix, printer), xiv
Actors, 347; charitable qualities of, 272
Adams, John (1735–1826), education of son, 334; hostility to Frenchmen, xx, 253; President's House at Philadelphia, refusal of, 358; Dr. Rittenhouse, 336; succeeded Washington, 138; visited when Vice-President, 213
Adams, John Quincy (1767–1848), education, 334
Adelaïde (servant), 8
Adet, Minister of France, arrival, 185; character, 275; trip to Albany, 220; visited, 213
Adolphe (ship), 301
Adrastes (cartel ship), Moreau's return voyage (1788), 252, 253, 255; deaths, 364–66; passage costs, 255–56; provisions, 255
Adrienne (ship), 180
African ducks, 61
Africans. *See* Negroes; Slavery
Agricultural Society of New York, 318
Aiguillon, Duc d' (1761–1800), 224
Aiguillon, Mme. d', letter *quoted*, 248
Albany, New York, French refugees, 144; snowfall (1798), 320
Alfalfa (luzerne), 172
Alien Bill, xx
Amboy, New Jersey, 110, 111
Amelia (schooner), 25, 26
America (ship), 224
American aid to France, 127–28
American men, 265; birth of a child, 289; conjugal relations, 289;

divorce, 290; giving the arm (custom), 289; indolent, 328; lawyers, 335; quarrelsome, 328; remarriage, 290; women's purchases, 283. *See also* Americans; American sailors; American women; Children; Houses and Homes; names of individual cities—trade, industry, commerce
American Philosophical Society, xvii, 178, 210, 225, 350–51
American Review (1802), *quoted*, 166
Americans: attach themselves to nothing, 279; beef, fondness for, 6; blend of Europeans and Indians, 269; bound out in service, 294; character, 7, 12, 267, 280; characteristics, 270–72; cleverness and knowledge, 334–35; commercialism, 269; complexion, 265; conjugal customs, 290; country dwellers, 279, 281, 311–12; courtship and marriage customs, 283, 285–86; divorce, 290; Eastern contempt for Southern states, 269; eels, no fondness for, 68; emigration, 279; English, detestation for, 267; friendship, indifferent to, 279; generosity, 270, 273–74; green fruit, eating of, 280; homes, *see* Houses and Homes; hospitality, 335; ice cream, fondness for, 323; improvident, 25; indolence, 272; lack of imagination, 272; laziness, 12; letters of introduction, 269; longevity, 282; love, indifferent to, 279, 285, 290, 355; manner of living, 265–66; manners, uncouth, 121; marriage customs, 283, 285–86, 290; meat consumption, 280; men of letters, 335; money, love of, 270–71; mourning customs, 68; origins, retain traces of, 272; ostentatious display, 363; oysters, passion for, 266; pride, 270; regional pride, 269; self-admiration, 334; self-respect, 264; sensitivity, 273; settlements, 269;

sleep too long, 280; starting a voyage on Saturday, 1; stomach powders, use of, 18; superstition about dove-cotes, 77; tobacco, use of, 279; traits, outstanding, 7, 12, 267, 272; trickiness, 269; uncharitable qualities, 72; want of integrity, examples, 274; work, capacity for, 280

American sailors: clothing, 6; consider themselves more skillful than French sailors, 7; discipline, 7–8; drink, 6; food, 6, 7; Gulf Stream, 19; lack of foresight, 4; pay, squandering of, 6; wages, 157

American ships: advice to Frenchmen coming to North America on, 37–39; badly fitted out, 4; Baltimore-owned, 80; berths, how to reserve, 82–83; cabins and their furnishings, 4–5; captains' wages, 161; carelessness with which fires are lighted, 4; Charleston packet, 164; cleanliness, 5; cost, 158; crew discipline, 7–8; drinks (water, tea and rum), 6; ferries, 167; figureheads, 362; food on, 9–11, 83; indentured servants, 293–94; mariner apprentices, 291; meals, 6; navigation, 5; Norfolk-built vessels, 51; religious services, 6–7; storage of supplies, 37; strongly built, 4; tea consumption, 38; toilet facilities, 5; ton equivalents, 163; types built, 362; water on, 14; wood used in, 362

American women: abortion, 293; aversion to certain words, 284; beauty, 281, 287; bedrooms, 289; body divisions, 287; bondwomen, 295; breasts, 283–84, 288; carriages, their importance to, 98, 111, 334; chemises, 288–89, 297; chignons, 302; childbearing, 289; cleanliness, 287, 288, 289; climate, influence on, 287; complexion, 265; confinement, cost of, 160; conjugal relations, 289; courtship and marriage, 285–86, 289–90; criminals, 166; dancing, 290–91; desertion, 289; divorce, 290; doctors' problems with, 287–88; dress, 287; false modesty, 284, 287; first suitors, 284; food, 287; hair, 282; health, 287; housekeepers, 285, 286; illegitimate children, 293; liberty they enjoy, 285;

love of adornment, 283; marriage, respect to, 289–90; married, seduction of, 284–85; matrimony, pleasures of, 287; meat carving, 286; menopause, 283; menstruation, 287; modesty, 284; Negro, 302–03; nervous illnesses, 282; not affectionate, 284; opinions of Frenchwomen, 287, 288; pastry making, 286; pregnancy, 287; Quaker, 280; reproduction faculty, 283; sailors' wives, 312; self-love, 285; shame, 293; skin eruptions, 287; stage traveling, 122; stomachs, weak, 287; tea, overuse of, 287; teeth, 282, 287; unnatural pleasures, 286; washing and bathing, 287, 289; white slave traffic, 302–03; white, 281–91; withdrawal from dinner table, 265. *See also* American men; Americans; Children; Houses and Homes; Prostitution

Anabaptists: Baltimore, 78; Brooklyn, 168–69; Negroes, 306; Portsmouth, 64; Wilmington (Del.), 88

Andros, Sir Edmund, colonial governor (1637–1714), 260

Anglican-Episcopal Church. *See* Episcopal Church

Animals: care of, 120; climate, effect on, 327

Annapolis, Maryland, 81

Apple pie, cost of, 319

Archives Coloniales, Paris, xi, xxi

Arthaud, M. (brother-in-law), 191, 194

Artibonite, Marquès de l', 192

Asia (ship), 214

Atheists, 338

Atlantic crossings, cost and passage time: Demeunier (1797), 233; Moreau (1793), 1–45; Moreau (1798), 255, 364 ff.; Talleyrand (1796), 223

Aubert family, 90, 250

Aurora (news sheet), 335

Azores, storms, 7; wind, 20

Bache's *General Advertiser*, xix

Back River Point, Virginia, 72

Badaminier of the Moluccas (catalpa tree), 106

Bad luck, 22

Bailly, Jean Sylvain, Mayor of Paris (1736–1793), xiii, 3

Baltimore, 76–81; anchorage, 78; Baltimore Street, 76; banks, 80; Calvert Street, 77; Cap François church bell, 274; churches, 78; commerce (with Philadelphia), 82; cotton mills, 81; distilleries, 81; dove-cotes, 77; exports, 80; French, liking for, 81; government, 81; Holyday Street, 76; horses, 77; hotels, 80; houses, 76; Howard Street, 77; Howard's Park, 75; Indian Queen Hotel, 74; industries, 81; Jones Falls, 76, 79–80; Lafayette Street, 76; markets, 78; mileage from Annapolis, 81; mileage from New York, 166; mileage from Philadelphia, 81; mileage from Richmond, 81; newspapers, 81; Norfolk packets, 71; pleasant air, peculiar to itself, 79; population, 78; port, 78; public buildings, 77; sidewalks, 76; street litter, 76; street lighting, 77; streets, 76, 77; theater, 79; wharves, 78; yellow fever, 80
Baltimore to Philadelphia trip (1794), 82–95
Bank of North America, 359–60
Bank of Pennsylvania, 360
Bank of Philadelphia, 360, 361
Bank of the United States, 80, 360
Baptist Church: at New York, 149; at Philadelphia, 337
Barbecues, 58
Barère, M. (patriot), 182
Barrels: cartage, 158; cooperage, 158; firkin, 163; freight, 159; hoops, 162–63; kinds, 163; packing, 158; staves, 158, 163; storage, 158–59
Bastille, fortress, xii, 204
Bastille — or Liberty Triumphant (play), 187–89
Bathtubs, 324
Baudry family, 42, 45, 252, 255, 367
Bayard, M. (merchant), 129, 165
Bayard, Mme., 45
Beaufort, Count de, 179; letters *quoted*, 182, 183
Beauharnais, Josephine de (1763–1814), xxi
Beaumetz, Bon Albert Briois (1759–1800?), 91–92; in New York, 125, 126, 145; in Philadelphia, 178; letter *quoted*, 186–89; marriage, 210–11, 213; voyage to Calcutta, 214; referred to, 181, 202, 204, 207, 209

Bedbugs, observations on, 21, 325
Bedford, Long Island, 173
Beef: American and English fondness for, 6; prices: (New York), 157, 158; (Norfolk), 55; (Philadelphia), 319
Belly, Daniel, 282
Bellyache, Antilles, 53
Bénézech, Pierre, 239
Bergen, settlement, New Jersey, 118
Berlin, M. (friend), 42, 75
Bermudas, fear of the waters near, 7, 19
Bernard, M., 365
Bernardy, M. (innkeeper), 122
Berwick, Maine, 282
Betting, 329
Beverley, his slaves, 305
Billets de plaisir (receipts), 271
Bingham, William, gift of statue of Franklin, 352
Birds, 5, 6
Birth control, 177–78, 315
Blaçon, M. (friend), 92, 215, 220, 240, 255, 371
Bligh, M., 306
Blisterflies, 324
Boardinghouses (*pensions*): in Brooklyn, 170; in New York, cost of, 128, 160; in Norfolk, 35–36, 53, 54–55; in Philadelphia, 317–18. See also Inns, Taverns and Hotels
Boarding schools, 292
Bolman, M. (friend of Lafayette), 212
Bomare, M., 106
Bonamy, M. (friend), 123, 125, 373
Bonaparte, Jerome, 186
Bonaparte, Napoleon. See Napoleon I
Bond, Dr. Phineas (Consul General), 268
Bondwomen, 295
Bonnechose, Brother (King's page), 3
Book of Prayers, 225
Bookstores, xvii, xviii, xix, xx, 52. See also Moreau de St. Méry & Co.
Boot cleaning, 80
Boozing ken, 57
Boston, Massachusetts: climate, 320; mileage to New York, 166; M. Nancrède, bookseller, 181; M. Pope, watchmaker, 336; Public Library, vi
Bottle tippling, Norfolk, 57
Boudier, Mlle. Popote, 177
Bougainville, Louis Antoine de, French navigator (1729–1811), 134

Boundées (English expression), 297
Boussenat, M. and Mme., 43
Bowdoin, James, American merchant (1726–90), 268
Boxing, 328–29
Brandy: cost of, 159; use in pancakes, 11
Brandywine Creek, Delaware, 87
Bridesmaids, 287
Bridges: Delaware, 101–02; Hackensack River, 117; Neshaming Creek, 99; Passaic, 115; Raritan, 109; Schuylkill, 99, 262–63, 278; stone, 99; wooden, 100
Bridgeton, New Jersey. *See* Rahway
Brière, M., 8, 14, 24, 32, 34, 45
Brine, making of, 162
Bristol, Pennsylvania, 100; Philadelphia, distance to, 100; Red Lion, distance to, 120; referred to, 99, 102, 135, 138; Trenton, distance to, 120
Brooklyn, Long Island: air, 169; carriage hire, 173; churches, 168; houses, 168; houses, country, 170; New York ferry, 167–68, 169–70, 173; peaches, 143; *pensions*, 170; population, 168–69; powder magazine, 169; referred to, 125, 134, 139, 140; rope-walk, 169; streets, 168; Tories, 168; vandalism of New Yorkers, 173; water, 169
Brown, M. (printer), burned to death, 332
Brunau, M., 241
Brunswick, Maine, 282
Brunswick, New Jersey. *See* New Brunswick
Buckets, cost of, 159
Bundling, 315–16
Bureaux de Pusy, Jean Xavier (1750–1805), 251
Burgomaster (bird), 6
Burlington, New Jersey, 100, 277; colonists, 102; houses, 100; population, 100
Burns, Sr., Dr., 128
Burr, Aaron (1756–1836), 138
Bynn, Mlle. Eléanore, 36
Byron, Claude, 300

Cadignan, M. (friend), 92, 226, 239
Cambefort, Baron de, 2, 75
Campan, Mme., 125
Cape Charles, Virginia, 28

Cape Haitien (Cap François), San Domingo, x
Cape Hatteras, 7, 19
Cape Henry, Virginia, lighthouse, 72; referred to, 28, 29, 43
Capron, Mme., her school, 113
Capuchins, work with Negroes, 48–49
Carey, Matthew (bookseller), 333
Carolinas. *See* North Carolina; South Carolina
Carpentier, M. (friend), 231
Carpets, use of, 264, 326
Carriages, importance to women, 98, 334; Philadelphia, 334; Rahway, 111
Carroll, John, American Roman Catholic prelate (1735–1815), 49, 340, 341
Cassan, M. (deputy), 50
Castor-oil plant, 172–73
Catalpa trees, 106
Cats, 327–28
Cazenove, M. (friend), letters *quoted*, 220, 225–26; referred to, 125, 126, 178, 202, 206, 214, 218, 254
Chamber pots, 25. *See also* Toilets
Champion, M. (friend), letters *quoted*, 227–30, 249–50
Charente (frigate), 30
Charleston, South Carolina: carpets, use of, 264; climate, 320; commerce in Negroes, 307–08; commerce with New York, 164; cruelty to Negroes, example of, 307; fire (1795), 308–09, 332–33; incendiaries (1800), 308; necessity of putting in at, 19, 21; packet, 164; to New York, mileage, 166
Charter Oak, Philadelphia, 277
Châtelet, Emilie, Marquise du (Emilie Montagne), 226, 240
Chemises, 288–89, 297
Chesapeake Bay, 27; Baltimore–Philadelphia commerce, 82; dangers, 74; ice-bound period, 82; navigation, 71 ff.; scenery, 84; true entrance, 72
Chester, Pennsylvania, 88, 277
Chignons, 302
Children: American families, 266, 280, 338; bastards, 293; boarding schools, 292–93; cradles, 291; delinquency, 121; education, 171, 291–93, 357, *see also* Education; favoritism, 290; firecrackers, 169; German families, 280; indentured, 294, 299; May Day, 336–37; mourning for, 345; naughty,

291; Negro, 291, 357; of indentured servants, 295; of slaves, 304; play in cemeteries, 343; punishment, law for, 311; school age, 292; snowball throwing, 291; spelling lessons, 177; son of Woodbridge innkeeper, 110; tenderness for, 290; treatment of Negroes, 303, 309; white, 291–93; willful, 291. *See also* Girls

Chimney sweeps, 61

Chinese collection (Van Braam), 251–52

Chopine (measure), 162

Christiania Creek, Delaware, 87

Church, John Barker, 145

Cider (beverage), cost in New York, 157; Newark, 114; New England, 55; with meals, 265

Cigars, 266

Circuit Court of the United States, Pennsylvania district, 213

Clarkson, M., of New York, 40

Clarkson, Matthew (Mayor of Philadelphia), 293

Claudot, M., guillotined, 43

Cliftord, Archer (innkeeper), 114

Clinton, Governor George (1739–1812): his house, 125; portrait, 154

Cobbett, William. *Pseudonym* Peter Porcupine (1763–1835), xvi, 211; *quoted*, 301

Cochon de Lapparent (1750–1825), 239

Cockade, 224, 225, 253

Cock fights, 329

Coffee, cost of, 160; mill, cost of, 160

Coffins, 343, 344, 345. *See also* Funerals

Cohocksink's Creek. *See* Philadelphia

Colic, 18

Collection Moreau de St. Méry, Archives Coloniales, xi, xxi

Colleges. *See* Columbia College; Princeton College

Collins, Dr., 179

Collot, General, 235, 241, 243, 248, 253

Collot, M., 323

Collot d'Herbois, M. (patriot), 182

Colonial, definition of, ix

Columbia (ship), 124, 334

Columbia College, New York City, 153

Columbus (ship), 193, 194

Combatz, M. de (clerk), 203, 245

Combis, Rear Admiral, 50

Commercial treaty (1795), with England, 271

Committee of Public Safety, 2

Commune of Paris, xiii, xiv

Concorde (40-gun frigate), 30, 71

Confinement, 289; cost of, 160

Congress, United States, in Philadelphia, 349; opening ceremonies, 349–50; relief to French *émigrées*, 273; visit to (1794), 90–91; Washington's opening address: (1794), 176; (1795), 209

Connecticut, slavery, 304

Constituent Assembly (1789), xiv, xv

Constitution (France), first copy in United States, 202

Constitution (United States): Hamilton, Alexander, 137; Thirteenth Amendment, 310; universal freedom, 310

Contraceptives, 177–78

Convention nationale, 2; slavery abolished, 17; Toulon, 30

Conventions, abolitionists, 303

Corday, Charlotte, French patriot (1768–93), 210

Courrier de la France et des Colonies (newspaper), edited by Gatereau, xviii, 206

Cradles, 291

Craig, Miss Janet, 68

Craney Island, 71

Creole, meaning of, ix, 236

Cucumbers, cost of, 159

Cult of Reason, 3

Cunningham, M. (neighbor), 224

Daedalus (frigate), 34, 58

Dairy products. *See* Foods

Damourien, M., 227

Dancing: Negroes, mania for, 60; white men and women, 290–91

Daniel Mérian & Co., xv

Danton, Georges Jacques, French Revolutionary leader (1759–94), 92–94

Dauzat (surgeon), 125–26

David (cabin boy), 8, 25

Debts, husbands not responsible for, 289

De la Danse (Moreau de St. Méry), xvi, 181, 216

Delaware: boundary, 85; ferry to New Jersey, 362; slavery, 304–05

Delaware Capes, 86

Delaware River, 87, 88; bridge, 101–02; ferry-boat service, 101–02; freezing, 320, (1779), 322; tide, 258, (1796), 326; width, 258; width at Bristol, 100

Delbens, M., 356

Demeunier, Jean Nicholas (1715–1814), letters *quoted*, 233–35, 246–47; referred to, 180, 202, 204–06, 207, 209, 237

Democrats, 271

Den Née Prove (ship), 214

Depression (1797), 235–36

Description topographique et politique de la partie espagnole de l'isle Saint-Domingue (Moreau de St. Méry), xvi, xvii, xviii, 212–13, 217, 221; Cobbett's translation, 211, 212

Description topographique, physique, civile, politique et historique de la partie française de l'isle Saint-Domingue (Moreau de St. Méry), v, vi, xvi, 221–22, 226, 227, 252

Desèze, M. (young man), 128–29

Desfourneaux, General, 242

Deslozières, Baudry (brother-in-law), 8, 24

Deslozières, Eléanore (niece), 8

Despioux, M. (compositor), 204

Destourelles, M. (refugee), 139

Diana (ship), 180

Dillon, Arthur, 123–24

Divorce, 290

Dogs, 327

Dolphin striker, 20

Domergue, François Urbain, 229; letter *quoted*, 221–23

Domestic servants. *See* Servants

Donne, Mlle., her pension, 135

Doughty, M. (Quaker), 168

Drinker, Edward, 278

Drowning, 272–73

Druggists, 335

Drunkenness. *See* Liquor, use of

Dubourg, M. (printer), 245–46

Duels with pistols, 329; Moreau, 183–84; threat of, 194–96

Dunmore, Lord, destruction of Norfolk, 47

Dupetit-houars, Aristide (relative), 243–44, 366

Dupont de Nemours, M., 250–51

Dupuy, M. (nephew), 1, 2, 11, 24

Dupuy, Mme. (sister), 8; need for wine, 14

Dusaulx, Jean Joseph (colleague, 1728–99), xiii

Dutch: avarice, 272; in Brooklyn, 168; indolence, 272; in Long Island, 172; in Newcastle (Del.), 86; in New York, 149, 304; niggardliness, 272; slaves, 272, 277

Dutchman (a seaman), 8

Dutch Reformed Church, 149

Eagle, of Charleston (brig), 274

Earl, M., 123

Easter, celebration of, 44–45

East River, 119; anchorage, 166; porpoises, 148; sharks, 148; tides, 148. *See also* Hudson River

Edenton, North Carolina, 43

Education: boarding schools, 292; children, 291–93; compulsory, 292; effects of parents, 171; effects on children, 171; lesson payments, penurious attitude toward, 270; literacy, 291–92; Long Island, 171; Moreau ideas on, 232–33; Newark, 113. *See also* Columbia College; Philadelphia; Princeton College; University of Pennsylvania

Eels, 68, 174

Eggs, fare paid with, 167

Elder-flower powder (insecticide), 325

Eliza (ship), 301

Elizabeth (Elizabethtown), New Jersey: houses, 111; money, reckoning of, 112; society, 111; to New York, 112; to Newark, 120; to Woodbridge, 120; referred to, 139

Elizabeth River, Virginia: channels, 46; depth, 62; ferry-boat service, 65–66; fish, 55; fortifications, 58; Norfolk and, 32, 46; referred to, 40, 47; shores, 33

Elk River, Maryland, 84

Elkton, Maryland, 85

Embuscade (frigate), 30

English: American similarities to, 6, 329; contempt for the United States, 267–68; influence, 276, 329, 334; representatives and ministers, 267–68; stomach powders, 18. *See also* Frenchtown; Newcastle (Del.); Norfolk (Va.)

English language, aversion to certain words, 284; in Virginia, 63, 69–70

Episcopal Church: Baltimore, 78; Brooklyn, 168; Frankfort, 97; Ne-

groes, 341–42; Newark, 112; Newcastle (Del.), 86; New York, 149; Norfolk, 47, 49; Philadelphia, 192, 337, 339, 341–42; Portsmouth (Va.), 64; Swedish, 88; Trenton, 102; Wilmington (Del.), 88
Essex County, New Jersey, 112
Estève, M. (friend), 233

Fall Island, 84
Families, 266, 280, 285, 338
Farmers, 100–01. *See also* Americans, country dwellers
Farrhit, M. (English citizen), 36
Fauchet, M. (French representative in United States), 275
Favorite (ship), 128
Feather beds, 280; bedbugs, 325
Federalist party, 252, 253
Fells Point, 76, 78, 79, 80
Fences (dry hedges), 86; Gosport (Va.), 69; kinds of, 121–22; New Jersey, 110; Philadelphia to New York, 20; tiresome sight of, 98. *See also* Hedges
Figureheads, 362
Fingernails, long, cultivation of, 63
Firecrackers, 169
Fireflies, 45
Fires, 61, 65, 230, 308–09, 331–33
Firkin (small barrel), 163
First Forty Years of Washington Society (M. B. Smith), quoted, 186
Fish and fish prices. *See* Foods
Flatbush, Long Island, 170
Flies, 316, 324–25
Flour, 158; barrel, 158; freight, 159; inspectors, 161
Flowers, artificial, 283
Foncin, M. (engineer), 227
Food: New York, 156 ff.; Norfolk (Va.), 55; Philadelphia, 329–30; prison costs, 165; sailors, 6, 7; women, 287. *See also* Meals
Forests, destruction of, 363
Fort Mifflin, 88–89
Fortune, Michael, translator, 231
Fournier-Pescay, xxi
France: ambassadors to United States, 275–76; Chouans (Breton rebels), 207; churches and places of worship closed, 4; cockade, 224, 225; Committee of Public Safety, 2; *Convention nationale*, 2; Council of the Five Hundred, 234–35; Cult of Reason,

3; Directory, 234, 235, 239, 252; emigrants, perpetually banished, 2, 208; events (1796), 223; feeling for America, 275; monarchy, 2; Negroes, 311; Reign of Terror, 2–3; Republic, 2–3; United States relations: (1797), 240; (1798), 246–47, 252, 253
Frankfort, Pennsylvania, 97, 99, 100; distance to Philadelphia, 120; distance to Red Lion, 120
Franklin (second mate), 8, 27, 28
Franklin, Benjamin (1706–90), 5, 27, 92; epitaph, 342; lightning rod, 321–22; open letter to King of England (1763), 295; "purloined letters," 268; statue, 352; stove, 326; tomb, 342
Franklin, Deborah, 342
Franklin Society, 357
Franklin stove, 326
Freemasonry: Newark, 113; Norfolk, 54; Philadelphia, 186
French ambassadors, 275–76
French Canadians, 180
French *émigrées*, 265; American faithlessness, 153, 274; impression left in United States, 276; feeling for America, 275; relief to, 273. *See also* individual cities
French party. *See* Democrats
French Pronunciation Determined by Invariable Signs (Domergue), 222
French Revolution, xii, xiii, xiv, xv
Frenchtown (La Ville Française), Maryland, 82, 85; cost of trip to Newcastle, 84; stages, 84, 85
Fruits. *See* Food
Funerals: coffins, 343, 344, 345; extravagance of, 345; Negro, 302; Norfolk, 53–54; Philadelphia, 253, 255, 338, 345. *See also* Mourning customs
Furniture, 263–64. *See also* Houses and Homes

Gage, Mrs. Aphen, 282
Gage, General Thomas, 282
Gallet, M., 233
Gannet (bird), 5
Gatereau, M., of San Domingo, 206, 209
Gauvain, M. (friend), 40, 43, 44, 75, 128, 183–84, 196, 200
Gazette (Philadelphia), 295

Geanty, M. (refugee), 75, 177

General Advertiser (Bache), xix

General or abridged outline of the sciences and arts for the use of the young, published by Moreau de St. Méry, 225; translation, 231–32

General Washington Tavern, 97, 98

Genêt, Minister of France to the United States, 125, 164, 275

Georges (friend), 95

Georgia: climate, 320; *émigrées* from San Domingo, 308; fires (1798), 308; public officials, 308. *See also* Savannah

German Calvinist Church, 78, 337

German Lutheran Church, 78; New York, 149; Philadelphia, 175; fire, 177, 337, 339

German Reformed Church, 78

Germans: barns, 99; Catholics, 340, 341; indentured servants, 295, 300, 301; of Pennsylvania, 260, 264, 280, 340, 341

Germantown, Pennsylvania, 362

Girard, Stephen (1750–1831), 360

Girls: boarding schools, 292–93; bond, 295; dancing, 290–91; first suitor, 284; hair, 283; indiscretions, 284; maturity, 282; nubility, 283; puberty, 283; social gatherings, 283; skirts, 283; sleeping with servants, 286; unrestrained life, 290. *See also* American women; education

Gironde (political party), 2

Glasgow, Delaware, 85

Gold, Captain, 71

Gosport, Virginia, 68–70; English language, 69–70; fences, 69; houses, 68, 69; mourning customs, 68; roads, 69; women, 69–70

Gourde, value of, 112, 358–59

Gouvernet, Marquis de, 144

Governor's Island, 119, 148

Goynard (sea captain), 8, 9, 10, 11, 12, 14, 16, 21–22, 24, 29, 31, 33, 35, 38, 40, 41–42, 45, 90–91, 123, 139, 145, 246, 247, 302

Grammatical Solutions, taken from the Journal of the French Language (Domergue), 223

Grand, Mme., 226

Grandprey, M. de, 210

Grassy, Dr., 334–35

Graves, 54, 344. *See also* Funerals

Greek, teaching of, 292

Greenway, Captain, of the *Welcome*, 277

Grim (a seaman), 8, 27, 28

Grimperel, M. (friend), 220

Grog (drink), 279

Guadeloupe, English seize, 42

Guerlain, M.: Moreau's duties as clerk, 123, 124, 125, 126–28; resigned, 126; referred to, 42, 45, 123, 145; settlement with, 134

Guillemard, M. (Englishman), 181, 245; letter *quoted*, 254–55

Guillotine, atrocious form of death, 209–10

Gulf Stream, 5, 12, 13, 19

Guspin, M., 44

Hackensack River, 115–16, 117; bridge, 117; ferry, 117

Hamilton, Alexander, American statesman (d. 1804): ambition, 136, 138; appearance, 138; background, 136; desire for presidency, 137–38; dinner for M. de Montier, 275; dinner with, 179; duel with Aaron Burr, 138; Lafayette's son, 206; lodgings, 135–36; manufacturers association (1791), 113; marriage, 137; portrait, 154

Hamilton, David (tavern keeper), 106

Hamilton, Elizabeth Schuyler, 145

Hammond, George, British Minister to the United States, 268

Hampton (settlement), 30

Hampton Roads, Virginia, 29, 32, 43, 312

Handwriting, teaching of, 291

Hartsfelder, Jurian, 260

Harwick (ship), 301

Hatteras, Cape, North Carolina, fear of the waters near, 7, 19

Haxkills, Pennsylvania. *See* Landslin

Hedges, living, 85–86, 120

Hédouville, General, 252, 253–54

Hericott, Mme. Elizabeth, 282

Hernes, Captain, 301

Heurtault La Merville, 369–70, 371

Homassel, M. (merchant), 255

Horsehair cloth, 263

Horses: cart, cost of, 159; cart drivers, 162; chestnuts, 162; decorative nets, 129; draught, 77; effect of climate on, 327; ferry-boat, dangers from, 101–02; fright at Hudson River swell (incident), 119; Maryland stallions, 77; Norfolk, 61; stud fees, 77; races (Jamaica), 145, 173; stage, 85, 96; use of, 69

Hospitals: at New York, 151–52; at Norfolk (Va.), 56–57; at Philadelphia, 354–56; at Portsmouth (Va.), 65

Hotels. *See* Inns, Taverns and Hotels

Houdet (priest), 191–92

Houses and Homes: bricks, 261, 267; carpets, 264, 326; comfort, 121; country, 121; decoration, 264; dining rooms, 266; doors, 122, 261; farm, 101; fire buckets, 331; fire screens, 327; formality, 289; furniture, 263–64; heating, 326; kitchens, 76, 146, 160, 166; lattices, 122; numbering of, 2, 261; ostentatious display, 363; outside view, everything sacrificed to, 121; painting, 280, 325; partitions, 122; porte-cochères, 261; repair of, 264; roofs, 147; servants, 264; shingles, 331–32; shutters, 147, 261; taste, 121; toilets, 264; water, piping into, 263; window panes, 147; window trims, 261. *See also* Food; Meals; individual cities

Howard, Colonel, his residence, 79

Howland, Reuben (first mate), 8, 20, 26, 44

Hudson River: ferries, 118–19; ice, 321; length of crossing, 119; passage time, New York to Albany, 321; porpoises, 148; sharks, 119, 148; ships of all sizes, 148; storm, 134; toll, 119

Hum, Thomas, 282

Hunter, M. (bookseller), 51, 144

Hutchinson, Governor of Massachusetts, 268

Ice, use of, 80

Ice cream, American fondness for, 155, 323

Idée générale ou abrégé des Sciences et des Arts (Moreau de St. Méry), xvi, 225, 231–32, 246

Indentured servants. *See* Servants

Independence Day, celebration (1794), 125, 164; celebration (1796), 218; no gaiety and most stores open, 336

Indian Queen Hotel, Baltimore, 74

Indians, 276, 310

Indigo, cultivation of, 307, 308

Industry (ship), 124

Ink, manufacture of, 362

Inns, taverns and hotels: bachelors, 138–39; bed curtains, 121; bed sharing, 121; City Tavern, Philadelphia, 354; ice, 107; Maryland to South Carolina, 335; Massachusetts to Maryland, 335; mosquitoes, 118; New York, 149, 160; Paulus Hook, 118; Philadelphia, 317–18; picnic dinners, 336; rats, 107; sheets, 107, 118; shoe and boot cleaning, 107; tipping, 298–99; water, 107; window curtains, 122. *See also* Boardinghouses

Insecticides, 325

Insurance companies, 2, 361; fire, 331–32

Introductions: letters of, 269; personal, 269

Irish: indentured servants, 299–300; priests, 339

Irujo, Chevalier d', Spanish Minister to the United States, 235, 241, 255; letters *quoted*, 242, 244

Jacobins (political party), 144, 271

Jamaica, Long Island, 145; horse races, 173

James (merchant ship), 125

James River, 29, 30, 46, 72

Jay, John, American jurist (1745–1829): commercial treaty with England (1795), 271; presidency, 137–38; Sir John Temple, 268

Jean-Bart (74-gun), 30, 31, 32, 33, 57

Jefferson, Thomas (1743–1826), election of, 138

Jeffersonians (political party), 271

Jerçay, M. de, 50

Jewel (ship), 9, 14

Jews: at New York City, 149; at Philadelphia, 337

Josephine, Empress (1763–1814), xxi

Jules (clerk), 237

Jupiter (ship), 50, 62

Kearsley, Dr. John, 356

Kensington, Pennsylvania, 97, 277

Key, John (first child born in Philadelphia), 278

Kina (astringent), 143

Kingston, New Jersey, 106–07, 138

Kitchens: Baltimore, 76; equipment, cost of, 160; New York, 146; wood, cost of, 166
Knowles, M., 34
Knox, General Henry (1750–1806), 178
Kosciusko, General Thaddeus (1746–1817), 245, 247–48

La Colombe (Lafayette's aide-de-camp), 92, 94, 125, 143, 205, 215, 218, 251
Lacroix de Chartres (member of the Convention), 92
La Dentu family, 1
Lafayette, G. W. Motier, 205–06, 213; letter *quoted*, 241–42
Lafayette, Marie Joseph, Marquis de (1757–1834), xiii, 212, 251
La Grange, M. (printer), 203, 246
La Haye, Sr., M. de, 193, 194, 204, 209, 229
Lamberton, New Jersey, 101, 102
Lameth, Baron Alexandre Théodore Victor de (1760–1829), 224, 225–26
Lameth, Comte Charles Malo François de (1757–1832), 224, 225–26
L'Ami, M. (from Cap François), 90
Landslin, Pennsylvania, 277
Langdon, senator from New Hampshire, 253
Lapaquerie, M. (friend), 241
La Roque, Martial, 180
Laundresses, their charges and demands, 160
Laveau, General, 243
Lavoisier, M., 43
Lawyers, 335; salaries, 335
Laziness, American, 12
Le Roy, M. (merchant), 129
Lesbians, 286
L'Espérance (schooner), 45
Letombe, Philippe Joseph (French Consul General to the United States), 241, 248, 255; letters *quoted*, 240, 242
Leyden Gazette, 241
Liancourt, François Alexandre Frédéric La Rochefoucauld, Duc de (1747–1827), 176, 179, 180, 181, 201–02, 203, 207, 209, 210, 215, 220, 224, 226, 227, 230, 231; *quoted*, 48, 236–37, 304
Lightning, 322

Lightning rods, 47
Liquor, use of, 14, 16, 22, 83, 266, 298
Liston, Robert, British Minister Plenipotentiary, 254
Literacy, 291–92
Lively (brig), 12, 14
Liverpool (ship), 47
Livingston, Chancellor, 123
Lobscouse (a stew), 10
Logan, Dr. James, 352
Loix et Constitutions des Colonies Françaises de l'Amérique sous le Vent (Moreau de St. Méry), xii
Long Island, 166–74; climate (1801), 320–21; crops, 172–73; fortifications, 174; frogs, 173; granite, 173; horse racing, 145; land values, 172; mosquitoes, 173; New York, communication with, 165; referred to, 125, 126; soil, 172
Longuemare de la Salle, M. (merchant), 14, 15, 35, 90, 95
Louis XVI, King of France (1754–93), executed, 2
Louis XVIII, King of France (1755–1824), xxi
Louisiana, 215–16, 239
Louisiana Purchase, 91
Louis Philippe, King of France (1773–1850), 224, 225, 226, 235, 240, 243
Loutherbourg, M. (painter), 175
Lowther, Captain George, 11, 13, 14, 15, 16, 21, 22, 23, 24, 27, 32, 37, 43
Lunatics, 355
Lunéville, Treaty of (1801), xxi
Lutherans: German, 78; New York, 149; Philadelphia, 284, 337; Swedish, 337; women's hats, 284
Luzerne, M. le Chevalier de la, 275, 322
Luzerne (alfalfa), 172
Lycée des Arts et des Sciences, xxi
Lydia Bailey (K. Roberts), problems in the writing of, v
Lynham, M. (merchant), 56
Lyon (Lyons), France, 3, 182
Lys, Mme. de, 140, 142

Madison, James (1749–1812), 49
Maidenhead, New Jersey, 102
Mangin, Abbé, 192
Mangs (birds), 6
Manhattan Company, 147

Manual labor, 295
Manufactory City, New Jersey, 113–14
Manx shearwater (bird), 6, 13
Marcombi, Colonel, 165
Marens Hook, 88
Marie Antoinette (1755–93): affair of the Queen's necklace, 130–31; clock of, 336; guillotined, 3
Marle, Mlle. de (fellow passenger), 8, 21, 31, 33, 35, 36, 42, 53
Marriage, 285, 295; bundling and, 315–16; Negro slaves, 306; second, frequency of, 290
Martinique, English seize, 42
Maryland: boundary, 85; Potomac River, 72; public officials, 307; slavery, 305; stallions, 77
Massachusetts, slavery in, 304
Massachusetts (merchant ship), 125; cost of, 158
Matthem, Colonel, 58
Maupertius, M. (relative), 112
May Day, 57, 336–37
Meals: beef, fondness for, 6; beverages, 265–66, 279; breakfast, 265; carving, 286; cider, 265; cigars, 266; desserts, 266; dinner, 265–66; flies, 325; ice cream, 155, 323; meat, 280; on shipboard, 9–12, 26, 72; oysters, 266; pastries, 266; tea, 266, 279; wine, 14–15, 266. *See also* Food; Liquor
Meat, 280; carving, 286; prices, *see* Food
Meaux, M. de, 322
Medicines, filling prescriptions, 335
Mémoirs du comte de Moré, xix–xx
Men of letters, 335
Menstruation, 287, 297
Mercer, General, 104–05
Merian, M. Daniel, xv, 41, 42, 126, 127
Merlin de Douai, Philippe Auguste (1754–1838), 239, 369–70, 371, 373
Merveilleux (fops), 234
Methodist Church: Baltimore, 78; Brooklyn, 168; Negroes, 48–49, 60, 306; New York, 149; Norfolk (Va.), 48–49, 60; Philadelphia, 337; Portsmouth (Va.), 64; Trenton, 102; Wilmington, 88
Michelton, Commodore, 274
Mifflin, Governor, 204, 358

Milestones, 85, 122
Milhet, M. (from Cap François), 90
Milhet, Mme. (mother-in-law), 189–91, 193
Millstone Creek, 106, 107
Milton, Lord, vi
Minerva (brig), 339
Mitchell, Dr. (chemist), 144–45
Mittelberger, Gottlieb, 299
Moccasin (snake), 73
Money, value of: Elizabeth (N. J.), 112; New York, 112; Norfolk (Va.), 62; Philadelphia, 270, 358–59; piastre gourde, 358–59
Montagne, Emilie (La Marquise du Châtelet), 226, 240
Montgomery, Major General Richard, 149–50
Montier, M. de, 275
Montmorin de Fontainebleau, M. de, 93, 94
Moon, eclipse of, 19
Moore, Captain Thomas, 87
Moravian Church, 149, 337
Moré, Comte de, xix–xx
Moreau de St. Méry, Amenaïde, 8, 17, 24, 367
Moreau de St. Méry, Médéric Louis Elie, French politician (1750–1819), ix–xxii; administrator of the states of Parma, Piacenze and Guastalla, xxi; Ambassador to Parma, xxi; ancestors, ix; arrest, order for his (Le Havre), 2–3; attached to French Legation, 240; *avocat au parlement*, x; Beaufort, Count de, suggested duel, 183–84; bookstore, xvii, xviii, xix, xx, *see also* Moreau de St. Méry & Co.; collection of laws, x, xi, xii; *conseiller d'état*, xx, xxi; *conseil supérieur*, x, xi; Creole, ix; dramatized in a play, 187–89; education, ix, x; exile in the United States, xv; family, xv; fever, 236; French Revolution, xii, xiii, xiv, xv; gout, 245, 249; hats, his affection for, 123–24; historiographer at the Ministry of the Marine, xx; lawlessness, opponent of, xv; legal training, ix–x; Legion of Honour, xx; Louis XVIII, gift from, xxi; Musée de Paris, member of, xii; Napoleon's disapproval, xxi; New York sojourn, xvi, *see also* New York; Norfolk sojourn, *see*

Norfolk; passport (1798), 253, 254, 255; pension granted by Empress Josephine, xxi; Philadelphia sojourn (1794–98), xvi–xx, *see also* Philadelphia; publications, xvi; return to France, 2, 364–74; Robespierre, xv; shipping agent in Norfolk, xv, xvi; undesirable foreigner, xx; weight lost on transatlantic trip, 40. *See also Sophie*, of Portland; Talleyrand

Moreau de St. Méry & Co., Philadelphia, xvii, xviii, xix, xx; catalogue, 180; depression (1797), 235; dismissal of clerk De Combatz, 203; medical supplies, 177–78; Roche, de la, quarrel with, 196–200; sign, 176

Morning Star (packet), 87; price of passage, 87

Morris, Robert, American financier and statesman (1734–1806), 101, 231, 336, 363

Morrisville, Pennsylvania, 101

Morse, Doctor, 209

Mortality rate, 282

Mosquitoes: Long Island, 173; New Jersey, 118; Norfolk (Va.), 53; Paulus Hook, 135; Philadelphia, 325

Motte, M. de la (merchant), 16, 22

Mouche, La (packet schooner), 255

Mountain (political party), 2

Mourgues, M., 252, 367, 372

Mourning customs, 68, 69; graves, 54, 344; tombstones, 341. *See also* Funerals

Mozard, M. (advocate), 185

Muhlenberg, General Pierre, 273

Mulberry Island, 29

Mullein, 110

Murray, M. A. (merchant), 87

Muscovy duck, 61

Myer, Moses (merchant), 34, 36, 40, 45, 71

Nancrède, M. (bookseller), 181

Nantes, France, atrocities at, 3

Napoleon, I (1769–1821): disapproval of Moreau, xxi; first made his name as a soldier at Toulon, 30; Talleyrand, 91–92, 226

Narbonne Lara, Comte Louis de (1755–1814), 92

National Assembly of Versailles, xii

National Convention. *See Convention Nationale*

Natural resources, 322

Navigation, of American ships, 5, 39

Necker, Jacques, French statesman (1732–1804), xiv

Ned (Edouard), the cook, 8, 9, 10, 11

Negroes, 301–03; baptized, 306; Capuchins, 48; churches, 48–49, 60, 306, 337, 341–42; dancing, mania for, 60; free men, 60; Norfolk (Va.), 54, 57, 59–61; Philadelphia, 301ff., 341–42; prejudice against, 304; San Domingo (1796), 219; treatment of, 73, 291, 302; yellow fever, 57, 236. *See also* Slavery

Neshaming Creek, 99

New Amsterdam. *See* Newcastle

Newark, New Jersey, 112–14; Academy, 113; cider, 114; Elizabethtown, distance to, 120; houses, 112, 113; inns, 114; New York, distance to, 120; New York stage, 114; public buildings, 112; shoe factory, 113

New Brunswick, New Jersey: boats to New York, 109; houses, 108, 109; inns, 109; population, 108; rents, 109; Six Mile Run, distance to, 120; Woodbridge, distance to, 120

Newcastle, Delaware, 82, 86–87; breakwater, 86; churches, 86; Court of Justice, 86; distance from Philadelphia, 86; Frenchtown, cost of trip to, 84; houses, 86; packet, 87–90; public buildings, 86; settlers, 277

New Hampshire, slavery in, 303

New Jersey: copper half sous, 117; ferry to Delaware, 362; mullein, 110; New York, communication with, 165; orchards, 108; shore, 88; slavery, 109

Newspapers, notices of deserting wives, 289. *See also* individual cities

New Utrecht, Long Island, 125, 171–72

New York, 146–74; banks, 164; bathing, 154; Battery, 120; Bowling Green, 151; Bridewell (house of correction), 152; Broadway, 125,

150, 151, 154; Brooklyn ferry, 167–68, 169–70, 173; buildings, 149–55; business district, 146; cellars, 146, 164; Chatham Road, 151; Charleston packet, 164; churches, 149–50; City Hall, 153–54; climate, 146–47, 156, (1801), 320–21; Columbia College, 153; commerce, 160–66; commercial paper, 163–64; confinement, cost of, 160; country houses (Brooklyn), 170; Cortlandt (Courtland) Street, 123, 124; cows, 146; crimes, 166; Custom House, 123, 154; domestics, 155; exposed in time of war, 161; fat people, 149; fish, 155; flies, 157; food inspectors (flour and meat), 158, 161; foods, seasons and prices, 156 ff.; French Consul (1798), 252; French *émigrées*, 153, 274; fur business, 164; Governor's House, 150–51; Greenwich, 129, 165; heat, 125; "Holy Ground," 156; hospitals, 128, 134, 151–53; houses, 146–47; houses of ill fame, 173, 315; ice cream, 155; Independence Day (1794), 125; inhabitants, 165; inns and *pensions*, 122, 149, 160; John Street Theater, 154; longitude and latitude, 166; Jewish synagogue, 149; Long Island, communication with, 165; markets, 154–55; meat, 155; mileage distance from Baltimore, 166; mileage distance from Boston, 166; mileage distance from Charleston, 166; mileage distance from Newark, 120; mileage distance from Philadelphia, 166; mileage distance from Richmond, 166; mileage distance from Savannah, 166; militia, 164; money, reckoning of, 112; moving mania (May 1), 165; mulattoes, 149; New Jersey, communication with, 165; Norfolk, passage cost to, 63; odors, 164; Park Row (Chatham Road), 151; *pensions* and lodgings, 149, 160; pigs, 146; population, 148, 165; port, 161; prices of general commodities, 160; prisons, 147, 151, 165; prostitution, 156, 173, 312, 315; Public Library, 154; public monuments, 149–55; public porters, 163; reservoir, 148; riots and treaty burnings (1795), 271; St. Paul's Chapel or Church, 149–50; servants, 155; sewers, cleaning of, 164; Sharpless, James, portrait painter, 245; shipping, 148; slaves, 148, 155–56, 166; slips, 148; stages (Philadelphia), 96–97; street walkers, 156; streets, 146, 147, 148, 164; Sunday amusements, 173; surroundings, 165; tea-water, 147; Temple, Sir John, 268; tide, 148; topography, 146; trees, 147; Trinity (Episcopal) Church, 129, 150, 152; Vesey Street, 153; wages, 157 ff.; water supply, 147, 148; weights and measures, 161; wharfs, 148, 162; window washing on Saturday, 146; yellow fever, 164, 165, 206. *See also* Long Island

Nicolite (New Quaker) Church, 78
Noailles, Count de, 92
Norfolk, Virginia, 46–64; anchorage, 46; Baltimore packets, 71; barbecue, 58; beef consumption, daily, 61; boardinghouses, 54–55; bookdealer, 52; boozing ken (bottle-tippling place), 57; chimney sweeps, 61; churches, 47–48; climate, 50, 52–53, 54, 57; commerce, 51; cost of living, 54; diseases, 53; docks, 46; English language, 63; fires, 61; fish, 55; food prices and seasons, 55–56; fortifications, 58; funerals, 53–54; government, 51; graves and gravestones, 54; horses and carriages, 61; hospitals, 56–57; house furnishings, 52; houses, 47; latitude and longitude, 46; love of luxury, 52; market, 46, 59; marriages, second, 54; May Day, 57, 58; men, 52, 54, 63; mileage distance from Philadelphia, 63; Militia, 57–58; newspapers, 50, 52; Other, French Consul, 241; passage cost to New York, 63; passage cost to Richmond, 63; pine buildings, 47; population, 51; port, 161; postal service, 62; printing houses, 52; public buildings, 51, 56; referred to, xv, xvi, 28, 29, 31, 32 ff., 42, 44, 45; rope factory, 62; San Domingan colonists, 49–50, 59; segregation, 54; sewage ditches, 47; slaughterhouses, 61; slaves, 59; square, 46; streets, 47; swamps, 61–62; sympathy for the French, 50, 58–59; theater, 54; tide, average rise of, 46; unemployment, 52;

warehouses, 47; weddings, 54; weights and measures, 62; wharfs, 47; women, 52, 54

Norfolk to Baltimore, trip by water, 71–75; cost, 71

Normande (frigate), 30

North Carolina: public officials, 307; slavery, 306, 307

Northern Liberties (suburb), Philadelphia, 260, 264

Northern Lights (1796), 325–26

North River. *See* Hudson River

Oak, American, 363

Oeuvre de Sept Jours, L' (Dusaulx), xiii

Ohio River, 322

Olive, M., 139, 140

Onion soup, 10, 11

Orléans, M. d' (Louis Philippe), 224, 225, 226, 235, 240, 243

Oster, Citizen, 42

Other, Consul at Norfolk (Va.), 241

Otis, James, 268

Overseers, 305–06

Oxen, use of, 69

Oysters: at Norfolk (Va.), 55; passion of Americans for, 266; street cries, 61, 266

Palatinate, 294, 300

Paper mills, 81

Papillon (gun-brig), 30

Paradé, Commissioner of Marine, 75

Parasols, 302; price of, 158

Parents, 283, 284

Paris, France: conditions (1796), 220; Constitution and Revolutionary compared, 233–34; in February (1797), 238–40; prostitutes, 234; street numbering, 261; watering carts, 263; women of the court, 234

Parker, Colonel, 90, 95

Parma, States of, street numbering, 261

Passaic River, 114–15; bridge, 115; cascades, 116; ferry-boat, 115

Pastry making, 286

Patapsco River, 76; freezing (1809), 81

Paterson, New Jersey, 113–14

Patterson, Elizabeth, 186

Patuxent River, 73–74

Paulus Hook, New Jersey, 118, 135

Peale's Museum, 180, 223, 335, 351–52

Pearlash, 163; inspection of, 161; tariff, 163

Peggy, of Frenchtown (schooner), trip from Baltimore to Frenchtown (1794), 82; berths, 82–83; food and drink, 83; passage price, 83; passengers, 84

Penn, William (1644–1718), 277–78

Pennsylvania: butter, 121; capital, 257; climate, 319 ff.; color prejudice, 309; death penalty, 353–54; government, rural, 281; House of Representatives, 348; population (1774), 300; receipts (assurance of solvency), 271; State House, 348; servants, indentured, 293, 299

Pennsylvania, University of, 356

Pennsylvania Hospital, Philadelphia, 354–55

Pensions. See Boardinghouses

Pérouse, Comte de la, 244

Petits Maîtres (fops), 234

Phaeton (frigate), 366

Philadelphia, Pennsylvania, xvi, xvii, 175–256, 257–363; actors, 272, 347; African Church, 341–42; air of North Philadelphia, 267; appearance, 257; balls, 333; banks, 337, 359–61; bastards, 293; benefit for American prisoners in Algiers, 272; Black Horse Alley, 278; boardinghouses, 317–18; Board of Health, 236; Bostoman and Cull's Tavern, 278; breweries, 361; brickyards, 361; Broad Street, 258, 259; buildings, wooden, 261; business transactions, 271; Callowhill Street, 236, 237, 317; canal, 263; capital of Pennsylvania, 257; capital of the United States, 257–58; carriages, 98, 279, 334; carts and wagons, 334; cemeteries, 302, 337, 340–41, 342, 343–45; central depot on docks, need for, 89; Charter, 257; Charter Oak, 277; children, punishment, 311; chocolate factories, 361; Christ Church, 89, 339; Christ Church Hospital, 356; churches, 179, 192, 337–43; Circuit Court, 349; circuses, 348; City Hall, 317, 337, 359; City Tavern, 337, 354; Clarkson, Mayor Matthew, 293; climate, 179, 266–67, 320, 321, 322,

324; coffins, 343, 344, 345; Cohocksink's Creek, 260; College of Physicians, 351, 356–57; color prejudice, 309; Comedy Theater, 323; commerce, 82, 257, 361–62; Congress, United States, 209, 349; contraceptives, first sale of, 178; Court House, 349; Court of Common Pleas, 349; Court of Errors and Appeals, 349; customs, melancholy, 280; debtors, 353–54; dews, evening, 322; dinner, 269; dispensary, 355; District Court, 349; dressmakers, 313; drinking water, 343; drowned persons, curious idea about, 273; druggists, 335; elevation, 260; Episcopal Church, 339, 342; everything is for sale, 279; factories, 361; federal government, seat of, 257–58; fires, 213, 230, 330, 331–32, 336; first child born in, 278; flies, 316, 324; flowers, 329; food prices, 329–30; foreigners, 264–65; Freemasons, 186; French colored women, 311; French *émigrées*, xvii, xviii, 265, 274; French styles in dress, 284; friendliness, 272; Front Street, 260, 263; fruits and fruit prices, 318, 329; 330; funerals, 338; German Lutheran Church, 332, 339; Germans, 260, 264, 280; girls, 281, 282–83; government, 359; Gray's ferry bridge, 263; hairdressers, 312; High Street, 258, 259, 263; Horse Market, 260; hospitals, 337, 354–56; House of Charity, 356; House of Correction, 353–54; House of Representatives of Pennsylvania, 348; houses, 98, 261–64, 266, 267, 278, 363; houses of ill fame, 302–03; 312; ice cream, 323; Indians, 276; industries, 361; influence of commerce on, 89; insurance companies, 337, 361; Irish Catholic Church and cemetery, 302; jail, 278; Jews, 337; Kensington, 97, 277; latitude and longitude, 257; length, 257; library, 352; Little Water Street, 259; location, 278; manner of living, 265–66; markets, 316–17, 318–19, 337; Market Street, 258, 278, 313, 316, 323, 336; marriage customs, 286–87; May Day, 336–37; meals, 265–66, 279; meat consumption, 155,

280; mint, 337, 358–59; morals, 311; Moreau's sojourn, xvi–xx, 175–256; mortality rate, 282, 323; mosquitoes, 325; Mulberry Street, 258, 259, 342, 344; museums, 337, 351–52; Negroes, 301 ff.; New Hall (theater), 345–46, 347; newspaper, 361; Northern Liberties, 260, 264; Northern Lights (1796), 325–26; Oak Street, 259–60; Oeller's Hotel fire (1799), 309; peaches, 318; Pegg's Creek or Run, 260; Penn Street, 259; Pennsylvania Hospital, 354–55; philanthropy, 272; Philosophical Society, 336, 350–51; Pine Street, 259; plays, 345–48; police supervision, 90; Poor House, 337, 356; population, 264, 276 *et seq.*; Potter's Field, 343–44; powder magazine, 361; Presbyterian Church, 336; precipitation, 321; President of the United States, house destined for, 358; prices of important commodities, 319; prisons, xviii, 179, 180, 302, 337, 353–54; prostitution, 311, 313–14; public instruction, 356–58; Public Library, 92, 225; librarian's wife and children killed in fire, 230; Quakers, *see that heading*; rents, 284; reservoir, 263; riots and treaty burnings (1795), 271; roads, 278; Roman Catholic Church, 339–40; rope-walks, 361; St. Mary's Church, 339–41, 344; schools, 337, 357; Schuylkill Bridge, 262–63; servants, 293–99; Sharpless, James, portrait painter, 245; shoemakers, 334; sidewalks, 259, 262, 263, sign painting, 176–77; skating, 272–73; sky, 32; sleigh-riding, 323; snobbery, 333; social service, 357; society, 280; Southwark, 260; Spruce Street, 353; Spruce Street fire (1794), 175; squares, 258–59; stages, 96–97; State House, 348; streets, 258–63, 273, 278; suburbs, 257, 260; Sunday observance, 317; Supreme Court, 349; Swan Hotel, 301; taverns, 318; theaters, 337, 345–48; to Frankfort, distance, 120; to New York, distance, 166; to Norfolk, distance, 63; tombstones, 341; trees, 262–63; vessels sailing from, 279; watchmen (town criers), 330; water, canal, 263; watering carts, 263; Water Street, 259, 260; water supply, 262, 343; Wayne, General Anthony, parade for, 211; weather, 323–24; weddings, 286–87; wharves, 89–90; 259; white men, 276–81; white population, 276–77; white women, 281–91; wood as fuel, 326–27; yellow fever, xix, 241, 258, (1797), 236–37, 256, 258. See also William Penn

Philadelphia–New York: route between (1794), 96–122; trips, natural scenery, 122

Philosophical Society. See American Philosophical Society

Piastre gourde (money), 358

Pickering, Timothy, Secretary of State (1745–1829)

Pigeon (ship), 176

Pillet (aide-de-camp to Lafayette), 94, 176

Pines, falling of pollen from stamens, incident of, 56

Planetarium, origin of, 336

Plum, M., his rope factory, 62

Point Comfort, 28, 29, 71

Poll tax, 302, 308

Pondichéry, capture of, 31

Pope, M. (watchmaker), 336

Port Royal, Martinique, 14

Portsmouth, Virginia, 64–67; boat service to Norfolk, 65–67; churches, 64; deer raising, 69; drinking water, 65; hospital, 65; house rents, 65; houses, 64; market, 64; population, 67; poverty, 67; prostitution, 67, 312; referred to, 33, 40, 42; roads leading to, 69; wharves, 65

Portuguese Johannes (money), 270

Postal service, 62

Potash, 159, 161, 163

Potomac River, width at mouth, 72

Pougers, Charles, 223

Powder of St. Germain (stomach powder), 18

Presbyterian Church: Baltimore, 78; Brooklyn, 168; New York, 149; Newark, 112; Newcastle (Del.), 86; Norfolk (Va.), 47–48; Philadelphia, 337, 339; Princeton, 103–04; Trenton, 102; Wilmington (Del.), 88

President (schooner), trip from Norfolk to Baltimore, 45, 71–74; berths, 72; cost, 71; Negroes, 73, 74; passage time, 74

Preston, Connecticut, 282

Prices, of important commodities, 160 ff., 319

Priestley, Dr., 212

Princeton, New Jersey, 102, catalpa trees, 106; healthfulness, 106; houses, 103; inns, 106; Presbyterian Church, 103; to Six Mile Run, distance, 120; to Philadelphia, distance, 106; to Trenton, distance, 120

Princeton College: curriculum, 105; enrollment, 105; fee, 105; laundry costs, 105; library, 104, 105; Nassau Hall, 104; planetarium, 104; painting of General Washington, 104–05; sport and licentious habits of pupils, 105

Prisons and jails. See individual cities

Prostitution, 122, 295, 302, 312–13, 314. See also individual cities

Protestant Episcopal Church. See Episcopal Church

Prussian stoves, 326

Public schools, 121

Puddings, 11

"Purloined letters," 268

Quakers: at Bristol, Pa., 100; color prejudice, 309; "Evil spirit," 313; House of Charity, 356; Kensington, Pennsylvania, 277; lecherous impulses, 312; men, 265; ministers, 339; Negroes, tolerance of, 302; New York, 149; Nicolite, 78; Philadelphia, 280, 337, 339; slavery, 304; syringes, use of, 315; Trenton, 102; Wilmington, 88; women's hats, 284; youth, 312–13

Quinine, excessive use, 53

Rachel (brig), 124

Rahway (Bridgeton), New Jersey, 111

Rain, days per annum, 321

Ramel, Finance Minister, 370, 371

Ramirez, Don Francisco, 256

Rappahannock River, 305

Raritan Bay, 111

Raritan River, 108, 109; bridge, 109, 110, ferry-boat, 109; width near bridge, 110

Read, Dr., 209

Receipt (assurance of solvency), 271

Red Lion Tavern, 97–98; melon frolic,

99; to Bristol, distance, 120; to Frankfort, distance, 120
Regnaud de Villevert, M., 374
Renslaer. *See* Van Rensselaer
Republican party, 252, 253, 271
Rhode Island, slavery in, 304
Ricard, General, 181, 208, 209, 219
Rice: barrels, 163; cost of, 159; shipping of, 161; tierce, 161
Ricepounds (puddings), 11
Richardet, M. (friend), 214
Richelet, M., of Maryland, 295
Richmond, Virginia: theater fire (1811), 309; to New York, distance, 166
Ricketts, John Bill (Scotch equestrian), 54, 348
Ridgley, Mlle., her *pension*, 75
Riene (servant), 8
Rising Sun (packet), 87
Rittenhouse, Dr. William (American astronomer), 95, 218, 225, 335, 336
Rivard, M. de (Italian engineer), 58
Robespierre, Maximilian (1758–94): beheading, 144; French terrorist, xv, 2–3
Robineau de Bugon, M., 233
Rochambeau, Dr., letter *quoted*, 218–19
Rochambeau, General, 103, 106
Roche, Frederick Frank de la (German nobleman), 128–34, 138, 175, 179; a busybody, 180; debt paid to, 245; duel episode, 195–96; letters, 196–201; meddler, 194; printing press, 194; referred to, xvi, xix, 125, 126
Roches, Champion des, 185
Rock Hill, New Jersey, 107, 108
Rohan, Cardinal Louis René Edouard de (1734–1803), 130–31
Roland, Mme. (1754–93), executed, 3
Romaine, Dr., 274
Roman Catholic religion: Baltimore, 78; burials, 345; German Catholics, 340–41; New York, 149; Norfolk, 49, 149; Philadelphia, 191–92; 337, 338–41
Ross, Dr. (Scotsman), 272
Rousseau, Jean Jacques, 313; ashes placed in the Panthéon, 43
Rouvray, 252–53
Rozier, French Consul at New York, 252
Rum: as a drink, 6; cask, 163; chopine, 163; in tea, 6; keg, 158

Rumford, Count (Benjamin Thompson), 166
Rush, Dr. Benjamin, 95, 336

Sailors. *See* American sailors
Sails and sail-patching, 23
St. Aubin, England, 3
St. Denis, royal sepulchre profaned, 3
St. Martin, M. (friend), 180–81
St. Paul's Chapel or Church, New York City, 118, 123, 149–50
St. Peter's Episcopal Church, Philadelphia, 192
Sally (ship), 301
San Domingo: colonists in United States, 34–35, 42, 49, 274; conditions (1796), 218–19; headmen, 219; men of color, 219. *See also* individual cities—French *émigrés*
Sandy Hook, 13; anchorage, 172
Sassafras beer, 134
Savannah, Georgia: snowfall (1800), 320; to New York, mileage, 166
Schmidt's Island, 27
Schuyler, Angelica and Elizabeth, 145
Schuyler, General Philip John (1733–1804), 145
Schuylkill River: bridges, 99, 262–63, 278; navigation, 257–58; Philadelphia water supply, 262
Scioto Land Company, 237
Scorpion (ship), 31
Seasickness, 2, 72
Seduction, 284–85; indentured women, 295
Séguin, M. (colonist), 75
Sémillante (40-gun frigate), 30
Servants, 264, 285, 286; indentured, 293, 294, 295, 296, 297, 298; white, 299–301, 302. *See also* Slavery
Shakers, 277
Shays' Rebellion, 136
Shearwaters (birds), 6, 13
Sherbets, American fondness for, 323
Shield, of Stockton (ship), 277
Shilling, value of, 112
"Shin-plaster" (money), 358
Ships. *See* names of individual ships; American ships
Shiver, Isaac (innkeeper), 107
Shoes and boots: cleaning, 80; costs, 157; factory, 81
Shortsightedness, American, 4, 6, 7
Sign of the Hunt, Inn, Newark, New Jersey, 114, 115

Six Mile Run, New Jersey, 107, 108, 135; to New Brunswick, distance, 120; to Princeton, distance, 120

Slaves and slavery, 303–11; abolition of, 17, 303, 357; Burlington (N.J.), 100; Carolina, 304; children, treatment of, 54; Connecticut, 304; criminals, 166; Delaware, 304–05; Dutch, 272, 304; Easter and Christmas vacations, 60; French colonies, 48; fugitives, reward for, 81; Maryland, 305; Massachusetts, 304; Methodists, 48; New Hampshire, 303–04; New Jersey, 109; New York, 148, 155–56; Norfolk, 59–61; North Carolina, 306, 307; Portsmouth, 67; Rhode Island, 304; South Carolina, 306, 307, 308; Virginia, 305, 306

Sleighs and sleigh-riding, 323

Smith, Mrs. Robert, party given by, 186

Smoking, 279

Snake Hill, New Jersey, 117

Snapper (turtle), 319

Snow, days per annum, 321

Snuff, use of, 279

Société libre d'agriculture, xxi

Sompérat, M. (of Jérémie), 71

Sonntag, William Louis, and Company, 133, 138, 139, 175, 179, 181, 184–85, 204, 209; his trouble with De la Roche, 230–31

Sophie, of Portland (brig), transatlantic crossing (1793–94), 1–45; bedbugs, 21; biscuit ration, 25, 26, 37; cabin stove, 10, 13; candles, exhaustion of supply, 13; chickens and turkeys, storage of, 9; constipation, 18; cost of passage, 8; crew, 8; diarrhea, 18; discomforts, 9; dolphin striker, breaking of, 20; fish, desire of passengers for, 9–10, 21, 34; hunger, experience of, 13; liquor, deprived of all spirituous, 14; morale of passengers, 23–24; music, 24; Norfolk, difficulties in attempting to dock at, 27–35; passengers, 8, 9; rain water, laxative quality of, 18; rigging, 20, 23; rolling of, 10; rudder tiller, 20; sails and sail-patching, 23; stomach powders, 18; storms, 9 *passim,* 15, 17, 21, 25; sugar, exhaustion of sugar supply, 11–12, 16; toilet facilities, 5, 25;

tonnage, 8; waste of fresh provisions, 37–38; water ration, 16, 37; weather, 9 *passim;* wine, search for, 14, 15, 16

South Carolina: abolition of slavery, 308; climate, 320; fleas, 325; poll tax, 308; public officials, 307; rainfall, 321; slavery, 306, 307

Southport (house), 46–47

Southwark (suburb), Philadelphia, 260

Sowels Point, 71

Staël, Baroness de, 187, 210, 369

Stage, travel by, 96–97; accidents, 97, 133; carriages, 96; changes, 108; courtesans, 122; drivers, 97; luggage (baggage), 96, 108; patronage, 102; women, 122

Staten Island, 110

Sternberg treatment for yellow fever, 236

Steuben, Baron, 334

Stomach powders, 18

Stony Brook, bridge, 103

Storms, at sea, 10, 15, 17, 19–22, 25; days per annum, 321

Stoves, heating, 326

Street cries, 61, 266

Sue, M., 209–10

Sugar, 6, 11–12

Sunday, observance of, 173, 317; hairdressers, 312; Negroes, 306

Superstitions, 1

Sureau, M. (colonist), 90

Sussex (American vessel), 2, 14, 35

Swannick (merchant), 333

Swedish Lutheran Church, 337

Syringes, 314–15

Talleyrand-Périgord, Charles Maurice de, French diplomat (1754–1838), xvi, xvii, xviii, xx, 91–92, 180, 181, 205, 209, 213, 368, 371, 372, 373, 374; Hamilton, Alexander, 179; Hugo, Victor, *quoted* on, 216–17; letters *quoted,* 145, 178, 181–82, 201–02, 202–03, 204, 205, 206, 207, 208, 210, 212, 217–18, 223–24, 226–27, 238–40, 251, 324, 367; Minister of Foreign Affairs, 249; New York, 125, 126; nomination, 237; Paris, 235; Philadelphia, 176; yellow fever, 206

Talon, M. (friend), 92

Taverns. *See* Inns, taverns and hotels

Taylor, Robert (Mayor of Norfolk), 59

Tea: as a drink, 6; girls, 283; overuse of, 287; rum with, 6; serving of, 266, 279; weddings, 386

Te Deum, singing of, 3–4, 27

Telescope, first made in America, 335

Temple, Sir John (1732–98), 267–68

Ternan, M. de, 275

Terrier, M. (friend), 95, 176

Theaters. *See* individual cities

Thunder, 321–22

Tiger (80-gun), 30, 57

Toasts, 266

Tobacco, factories, 81; raising of, 74; use of, 279

Toilets and toilet habits: American ships, 5, 25; at dinner parties, 266; chamber pots, 25; Philadelphia, 264, 266

Toise (measure 2.1315 yds.), 87

Tolls: bridge, 99; Hudson River ferry-boats, 119; Raritan River, 109

Tom (carpenter), 8

Tombstones, 342

Tot, M., his academy, 171

Toulon, France, surrender of, 30

Toussaint l'Ouverture (Governor General of San Domingo), 219, 232

Town criers, 330

Trenton, New Jersey, 100, 101; houses, 102; inns, 102; to Bristol, distance, 120; to Princeton, distance, 120

Trigant, Mme., 112

Trinity Episcopal Church, New York City, 124, 129, 150, 152

Turlutine (lobscouse), 10

Turtle Island, 274

Union (ship), 301

United States Army: New Brunswick barracks, 109; soldiers' pay, 109

Universalist Church in Philadelphia, 337

Upland, Pennsylvania. *See* Chester

Valentine, Dr., 143

Van Braam (Dutchman), 214, 218, 220, 225, 230, 238, 241, 246, 247, 251, 254, 374

Van Rensselaer, Stephen, 137, 145

Varenne, M. de (intimate friend), 139–43; 144; referred to, 125, 214

Varens, Mme. de, 313

Vaustable, 56, 65, 312

Vaughan, John, 179, 333

Vegetable prices. *See* Food

Ville Française. *See* Frenchtown

Vinegar, 159

Virginia: birth rate, 308; character of the people, 62–63; children, treatment of, 54; climate, 320; finger-nails, cultivation of long, 63; first bishop of the Protestant Episcopal Church, 49; fleas, 325; horses, 61; mulattoes, 305; Potomac River, 72; slavery, 305, 306; women, 69. *See also* Norfolk; Portsmouth; Gosport; Richmond

Virtue, 285

Volney, 206, 207, 214, 221, 222, 226, 253, 372

Voyage dans les Etats-Unis d'Amérique (La Rochefoucauld), 176

Voyages, Saturday an unlucky day to start, 1

War of Independence: arming of, 44; Long Island fortifications, 174; Norfolk's destruction, 47

Washington, George (1732–99): appearance, 350; birthday ball, 179, 333; Congress, opening of, 176, 209, 349–50; painting at Princeton, 104–05; portrait in City Hall, New York, 154; universal freedom, 310

Washington Tavern, Princeton, 106

Watchmakers, superiority of French, 336

Water: as a drink, 6, 65; cold, effects of drinking, 16, 323, 324

Water supply. *See* individual cities

Wayne, General Anthony (1745–96), 211

Weather reports and forecasting, 330

Wedding customs, 54, 286–87

Weights and measures, New York, 161; Norfolk (Va.), 62

Welcome (ship), 277

Wheat harvesting, 322

Whitethorn, beauty of, 85

Wild-pig hunting, 117

William (ship), 301

William and Mary College, Virginia, 49

Willington, New Jersey, 110

Wilmington, Delaware, xvi, 87–88

Wilmington, North Carolina, fire (1798), 333

Wilson, Colonel, 45, 66, 68, 90

Wine. *See* Meals

Woodbridge, New Jersey, 110, 135; inn at, 110; to Elizabethtown, distance, 120; to New Brunswick, distance, 120

Yale University Press, vii
Yellow fever, 144; *Adrastes*, 364; Baltimore, 80; Negroes, 51; New York, 164–65, 205, 206; Norfolk (Va.), 53; Philadelphia (1797), 236–37, 256, 258; Sternberg treatment, 236
Yorktown, attack on, 136
Youth, 24–25

ARUNDEL

A CHRONICLE OF THE PROVINCE OF MAINE

RABBLE IN ARMS

A CHRONICLE OF ARUNDEL

CHRONICLES OF ARUNDEL

THE LIVELY LADY

NORTHWEST PASSAGE

NEW YORK TIMES:

"It is the eternal pageant of the 18th Century that keeps one reading *Northwest Passage* to the very end. Of Robert Rogers Ann says: 'Ah, no! You can't kill what was in that man!' And it seems you can't—not with Kenneth Roberts to bring him back out of the star dust and make him again so real."
—*R. L. Duffus.*

SATURDAY REVIEW OF LITERATURE:

"The first half of *Northwest Passage* deals with one of the most agonizing marches in history. The second half you will read with as much satisfaction as you ever got from *The Virginians*. The hunger and desire of the nation just about to break westward into the untrodden lands, the tangle of cupidities and venalities and stupidities that in great part conditioned them—they are in *Northwest Passage* as they have not been in our fiction before. The second half is not only a good story; it moves on a plane of understanding and perception that only the best kind of historical fiction achieves."
—*Bernard De Voto.*

ATLANTIC MONTHLY:

"*Northwest Passage* is a great novel, since in its pages an era comes to life, complete with people and with things. When Kenneth Roberts wrote *Arundel*, he produced a novel which for most writers would have been a culmination. In *Rabble In Arms* and in *Northwest Passage* he has proved that *Arundel* was no more than a promise now bountifully fulfilled."
—*Ben Ames Williams.*

PROVIDENCE JOURNAL:

"So rich is *Northwest Passage* that I can do no more than recommend it with all my heart. In it Mr. Roberts has created an unforgettable figure. Robert Rogers has come to stay, to be despised, loved, abhorred and warred about, and withal saluted as an undoubted hero."
—*B. K. Hart.*

CLEVELAND PRESS:

"Kenneth Roberts' *Arundel* proved that he was the best historical novelist now practicing in America. Its sequel, *Rabble In Arms*, continued the proof. Consensus of critical opinion still is that each of these books should have received the Pulitzer Prize. *Northwest Passage* proves him to be not only the best historical novelist now practicing in America; but as far as American readers are concerned, the best that ever practiced anywhere, used any subject matter."
—*Elrick B. Davis.*

BROOKLYN EAGLE:

"*Northwest Passage* is accurate history, graphically told. Here is scope and power of writing. Here is the accuracy of a camera, the warmth and life of oils, the detail of an etching; the story of great men attempting great deeds."
—*Virginia Bird.*

MINNEAPOLIS JOURNAL:

"Towering above all else in the swirling 700 pages of *Northwest Passage* is that indestructible giant, Robert Rogers, a prodigious creation, a character bristling and sounding with life, a vivid portrait for your literary gallery. *Northwest Passage* will give you three novels' worth of entertainment."
—*Charles Lee.*

CHICAGO HERALD TRIBUNE:

"*Northwest Passage* chronicles a hero of gargantuan proportions and brings alive scenes and people from the forgotten pages of history. It is an enormous tale in every sense of the word—in length, breadth of action and intensity. The pages that describe the raid on St. Francis are as tense and lyric as a taut harp in a gale. It is a memorable and impressive book—a tremendous story."
—*Fanny Butcher.*

BOSTON POST:

" 'Magnificent' is the word for Kenneth Roberts' glorious story, *Northwest Passage*."

WORCESTER TELEGRAM:

"The clarity with which the characters emerge from the past, the drama of its campaigns, will fix the period in our memories for all time. The pictures in this story of gallantry and endurance are more vivid and unforgettable than any set pieces of fireworks."
—*Helen Beals.*

OLIVER WISWELL

NEW YORK TIMES:

"Behind the innocent title *Oliver Wiswell* there lurks, if that is the proper word, a bomb-shell. . . . It is history, for all its fictional form, and will startle every man, woman, and child who has been taught to believe that the American Revolution was fought and won by bands of angels. In it all the bitterness of a horrible civil war is powerfully and dramatically brought back to life."
—*R. L. Duffus.*

SAN FRANCISCO CHRONICLE:

"The story of the Royalists in the American Revolution has never been adequately told in fiction form. Now, after 160 years, Kenneth Roberts has undertaken this herculean task in *Oliver Wiswell*. No one excepting a man of Mr. Roberts' stature as a writer could lay before us the case of the American Royalists. It takes industry and unending research to accomplish the bare skeleton of such a book; it takes a high form of imagination, finished technique, and courage to carry the task to a successful conclusion. Yes, courage; for even after the passing of centuries, old prejudices still persist and cloud issues. It requires something greater than good writing and technique to hold up for examination a lost cause, and turn the dead past into a living present. This Kenneth Roberts has done. He has given life to people who were only names on a page of history, and summed up a case for Americans whom we had forgotten were Americans."
—*Inglis Fletcher.*

PROVIDENCE JOURNAL:

"If you do not read *Oliver Wiswell* it will be like not reading the *Odyssey* or *Pilgrim's Progress* or any other work that greatly states a changed view and begs both tolerance for the past and sympathy for friends in a vexed hour."
—*B.K.H.*

BOSTON HERALD:

"Adjectives pale before the superb drive and force of *Oliver Wiswell*. Only a great American and a great historian could have written this book; but only a great novelist could have woven his facts into such a fabric. America should be grateful to Kenneth Roberts."
—*Alice Dixon Bond.*

PHILADELPHIA RECORD:

"As you read *Oliver Wiswell*, you are before long intensely aware that you are reading an historical classic; you feel certain that this is a book your descendants will be dog-earing fifty and one hundred years hence. It has done better than a Pulitzer award because it has already won the more lasting prize of America's attention. And it will forever hold it."
—*Charles Lee.*

NORFOLK LEDGER-DISPATCH:

"Kenneth Roberts stands out among writers like Saul among the Israelites. *Oliver Wiswell* is one of the really great books that have been written since Mark Twain decided to call it a day."
—*Jay Lewis.*

NEW YORK SUN:

"No reader who owns *Arundel* and *Rabble in Arms* should fail to put *Oliver Wiswell* beside them on his shelf. When he has read all three he will know something important about the American Revolution—and perhaps about the course of history."
—*Margaret Wallace.*

A PRISONER OF THE JAPANESE:

"Brigadier General Lewis Beebe and I had taken a few books [into captivity] with us from the library of the University Club in Manila. They were handed around like rare treasures, read and reread, even committed to memory. One that especially stands out in my mind was Kenneth Roberts' *Oliver Wiswell*, which did more to take me out of myself than any other book I read."
—*Gen. Jonathan Wainwright;* THIS IS MY STORY.

TRENDING INTO MAINE

"Roberts knows his Maine, its history, geography, literature, legend, tradition, and people. It is his other Eden, his more than demi-paradise. For him it has a better than happy breed of men. It is the one spot beloved over all. He writes, therefore, something more than a native's appreciation, something better than a nicely tempered panegyric, a something which in its masculine passions disproves the old notion that a Maineman's reach cannot exceed his grasp. *Trending into Maine* is an exhilaratingly lyrical book, with a warm glow over it, and a clean wind through it, and an unspoken challenge and invitation in it that sets a man's eyes gazing northward."—*Charles Lee.*

"Readers who have made Mr. Roberts' acquaintance in one of his novels will recognize him in *Trending into Maine,* but with a difference. Freed from the trammels of plot, sustained character, and stylistic pattern, he lets his hair down, puts his feet up, and talks about what interests him most. He can't look at a bit of Maine scenery without having his mind filled with stories and people: 'Red men puttering about their lodges'; 'long, unhappy lines of women and children . . . trudging silently through the snow to the eastward and to Canada, pushed and shouted at by painted Indians'; 'wives and children of sea captains, waiting patiently through long Winters for those sailing on far-off waters'; 'Arnold's men, hunkered uncomplainingly among their bateaux on the river bank above Augusta . . .' It's a rambling, eloquent, colorful, lovable book."—*R. L. Duffus.*

"When Kenneth Roberts isn't writing an historical novel (which isn't often), he takes one peck of ripe tomatoes, puts them through a sieve, and adds vinegar, allspice, mustard, and powdered cloves. The result is ketchup. Or he rows out between the ledges at half tide and fishes for cunners. Or he retraces Arnold's route to Quebec. Or he mixes up a batch of letters, notes, and clippings and produces a book like *Trending into Maine,* into which he pours some of his ketchup, most of his great-great-grand-mothers, and every ounce of his passionate admiration for the state of Maine. *Trending into Maine* is not so much a book as it is a visit with Kenneth Roberts. He takes you into the kitchen, sits you down by the stove, hands you a doughnut, and stuffs you full of Arundel, Maine traditions, Maine smells, Maine people, the hardships of soldiering, the pleasures of ducks' breasts, the bravery of sea captains' daughters."—*E. B. White.*

MARCH TO QUEBEC

"Bringing together, in *March to Quebec,* the journals of the Quebec Expedition is an exceedingly valuable contribution to the Americana of the Revolution. . . . Many have been practically inaccessible. . . . Only a few libraries in the country have them all, and he who would buy them for himself would be obliged to spend a large sum of money and wait for a year or so before some dealer in rare books could accumulate all of them."

"Readers who enjoy weighing evidence ought to find much in *March to Quebec.* It has a suggestion of the thrill of a mystery story, not because the main outlines are in question but because motives and characters are deeply involved."

LYDIA BAILEY